Peter Cushing

Peter Cushing

*The Gentle Man of Horror
and His 91 Films*

Deborah Del Vecchio *and*
Tom Johnson

*with a foreword by
Barry Morse with Sydney Morse*

McFarland & Company, Inc., Publishers
Jefferson, North Carolina, and London

The present work is a reprint of the library bound edition of Peter Cushing: The Gentle Man of Horror and His 91 Films, *first published in 1992 by McFarland.*

LIBRARY OF CONGRESS CATALOGUING-IN-PUBLICATION DATA

Del Vecchio, Deborah, 1950–
    Peter Cushing : the gentle man of horror and his 91 films /
by Deborah Del Vecchio and Tom Johnson ; with a foreword by
Barry Morse, with Sydney Morse.
        p.   cm.
    Includes bibliographical references and index.

    ISBN 978-0-7864-4495-3
    softcover : 50# alkaline paper ∞

    1. Cushing, Peter, 1913–   — Criticism and interpretation.
I. Johnson, Tom, 1947–   .   II. Title.
PN2598.C94D4   2009
791.43'028'092 — dc20   92-50302

British Library cataloguing data are available

On the cover: Peter Cushing in *Frankenstein Must Be Destroyed,*
1969 (Photofest); lightning ©2009 Shutterstock

Manufactured in the United States of America

*McFarland & Company, Inc., Publishers
    Box 611, Jefferson, North Carolina 28640
    www.mcfarlandpub.com*

For my husband Carl,
who makes all my dreams realities.

To all the former members
of the American Peter Cushing Club,
for many happy memories.

To Peter Cushing, who made the films.

And Tom Weaver, who showed that
it is possible to write about them.

Contents

Foreword

(Barry Morse, with Sydney Morse)

It all goes back to my wife, whose professional name was Sydney Sturgess and who has known Peter longer than I have; in fact, although my wife and I have been married now more than fifty-one years, Sydney had actually met and worked with Peter about a year before she and I met.

Her remembrance of Peter goes back to 1938 when, around the spring of the year, Sydney and Peter were young members of a theater company, the Theatre Royal, in the city of Nottingham (shades of Robin Hood), which in those days was run as a repertory theater by an enterprising gentleman by the name of Harry Hanson. Hanson was one of the leading figures in the repertory theater movement before the Second World War. He had established a number of companies in different parts of the United Kingdom in which he presented plays — a new play every week — performed twice nightly (performances were usually at about 6:30 and 8:45 or 9:00 p.m.); and this was perhaps one of the most important aspects of his theater policy, that he was able to present plays briskly produced, tidily presented, and, more or less, skillfully acted.

This was a period in which the live theater was under considerable threat from the movies. Television had not yet taken hold of the public, but it did exist in England. The age of television began in the United Kingdom, on a more or less experimental basis, in 1935, but it hadn't taken a very firm hold. Live theater was very much under threat from the movies, and companies in the so-called legitimate theater, such as those run by Hanson, were the first to fight back against the movies. Presenting up-to-date plays (plays that had only recently ended their runs in the West End of London), they performed in handsome, well-run theaters and the ticket prices compared quite adequately with the prices which it would cost an audience to go to the movies. In those days the range of ticket prices was from sixpence to two shillings and sixpence.

There was immense popularity for such theaters. Because the audience was encouraged to buy season tickets, there also grew up an enormous affection and loyalty toward the individual actors in a company. In any of twenty or thirty of the larger cities in the United Kingdom, there would be established companies of this kind in which the members of that local repertory theater company would be every bit as popular in their way as the most famous movie stars.

It was quite a unique species of entertainment which, unfortunately, did not survive very long. The repertory theater continued to be popular up to and, more or less, through the Second World War. But with the growth of popularity of television on a national scale this type of theater inevitably pretty well ceased to exist by the time the mid–1950s came along.

Mostly young people were in these companies because the work load was enormous — playing and producing a different play every week virtually throughout the whole year. These young people were mostly actors who were expected to spend their apprenticeship years playing in repertory. In addition to the two performances that they had to give every night, there was also the task of rehearsing and preparing the new play which was to be performed the following week. The day's timetable would begin at either 10:00 or 10:30 A.M. when rehearsals would begin and would go on for four or five hours perhaps to the middle of the afternoon. Then there would be a short break of a couple of hours before they all had to assemble at the theater to prepare themselves for the first of two evening performances. Above and beyond all of that, there was the by no means negligible matter of having to learn the lines. All of them had to learn whatever dialogue was involved in a new, full-length play each and every week of the year. They were also obliged to provide all of their own clothes.

Now in the case of the men that was mostly a matter of what you could afford to assemble in the way of a wardrobe which would take you through every conceivable kind of play and kind of part that you might be called upon to play. But in the case of the girls, when you are considering plays which in some instances would oblige girls to provide three or four different changes of clothes during its course, they couldn't repeat with the same clothes that the audience had seen last week or the week before. So a great many of the young ladies became very skilled dressmakers, and in whatever spare time they could manage to scrounge they would actually make their own clothes.

It was a rather extraordinary life that those of us who were actors in those days lived because today's young actors would find it hard to believe that there was such a work load. It amounted to sometimes sixteen, eighteen, or twenty hours of work a day, and yet we did manage to have a bit of spare time and some enjoyment of our own.

In those days the repertory companies would play for the whole of the year except for the season that was occupied by the Christmas pantomime. Therefore, in a season of about forty-five weeks the company would have produced forty-five different plays. The young people in the company would have played no less than forty-five different parts. It's an astonishing realization when you consider that today, in many instances, all sorts of famous actors don't play that many parts in their whole lives! Here was an instance where people were learning their trade by playing that many parts in one year.

Anyway, the 1938 season was tremendously successful and everyone in the company became the darlings of the Nottingham audience. The particular individuals in the company would become so affectionately regarded by this audience which came to see them week after week that when each and every one of them made their first entrance, they were greeted by a warm round of applause as if they were old and established favorites. It was a phenomenon of a kind which never really existed before and I suppose never will again.

In this very happy and productive kind of atmosphere, Peter and the rest of us learned our trade. Among the others in that company whose names we remember very fondly was a young man named Peter Gray who worked as an actor for a number of years and with whom Peter Cushing was particularly friendly. They were known within the group as "the Peters."

Although the hours of the day were fully occupied, there still was a certain amount of time left for what we might call recreation. The two Peters were always the leading spirits in the company trying to make sure that people got exercise and fresh air. Of course, the actor's life is not a notably healthy one — so much of our days having to be spent in darkened theaters, a rather unhealthy atmosphere. But the two Peters, in particular, were always very keen to encourage the rest of the group to go swimming in whatever free hours they had during the afternoon in the River Trent, which flows through Nottingham. At that time, of course, there would be various other people swimming there. Among them, Sydney remembers, there would be coal miners. Young fellows who were working on the night shift digging away for coal all night and would come off perhaps at 6:00 A.M., go home to sleep, and would come out in the afternoon for their recreation and exercise.

Sydney recalls an encounter in which Peter Cushing took part when they had seen these young miners swimming in the river alongside of them on a number of occasions. It was obviously exercising the curiosity of these miners as to who these other young people were who apparently had leisure to swim in the middle of the afternoon in the river. One of them approached Peter Cushing and, I suppose in the local Nottingham-shire dialect accent, said, "Hey, what you young fellows and girls doing down here then swimming in the middle of the afternoon? How'd you get

off work to come and swim at this time of day?" And Peter, apparently
with some pride, said, "Oh, well you see we, we are actors! We're actors,
from the Theatre Royal here in the repertory company. That's what we
are. We are actors." And the young fellow sort of nodded his head en-
couragingly and said, "Oh, oh, oh well. There's no shame in it, is there?"
It was rather deflecting for Peter but they obviously all had a very good
time.

Now, next door to the Theatre Royal where I later played (I was not
in the same company with Peter), there was a music hall (a vaudeville
house as it would be called in the United States) called the Empire where
all sorts of different variety entertainers would come to perform (comedi-
ans, musical acts, jugglers, acrobats, and specialty entertainments of
different kinds). The two theaters were, quite literally, back to back, so
that the two stage doors were on opposite sides of an alley. It so happened
that during this season one of the vaudeville bills was an entertainment
which was composed of Hollywood doubles. There was a whole collection
of people who were apparently lookalikes for various Hollywood stars of
the day. They were apparently mostly young American performers who
had been selected because they looked like Norma Shearer, Greta Garbo,
Clark Gable, and others. There was always a certain amount of camara-
derie between the two companies. On this occasion Peter, because he was
always very much interested in what was going on in Hollywood, came to
know some of these young people since they were from the United States
and he was interested in what life was like over there. It was as a result
of this that he was encouraged and did shortly thereafter make his way
to California.

It was in Hollywood that he came to know Ida Lupino and her then
husband, Louis Hayward, and was encouraged and helped by them. That
was a time during which we didn't see Peter. We did not meet again until
Peter was back in the United Kingdom in 1942, when we both appeared
in a stage production of Tolstoy's great novel, *War and Peace*. We were in
the depths of the war, and Russia was a very important ally of the United
Kingdom and of the United States. There had been a radio production of
War and Peace which captured the imagination of the British public very
strongly and encouraged someone to come up with a stage adaptation of
this vast novel.

Needless to say, because of the range of the subject, it was a large-
scale production with a cast of over 100. We played a couple of other
places outside London before we actually opened in London but we didn't
have a very long run, partly because the economics of the show were such
that I don't think one could have broken even unless we played three
times a day at Yankee Stadium. It was that kind of ambitious event. But
since Sydney was an old friend of Peter's, we became great friends. Peter

at that time or shortly afterwards had married Helen and so we all four became great friends.

As it happened, during the war we were neighbors because we all lived in the Kensington district of London and it was during that time that Peter, Sydney, and I were involved in an extraordinary wartime escape. It was during the time when Hitler had launched the flying bombs on London. These flying bombs, otherwise known as buzz bombs were a form of guided missile or pilotless aircraft which did do regular damage on London in the latter part of the war. They carried considerable explosive power and they were heard approaching, but you could never be entirely sure where they would fall. They were not like the ordinary high-explosive bombs that were dropped by aircraft. They were in effect small aircraft themselves packed with explosives but without a pilot. This adventure which we went through together happened during the summer of 1944 when I was playing in a theater in London and Peter and Sydney had come to see this particular performance.

We were all traveling back together from the theater sitting on the top of a London double-decker bus. By this time we had become more or less immune to the perils of the flying bombs because they were rather unpredictable and nobody took too much notice of them because if you took notice of every air raid warning that sounded, you wouldn't get much done during the day.

On this particular evening we were in a district called Hammersmith and flying bombs were apparently coming over. You could hear these flying bombs if they were at all close because they made a rather growling kind of exhaust noise when they came closer to the ground. The only danger was when the exhaust noise cut out because that meant that the bomb was about to drop. When the engine cut out they fell straight to the ground.

Well, we were going along on top of this bus and not paying too much attention when we heard the approaching sound of one of these flying bombs, and then it stopped! Which meant that it was very close over our heads and about to drop. We were undecided what to do. Our lives were almost literally in the hands of the bus driver who had three options. To stop, go backward, or to go forward. He elected, he told us afterward purely by instinct, to go forward as fast as he could. He put his foot down and the bus accelerated up the road. When it was about a 100 yards ahead of where we had first heard this engine cut out, we saw the bomb actually come down and hit a church, St. Mary's, which was almost completely destroyed. It has since been rebuilt and my wife and I very often go past it, and every time we do we think of that occasion. What is it now? Forty-six years ago when we were on that bus with dear Peter and, by the grace of—who knows—God, Providence, a London bus driver, we escaped being destroyed by that flying bomb. It is always built into our remembrances of Peter.

Well, as I say, at this time we were reasonably close neighbors and we met very frequently. We would have meals or coffees or visits with each other. On one of those occasions (I think this was just after the war) there was an outbreak of a rather virulent strain of influenza which was called Hong Kong or Spanish flu. I often used to wonder what people in Hong Kong or in Spain would call flu when they got it there. Would they called it British flu? Anyway, Sydney and I were having dinner with Peter and Helen in their flat and I was feeling a bit feverish. I didn't know, of course, that I was suffering the onset of this strain of flu.

During the course of the meal, I didn't feel much like eating but I was enjoying myself and I hung on as long as I could. I began to feel more and more ill and before the end of the evening just when I was beginning to think it was about time I should start to make my way home, I passed out, completely passed out. Later, I became delirious and the next thing I knew was that very late the next day, nearly twenty-four hours later, I was still in Peter and Helen's flat tucked up in a bed that they made up for me on the sofa of their living room. I always remember that and their kindness very vividly.

I also remember that at that time Peter was not all that busy professionally. But, never being one to let the grass grow under his feet, he occupied himself by making beautiful model settings of all kinds of imaginary productions of stage plays, rather as a stage designer might do when preparing a set. He would make exquisitely finished designs for models of stage settings with scale models of human characters to place within the set. But it was not long after that he met Laurence Olivier and it was with Olivier that Peter traveled to Australia and played in *Hamlet* as Osric, which subsequently led to his very distinguished film career.

Not long after that time Sydney and I went to North America. We didn't see very much of Peter and Helen. In fact, we were not in England at the time when Helen died because I had been working predominantly in Canada and the United States during this period. Peter and I didn't work together again until the film *Asylum*, when we had quite a few scenes together. That was a great reunion, although by that time I was sad to see that Peter was feeling, I think very deeply, the loss of Helen. I always remember that over the years we would exchange Christmas cards and even after Helen had died he would always sign his cards from Peter and Helen, which was a rather tragic footnote to the way that he felt about his bereavement.

We did work together again in *Space 1999* and also in *The Zoo Gang* and we've kept, albeit rather distantly, in touch with each other. I know that Peter is not in the strongest health these days, although we are glad to see from his occasional appearances on television talk shows that he seems to keep his spirits up and we're very glad to see that someone is paying this sort of tribute to Peter that ought to be paid; because in our view he represents the very best kind of traditions of what we used to called real "pros."

A real pro, in the old-fashioned actor's use of that phrase, was held to be someone who not only was a polished and conscientious artist but someone who in his own private life upheld the best traditions of our profession in terms of loyalty and consideration for his fellows. I'm afraid that all too often in our profession nowadays we don't see those standards upheld very much. All too often, alas, self-seeking and self-promotion, greed and grabbing become the order of the day. But we're always grateful to remember people like Peter and remember the kinds of standards that we established for each other all those years ago. Sydney and I are very happy to be a part of this tribute to Peter and his life's work in a profession which is often so deeply misunderstood. We are very proud to have had a part in such a very worthwhile career.

London
October 21, 1990

Acknowledgments

Whenever anyone attempts to write a book of this type, there is always the hope that others will lend a hand to try to make it the best it can be. We were more than fortunate in this instance. We found, not surprisingly, that the mere mention of Peter's name invariably brought out the best in people. We owe a debt of gratitude to each and every one who gave so selflessly of their time and talents.

First and foremost, we would like to thank Peter Cushing — for all the obvious reasons — but also for having an unswerving faith in us and for his enthusiasm and assistance.

To Barry and Sydney Morse, whose friendship with Peter goes back some fifty-three years and who so generously provided us with inestimable insight into this very special association.

Many of Cushing's former coworkers willingly shared their personal memories exclusively for this tribute. Our grateful thanks to: Samuel Z. Arkoff, Desi Arnaz, Jr., Maxine Audley, Ian Bannen, Shane Briant, Veronica Carlson, Roy Castle, Hazel Court, Peter Duffell, Richard Gordon, Don Henderson, Alex Hyde-White, Deborah Kerr (my namesake!), Francis Matthews, Ferdy Mayne, Sir John Mills, CBE, Maureen O'Sullivan, Fred Olen Ray, Clive Revill, Peter Graham Scott, Thorley Walters, Sam Wanamaker, Douglas Wilmer, and Edward Woodward, OBE.

A special thank you to the staff at the British Consulate in New York who, when we asked for information on Peter's recent OBE award, without hesitation, said, "Yes, but it should have been a knighthood!"

To Anthony Timpone, editor of *Fangoria* magazine, who gave me my first professional byline and who came through with a still from *Biggles* after we exhausted every other possibility and had given up all hope; to the editor of *Midnight Marquee* (formerly, *Gore Creatures*), Gary Svehla (a friend for more years than either of us will *ever* admit!) for arranging a personal interview with Veronica Carlson; and to Dick Klemensen, also a friend for many a "yere," who offered encouragement and whose fanzine, *Little Shoppe of Horrors*, has given so many Hammer Film aficionados an outlet to keep alive the memory of that beloved studio's many contributions to the genre. Thanks fellas!

We would also like to extend our profound thanks to Nick Gadd and fiancée, Cathy Fleming, for providing us with enough information on Cushing to fill an encyclopedia and who shared with us their mutual devotion to Peter and his career.

A very special thank you to Peter's secretary, Joyce Broughton, and her family. This lovely lady has remained a steadfast friend ever since that "pesky kid" from America formed her fan club. Mrs. Broughton came to the rescue countless times. I will always be grateful to you, Joyce, for your many kindnesses.

Our thanks to Mark Martucci, who made his *vast* video library available for our use. To an old friend, Randy Vest, who was always there when we needed him. To Gloria Pasquini, for typing her fingers to the bone transcribing taped interviews, and to her husband, Richie, who understood when she suddenly affected a British accent! To Becky and Brent Worley, for taking in a "star boarder" and for offering their advice. To Debbie Hart, Elaine Hahn, and Gloria Vargas, for patience and endurance! To Geri Schutzwohl and Jim Didyoung for lending their special expertise in the translating and photographic departments. Thanks also to Greg Mank for his hospitality and much appreciated advice as well as John Skillin for tracking down a print of *The End of the Affair* for us.

And finally to those dear folks without whom neither of us would be possible. To Raymond and Edna Bennett and Jeanne and Paul Johnson. I would also like to add Ann Del Vecchio (my surrogate mom). Thanks Moms and Dads—for everything!

*　　*　　*

All stills and advertising material used in this volume are from the private collection of Deborah Del Vecchio and appear through the courtesy of their respective production and or distributing companies, which hold exclusive copyrights.

Quotes from Peter Cushing which are not credited are excerpts from personal correspondence and interviews.

Deborah Del Vecchio
Tom Johnson
July 14, 1992

Introduction
(Deborah Del Vecchio)

Why Us?

For many years we had gone to bookstores wistfully hoping that a book on Peter Cushing's films would be there. Certainly there was no shortage of this type of book in the market, including enough information on such notables as the Three Stooges and James Dean to stock a library! After many disappointing visits, it gradually began to dawn on us that the reason the book wasn't there was because we hadn't written it yet. And, if not us, who would write it? However, for countless reasons, we hesitated...

The publication of Peter Cushing's two volumes of autobiography in England disappointed many readers to a certain degree. Although these books contained a wealth of personal information, there was not nearly enough space devoted to his film career to satisfy most fans — including us.

Once again, we considered writing the book; however, our main concern was, as fans, did we have the right to coauthor a "films of" book? If not us, who else should have that right? Would — or could — we be objective enough to present a rational view of his career? Would our admiration for Peter Cushing as a person cloud our view of him as an actor? Were we up to the vast amount of research necessary to compile a competent overview of his rich and varied career? And, more importantly, would anyone actually be willing to publish the work of two first-time authors?

The answer to all of the above is, obviously, yes.

First Impressions

When we first began working on this book each of us thought back to the very first time we saw Peter Cushing on the screen and our interest in his career began. Here is Tom Johnson's reminiscence:

1

"To a boy of ten, seeing Peter Cushing in *The Curse of Frankenstein* had a far greater impact at the time than I could have possibly guessed. He was unlike anyone I had ever seen before—on or off the screen. I was completely fascinated by his appearance, his manner, and his accent. He seemed to be in total control, which was very attractive to a child who was not. Although I realized that Frankenstein was not a good man, I somehow sensed that Peter Cushing was. While the character frightened me, the actor did not.

"I have no explanation as to why I was drawn to him, but I dimly remember being unable to think of much else for days. Every child needs a role model, I guess, and mine was Victor Frankenstein!

"I now recall, with some embarrassment, going to a local butcher and obtaining, under false pretenses, a calf's brain. Garbed in one of my father's white shirts (standing in as a lab jacket), I placed the brain inside a plastic model of a human skull in my makeshift basement laboratory. My parents were not amused. The butcher was duly warned and the transplants ended. Fortunately, the voice of reason prevailed and I stopped short of robbing graves!

"Since I have become, as an adult, a relatively harmless and productive member of society, my early career as a medical adventurer can be written off as good, clean(?) fun. However, my admiration for Peter Cushing did not abate."

As a girl of seven, my own initial reaction to Christopher Lee as Dracula in his horrifying close-up—blood-drenched mouth, exposed fangs, and bloodshot eyes spewing fire and hate—in Hammer's *Horror of Dracula*, sent me literally screaming up the aisle and very nearly out of the theater! My father caught up with me at the door and brought me back to my seat. I don't recall much of the action after that—having decided that this was all too much for my tender years—and found refuge behind tightly closed eyelids until my ears picked up the sound of a music box playing. Cautiously, I raised up one eyelid and beheld a kindly looking man wearing a fur-trimmed overcoat. He spoke softly and carried himself with an air of reassurance.

Later in the film this same, gentle man spoke to a young girl (who was about my age) and assured her that everything would be made right again. He then placed his fur-trimmed coat around her shoulders and gave her a crucifix to hold tightly in her grasp. After comparing her to a teddy bear (my favorite toy), he told her that the sun would be coming up soon to chase away the shadows.

Though Peter went ahead with his grisly task (of staking vampires), somehow the horror of what was happening didn't seem so bad to me after that. This man was doing something good and he would prevail. He didn't wear a white hat or ride a snow-colored horse, but to me he was a gallant hero all the same.

Approximately fourteen years later, after having followed Peter Cushing's film career, I found myself writing to him about the possibility of starting a fan club in his honor and, to my joy, he agreed. Among the first members of the organization, which I dubbed the American Peter Cushing Club, were two young men. One I would eventually marry and the other was to become the coauthor of this book.

During the eight highly successful years I headed my club for Peter (which had a devoted membership and spanned the globe), I met him on two occasions. The first time was back in 1973 when he invited several of the club's officers and members to a luncheon and tour of Shepperton Studios outside London. Having had some less than pleasant experiences with so-called film personalities, whose egos far outweighed their talents, I found myself hoping for the best and expecting the worst. Happily, I was never more misplaced in my suspicions. What I did find was that Peter Cushing in person was a very down-to-earth individual who treated the club's officers and myself like family!

We met again in the fall of 1975 when the club's officers were given the honor of being his personal escorts during the legendary Second Famous Monsters Convention held at the Hotel Commodore in New York City. I watched as Peter Cushing signed literally hundreds of autographs and never once complained. In fact, he insisted on remaining until everyone was accommodated. I stood near the podium when he addressed the audience and received the deafening applause of thousands of fans. I saw the emotive tears in his eyes and at that moment I knew that that seven-year-old girl was right. Peter Cushing would indeed prevail and would be fondly remembered by many for a long time to come.

Lasting Impressions

To meet Peter Cushing, on-screen or in person, is to experience him. It is an odd phenomenon that is, at best, difficult to explain but anyone who has ever had the privilege will no doubt agree with this analogy.

Peter has been called "an honest man," "a charming man," "a man of mystery," and "a saint" by his peers. He impresses everyone in different ways, but all will freely admit that, as an actor, he is totally professional in everything he lends his name to whether it be a guest spot on a radio talk show, a theatrical performance, or as the star of a television broadcast or a motion picture. Add to this sincerity a sense of humor, a love of all humankind, and an abiding faith and you have some measure of the man.

"His name on a poster is as important as anyone's," former American International Pictures head Samuel Z. Arkoff once said when asked about his impressions of Peter Cushing, and film audiences worldwide proved that his claim was accurate. Whether or not a film itself was eventually worthy of him may have been debatable, but never Peter's performance in it.

The simple fact of the matter is that Peter Cushing has never given a bad performance. As hard as that may seem to anyone who has never seen one of his films, to those who have followed his career this is common knowledge. Peter's characters easily come to life for his audiences. Viewers find they have a relatively easy task suspending their disbelief.

It seemed perfectly acceptable that Dr. Van Helsing had indeed devoted his life to the destruction of Dracula and all his kith and kin, despite the audience's knowledge of the fact that vampires don't exist. Not one of us had difficulty following Dr. Victor Frankenstein's exploits as he tirelessly attempted to improve on God's model, and, although he ultimately failed, he was always eager to begin anew in the next installment. Not surprisingly, we were just as eager for him to succeed! Many of us breathed a collective sigh of relief when his Sherlock Holmes was on the case since we knew he wouldn't let the villain go unpunished. Yet not a single one of us blinked when the malevolent Moff Tarkin coolly destroyed an entire planet, then turned to an astonished Princess Leia and with a cynical Mona Lisa smile whispered, "You're far too trusting!"

Perhaps *trust* is the key word. Peter Cushing could be relied on and never minimized his performance. Whether the part was a simple walk-on or he was in every scene, Peter never cozened his audience or his role.

Cushing has often been asked, "What's your favorite film, your favorite role?" His answer is invariably the same. "All of 'em! I love them all!" And he truly does. It is more than likely that he would say that he could have done it better, never being totally satisfied with a performance. He would never single out a particular role or a certain film of his as being of any singular worthiness. It is not a matter of disinterest—far from it. It's simply his modesty coming to the fore. Peter is more interested in pleasing his audiences than being pleased by them.

No film is perfect. Each and every one has something wrong with it. Horror and fantasy films regularly suffered the brunt of film critics' reviews and, like hungry jackals, they fell to the meal over and over again simply on the basis of the films' genre. However, more often than not, Peter Cushing's performances were lauded. In many cases his performance alone saved a film and critics were always quick to point this out. For once, both fans and critics could agree on something.

Film company moguls themselves were very much aware of Peter

Cushing's box office appeal. There were occasions when he was obviously exploited by producers who knew the value of his name but willingly overlooked his enormous talent by offering him roles that were inferior. Although Cushing himself is partly to blame for this, since after the death of his wife Helen in 1971 he needed work to divert him from his grief. One cannot help but speculate as to why these unworthy parts were offered to him in the first place other than to enhance an otherwise mediocre film. This was simply another case of the industry taking advantage of a good thing, as many a respected film star will be quick to point out.

However, voracious film executives aside, Peter Cushing's film career provided us all with a rich legacy. There is only one actor in modern motion picture history who has made such characters as Baron Frankenstein, Dr. Van Helsing, and Sherlock Holmes, among so many others, uniquely his own. An actor with whom each of these roles are immediately identified by an entire generation of film goers; a single performer who breathed new life and vitality into these classic literary personalities to the delight of countless movie buffs around the world; and a man whose classic looks and old-world charm wove a magic spell around each and every role he played.

Peter Cushing could be coldly cynical, compellingly romantic, or wildly eccentric when called upon; warm the heart with a smile or freeze the blood with a glare. He could play the wise old professor, the mad scientist, the pirate, or the priest with equal aplomb, as well as lend an air of authenticity to the most ambiguous or absurd lines of soliloquy.

One of the true masters of improvisation, Peter was also capable of manipulating both props and fellow cast members with the expertise of a premier illusionist. Yet he never allowed himself to overshadow his colleagues, nor did he have to resort to such subterfuge since Peter could draw all eyes to him simply by his presence in a film.

Part of Cushing's genius lay in his approach to his work. He played Stoker and Shelley in the same way he did Shakespeare. He would also meticulously research his character, delving not only into the psyche of the man but learning all he possibly could about the period and life-style he lived in or the profession of his object of study so that his performance would be as accurate and as faithful to the story as he could possibly make it.

Peter Cushing made a total of ninety-one feature films, all of which will be covered in this book. Although he was certainly not limited to his work in the cinema, it will be in this medium that he will be most remembered by many. Though his film work was certainly not limited to appearances in fantasy films, it will doubtless be in this particular genre that he will be most fondly cherished by all.

But no matter in what way or in which respect Peter is held, he will always be what he always was above all else—a gentleman and a gentle man.

Some Notes of Explanation

The authors have made every effort to include cast and technical credits information which are as complete as possible for each of Peter Cushing's films. In most cases numerous sources had to be consulted to achieve our goal.

It should be noted that many of Cushing's films underwent title changes (in some instances, several times!) before, during, and after the film was produced. Titles were very often changed from country to country and, in some cases, even from area to area within the same country! To give an example of this lunacy, *Trial by Combat* (1975) was originally known as *Choice of Weapons*, yet when it was released in the United States it was called *Dirty Knight's Work* in some Western states!

Blood Beast Terror (1967) was also released as *The Vampire-Beast Craves Blood* and *Death's Head Vampire*. John Gilling's *Mania* (1959) probably holds the record for the most title changes. It was released in England as *Flesh and the Fiends*. It also resurfaced over the years under such titles as *The Fiendish Ghouls* and *Psycho Killers*.

More recently, videotape releases of Cushing's films have carried on the tradition and added to the confusion. A prime example of this is Hammer's 1971 production, *Fear in the Night*. Due to Joan Collins' popular television soaper, the video version was released in the United States as *Dynasty of Fear!*

We have referred to all of Cushing's films by their U.S. release titles with a few exceptions. However, all alternate titles, where known, have also been noted. In addition, due to the fact that many of his films had delayed release dates (in some cases, delays lasted years), we decided to list them according to the year they were produced.

Whenever possible, we have attempted to include all known television (including made-for-TV movies), stage, and radio appearances made during the course of Cushing's film career. In order to give readers some added perspective of his versatility and demand in the industry, we included notes regarding these appearances within the context of our individual film commentaries which correspond to the year these appearances were made. Again, various sources were consulted and though these may not be conclusive they are as near to complete as we were able to gather during our research. Should any of our readers have additions or corrections, we would appreciate your input. Letters should be addressed to us in care of the publisher.

Double Takes

For those readers who, like us, are absolute sticklers or just plain trivia buffs, there are some additional motion pictures in which Peter Cushing made an appearance (of sorts) but did not receive any screen credit. In Vincent Price's black comedy, *Theatre of Blood* (1973), Peter appears as Osric in a film clip from Laurence Olivier's *Hamlet* (1947). A clip from *The Curse of Frankenstein* (1956) is shown during Stanley Kubrick's controversial film, *Lolita* (1962); and in *It Came from Hollywood* (1982), a trailer featuring Baron Frankenstein from *Frankenstein and the Monster from Hell* (1972) is highlighted. Hammer Films reprised the exciting climax of *Horror of Dracula* (1957) as the opener for their sequel, *Dracula — Prince of Darkness* (1966); and Van Helsing appears again in Sean Connery's *Cuba* (1979). Lastly, in *Goliath Awaits,* a 1981 television movie, Peter's character Palimedes from *The Black Knight* is erroneously credited to John Carradine, who plays an actor in the teleplay.

A Profile of Peter Cushing

Beginnings

Peter Wilton Cushing was born on Monday morning, May 26, 1913. His birthplace—Kenley, Surrey, England—is, as he puts it, "between the towns of Ham and Sandwich." His parents, George and Nellie (King), were products of the Victorian era so it is not difficult to trace their son's courtly manners.

"My father was a practical man," recalls Peter. "He was a quantity surveyor which is all to do with mathematics. I can't add up two and three and get it right."[1]

The family had a theatrical background, especially his step-uncle, Wilton Herriott, for whom Peter was named. Despite the family history on the stage, George Cushing was not enamored of the profession because, according to Peter, "It was still a period when they regarded all actors as rogues and vagabonds."[2]

World War I was raging soon after Peter's birth and his few memories of it include zeppelins caught in spotlights. A more significant childhood memory is of a Christmas visit to London to see *Peter Pan*, about which many of his childhood fantasies revolved.

Peter's schooling began in the Dulwich kindergarten, as also did his acting career as, oddly enough, a goblin. He was often ill as a child, suffering from pneumonia several times. He collected cigarette cards, rode bicycles with his older brother David, and considered himself a loner. His nickname was "Brighteyes."

Every child has a hero, and Peter had two—both of them named Tom. Tom Merry was a fictional adventure character on whom Peter based his code of conduct. Tom Mix was a Hollywood cowboy. "You see," says Peter, "I thought that all Americans were cowboys. Mix was the Clint Eastwood of my youth, so I always wanted to go to Hollywood."[3] As fate would have it, he met his cowboy idol in Hollywood years later and was even a witness to a contract signed by the famous silent film star.

"I always used to dress up and play 'let's pretend,'" Peter recalls. "Some of my earliest memories were of dressing up in my mother's clothing

9

and playing old farmer ladies."⁴ He also put on puppet shows—for profit. "I'd do these terrible performances in a high squeaking voice," he admits. The shows were so bad that his audience would be admitted for free, but had to pay to leave. Peter's desires to dress up and to pretend are, as he puts it, "the basic principals of acting."

As an older student, Peter's main interests were in athletics and art. "Academically, I was no great shakes," he confesses; "but, the athletic pursuits have served me well because I am rarely in a film in which I don't either fall or get knocked down."⁵

Although Peter, as a young adult, knew that he wanted to act, the actual entry into the profession was far from easy. He first tried the practicality of a regular job without success. "I was in an office for four years as a so-called Surveyor's Assistant," he recalls. This was with the Coulsdon and Purley Urban District Council. Peter revealed that "I was always the last to check on and the first to clock off. I wasn't very popular."⁶

Peter finally made the decision to make a real attempt at acting. It was a difficult move but, as he honestly states, "I knew it was the only thing I was capable of doing. [My father] didn't put any barriers in my way, but he wasn't able to help, and he was always a little worried."⁷

One obstacle was his strong Surrey accent. When he took a class at the Guildhall School of Drama and Music, his professor threw up his hands, "Get out!" he cried. "Your voice offends me!"⁸ As a result, Peter attended a special class in London to correct his accent—obviously with excellent results.

Minus his accent, Peter still found that roles were not going to come his way without more effort. His next step was to lose his name.

"I was in the throes of first love at the time," he says sheepishly, "and the word 'darling' was naturally used a lot, so I thought 'I'll call myself Peter Ling.'"⁹ Since the casting directors now thought him to be Chinese, his fortunes did not improve. His first actual job in the theater was not as an actor but as an assistant manager with the Worthing Repertory Company.

Peter bombarded Bill Fraser, the director of the Connaught Repertory Company, with endless requests for an audition. He was delighted to finally receive an invitation. He was crushed, however, to learn that the invitation was to ask him to stop requesting auditions. Peter burst into tears and Fraser "took pity on me and put me on the stage that very night in J. B. Priestley's *Cornelius* in which I played a creditor. It was my first professional appearance."¹⁰

That performance, in June 1936, was not without incident. Lacking any lines of note, the young Cushing chose to draw the audience's attention by improvising some stage "business" of his own. Fraser was not amused.

Although he worked in other repertory companies, the lure of Holly-wood, with its magical films and stars, had long tugged on Peter Cushing's sleeve. He managed to save £50 and his father generously paid for his ticket to America—one way only. "It bothered me a bit at the time," he recalls. "I think he thought I could swim home."[11]

Peter had a realistic view of his chances for success. "I went with a carefree attitude," he admits. "If I landed film parts, fine! If I didn't, well, I was young and would be able to come back to Britain and try again."[12]

What was unrealistic was Peter's misreading of the world situation. He was, apparently, oblivious to the coming world catastrophe. When he left for New York on January 18, 1939, World War II was on the horizon.

The beginning of Peter Cushing's film career in Hollywood (1939–41) could be described as a combination of luck and missed opportunities. Since the start of the film industry in America, countless young hope-fuls—like Peter Cushing—have arrived in Hollywood with stars in their eyes. Most never got past the studio gates.

Peter's good fortune began with a chance meeting with Columbia film executive Larney Goodkind in New York. Goodkind (who lived up to his name) provided Peter with a letter of introduction should he ever actually reach Hollywood. The letter probably meant very little, but gave the young Cushing "a wonderful sense of encouragement."[13]

He arrived, broke, at a YMCA in Los Angeles with little more than an obvious willingness to work and a likable personality. Peter took these with him and went studio hopping. He found himself at a studio where the Edward Small Company was about to begin *The Man in the Iron Mask*. Peter announced to a guard, "I've come to get into pictures and I *must* see someone." Incredibly, he was allowed inside.

Peter Cushing believes that there is a plan that we all follow which he feels explains his being—more than once—in the right place at the right time. This is certainly illustrated by his being accepted by director James Whale to appear in the film and by his being befriended by star Louis Hayward. Hayward and his wife Ida Lupino provided Peter with not only a place to live, but almost certainly with introductions to others in the film industry. As two of Hollywood's up-and-coming young stars, the Haywards were capable of opening doors to which Peter Cushing lacked the key.

As a young man with a proper British accent, Peter filled a type that often needed filling as many English actors were being called home to fight. Since Peter was exempted from military service due to athletic in-juries from his school days, he was able to fill the void.

Peter Cushing's only major Hollywood role was in RKO's *Vigil in the Night* (1939)—a role secured through the help of a friend. His one big scene—for which he received his only critical notice—was specifically

Groomed for stardom? Peter Cushing as Clive of India in the MGM short *Your Hidden Master* in the series *The Passing Parade* (1941).

written for him by director George Stevens. Another director might not have been as generous.

Peter's Hollywood feature career ended where it began, being directed by James Whale. *They Dare Not Love* (1941) was also Whale's last feature film. By this time, Peter's fine work in *Vigil in the Night* was common knowledge in Hollywood and he had attracted the attention of MGM. The studio was producing a series of short films entitled *The Passing Parade* that were, in a sense, screen tests. According to Peter, he was being groomed by MGM, and was cast as Clive of India in *Your Hidden Master*, directed by Sammy Lee. His performance was a success and he was poised for a breakthrough. Then — on the brink of stardom — he left Hollywood.

A combination of homesickness and the war pulled Peter Cushing back to England. While it is not our intention to mitigate the importance of World War II to Peter Cushing's career, it is still interesting to wonder what direction his career might have taken without the war.

Based on his excellent reviews for *Vigil in the Night* and MGM's interest in developing him, it's possible that Peter might have become a star along the lines of, say, David Niven or James Mason. Then again, perhaps not. There are few certainties in the film industry.

When Peter reached New York on his return to England, he found himself unable to get transport across the Atlantic — and unable to pay for it even if he had found it. Then, down on his luck, he met actor John Ireland, who recognized Peter from having seen *Vigil in the Night*. "He pointed out," recalled Peter, "that, since I had worked in Hollywood, I must have made Social Security payments. These entitled me to relief. I went to the relevant authorities. They allowed me, to my joy, $18 a week. Eventually I reached home by taking the place of a deserter on a cargo boat from Halifax, Nova Scotia, and for the two-week voyage, I was a so-called deckhand."[14]

After an arduous struggle, Peter Cushing reached England in March 1942 but he would not appear in a film until 1947. During and just after the war his acting would be limited to the stage. It was, perhaps, this experience that truly shaped him as an actor and laid the groundwork for his future success.

Soon after his return Peter joined ENSA (Entertainment National Service Association — also known as "Every Night Something Awful"). The company toured military bases entertaining the troops and provided young performers with all the experience they could handle.

In May 1942 Peter Cushing met Helen Beck while waiting for the company bus outside the Drury Lane Theatre. Beck had replaced Sonia Dresdel in the cast of Noel Coward's *Private Lives* and the two ran their lines together on the train to Colchester.

They were married on April 10, 1943, at the Kensington Registry

Office. Peter recalls that, "For a while we lived with Helen's parents in Kensington. Then we found a flat nearby. Although it was a lovely flat, it had a lot of windows . . . it was hardly the place to be during an air raid!"[15] He freely admits that he married Helen for her money. "She had thirty pounds, and I had about twenty-three."

Peter returned to films in much the same way as he entered, but in a far more prestigious production. He was, again, in the right place at the right time. As Osric in Laurence Olivier's *Hamlet* (1947), Peter Cushing had finally reached the big time. Or had he? After completing the film, it would be another six years until his next one. A combination of ill-nesses — both his and Helen's — and touring in stage productions limited his opportunities for film work. Then, in 1951 he became a television star — in fact, England's first.

Television was as hungry for talent as Peter Cushing was for success, and the two meshed perfectly. Between 1951 and 1956 he would appear in twenty-three television plays and would be chosen as England's finest television actor. During this period he performed in four films, most notably as Deborah Kerr's sad husband in Graham Greene's *The End of the Affair* (1954). His many television appearances — and awards for them — brought him to the attention of Hammer Film Productions.

Hammer often based their films on successful television shows, so it was only natural that the studio's greatest star should come from that medium. Hammer had long desired Peter Cushing's services and, when they announced their remake of *Frankenstein,* they got him.

With his success in *The Curse of Frankenstein* (1956), Peter Cushing became an overnight international star — after only twenty years of hard work, setbacks, and interruptions. He had now achieved a success that few actors would even dream of. However, by the decade's end he had in a sense created his own monster.

"I don't mind at all that people may refer to me as a 'horror actor,'" he says, "because in this unpredictable profession actors are awfully lucky. They're doing something they love, they're earning a living by it, and the end product, we hope, gives pleasure. But for any actor to be associated with a form of success like Hammer's I think it is absolutely wonderful and if that means being thought of as a horror actor, then I think it's the most marvelous thing that could happen to me."[16]

Perhaps so, but an actor of Peter Cushing's talent and range could not have been completely pleased with the restrictions of the horror genre. A cursory glance at his credits indicates that in the early 1960s he was not appearing in the type of film that had made him famous. Since the horror film in general was booming, one can assume that he had been offered parts that were not accepted.

Peter Cushing's brief absence from horror films produced some excellent performances in some interesting films, but nothing like his initial success with Hammer. In 1963 he returned to Gothic horror in *The Gorgon* and there, with few exceptions, he remained.

During the 1960s the quality of his films began to fade, but the quality of his performances remained high. Peter's stage and television work (with the exception of the BBC Sherlock Holmes series) began to dwindle but, whatever the role, he treated it—and the audience—with respect.

As his film career seemed to be winding down, a personal tragedy occurred which revived it. Helen Cushing had been ill for long periods since the 1940s and died in January 1971. Her passing was a blow from which Peter never truly recovered. He turned to film work as therapy, appearing in twelve films in a twelve-month period. During the early 1970s he gave some of his greatest performances, most notably in *Tales from the Crypt* (1971) and *The Creeping Flesh* (1972). However, by the mid–1970s the unprecedented success of big-budget horror-fantasy films had helped destroy the B-budget market for Hammer and Amicus, and Peter's output began to slow down.

In 1975 he appeared in his final stage production, touring in *The Heiress*. Of his role Peter said, "I do not really have a favorite role, but one which I will always think of is my part in *The Heiress* at a provincial theatre in Basingstoke. In that play I think I got as near to giving a performance which pleased me as I have ever done."[17]

Peter Cushing's appearance in *Star Wars* (1976) gave his film career a boost, introducing him to a new generation of fans. (When seeing one of his old films on television, some thought the actor playing Baron Frankenstein was Peter Cushing's son!) Unfortunately, *Star Wars* had little long-term effect on his career. Of his remaining eleven films, only *Top Secret!* (1983) had a wide release, and four were, seemingly, never released at all in the United States.

As of this writing, *Biggles—Adventures in Time* (1985) marks Peter Cushing's last film appearance. But if *Biggles* is indeed his last film, Peter Cushing has nothing to regret. "An actor's last job is his last job," he says. "The job he finishes may be his last for a week, a year, two years, you just don't know."[18]

Summing up his own career, Peter Cushing states, "When you're dealing with these pictures which are dealing with the impossible, you have to believe in it and love it yourself if you're going to try and get an audience to believe it with you.... That's the only way to approach any work."[19]

As an actor, Peter Cushing's goal was to provide entertainment for his audience. He entertained a vast number of people for a very long time. Despite not receiving the recognition due him, pleasing his audience was and still is, perhaps, the award he wanted most.

Pastimes and Pleasures

As a youth, I based my code of conduct upon a fictitious schoolboy named "Tom Merry" whose adventures I read each week in a boy's paper — Peter Cushing

Peter Cushing's hobbies and interests give one some significant insights into his off-screen personality.

Peter was always an avid reader. In his youth he would spend most of his pocket money on comics and story picture books, graduating to biographies and reference books on a variety of subjects in his adult years. Some of Cushing's favorite authors include A. J. Cronin, R. F. Delderfield, Howard Spring, Nevil Shute, and Frederick Forsythe. According to Peter's secretary, Joyce Broughton, he would "rather buy a book than eat!"[20]

The art of the miniature has always delighted Cushing. As a child he collected toy lead soldiers and farm animals. Once he began his acting career Peter took a great interest in stage set designs and in his spare time would construct miniature model sets. Each of the sets he designed took him about one year to complete. Peter also constructed a model theater stage, which included a working curtain that could be raised or lowered with the flick of a switch, six tiny floats or footlights in addition to its self-contained lighting system, and three small box seat stalls on either side of the structure.

The sets themselves represented a variety of subjects from a Japanese garden to the deck of a sailing ship. Peter even designed authentic interior sets based on actual productions, including *Pride and Prejudice* and *An Ideal Husband.* Other sets included a forest scene from Robin Hood, a medieval castle interior, and an old-world village. Every one of his miniature sets included minute figurines in full costume, appropriate furnishings, and bric-a-brac which Peter himself designed to scale. Each of these sets were no bigger than a shoebox and were made to fit snuggly behind the model theater stage to complete the illusion. "I love to put up a set," Peter revealed. "Light it, then sit back with some suitable music on the record player."[21]

Aside from his model sets, Peter also enjoyed making model airplanes and collecting model steam trains, tropical fish, and cigarette cards.

An avowed audiophile, Cushing admitted his tastes in music were always eclectic, ranging from Gilbert and Sullivan to Puccini, Strauss, Wagner, and Sibelius, as well as Dixieland Jazz and Grand Opera.

A man very much interested in nature, Peter developed an interest in ornithology as a child, and for many years collected various species of

A look inside one of Peter's model sets.

birds' eggs and skeletons for study. Peter also was very active in the conservation movement in the United Kingdom. Both Peter and his wife Helen enjoyed gardening and for years filled their Whitstable garden with many varieties of flowers, trees, and shrubs. Their favorite plants, however, were always roses and lavender.

But of all his many pastimes, Peter's main passion was his artwork. While still in his teens, Cushing had studied art at the Croydon School of Art where he developed an interest in the Impressionists' style. In 1958 the Fine Art Society in London held an exhibition of his watercolor landscapes entitled "Here and There." More recently, in 1987, Britain's Prince Edward accepted one of his works for a charity auction the prince was sponsoring.

Peter's artistic talents have also served him well throughout his film career. In addition to submitting costume designs for some of his films, Peter has also designed jewelry, ties, and scarves. During the 1940s, which Peter referred to as his "lean years," he supplemented his income designing scarves for a textile manufacturer. At the premiere of *Hamlet* in 1948 Peter presented Queen Elizabeth (now the Queen Mother) with a scarf he had designed especially to commemorate the event.

Yet another side of this man's character is his charitable works. For many years Peter has recorded talking books for the blind and has reverted any fees for his services back to the foundation. When his autobiography was published, Peter donated signed copies of his book to a branch of the Guide Dog Association to raffle. He has also been a longtime supporter of England's Muscular Dystrophy Foundation and is widely admired for his compassionate nature that has benefited some of his less fortunate fellow actors.

On Acting and Horror Films

> There is little chance for a person to exercise the imagination to-day in this complex, programmed society we have. These movies allow people of all ages to experience wondrous things and a good fright never hurt a healthy person — Peter Cushing

Peter Cushing admits that he had always aimed for a career in films. Although he felt that his years in repertory and on the London stage were excellent platforms for his basic training as an actor, it was films that Peter had had his heart set on all along. The main reason was his dislike of repetition. Peter once compared his stage performances to a newspaper reporter who is forced to write the same article every night.

"On the stage," Peter admitted, "naturally one wants to be in a long run.... But I can't bear the repetition. After about three weeks I'm ready to give up and I know my performance deteriorates in a long run."[22]

Films offered Peter Cushing much needed versatility and the added benefit of additional takes if he was dissatisfied with his delivery in a particular scene, although on most occasions his directors were quite satisfied with Cushing's performance on the initial take. "My preference for films also follows from my striving for perfection. With a little more time ... you can get as near as possible to it, and if anything goes wrong, you can do it again."[23] However, Peter felt, even with the added benefits film offered an actor who is ever striving for excellence, he still could have improved his performances. "If the time ever comes when I'm actually pleased with one of my performances, that will be the time I start slipping!"[24]

Although Cushing preferred making films, they too had their drawbacks as far as this actor was concerned.

> I don't care for location work because film is such a make-believe medium that put me on a set where I know behind it is all plaster, packs of sandwiches and where the *Daily Mail* is tucked in and people are having cigarettes..., then I know it's all make believe. But put me up against a real lovely wood, a real church, or along a real road, and I find it much

more difficult to pretend because that's what acting is — let's pretend. Against the real thing, I'm not so happy.[25]

To his credit, Cushing has never downgraded his career in horror films. In fact, Peter was grateful for the positive audience response to his appearances in this much maligned genre. "Horror films . . . can be just as intelligently made as anything else. . . . They have helped to keep me working and have given pleasure to thousands."[26] "Once you make any kind of impact, film people only see you in that particular light. . . . This bothered my wife, Helen. She'd seen everything I'd done and knew the variety of my work. . . . I was worried about the future and here was an answer."[27]

Although Cushing has worked for a number of film companies, he always believed that his years at Hammer's Bray Studios were some of his happiest.

> It was certainly a great team . . . and . . . the more they played together, the better they became. What was important was that everybody got on so well together. I think [that extended] from the top . . . to the call boy. I have a great affection for those days at Bray . . . and I miss it greatly. . . . When they did move to places like Shepperton and Elstree the same people were there and the atmosphere was so very nice but it wasn't . . . home.[28]

Quick to play down his own genius as an actor, Peter believed that his enduring popularity as a horror film star stemmed from the effect of the genre itself on the public. "The one type for which there is always a market is horror [films]. Love stories come and go . . . Westerns are out, but there is always an audience for horror."[29] "I don't think of myself as famous. Whatever fame I've got has come through what I've done and associations of things I've done. If you are associated particularly with films that make a sensational impact and which make a great deal of money, then fame is thrust upon you. . . . I didn't go into the business to seek fame but I'm glad it's there because if you're famous it means you're wanted."[30]

However, out of all those who have helped Peter's career beyond the screen, Peter has consistently credited his fans.

> Sincere fans represent a section of society who go to see the films made by their particular favorites and — as such — they are a most important factor. Without an audience no actor could survive in his chosen profession, and it is really for them that we work. . . . I am indebted to them, and most grateful and will always endeavour to deserve their devotion, praise and affection. As my beloved wife said, "we are public servants who are pleased to serve and serve to please."[31]

Notes

Any personal references not noted are from Peter Cushing, *Peter Cushing, An Autobiography* and interviews with the authors.

1. James Kravall, video interview in *Little Shoppe of Horrors* 8.
2. Ibid.
3. Rosemary Collins, *Radio Times,* July 2, 1970.
4. Kravall, *Little Shoppe of Horrors* 8.
5. *Three Crowns* 27, Christmas 1974.
6. Collins, *Radio Times,* July 2, 1970.
7. Kravall, *Little Shoppe of Horrors* 8.
8. *Three Crowns* 27, Christmas 1974.
9. John Player lecture, delivered by Peter Cushing at the National Film Theatre, London, January 1973.
10. Ibid.
11. Ibid.
12. Dick Tatham, *My Weekly,* August 23, 1969.
13. John Player lecture, January 1973.
14. Tatham, *My Weekly,* August 23, 1969.
15. Ibid.
16. John Player lecture, January 1973.
17. *Whitstable Times,* March 20, 1986.
18. John Player lecture, January 1973.
19. Ibid.
20. *TV Times,* June 3–9, 1989.
21. Peter S. Haigh, "Peter Cushing's One-Man Show," ABC *Film Review.*
22. Interview with Fred Jones, *Radio Times,* November 14, 1968.
23. Ibid.
24. Steve Swires, "Peter Cushing—The Baddie with the Heart of Gold," *Starlog* 96.
25. Chris Knight and Peter Nicholson, "A Chat with Peter Cushing about 'Dracula Today,'" *Cinefantastique,* Summer 1972.
26. Dick Tatham, "Peter the Great," *My Weekly,* August 23, 1969.
27. Eileen McCarroll, "Peter Cushing and the Power of Goodness," *Woman's Weekly,* 1988.
28. Chris Knight, "Talking with Peter Cushing," *L'incroyable Cinema* 5.
29. Interview by Dane Lanken, *The Gazette,* November 19, 1976. Montreal.
30. Knight, "Talking with Peter Cushing," *L'incroyable Cinema* 5.
31. Daphne Ayles, "Are the Fans Framed?" *London Calling,* Winter 1974.

Hollywood (1939–1941)

The more I do the more I feel the need and urge to improve standards, always with the feeling of never achieving such ideals. Your combined loyalty and constructive criticism do much to sustain my efforts — Peter Cushing

The Man in the Iron Mask
(1939)

Credits and Cast

Released July 1939; 110 minutes; Black and white; An Edward Small Production; released through United Artists; filmed in Hollywood. Director: James Whale; Producer: Edward Small; Screenplay: George Bruce; Based on Alexandre Dumas' novel; Music: Lucien Moraweck; Director of photography: Robert Planck; Art director: John D. Schulze; Production manager: Val Paul; Editor: Grant Whytock; Sound recordist: W. H. Wilmarth; Costumes: Bridgehouse; Fencing instructor: Fred Cavens; Special effects: Howard Anderson.

Louis Hayward (Louis XIV/Philippe), Joan Bennett (Maria), Warren William (D'Artagnan), Joseph Schildkraut (Fouquet), Alan Hale (Porthos), Walter Kingsford (Colbert), Bert Roach (Athos), Marian Martin (Mme. de la Vallière), Montague Love (Ambassador), Doris Kenyon (Queen Anne), Albert Dekker (Louis XIII), Nigel de Brulier (Richelieu), William Boyle (Commandant), Boyd Irwin (Constable), Howard Brooks (Cardinal), Reginald Barlowe (Jean Paul), Lane Chandler (Captain of the Guard), Wyndham Standing (Doctor), Dorothy Vaughan (Midwife), Sheila D'Arcy (Maid), Robert Milsasch (Torturer), D'Arcy Corrigan (Prisoner), Harry Woods (First Officer), Peter Cushing (King's Messenger), Emmett King (Chamberlain).

Synopsis

> *How could I mistake it — I've been here before —*
> Peter Cushing's first line in films.

Prince Philippe of France is born minutes after his twin Louis. Since Philippe will be denied the throne and become a political liability, his

21

Cushing's first screen appearance in James Whale's *The Man in the Iron Mask*.

father, King Louis XIII (Albert Dekker) makes a difficult decision. Philippe will be given to faithful musketeer D'Artagnan (Warren William) to raise in isolation.

The years pass. Having succeeded his father, Louis XIV (Louis Hayward) becomes a tyrant and Philippe (also Hayward), unaware of their relationship, leads a revolt against him. Philippe is captured and Louis — astounded at their resemblance — uses him as bait for assassins. Philippe is also used to court Louis' intended bride Maria (Joan Bennett), as the king has other romantic interests.

When Louis discovers that they are brothers, he orders Philippe placed in an iron mask and imprisoned for life in the Bastille. With the help of D'Artagnan and the musketeers (Alan Hale, Bert Roach, and Miles Mander), Philippe escapes.

Philippe captures his twin and imprisons him in the same manner, hoping to have the chance to right his brother's wrongs. As Philippe and Maria are about the wed, Louis escapes and leads an attack to regain the throne. In the ensuing battle Louis is killed when his carriage overturns. D'Artagnan, mortally wounded, dies in Philippe's arms as the new king vows to restore France to its former glory.

Commentary

On Wednesday, January 18, 1939, Peter Cushing boarded the SS *Champlain* in Southampton, bound for America. The twenty-five-year-old would-be actor was on his way to Hollywood on a one-way ticket provided by his father. During a brief stay in New York he met Larney Goodkind of Columbia Pictures, who had a contact in Edward Small's production company.

Armed with a letter of introduction, he arrived in Los Angeles on February 10 and, after a four-mile walk, found himself at the North Hudson Street YMCA. By the end of the month he was "in the movies."

The letter admitted him to the studio where *The Man in the Iron Mask* was to begin filming. He was hired at $75 per week to play opposite Louis Hayward in the split screen process used to produce the illusion of twins. Since Peter Cushing would always be playing the "other" twin (to give Hayward someone to react to), his scenes would be discarded.

Director James Whale—ironically the director of the 1931 *Frankenstein*—was pleased with the young actor's efforts and rewarded him with a small part as the King's Messenger. In order to get the part, Peter Cushing, well, misrepresented himself as an accomplished swordsman. He was instantly found out by the film's fencing master, Fred Cavens. Sensing a willing pupil, Cavens taught him a skill that was soon mastered and would be used often during his career.

Peter Cushing was horrified at his first glimpse of himself on screen. "I nearly fainted on the spot when I saw myself for the first time. I had a dreadful voice and was as round as a dumpling," he recalled.[1] He fared little better on horseback, being thrown from his uncooperative mount.

Fellow Englishman Louis Hayward befriended his "twin" and invited him to dinner. "I spent many enjoyable weekends there," Cushing said, "and finally they kindly invited me to stay with them for as long as I wished."[2] The guest was soon being introduced by Mrs. Hayward (Ida Lupino) as her "son."

The film was a great success and is still enjoyable today, despite its familiar subject matter. The reviews were less than generous, but audiences loved it.

The *New York Times* (June 26, 1939) found it "Not quite the swashbuckling tale we had expected ... nevertheless a moderately entertaining costume piece." The *New York Daily Mirror* (June 29) felt that "Mr. Small gave the fans a dashing cast and a gifted director." *Variety* (June 28) called it a "highly entertaining adventure melodrama ... picture holds lightness and romance, all neatly interwoven."

This small beginning started Peter Cushing off on a career that would include ninety more films and would span six decades—a record equaled by few performers.

Notes

1. John Player lecture, January 1973.
2. Cushing, *An Autobiography*.

A Chump at Oxford
(1939)

Credits and Cast

Released February 1940 (U.S.); 42 minutes (U.S.), 63 minutes (U.K.); Black and white; A Hal Roach Production; Released through United Artists. Director: Alfred Goulding; Producer: Hal Roach; Associate producer: Hal Roach, Jr.; Original story and screenplay: Charles Rogers, Felix Adler, Harry Langdon; Production manager: Sidney S. Van Keuran; Photography: Art Lloyd; Photographic effects: Roy Seawright; Editor: Bert Jordon; Art director: Charles D. Hall; Set decorations: William L. Stevens; Wardrobe supervision: Harry Black; Sound: William Randall; Musical score: Marvin Hatley.

Stan Laurel (Stan Laurel/Legendary Lord Paddington), Oliver Hardy (Himself), Forrester Harvey (Meredith), Wilfred Lucas (Dean Williams), Forbes Murray (Bank President), Frank Baker (Jenkins), Eddie Borden (Student Ghost), Peter Cushing (Jones), Charlie Hall (Hector), Gerald Fielding (Brown), Victor Kendall (Cecil), Gerald Rogers (Johnson), Jack Heasley (Hodges), Rex Lease (Bank Robber), Stanley Blystone (Officer), Alec Harford (Cabdriver).

Synopsis

What is it?—Peter Cushing upon seeing Stan Laurel.

Stan and Ollie (Laurel and Hardy), two bumbling street cleaners, are convinced that their lack of success is due to a lack of education. After accidentally capturing a bank robber (Rex Lease), they are rewarded with a free Oxford education by the grateful bank president (Forbes Murray).

After arriving at Oxford, they are subjected to a brutal hazing by several upperclassmen (including Peter Cushing) which nearly causes the duo to be expelled.

When hit on the head by a falling window, Stan loses his memory and becomes Lord Paddington, an outstanding scholar-athlete who disappeared years earlier after being hit by the same window! Stan is now the toast of Oxford.

Disgusted by his friend's pretentious behavior, Ollie plans to return to America. Just in time, the fateful window bonks Stan again, restoring both his memory and their friendship.

Commentary

One of the most fascinating aspects of Peter Cushing's brief Hollywood career is that he found himself — as an actor with no background in films — working with an assortment of film legends.

In *The Man in the Iron Mask* and *They Dare not Love* he was directed by James Whale. He acted with Cary Grant in *The Howards of Virginia* and with Carole Lombard in *Vigil in the Night*. And, in *A Chump at Oxford*, he appeared with Laurel and Hardy.

The screen's most famous comedy duo first appeared together — quite by chance — in *Lucky Dog* (1917). In all they appeared in over 150 films, 27 of which were of feature length.

Ephraim Katz described their secret of success as "representing a level of naivete and stupidity that almost anyone in the audience could feel superior to. They would constantly get into trouble as the result of a brainless act, usually on the part of Laurel, and sink into a deeper and deeper mess."[1]

Oliver Hardy, usually Stan's straight man, was "a study in frustrated dignity. His exasperation with Laurel's follies was typically registered by a frustrated, incredulous gaze into the camera."[2]

They were associated for most of their careers with the Hal Roach studio. This collaboration ended after the filming of *A Chump at Oxford*. By 1945 their film careers were, for all practical purposes, finished.

While *A Chump at Oxford* may seem less than hilarious today due to changing comedic tastes and styles, it was well thought of in its time. Graham Greene noted in *The Spectator* (February 23, 1940) that "*A Chump at Oxford* ranks with their best pictures." *Variety* (February 21) felt that "They have more witty dialogue than usual."

For his second film role Peter Cushing was cast as an Oxford student both in the film and in press book publicity: "Numbered among these real-life Oxonians are Peter Cushing." Cushing must have been surprised at his easily won degree.

Peter Cushing enjoyed working with the famous pair and has always considered the experience as a highlight of his career. Always admitting that he is a fan as well as an actor, Cushing was often in awe of the legendary figures he encountered in Hollywood. He describes his experience thus:

> A few days after completing my stint on *The Man in the Iron Mask*, I was at [Schwab's drug store] enjoying a milkshake, and it was there that I heard Hal Roach was needing English type actors for a Laurel and Hardy film. . . .
> I lost no time in making contact with his studio and I was accepted. My part was little more than an "extra," but I was so proud to be with two of the greatest comedians the cinema has ever produced.[3]

After a scene in which several cast members — including Peter Cushing — fell into a pool, the famous duo "made quite sure there were towels, blankets, and hot drinks available for all of us when we climbed out of the water. Such was their thought for others."[4]

Cushing summed up his feeling for Laurel and Hardy by saying, "I was only with them for a week. It is one that I treasure."[5] He also treasured an award presented to him in 1971 from the Sons of the Desert Society — a group dedicated to the films of Laurel and Hardy.

Initially, *A Chump at Oxford* was released in America as a forty-two-minute featurette. It contained added footage (to sixty-three minutes) when released in England. This longer version is currently available on prerecorded video.

Director Alfred Goulding, an Australian, was a director for the Roach studio. It was he who, after catching Laurel and Hardy in a vaudeville act in Los Angeles, suggested to Hal Roach that they be signed for a five-film series.[6] The rest, as they say, is history.

The 1940s were, more or less, a golden age of double features — a concept sadly out of fashion today. *A Chump at Oxford* found itself paired with two rather unlikely co-features (as, no doubt, did many other films). At New York's Rialto Theater the Laurel and Hardy comedy was paired with *The Siege of Warsaw* — a deadly serious and rather controversial documentary of the Nazi bombing of Poland! Equally absurd was the double feature at Boston's Trans Lux — *A Chump at Oxford* and Bela Lugosi's *The Human Monster*.

Notes

1. Ephraim Katz, *The Film Encyclopedia*.
2. Ibid.
3. Cushing, *An Autobiography*.
4. Ibid.
5. Ibid.
6. Video Treasurers Classic Collection, *A Chump at Oxford*, 1991.

Carole Lombard, Brian Aherne, Peter Cushing, and Anne Shirley in *Vigil in the Night.*

Vigil in the Night
(1939)

Credits and Cast

Released April 1940 (U.S.); 96 minutes; Black and white; A Pandro S. Berman Production; Released through RKO; Filmed in Hollywood. Producer and director: George Stevens; Screenplay: Fred Guiol, P. J. Wolfson, Rowland Leigh; Based on the novel by A. J. Cronin; Director of photography: Robert DeGrasse; Music: Alfred Newman; Art director: Van Nest Polglase; Editor: Henry Berman; Costumes: Walter Plunkett; Technical advisers: Albert Hemming, Cecil E. Reynolds; Set director: Darrell Silvera; Sound recordist: Richard Van Hessen.

Carole Lombard (Anne), Brian Aherne (Dr. Prescott), Anne Shirley (Lucy), Julien Mitchell (Mr. Bowley), Robert Coote (Dr. Caley), Brenda Forbes (Nora), Rita Page (Glennie), Peter Cushing (Joe Shand), Ethel Griffies (Matron East), Doris Lloyd (Mrs. Bowley), Emily Fitzroy (Sister).

Synopsis

> *Why couldn't you have kept your blasted notions to yourself?* —
> Joe Shand.

Anne (Carole Lombard) had dedicated her life to nursing, but her younger sister Lucy (Anne Shirley) has entered the profession only to please her sister. She is uncomfortable with her responsibilities and rebels against the monotony.

While attempting to earn her certificate, Lucy becomes fatigued by overwork. Charged with the care of a seriously ill child, she falters. Her carelessness causes the child's death, but Anne takes the blame so that Lucy can become certified. However, Lucy has had enough and, despite Anne's sacrifice, leaves for London with Joe Shand (Peter Cushing) to start a new life. Anne must now bear the shame and responsibility alone.

She leaves that hospital in disgrace and finds a position at another, less affluent one. There Anne meets Dr. Prescott (Brian Aherne) and the two join in a struggle against inadequate funding and a smallpox epidemic. Mr. Bowley (Julien Mitchell) controls the hospital funds but he refuses to increase the meager budget until his own son is stricken.

Lucy, feeling guilty about Anne's sacrifice and her own lack of dedication leaves London — and Joe — to work with Anne once more. She volunteers to care for the smallpox victims and contracts the disease herself.

After Lucy's death, Joe hysterically blames Anne, claiming that Lucy was never cut out to be a nurse and forced into it — and her death. As Joe regains control of himself, Anne and Dr. Prescott hurry to the operating theater to aid miners injured in an explosion.

Commentary

Of Peter Cushing's seven Hollywood features from 1939 to 1941, this was the only one in which he made an impact. For his key role as Joe Shand he received the following review from Kate Cameron in the *New York Daily News* (May 2, 1940): "Peter Cushing dominates two dramatic scenes.... His acting has the same forceful quality that distinguishes Spencer Tracy's performances."

Cushing was cast with the help of fellow actor (and cricket player) Robert Coote who suggested him to director George Stevens. However, as shooting began in July 1939 misfortune struck in a manner not unlike the film's plot. Star Carole Lombard had to be operated on for an acute appendicitis, halting the production for six weeks.

Opposite page: **Peter Cushing's first star billing.**

During the interim Peter Cushing was offered roles in two (unknown) films, which he turned down because he would have had to abandon his role in *Vigil in the Night*. Since only three days of filming had been completed, this was quite a show of dedication. As a life-long movie fan, he was in awe of Carole Lombard (Mrs. Clark Gable) and valued the opportunity to act with her.

While the production was shut down, Peter Cushing went to Palm Springs with the Haywards and was lucky enough to grab the lead in a stage production of *Love from a Stranger*. His character was to have blonde hair, so he bought gold luster from an art store. "It was most effective," he recalls. "It also turned my scalp bright green."[1]

When the production resumed, Peter Cushing found himself in a somewhat prophetic situation. "One morning, I saw a prop man carrying a succulent side of bacon into the Operating Theatre set. 'Lunch?' I inquired, hopefully. 'Nope,' he replied laconically, 'operation.'"[2] In a manner that Cushing would often duplicate later in his career, the bacon was to be placed on an actor's stomach to give the "surgeon" something to realistically cut through.

While well done in all areas, the film was not a success. Lombard, famous for her wacky comedy roles, was not accepted in this straight role. The story itself is depressing and provided little relief from the stressful outbreak of World War II.

The *New York Times* (May 2, 1940) felt that the author (A. J. Cronin—a doctor) "feels strongly about something—so strongly that he never gets around to saying it." *The Times* (London, May 27) stated that the film "has been made with a pains-taking sincerity and both acting and directing are level headed and restrained, but inspiration is lacking and the film never touches the heights."

After the film's release, Peter Cushing was interviewed by the *New York Journal American*. Asked whether he had "gone Hollywood," Cushing said that his home had a swimming pool, tennis court, and gym. "Do you own it?" asked the interviewer. "Why I merely rent a room there," he replied. "I live at the YMCA."

The following appeared in the somewhat massive RKO press book and, although it may be typical publicity hype, it has the ring of truth. It indicates the potential Hollywood career that might have been Peter Cushing's had he not returned to England. It reads:

> One scene does not make a screen star, but more than one Hollywood luminary received his first impetus toward stardom by a single starkly dramatic sequence.
> Such a scene as that . . . may well launch English new-comer Peter Cushing on a top flight career.
> Cushing, who landed in Hollywood with less than one dollar in his

jeans, plays Anne Shirley's husband in the story. So highly did Producer-Director George Stevens regard Peter's work in the early scenes that he had a sequence written into the script which gives Cushing the chance every aspiring young actor dreams about. It is a scene with the young actor ranting and raving at Carole Lombard as a nurse and Brian Aherne as a doctor.

More than one male star has hit his stride with just such high keyed histrionics.

In Cushing's first appearance in a feature article, Elizabeth Copeland headlined the young actor in her "Reel News from Hollywood" column:

> Peter Cushing, by Skimpy Living, Manages to Wait for Carole Lombard Film. . . .
>
> Peter Cushing's long standing admiration for Carole Lombard has cost him a number of good roles and a sizable addition to his bank account.
>
> During his London stage career [*sic*], Cushing conceived his admiration for the blonde actress. When he decided to come to Hollywood, one of the motivating factors was the hope that he might have a chance to play in a picture with her.
>
> After four months in this country he was selected by Director George Stevens for a featured role in *Vigil in the Night*, . . . but after only three days of shooting at RKO Radio Studios, Miss Lombard was stricken with appendicitis and her ensuing hospitalization caused a six-week production halt.
>
> Cushing had arrived in the country almost flat broke, and he could weather this production delay only by the most skimpy living. During the six-week interim, he was offered substantial parts in two other pictures but his acceptance of them would have caused him to abandon his part in the Lombard film. It was a temptation, but he struggled through and at length realized his ambition in scenes before the camera with Miss Lombard.[3]

Notes

1. Cushing, *An Autobiography*.
2. Ibid.
3. Elizabeth Copeland, *Richmond News Leader* (date unknown).

Laddie
(1940)

Credits and Cast

Released 1940 by RKO; Filmed in Hollywood. Director: Jack Hively; Producer: Cliff Reid; Screenplay: Bert Granet; Based on the novel by Gene Stratton Porter; Music:

Roy Webb; Photography: Harry Wild; Special effects: Vernon Walker; Art director: Van Nest Polglase; Editor: George Hively; Costumes: Renie.

Tim Holt (Laddie), Virginia Gilmore (Pamela), Spring Byington (Mrs. Stanton), Robert Barrat (Mr. Stanton), Miles Mander (Mr. Pryor), Joan Carroll ("Little Sister"), Esther Dale (Bridgette), Martha O'Driscoll (Sally), Mary Forbes (Mrs. Pryor), Peter Cushing (Robert Pryor).

Synopsis

> *Rugged manhood ... flowering womanhood.* — RKO publicity

The Stanton family live on an Indiana farm in the late 1800s. Laddie (Tim Holt), the oldest son, is admired and respected by everyone in the small farming community. His life is pleasant and uncomplicated until the Pryors buy a large estate nearby.

Mr. Pryor (Miles Mander) had brought his wife (Mary Forbes) and daughter Pam (Virginia Gilmore) from England to forget a family scandal brought about by his son, Robert (Peter Cushing). The young man had disgraced both himself and his family in a notorious episode in the military.

Laddie has fallen in love with Pam and invites her to his sister Sally's (Martha O'Driscoll) wedding, where he proposes. However, Mr. Pryor disapproves because of Laddie's much lower social standing.

Pryor does, however, agree to sell Laddie some acreage from the estate. Laddie's young sister (Joan Carroll) prays for a miracle. While walking in the forest, she spots Pam in earnest conversation with a young man. Robert has come to the United States to convince his father of his innocence in the scandal, but the long journey has weakened him and his is dangerously ill.

"Little Sister" (as she is called) gets Laddie, who takes the stricken Robert to the Stanton farm where he is nursed back to health. She then informs Mr. Pryor that his son is at her family's farm. Angered, he rushes to confront Robert, but is intercepted by Laddie. Pryor is convinced by Laddie that he has never really heard Robert's side of the matter and agrees to be forgiving.

Softened by the reunion with his son, Pryor gives Laddie and Pam permission to marry.

Commentary

This was the third filming of Gene Stratton Porter's popular novel (2.5 million copies sold), previously filmed by RKO in 1935 by director

George Stevens. Its sentimental plot would probably be viewed today as camp, but it provided simple, family oriented entertainment in increasingly troubled times.

To recreate the rural 1870s RKO covered two of its sound stages with over 100 tons of soil and even planted trees and shrubbery. This seems rather pointless, due to the modern use of natural location shooting, but made perfect sense during the 1940s.[1]

Released soon after the outbreak of World War II — but before American involvement — the interplay between British and American characters was an important issue of the day and would become a common plot device of the early 1940s.

Star Tim Holt (son of actor Jack Holt) is best remembered today for his roles in Orson Welles' *The Magnificent Ambersons* (1942) and John Huston's *Treasure of the Sierra Madre* (1948), but the bulk of his career was spent in B westerns like *The Mysterious Desperado* (1949).

Peter Cushing's small — but key — role as Robert went unnoticed by both audiences and critics, as did the entire film. He probably secured the role because of his accent and to keep him busy on the RKO lot after his fine performance in *Vigil in the Night.*

An unidentified newspaper clipping (almost certainly from the period of *Laddie*'s release) reveals that "Peter Cushing, the young English actor who recently completed a role in *Vigil in the Night* is being tested by Gene Towne and Graham Baker for *Tom Brown's School Days.*"

The latter film was released by RKO in 1940 — without Peter Cushing. It is not clear whether Cushing ever actually tested for the film or was rejected. It is also worth wondering whether he was considered for other parts during this period or actually appeared in a small role in a film that has still gone unnoticed. Due to his appearance in *The Howards of Virginia*, a film that is not part of his filmography in any source book, anything is possible.

Note

1. RKO press book.

The Howards of Virginia
(1940)

Credits and Cast

Released 1940; 117 minutes; Black and white; Released through Columbia; Filmed in Hollywood and Williamsburg, Virginia. Director and producer: Frank Lloyd;

Associate producer: Jack H. Skirball; Screenplay: Sidney Buchman; Based on the novel by Elizabeth Page, *The Tree of Liberty*; Music: Richard Hageman; Director of photography: Bert Glennon; Editor: Paul Weatherwax; Montage: Slavko Vorkapich; Art director: John Goodman; Set decoration: Aloward Bristol; Technical adviser: Waldo Twitchell. Released in U.K. under title *The Tree of Liberty*.

Cary Grant (Matt Howard), Martha Scott (Jane Peyton), Sir Cedric Hardwicke (Fleetwood Peyton), Alan Marshal (Roger Peyton), Richard Carlson (Thomas Jefferson), Paul Kelly (Captain Allen), Irving Bacon (Norton), Elizabeth Risdon (Clarissa), Anne Revere (Mrs. Norton), Richard Alden (James Howard), Phil Taylor (Peyton Howard), Rita Quigley (Mary Howard), Libby Taylor (Dicey), Richard Gaines (Patrick Henry), George Houston (George Washington), Peter Cushing (Leslie Stevens), Ralph Bird (Jason), Roy Gordon (Col. Jefferson).

Synopsis

Your servant, sir. — Leslie Stevens

As America moves close to a revolution against British rule, backwoodsman Matt Howard (Cary Grant) comes to Williamsburg, Virginia. Through the help of his friend Thomas Jefferson (Richard Carlson), Matt obtains a job as a surveyor and is introduced to Williamsburg society (including Leslie Stevens, played by Peter Cushing). Although Matt seems to prefer the wilderness, he tries to adjust to his new life.

After working for the wealthy Fleetwood Peyton (Sir Cedric Hardwicke), Matt falls in love with his employer's daughter, Jane (Martha Scott). They marry and soon return to Matt's beloved frontier.

Encouraged by Jefferson, Matt enters politics and, when revolution breaks out, sides with the colonies. Now a soldier, Matt is involved in many important battles, including the final defeat of the British at Yorktown. His duty done, he returns to Jane and their children.

Commentary

Peter Cushing never listed this film among his credits and it's not hard to see why. By the time his film career really got moving in the mid–1950s his five-second appearance in a fifteen-year-old film was easily forgotten.

In truth, he does not even make the most of the five seconds. His inexperience is painfully obvious and he exhibits none of the screen presence that would be his in the future. He sits, rather stiffly, as Richard Carlson introduces him to Cary Grant as "a great talent with music, practically

Peter cuts a dashing figure as Leslie Stevens in *The Howards of Virginia* (U.K. title, *The Tree of Liberty*).

none with the ladies." He answers with an awkward bow. Peter Cushing was not mentioned in the film's lengthy cast list.

What is fascinating here is whether Peter Cushing appeared in other films—perhaps in crowd scenes—that have not yet been noticed. *The Howards of Virginia* was a Columbia release of 1940, while his other films of 1939-40 were through United Artists, Hal Roach, and RKO. It's more than likely that a young man with an English accent was needed for the small part and Cushing was simply in the proverbial right place at the right time. At any rate, one can't help wondering.

The film itself is not very good, either. Cary Grant, cast against type as a backwoodsman, failed miserably in his rare "stretch." His attempt at rough speech and mannerisms is laughable and gives the entire film a false look and feeling that fine production values can't overcome. Possibly the best thing about the film is its location filming in Williamsburg, Virginia.

Newsweek (September 2, 1940) felt that "Obviously miscast, Cary Grant meets the exigencies of a difficult role with more gusto than persuasion. . . . While ambitious, expensive, and generally interesting [it] comes to life all too infrequently." The *New York Times* (September 4) agreed that the film was "deficient in dramatic action. The only disappointment — and it is a major one — is Cary Grant."

Women in War
(1940)

Credits and Cast

Released 1940 (U.S.), February 1942 (U.K.); 71 minutes; Black and white; A Republic Picture; Filmed in Hollywood. Director: John H. Auer; Producer: Sol C. Siegel; Screenplay: F. Hugh Herbert, Doris Anderson; Music: Cy Feuer; Director of photography: Jack Marta; Special effects: Howard Lydecker; Editor: Edward Mann; Wardrobe: Adele Palmer.

Elsie Janis (O'Neil), Wendy Barrie (Pamela), Patric Knowles (Lt. Larry Hall), Mae Clarke (Nurse Halliday), Dennie Moore (Ginger), Dorothy Peterson (Frances), Billy Gilbert (Pierre), Colin Tapley (Captain Tedford), Stanley Logan (Colonel Starr), Barbara Pepper (Millie), Pamela Randell (Phyllis), Lawrence Grant (Gordon), Lester Matthews (Sir Humphrey), Marian Martin (Woman), Holmes Herbert (Justice), Vera Lewis (Pierre's Wife), Charles D. Brown (Freddie), Peter Cushing (Captain Evans).

Synopsis

> Bombs rain from the sky! Tanks charge with fury! But brave women, resigned to fate, stand side by side with their men. — Republic poster publicity

A drunken British officer (Colin Tapley) makes a violent pass at headstrong American Pamela (Wendy Barrie) who, defending herself, pushes him over a balcony to his death.

At her trial things look bleak until O'Neil (Elsie Janis), her estranged mother whom she has not seen for years, secretly arranges for her to join the Overseas Nursing Corps. This sways the jury and Pamela is acquitted. For reasons of her own, however, O'Neil does not reveal her identity to her daughter after the trial.

After joining the Nursing Corps, Pamela encounters more problems. She is accused by Halliday (Mae Clarke) of trying to seduce Larry (Patric Knowles), her fiancé. Innocent but angered, Pamela decides to do what she was accused of. Larry falls for her but Pamela, realizing that she is in the wrong, rejects his proposal.

Halliday, unaware of Pamela's change of heart, tries to commit suicide and kill Pamela at the same time by driving an ambulance into a bombing attack. She learns the truth too late to save herself, but Pamela is saved by O'Neil who then reveals her identity.

Cushing does his bit for the war effort in *Women in War*.

Commentary

When *Women in War* opened at New York's Criterion Theater in May 1940, American entry into World War II was still a year and a half away. As such, it was one of the first films to use American involvement in the war as a plot device.

The film received quite a bit of notice for featuring Elsie Janis—a former stage star—in her comeback role as O'Neil. Now forgotten, Janis had been a celebrated actress in the early 1900s.

She began her career at age five, and from 1907 to 1917 she was one of the most popular actresses in both America and England. After making two films in 1916, she went to Europe and entertained troops until World War I ended in 1918. For her sacrifices made on behalf of the troops, she was known as the Sweetheart of the American Expeditionary Forces. After the war, she returned to the stage but made no film appearance until *Women in War*. Janis survived a personal horror during the war when her fiancé was killed in a fall from an observaton balloon.

Mae Clarke (Elizabeth in James Whale's *Frankenstein*, 1931) also made a comeback of sorts after a three-year absence from films.

Peter Cushing, last billed as Captain Evans, had another small role in the wake of his success in *Vigil in the Night* and made no impression on either audiences or critics.

Many of the reviewers commented on the realism of the battle scenes. Not all were pleased. Lee Mortimer in the *New York Daily News* (May 30, 1940) said, "The worst that can be said about *Women in War* is that it packs too much punch." *Variety* (May 29) felt that the "Picture is unfolded in a episodic manner, skimming over the thin story structure at a fast pace. Special effects and miniature work accentuate the regulation village bombing scenes." Bosley Crowther in the *New York Post* (May 30) was not impressed. "Neither can we say very much for the shell shocked blatancy of *Women in War*. But with matters of taste aside, we can't say much for the picture either."

Two uncredited reviews were even more blunt. "Nerve wracking intensity, noise, and horrors of war. Unnecessary drinking and cheap moral standards." And finally, the ludicrous: "If this is the best the war can inspire [??], let's do without war pictures."

The battle scene that unnerved most reviewers and, presumably, audiences, took sixteen hours to film, but lasted less than four minutes on screen.[1]

Exploitation played a large part in promoting the film. One idea seems to have gone a bit too far. At the Criterion the outer lobby featured a machine-gun pit with sandbags and loudspeakers blaring sounds of machine-gun fire, bursting bombs, and the whine of shells!

The film today seems "lost" — a category that, unfortunately, fits more than a few of Peter Cushing's films. Lacking a real star or high-powered director, the film has probably not been seen since the 1940s.

Note

1. Republic press book.

They Dare Not Love
(1941)

Credits and Cast

Released 1941; Black and white; 75 minutes; A James Whale Production; Released through Columbia; Filmed in Hollywood. Directors: James Whale and Charles Vidor; Producer: Samuel Bischoff; Screenplay: Charles Bennett, Ernst Fajda; Director of photography: Franz F. Planer; Editor: Al Clark; Music: Morris Stoloff.

George Brent (The Prince), Martha Scott (Marta), Paul Lukas (Von Helsing), Egon Brecher (Professor Keller), Roman Bohnin (Baron Shafter), Edgar Barrier (Captain

Ehrhardt), Kay Linaker (Barbara), Frank Reicher (Captain), Peter Cushing (Sub-Lt. Blacker), with Lloyd Bridges.

Synopsis

> *The breathtaking drama of two hearts beating to the terrifying tempo of a world in flames.* — Columbia poster

Prince Von Rostenberg (George Brent) leaves Austria as the Nazis attack. En route to America he meets Marta (Martha Scott) but they are soon separated. He is tracked by a Gestapo agent, Von Helsing (Paul Lukas), who is to prevent the prince from returning to Austria to lead a revolt.

The prince discovers that Marta and her father (Egon Brecher) are helping Austrians escape and decides to exchange himself for the release of seven prisoners, one of who is Marta's fiancé.

Marta discovers that her lover is, in fact, a Gestapo agent and prevents the prince from needlessly sacrificing his life.

Commentary

Peter Cushing's feature film career in Hollywood ended with this indifferent effort from famed *Frankenstein* director James Whale. Strangely, it was also Whale's last feature and ended that often brilliant career of the director of Peter Cushing's first film.

James Whale was as instrumental as anyone in the creation of Universal's horror cycle of the 1930s. He directed Karloff in *Frankenstein* (1931), *Bride of Frankenstein* (1935), and the *Old Dark House* (1932), in addition to Claude Raines in *The Invisible Man* (1933). After *Showboat* (1936), his career began to slip and, as usual in such cases, some of his less than endearing mannerisms became less easily tolerated.

Gregory Mank reported that Whale was often insensitive to and jealous of Boris Karloff and referred to him — privately — as a "truck driver."[1] Attitudes like that on the set seemed to increase as his talent waned, and a blowup on the set of *They Dare Not Love* resulted in his replacement by Charles Vidor. James Whale never directed another feature film. He died, an apparent suicide, in 1957 — the year that *The Curse of Frankenstein* was released.

Peter Cushing did not appear until the climax, leading a party to rescue Brent and Scott.

The *Baltimore Evening Sun* (April 23, 1941) found the play "scarcely inspired and, although it pains us to say so, the work of an ordinarily able cast will do nothing to enhance its members' reputations. The *New York*

Herald Tribune felt "James Whale's direction is deliberate and fails to take fullest advantage of suspenseful opportunities in the script."

Going to the movies, naturally, was an entirely different experience in 1941 than it is today. We present the following (somewhat trivial) information to give the reader an idea of what one would have encountered seeing *They Dare Not Love* on its original release. In addition to the standard cartoon, newsreel (World War II events), and short subject (possibly on baseball), audiences at the Loew's State in New York City were treated to a performance by Dick Stabile's Orchestra and a vaudeville act featuring Henry Armetta and Edith Shutta. The good old days!

Peter Cushing's Hollywood career ended with this—another small role. His seven appearances—with the exception of *Vigil in the Night*—made no impact, and he was growing homesick. At the outbreak of World War II he had reported for a physical for induction in the British Army but, "due to a couple of injuries sustained during my rugger playing days—torn ligaments in my left knee and perforated left ear drum—I was . . . told to stand by. They are not in need of cannon fodder yet, the cheerful M.O. informed me."[2]

After leaving Hollywood, Cushing earned money for his passage home by appearing on the stage. His work in a summer stock troupe in Warrensburg, New York, (six plays) led to his first—and only—Broadway play.

The Seventh Trumpet premiered at the Mansfield Theater on November 21, 1941. Written by Charles Rann Kennedy, it is described on its dust jacket as "a subtle harmony of high comedy, profound poignancy, and spiritual exaltation." It closed, after eleven performances, on November 29.

Reviews for the religion-oriented production were quite favorable from church groups. The New York Federation of Churches, for example, reported that, "The Seventh Trumpet is tremendous!" The Free Synagogue called it, "A beautiful and noble utterance."

Unfortunately, the mainstream critics—and audiences—were not impressed. Burns Mantle, in *The Best Plays of 1941–42* said, "Charles Rann Kennedy tried to stir the faithful to a new declaration for Christian socialism . . . but found the faithful too busy to attend its call."

Peter Cushing played Percival, a London bobby. In a cast of unknowns (both then and now), he was listed fourth. Sadly, it was his only Broadway role.

Notes

1. Gregory Mank, *Karloff and Lugosi.*
2. Cushing, *An Autobiography.*

England and the World (1947–1985)

Hamlet
(1947)

Credits and Cast

Released May 1948; Black and white; 142 minutes; A Two Cities Film; Released by Rank (U.K.), Universal International (U.S.). Director: Laurence Olivier; Associate producer: Reginald Beck; Assistant producer: Anthony Bushell; Supervised by: Filippo Del Guidice; Director of photography: Desmond Dickinson; Editor: Helga Cranston; Camera: Ray Sturgess; Designer: Roger Furst; Art director: Carmen Dillon; Production supervisor: Phil C. Samuel; Production manager: John Gossage; Sound: John Mitchell, L. E. Overton; Special effects: Paul Sheriff, Henry Harris, Paul Whitehead; Mime: David Paltengh; Swordplay: Dennis Loraine; Makeup: Tony Storzini; Hairstyles: Vivienne Walker; Set dresser: Roger Ramsdell; Continuity: Elizabeth Everson; Electrician: James Hamilton; Music: William Walton, Muir Matheson.

Laurence Olivier (Hamlet), Eileen Herlie (Gertrude), Basil Sydney (Claudius), Jean Simmons (Ophelia), Felix Alymer (Polonius), Norman Wooland (Horatio), Terence Morgan (Laertes), Peter Cushing (Osric), Harcourt Williams (First Player), Patrick Troughton (Player King), Tony Tarver (Player Queen), Stanley Holloway (Gravedigger), Russell Thorndyke (Priest), John Laurie (Francisco), Edmund Knight (Bernardo), Anthony Quayle (Marcellus), Niall MacGinnis (Sea Captain), The Ghost (John Gielgud), with Anthony Bushell and Christopher Lee (?).

Synopsis

> *Dost' know this waterfly?* — Said of Osric by Hamlet.

Elsinore, Denmark. The king is dead, but his spirit walks the battlements by night, observed by Horatio (Norman Wooland), Francisco (John Laurie), and others. After much discussion, they decide it would be best to tell Prince Hamlet (Laurence Oliver).

We know this "waterfly"! Peter Cushing as Osric in Olivier's *Hamlet*.

The king's brother, Claudius (Basil Sydney), has replaced him not only as ruler of Denmark, but as husband to Queen Gertrude (Eileen Herlie). Hamlet has been unable to accept his father's death and this new arrangement and he broods. He speculates that his mother's remarriage — within a month — is not only heartless but incestuous, but holds his tongue.

The Prince loves Ophelia (Jean Simmons), daughter of Polonius (Felix Alymer), the lord chamberlain of the court. She is warned, both by her father and brother Laertes (Terence Morgan) that it will come to nothing due to Hamlet's social position and deteriorating mental state.

Horatio reveals the sighting of the spirit and Hamlet decides to meet them on the battlements during their midnight watch. The spirit appears during a revel in Claudius' honor and speaks to Hamlet.

The spirit is doomed to walk the earth, for the king died a sinner, unforgiven his sins. Worse, the spirit reveals that the death was not a natural one—he was poisoned by Claudius. He must be avenged before he will find peace, but Hamlet cannot act.

Polonius informs Claudius and Gertrude that he suspects Hamlet is mad. While he expounds on Hamlet's strange behavior and unseemly advances toward Ophelia, the prince hears all, hidden in a staircase. When Hamlet later fails to recognize Polonius, the chamberlain is convinced of his madness—a role Hamlet seemingly encourages. After further abusing Ophelia—this time observed by Claudius—plans are made to send the prince to England.

High on the battlements, Hamlet contemplates suicide but is, typically, unable to make a decision or follow a course of action.

When told that a troupe of actors has arrived, he requests that at the evening's performance some lines of his own might be inserted to mirror his father's murder. He asks Horatio to observe Claudius closely. As the play proceeds, Claudius reacts violently and Hamlet is almost delirious with joy.

Alone, Claudius castigates himself for his evil deed. As he prays for forgiveness, Hamlet stalks him from behind, but decides not to kill him at prayer ... better to wait to kill after a sin.

Hamlet confronts his mother in her chamber and sees a movement behind a tapestry. He stabs it, killing the inquisitive Polonius. When questioned about the killing, he answers in foolish riddles about worms, appearing to those assembled as mad. Claudius now makes the final arrangement to send Hamlet to England—and his death.

Ophelia has broken under the strain and has gone mad, sobbing and shrieking in the hallways. A servant, Osric (Peter Cushing), delivers a letter to the queen from Hamlet. Horatio also receives a message from his friend, telling of a battle at sea against pirates who have promised to return him to Denmark.

Laertes is horrified at Ophelia's condition and swears vengeance on Hamlet. Her death by drowning soon follows, intensifying his anger. When Hamlet returns from the sea, he witnesses, by accident, her burial.

Claudius and Laertes plan to kill Hamlet by poisoning him in a "duel" for wager. Osric informs Hamlet of Laertes' challenge and his goading, insinuating manner causes Hamlet to accept. In his haste to report his success, Osric tumbles down some steps.

As the onlookers assemble, Osric, with a smirk, hands out the rapiers. One has been dipped into a poisoned cup. As they lunge, Osric serves as judge to score the hits of the supposedly harmless weapons. As Hamlet scores first, Gertrude drinks from the cup.

With a glance at the now serious Osric, Laertes cuts Hamlet's arm. The prince wrests the sword from him and stabs his wrist as Gertrude, dying, falls from her chair.

Laertes, dying in Osric's arms, blames Claudius' treachery for all that has happened. Hamlet leaps upon the king and kills him.

Hamlet and Laertes make their peace, and both die, victims of Claudius' ambition and Hamlet's indecision.

Commentary

This is probably the most famous filming of a Shakespearean play, and rightly so. Star and director Laurence Olivier's film received many awards, including Academy Awards for Best Picture, Best Actor (Olivier), Best Set Design, and Best Costume Design. It was also chosen Best Picture by the British Film Institute.

To be associated with such a film at this (or any) point of his career was a great achievement for Peter Cushing. His casting indicates the standing he enjoyed among his peers. "I got a phone call from [producer] Tony Bushell," Cushing recalled, "saying that he and Laurence would like me to consider playing something in the film of *Hamlet*. So I said, 'I suppose Hamlet's cast?' and he said, 'Yes, Laurence is playing that. The only one left is Osric.' And I said, 'Well, that's me, obviously.'"[1]

His casting, however, was no accident. He had impressed Sir Laurence with his talent and honesty in an earlier association and was promised that he would be given an opportunity in a future production. Lord Olivier thought highly of Peter Cushing, praising him as "one of the best screen actors."[2]

Both Peter Cushing and Laurence Olivier used their own hair but, according to Sir Laurence, "We were the only two in the cast that looked like we were wearing wigs."[3] A recurring problem with his teeth caused Cushing some difficulty during a dialogue delivery. Lord Olivier remarked, "You are not using your lips because you are afraid you might spit. Now drown me! It will be a glorious death so long as I can hear what you are saying!"[4]

After the filming was completed, Peter and Helen Cushing were invited by Sir Laurence to join the Old Vic Theatre Company's tour of

Australia and New Zealand. Before leaving, Cushing designed a scarf that portrayed the main performers of *Hamlet* in costume. The scarf was accepted as a gift by the queen at the film's premiere at London's Odeon Theatre.

The American premiere was also quite an event. Its opening at Boston's Astor Theater on July 13, 1948, was picketed because — believe it or not — civic and religious groups objected to its "bawdy language" and demanded cuts. During its first run the film commanded a $2.40 admission, far in excess of the norm. Sir Laurence appeared on the cover of both *Time* and *Life* to herald the film's release.

Hamlet was the first film to feature both Peter Cushing and Christopher Lee — maybe. Many viewers find it difficult to spot the 6' 4" Lee, and for good reason. Lee recalls: "I smuggled myself onto the set as a soldier in order to watch Olivier directing. It was a totally unauthorized appearance."[5]

Naturally, reviews were ecstatic, but not without one controversy. *Time* (May 17, 1948) felt that "mostly as a result of cutting, their *Hamlet* loses much of the depth and complexity it might have had." However, the play in its entirety runs four hours, so some cutting was unavoidable. *The Times* (May 5) praised Lord Olivier's choice of actors: "The casting was admirable — nothing less than a masterpiece." *Variety* (May 12) called it "picturemaking at its best.... At a cost of $2,000,000, it seems incredibly cheap compared with some of the ephemeral trash that is being turned out."

Peter Cushing offered his own review: "If *Hamlet* had been a Hammer film, they'd say, 'This is disgusting! I mean, dreadful — all these deaths! Think of the bodies littering the floor!'"[6]

In a 1969 interview by Dick Tatham, Peter Cushing revealed that soon after the completion of *Hamlet* he was taken ill. He was stricken while rehearsing with Lord Olivier and John Mills for the play *The Damascus Blade*. "I knew Olivier had been thinking about putting me under contract.... He did so — the day after I had been ordered to bed. He paid me ten pounds a week during the six months I was ill. What I would have done without this, I can't imagine."[7]

This began an eighteen-month dry spell in 1949–50 in which Cushing could find no acting work. He continues: "So, I fell back on doing designs for a scarf-making firm. When nine months passed, I decided to give up acting. Helen was ill and the main thought in my mind was to concentrate on getting a reliable income."[8]

The dry spell ended with a phone call from Robert Helpmann for a role in the play *The Marriage Bureau*. "It only ran three weeks," Cushing recalled, "but it was enough to bring me back into circulation."[9]

Although he would not appear in another film until *Moulin Rouge*

(1952), he was kept busy on the stage, appearing in *Richard III*, *School for Scandal* (both in 1948–49), *The Gay Invalid*, *Caesar and Cleopatra*, and *Anthony and Cleopatra* (all in 1951).

Notes

1. Cushing, *An Autobiography*.
2. Laurence Olivier, *On Acting*.
3. Ibid.
4. Ibid.
5. Robert W. Pohle, Jr., and Douglas C. Hart, *The Films of Christopher Lee*.
6. "Peter Cushing—A One-Way Ticket to Hollywood," BBC Television, 1989.
7. Cushing, *An Autobiography*.
8. Ibid.
9. Ibid.

Moulin Rouge
(1952)

Credits and Cast

Released December 1952; 118 minutes; Technicolor; A Romulus Films Production; Released through United Artists (U.S.); Filmed on location in Paris, France, and at Shepperton Studios, England. Director and producer: John Huston; Screenplay: Anthony Veiller, John Huston; Based on the novel by Pierre la Mure; Associate producer: Jack Clayton; Production manager: Leigh Aman; First assistant director: Adrian Pryce Jones; Director of photography: Ossie Morris; Sound mixer: A. E. Rudolph; Art director: Paul Sheriff; Costumes and decor: Marcel Vertes; Editor: Ralph Kemplin; Music composer: George Auric; Special color consultant: Eliot Elisofon.

Jose Ferrer (Henri de Toulouse-Lautrec/Comte de Toulouse-Lautrec), Colette Marchand (Marie Charlet), Suzanne Flon (Myriamme), Zsa Zsa Gabor (Jane Avril), Katherine Kath (La Goulue), Claude Nollier (The Countess de Toulouse-Lautrec), Muriel Smith (Aicha), Georges Lannes (Patou), Walter Crisham (Valentin Dessosse), Mary Clare (Madame Loubet), Lee Montague (Maurice Joyant), Harold Gasket (Ziller), Jill Bennett (Sarah), Maureen Swanson (Denise), Jim Gerald (Père Cotelle), Rupert John (Chocolat), Tutti Lemkow (Aicha's Partner), Eric Pohlman (Proprietor—First Bar), Christopher Lee (Seurat), Peter Cushing (Marcel de la Voisier), Jean Landier (Anquetin), Robert le Fort (Gauzi), Jean Claudio (Drunken Reveller), Suzi Euzaine (Lorette), Guy Motchen (Delivery Boy), Monsieur Ledebur (Maitre d'Hotel Maxims), Monsieur Tabourno (Maitre d'Hotel–Pre Catalan), Fernand Fabre (General), George Pastell (Man–First Bar), M. Valerbe (Sommelier), Jean Ozenne (Felix), Francis de Wolff (Victor), Michael

Balfour (Dodo), Terence O'Regan (Bevert), Arissa Cooper (Giselle), Jaques Cey (Girard), John Serrat (Art Dealer), Raf de la Torre (Filibert), Pamela Deeming (Midinette), Donovan Winter (Guardsman), Bernard Rebel (Playwright), Christopher Rhodes (Second Man), Rene Laplat (Writer), Maria Britnieva (Woman), Ina de la Haye (Beautiful Young Man), Richard Molinas (Drunken Man), Isabel George (Lovely Companion), Paul Homer (Footman), Tim Turner (First Artist), Michael Seavers (Second Artist), Moyra Fraser, Hilary Allen, Maria Sanina, Sari Luzita, Sheila Nelson, Aleta Morrison (Can-Can Dancers).

Synopsis

In the Paris of the gay 1890s, Parisians from all different walks of life gather together for an evening of entertainment at the Moulin Rouge.

One of the cabaret's regulars is French painter Henri Toulouse-Lautrec (Jose Ferrer), a misshapen, strange little man who was destined to become one of the world's most celebrated artists.

Seated at his usual table near the dance floor, Lautrec sketched the wild and colorful can-can dancers, the singers, and the club's patrons, who, for a few hours every night, are able to shed all their inhibitions and enjoy the Bohemian flavor of the Moulin Rouge. As Lautrec's drawings take form, some of his most famous subjects pause at his table for some brief discourse. Among them are the club's stars: dancers La Goulue (Katherine Kath) and Aicha (Muriel Smith)—whose constant and sometimes violent jealousy for one another provides added entertainment for the crowds—and the beautiful singer Jane Avril (Zsa Zsa Gabor)—whose fickle nature leads her through a succession of meaningless romances in her seemingly endless search for the one true love of her life.

Toulouse-Lautrec has more than his own share of burdens. Born to one of the oldest and wealthiest families in France, Lautrec suffered a tragic accident as a child which left him permanently crippled and hideously deformed. Henri disgraces his aristocratic father when he decides to pursue a career as a painter, and abandons his heritage to make Paris and the Moulin Rouge his new home.

One evening, as Lautrec leaves the cabaret for his apartment studio, he meets a homeless woman named Marie Charlet (Colette Marchand), and he falls in love with her. His desperate lifelong hope to find the one woman who might love him in spite of his deformity is soon dashed when Marie proves unfaithful. Lautrec attempts suicide but decides against taking his life when he realizes that he can find solace in his paintings. However, the heartache and depression eat away at him, leaving Henri even more cynical and tenacious of life than before. Lautrec returns to the Moulin Rouge and his favorite cognac to help him ease the pain.

Henri's life takes a turn for the better when he is commissioned to design posters for the cabaret. Overnight, both Lautrec and the Moulin Rouge become sensations. Lautrec's paintings are exhibited and the showing is a tremendous success. At the same time Lautrec meets another woman named Myriamme (Suzanne Flon), a very popular fashion model. Myriamme has just ended a painful relationship with a wealthy young man named Marcel de la Voisier (Peter Cushing) who had offered to make her his mistress but not his wife. Myriamme and Lautrec become good friends. Myriamme grows to love Lautrec but Henri cannot forget what happened to his relationship with Marie and keeps their affair cool and noncommittal. Myriamme soon realizes the hopelessness of their love and leaves Lautrec for Marcel, who now wants her back on her terms. Myriamme sends a letter to Lautrec, telling him of her marriage.

This news breaks Henri and one night he drinks himself into a stupor, falling down a flight of stairs. His parents are notified and they bring him back to the family home.

Lying on his deathbed, his father admits he was wrong about his son's talent and proudly tells Henri that he is to be honored with a collection of his works at the Louvre. Henri is to be the first artist to be so honored while still living. Near death, Henri sees visions of the stars of his beloved Moulin Rouge who all bid him a fond farewell.

Commentary

> Helen had watched the transmission.... ["Eden End," 1951] She'd said I'd given a fine performance. But I was convinced, despite the fact that she had always been my most honest critic, that it had been the worst in my career. I spent a sleepless, miserable night. But [the] next morning a BBC producer rang to offer me a play at Christmas ["When We Are Married"]. Similar offers followed. It was the start of a most pleasant spell in TV."—Peter Cushing[1]

What Peter Cushing described as a "most pleasant spell" resulted in no less than thirteen television plays (including two six-part serials) between 1952 and 1953.[2] In addition to his television plays, Peter also found time to work again on the London stage in Robert Helpmann's 1952 production of *The Wedding Ring*.[3] Peter also landed a small role in *Moulin Rouge*, American filmmaker John Huston's acclaimed biography of the French painter Toulouse-Lautrec.

Released by United Artists, Huston filmed *Moulin Rouge* almost entirely in Paris; concentrating on the back-street boulevards and bistros that Lautrec was known to have frequented.

Time (January 5, 1953) described the film as "a fictionalized biography of famed French painter Henri de Toulouse-Lautrec (1864–1901). The son of a nobleman, Lautrec was crippled in childhood and grew up an ugly, aristocratic dwarf who tried, in cognac and in the brothels . . . of Paris, to forget the pain in his legs and heart. When he died at 37, after a feverish lifetime that included a sojourn in a madhouse, he left behind him a vivid record of the lower depths of Paris, its harlots and hunted, defeated and disfigured, drawn with artistry, insight and compassion."

John Huston, whose previous release was United Artists' *The African Queen* (1951), photographed *Moulin Rouge* using the same smoky pastels and shadings for which Toulouse-Lautrec's posters and paintings were famous. Huston hired *Life* photographer, Eliot Elisofon to serve as "special color consultant" on the film. By using special color filters over the camera lens, Huston was able to duplicate the dominant colors of Lautrec's paintings — blue to blue green, pink, and purple. The result was very much like a living, breathing canvas of many of the subjects Lautrec had immortalized during his lifetime.[4]

Starring as Toulouse-Lautrec, Jose Ferrer could also be described as a man who suffered for his art. Standing 5' 11", Ferrer was required to cut his size down to Lautrec's 4' 8" height for the film. In order to accomplish this illusion, Ferrer had to wear a specially made device which the actor himself described as his "torture boot." Required to walk literally on his knees, Ferrer was dressed in heavy leather "boots" which were fitted tightly over his kneecaps and were held in place by leather straps suspended over his shoulders. He was then dressed in tiny trousers, which had been fitted around his knees and thighs. With his own legs hidden behind him and out of camera view, Ferrer was transformed into the misshapened artist. However, because of these tight-fitting boots, Ferrer could only wear them for twenty-minute stretches and had to have them removed periodically since they cut off his blood circulation.[5]

Peter Cushing's miniscule role in *Moulin Rouge* was the dapper Marcel de la Voisier, who had supposedly lured one of Lautrec's loves away from him. Also featured in the cast was Christopher Lee, who played the painter Georges Seurat. Little did either of them know that within a few years of their appearance in this film both would find themselves international stars, not only in their own right, but as costars and partners in fame in twenty-one other feature films.

Moulin Rouge was nominated for seven Academy Awards including: Best Picture, Actor, Director, Editing and Supporting Actor. However, it would eventually only glean two — one for Art Direction/Set Direction and another for Costume Design. Both well deserved. The film would also be honored with a Silver Lion award at the Fourteenth International Film Festival held annually in Venice, Italy.[6]

Critical reviews for *Moulin Rouge* include that in *Variety* ("Gene," December 24, 1952) which reported that "On artistic grounds . . . a standout all the way . . . John Huston's direction is superb in the handling of individual scenes . . . each scene has a framed appearance which richly sets off the action . . . lighting and camerawork are excellent." Bosley Crowther of the *New York Times* (February 11, 1953) also cited the film's overall look in his review: "If the measure of the quality of a motion picture merely boils down to how much the screen is crowded with stunning illustration, then John Huston's *Moulin Rouge* well qualifies for consideration as one of the most felicitous movies ever made . . . a bounty of gorgeous color pictures of the Parisian Café world at the century's turn and of beautifully patterned compositions conveying sentiments, moods, and atmosphere." Otis Guernsey, Jr., of the *New York Herald Tribune* called it "A magnificent motion picture achievement. . . . A monumental piece of work!" Wanda Hale of the *New York Daily News* gave it "Highest Rating. . . . Will cast a spell over audiences and live endearingly in the memory of the viewers." The *Los Angeles Mirror* (Dick Williams) felt that it "Starts the new movie year off in rousing fashion!" Edwin Schallert of the *Los Angeles Times* predicted that the film was "Bound to shed new luster on John Huston as a creator of motion pictures." And Archer Winston of the *New York Post* raved, calling it "Very probably the most beautiful picture ever made. . . . Beyond compare!"

Notes

1. "Peter the Great" interview with Dick Tatham, *My Weekly*, August 23, 1969. Peter's character in *Eden End* was Charles Appleby. His fee for the performance was a mere 30 shillings — which included 3 weeks rehearsal money! Cushing's character in "When We Are Married" was Gerald Forbes.
2. 1952 Television performances: "Pride and Prejudice," as Mr. Darcy (six-part series began February 2, 1952); "Bird in Hand," as Cyril Beverly; "If This Be Error," as Nick Grant; "The Silver Swan," (character unknown); and "Asmodee," as Blaise Lebel. 1953 Television performances: "Number Three," as Mr. Simpson; "Epitaph for a Spy," as Vadassey (six-part series began March 14, 1953); "A Social Success," as Henry Robbins; "Rookery Nook," as Clive Popkins; "The Road," as Antoine Vanier (aired June 21, 1953); "Anastasia," as Piotr Petrovsky (aired July 12, 1953); "The Noble Spaniard," as Duke of Hermanos; and "Portrait by Peko," as Seppi Fredericks.
3. Peter's character in *The Wedding Ring* was Cyril Soames.
4. United Artists publicity manual.
5. "Actor Plays Most Bizarre Role since Chaney," *Portland Oregon Journal* (September 28, 1952).
6. August 20–September 4, 1953.

The Black Knight
(1954)

Credits and Cast

Released September 1954; 85 minutes; Technicolor; A Warwick Production; Released through Columbia; Filmed in England, Wales, and on location in Spain. Director: Tay Garnett; Producers: Irving Allen, Albert R. Broccoli; Story and screenplay: Alec Coppel; Director of photography: John Wilcox; Editor: Gordon Pilkington; Music: John Addison; Conducted and played by Muir Mathieson and the Royal Philharmonic Orchestra; Ballad, "The Bold Black Knight," Lyrics composed and sung by Elton Hayes; Additional dialogue: Dennis O'Keefe, Bryan Forbes; Assistant director: Phil Shipway; Production supervisor: Adrian Worker; Art director: Vetchinsky; Associate art director: John Box; Production controller: Arthur Alcott; Camera operator: Ted Moore; Costumes: Beatrice Dawson; Wardrobe supervisor: John McCorry; Continuity: Betty Harley; Technicolor color consultant: Joan Bridge; Editor: Gordon Pilkington; Makeup: Fred Williamson; Hairdresser: Gordon Bond; Sound recordists: Charles Knott, J. B. Smith; Archery expert: George Brown; Choreographer: David Paltenghi; Associate producer: Phil C. Samuel; Horse wrangler: Paul Bexley.

Alan Ladd (John), Patricia Medina (Linet), Peter Cushing (Sir Palamides), Harry Andrews (Earl of Yeonil), Andre Morell (Sir Ontzlake), Lawrence Naismith (Major Domo), Patrick Troughton (King Mark), Anthony Bushell (King Arthur), Ronald Adam (Abbot), John Laurie (James), Basil Appleby (Sir Hal), Olwen Brookes (Lady Ontzlake), Jean Lodge (Queen Guenevere), Bill Brandon (Bernard), Pauline Jameson (Countess Yeonil), Tommy Moore (Apprentice), John Kelly (Woodcutter), Elton Hayes (Troubadour), David Paltengli (High Priest).

Synopsis

> There is a saying in my country. When a puppy yelps at his master,
> it is time to cut off his tail. — Sir Palamides

During the legendary days of King Arthur and his Knights of the Round Table, a blacksmith named John (Alan Ladd) is dismissed from his work when the lord of the castle, the Earl of Yeonil (Harry Andrews) finds him in the embrace of his daughter, Lady Linet (Patricia Medina).

As John prepares to leave the castle, the fortress is attacked by a force of men dressed as Vikings. John, unskilled as a fighting man, is unable to save his master and rides off to Camelot to seek the king's help. Linet sees John leaving the castle in the heat of battle and wrongly accuses him of cowardice.

John seeks the help of a sympathetic knight, Sir Ontzlake (Andre

The dastardly Sir Palamides in Warwick's *The Black Knight.*

Morell). Both men suspect King Arthur's rival, King Mark of Cornwall (Patrick Troughton) and his henchman, Sir Palamides (Peter Cushing) of conspiracy to dethrone Arthur (Anthony Bushell) and to abolish Christianity, returning England once again to the old religion practiced centuries before by the Druids.

Sir Ontzlake secretly trains John in the knightly arts. Disguised as the Black Knight, John thwarts King Mark's and Sir Palamides' schemes and is rewarded by his grateful king with a true knighthood as well as the hand of his lady love, Linet.

Commentary

The year 1954 would mark another turning point in Peter Cushing's career. Demand for his talents were evidenced by his television appearances in BBC adaptations of "Tovarich," "The Face of Love" and as the title character in Anotole de Grunwald's play, "Beau Brummell,"[1] (which also featured Ferdy Mayne — *The Vampire Lovers* [1971] — and David Peel — *The Brides of Dracula* [1960] — in supporting roles). But it was his riveting portrayal of Winston Smith, the tormented antihero of George Orwell's "1984,"[2] that would make Cushing's name a household word in England and would earn Peter the nickname of "the Horror Man." For his outstanding performance, Peter was given the Guild of Television Award for Best Actor (England's equivalent of an American Emmy) in 1955.

In addition to his television appearances, Cushing also appeared in the stage production of *The Soldier and the Lady*, directed by Sam Wanamaker. Wanamaker, who also has numerous films to his credit both as actor and director, recalled that his work with Peter many years ago in the play was, in his words,

> a most pleasurable experience and I regret he did not do more on the stage.
> My recollection of our work together was that he was meticulous in rehearsal in working out every detail, gesture and reading. He would work these things out ... and bring that precision to the rehearsal.
> I was a director and actor trained in the Stanislavsky and Group Theatre and Actor's Studio method in America of improvisation with emphasis on the inner life of the character and his emotions. Peter's approach was exactly opposite to the methods I used both as an actor and a director.
> Peter found great difficulty adapting to my demands which were to free the actor from preconceptions about result which inhibited a sense of happening for the first time at each performance. In spite of these quite different — indeed extreme differences in approach — Peter's performance in the play was exemplary.

In an article that appeared in the "American Peter Cushing Club Journal" (number 5), member and contributor Rukmani Singh Devi gave this eyewitness review of the play and Cushing's performance:

> A satire on a mythical Ruritania-like kingdom. Most impressive was the soldier — Peter Cushing. At one entrance something essential began to formulate: a concept about what acting could and should be. His presence

> was . . . striking. The Proto-Attic profile, the knowing modulation of wry humour, and an incandescent smile . . . one's attention was drawn . . . to the sound of Mr. Cushing's speech; his ability to "sing" his dialogue. The lilt of his voice, its resonance and infinite rhythms. All moulded into a delivery at once cognizant of the musical patterns of the words but without sacrificing their context or meaning.

In the same year Peter Cushing was to appear in two feature films with widely diverse themes: *The End of the Affair* (based on the novel by Graham Greene) in which he portrayed Henry Mills, the cuckold yet forgiving husband of Deborah Kerr. And as Sir Palamides in *The Black Knight*, which starred Hollywood leading man, Alan Ladd. Both films were released under the Columbia Pictures banner.

The Black Knight, a Warwick Production filmed in England and Wales with additional location shooting in Spain, was a costume drama set during the mythical days of King Arthur and his knights. Jumping on the bandwagon of other major Hollywood studios such as Universal, Fox, and Warner Brothers, who also released similiar medieval adventures that year, producers Irving Allen and Albert R. Broccoli commissioned Tay Garnett to direct Alec Coppel's screenplay. Garnett, whose previous screen credits included *The Postman Always Rings Twice* (1946) and *A Connecticut Yankee in King Arthur's Court* (1949), started in films in 1920 as a screenwriter for both Mack Sennett and Hal Roach before joining the DeMille unit at Pathé in 1927 and moving up to the directorial chair.

In addition to Peter Cushing, the cast assembled included such distinguished performers as Andre Morell and Harry Andrews (in his second film appearance). Sets, costumes, and locales[3] (which included some extraordinarily good matte paintings of Camelot and the fire-damaged keep of the Earl of Yeonil), were all impressive. The film was beautifully lensed in technicolor by John Wilcox. And yet, with all these factors in its favor, the film suffered from four major flaws.

First and foremost was its unbelievably miscast star, Alan Ladd. Then there was the obvious irreverence of the director for the film's content and themes, which was quite evident throughout. The weak, ill-conceived, occasionally laughable screenplay was also a handicap as well as the choppy, rushed editing which greatly harmed the film's flow in its attempt to highlight the action scenes.

Morell and Andrews somehow rose above their material and were badly needed assets, but it was Cushing who literally saved this calamity with his masterful performance as the villain, the dreaded Saracen, Palamides. His affected Arabic accent and hand gestures, as well as his villainous looks make for a performance well worth the effort to watch.

Evidently, the filming of *The Black Knight* was not without its minor mishaps. Patricia Medina, Lady Linet, sustained a couple of cracked ribs during one of the scenes when she was attacked by Cushing's servant, Bernard (exwrestler, Bill Brandon). In typical Hollywood style, Medina's chest was bandaged and she went on with the scene, no doubt in considerable pain. Another incident took place during the Druid ceremonies at "Stonehenge." A stuntman who was hired to play one of the sacrificial monks was nearly roasted alive when the basket he was suspended in caught fire and his costume began to smolder.

Some reviews of *The Black Knight* included that in *Variety* by "Mayo" (September 8, 1954), who wrote, "British-made action spectacle, produced in lush technicolor and vigorously directed by Tay Garnett . . . lensed on a lavish scale with big-scale battle scenes. . . . Expensive decor, magnificent rural scenery . . . are some of the scenic highlights. This compensates for the necessarily juvenile nature of the plot. . . . There's no let up in the action. . . . Peter Cushing does a sterling job as Sir Palamides, the principal villain. . . . Other principle roles are enthusiastically played by a competent team of British performers." Bosley Crowther of the *New York Times* (October 29, 1954) called it "a standard but spirited account of treachery at Camelot. . . . Warwick Productions . . . has taken the trouble to film all this chivalry and derring-do in such colorful areas as England and Spain to give the audience pleasing and authentic scenic effects. . . . Peter Cushing and Bill Brandon as Saracen schemers . . . make their conspiracy against King Arthur obvious but properly hateful. . . . Credit the producers with some truly imaginative touches." The *Christian Science Monitor* critic, Rod Nordell, in his November 9, 1954, review, reported that *The Black Knight* "decorates an elementary action story with beautiful photography. It takes a moment to become adjusted to Alan Ladd using such language as 'Your Majesty. I ask a boon.' . . . Tay Garnett has directed the riding, swordplay, and rough and tumble with an eye for theatrical effect rather than brutality. Alec Coppel's script requires few pauses for dialogue and romance."

Peter in his autobiography remembers his association with Alan Ladd as being amicable, citing Ladd as being "a shy, reserved person" who had "kind thoughts for others."[4] Peter had given Ladd a toy replica of his character, the Black Knight, which according to Cushing, started Ladd in his own collection of model soldiers.

It is interesting to note that twenty-three years later, Alan Ladd's son, Alan Ladd, Jr., who then headed 20th Century–Fox, took the chance on a young filmmaker's dream — one that every other major studio had turned down and which eventually became one of the largest grossing and much beloved motion pictures of all time, *Star Wars*. Even stranger still is the fact that one of Alan Ladd, Sr.'s costars, Peter Cushing, would star in the George Lucas film production as Governor Moff Tarkin.[5]

Notes

1. Original air date, March 12, 1954.
2. Original air date, December 10, 1954.
3. Spanish locales included the castle at Manzares el Real, Guadmud Castle near Toledo, and the walls surrounding the eleventh-century city of Avila. The latter was used to represent the walls of Camelot. Also used was Castle Coch in South Wales.
4. Peter Cushing, *Past Forgetting—Memoirs of the Hammer Years.*
5. George Lucas, who wrote and directed the film.

The End of the Affair
(1954)

Credits and Cast

Released February 1955; 106 minutes; Black and white; A Coronado Production; Released through Columbia; Filmed at Shepperton Studios, England. Director: Edward Dmytryk; Producer: David Lewis; Screenplay: Lenore Coffee; Based on the novel by Graham Greene; Music: Benjamin Frankel; Director of photography: Wilkie Cooper; Art director: Don Ashton; Production manager: Ernest Holding; Sound recordist: John Cox; Camera operator: Alan Hume; Assistant director: Christopher Nobel; Continuity: Betty Forster; Costumes: Julia Squire; Makeup: Neville Smallwood; Hairdresser: Maud Onslow.

Deborah Kerr (Sarah Miles), Van Johnson (Bendrix), John Mills (Parkis), Peter Cushing (Henry Miles), Stephen Murray (Father Crompton), Nora Swinburne (Mrs. Bertram), Charles Goldner (Savage), Michael Goodliffe (Smythe), Joyce Carey (Miss Palmer), Frederick Leister (Dr. Collingwood), Mary Williams (Maid), O'Donovann Shiell (Doctor), Elsie Wagstaff (Landlady), Christopher Warbey (Lancelot), Nan Munro (Mrs. Tomkins), Josephine Wilson (Miss Smythe), Shela Ward (Old Woman), Stanley Rose (Fireman).

Synopsis

> They always say, don't they, that the husband is the last person to know. — Henry Miles

Bendrix, (Van Johnson), an American author, is wounded during World War II and discharged from the army. He remains in London to write about the British Civil Service and is introduced to a neighbor Henry Miles (Peter Cushing). Henry is a civil servant and Bendrix intends to use him as a model.

The marriage of Henry and Sarah Miles (Peter Cushing and Deborah Kerr)
shatters in *The End of the Affair,* from the novel by Graham Greene.

Henry invites Bendrix to a house party where the author meets
Henry's wife, Sarah (Deborah Kerr). Bendrix is attracted to her and his attraction is heightened when he glimpses her, in a mirror, kissing a man
at the bottom of the stairs. The sadly trusting Henry suggests that Bendrix
interview Sarah for more details.

The two meet in a restaurant and discuss their confused emotions.
While walking home, Bendrix hails a cab and they go to the Albian Hotel.

A week later they meet at Sarah's house. As they embrace in the drawing room, Bendrix admits to being concerned about Henry's return from
the office. Sarah dismisses his fears, saying that they will hear him on the
stairs — there is a step that "always creaks."

Bendrix is disgusted by his behavior toward the kindly Henry, and
angered at Sarah's apparently living only for the moment. He fears the
end of their relationship, yet seems determined to destroy it with his
jealousy.

One night, in Bendrix's flat, a bomb hits while he is downstairs and
he is trapped under a fallen door. When he frees himself and goes back
upstairs he finds Sarah on her knees. She is startled at his appearance and

VAN
JOHNSON
DEBORAH
KERR
-UNFORGETTABLE AS LOVERS!

THE **END**
OF THE
AFFAIR

with **JOHN MILLS**
PETER CUSHING

COLUMBIA PICTURE

Peter Cushing in good company with three established stars.

prepares to leave, vague about when they will meet again. As they part, Bendrix feels a weird sense of having returned from a long journey.

After a stay in the hospital for shock, Bendrix is unable to reach Sarah. He thinks that she is unhappy that he survived the blast—that she wanted to end the affair without guilt. He leaves London to forget her.

When Bendrix returns one year later, the war has ended and he is at work on a new book. One night, as he walks in the rain, he sees Henry trudging gloomily ahead. Henry is upset and worried about Sarah's un-explained absences and asks Bendrix for advice. He confesses that he has considered hiring a private detective but finds it distasteful. Bendrix offers to go in his place as Sarah returns, drenched, from her "walk." Despite Henry's objections, Bendrix goes to the detective agency the next day.

Later that day Bendrix arranges a "chance" meeting with Sarah on the street, observed by a furtive little man and a boy. The man, Parkis (John Mills), is a detective from the agency and reports Sarah's encounter on the street to Bendrix, whom he clumsily fails to recognize.

Parkis calls Bendrix to meet him at an address frequented by Sarah. After watching her enter, he calls Henry and arranges to meet him. He confesses what he has done and gives Henry a report of Sarah's activities. Shattered, Henry tosses the paper into the fire.

While crashing a party at the Miles' home, Parkis steals Sarah's diary and brings it to Bendrix, along with the information that she is quite ill. Bendrix dismisses the detective and begins to read the diary.

According to Sarah's notes, when the bomb struck, she investigated and found him dead. She returned upstairs and prayed that if God would restore Bendrix's life, she would end the affair. Stunned by his appearance upstairs, she rushed out of the flat and found refuge in a Catholic church. Sarah explained her plight to Father Crompton (Stephen Murray) who told her that she need not keep a bargain made with someone she did not believe in. Upon her return home, she attacked Henry about his own beliefs, and he was as unsure as she.

The next day she heard Richard Smythe (Michael Goodliffe) an atheist, speaking to a crowd at Hyde Park Corner. She visited him, hoping he could destroy her half belief.

After hearing a speech from the queen at the war's end, Henry and Sarah strolled through a park as Henry discussed his and their fortune, which included a possible knighthood. The prospect of their lives together repulsed her. Out for a walk in the rain, she returned home to find Henry and Bendrix.

As he finishes the diary, Bendrix realizes that he has been wrong about everything. Sarah has decided to return to Bendrix, whatever the consequences. But as she packs to leave Henry, she falters. He returns home from his meeting with Bendrix completely shaken and begs her to stay with him.

Sarah's illness — both physical and spiritual — finally takes its toll. They meet in a driving rain at the church and she tells him it is too late.

When Bendrix next visits the Miles' home, Sarah is dying. He chats with her mother (Nora Swinburne) who tells Bendrix that Sarah as a child was baptized a Catholic. As they talk, Henry walks down the steps, ashenfaced. Dr. Collingwood (Frederick Leister) tells Bendrix that Sarah's life just ran out of her.

Alone in his flat, Bendrix reads a letter from Sarah in which she states that she fell into belief like she fell into love.

Commentary

Graham Greene's 1951 novel is considered to be among the best of the great author's work, but it was a difficult book to film. Dealing with a complex religious experience, the novel was a questionable basis for a commercial movie. Also, the sexual aspects of the novel would not escape the film censors. As a result, the film is a much lesser work than the novel.

Another problem was the miscasting of Van Johnson, an opinion held by Graham Greene himself. When he visited the set at Shepperton Studios in August 1954, Greene was not pleased with the actor's playing of a scene. "They were trying to do those shots," said Greene, "where you get the same scene from each person's point of view: you had Johnson embracing Deborah Kerr with the camera on him and the camera moved to be on her in the same close embrace. Anyway, while the camera was on her, he put chewing gum in his mouth."[1]

The author had previously been against Gregory Peck's casting in the role. "I stymied Gregory Peck," he recalled. "But to then find that Van Johnson took his place was a disaster."[2]

The film's main problem, however, was the decision by Columbia to alter its structure prior to the release. Like the novel, the film was told in flashbacks. Director Edward Dmytryk was taken aback when "Columbia was worried that a story that was told out of chronological order would confuse the mass audience."[3] The film was recut against the wishes of all concerned.

The End of the Affair was an important film for Peter Cushing. His inclusion in an "A" production of a best-selling novel indicates his rising status in the eyes of the British film industry. The role and the film remain personal favorites.

Always concerned with authenticity, Peter Cushing was pleased with the attention to detail taken by hairdresser Maud Onslow. He was given a special haircut which produced two small tufts of hair on either side of his head—the mark of someone wearing a bowler hat typical of the character he portrayed.[4]

Given special billing, Peter Cushing emerged from the film with a personal success. His performance as Henry is one of his best and was duly noted by the critics. The *New York Times* (March 1, 1955) felt that "Peter Cushing as the lady's cryptic husband shows exceeding potential." *The Times* (February 23) observed that "Mr. Dmytryk undervalues Henry and Mr. Peter Cushing does a gallant job standing up for what is left."

Opinions on the film, however, were mixed. *Variety* (March 3) stated, "What might have been a poignant romantic drama develops into a bewildering discussion of faith versus reason." *The Picturegoer* (February 25) found it "an unusually distinguished film that provokes and excites."

Deborah Kerr shared her thoughts on Peter Cushing with the authors. "I only wish we had worked more together, but Peter gave a lovely understated performance as my shy and retiring husband. The last time we met was some years ago in the coffee shop at the Castelanna Hilton in Madrid. We sat over tea and reminisced over the years. Such a sweet man."

As Henry Miles, Peter Cushing delivers what is one of his finest screen performances. Here we see his career as it might have been if not for his association (for better or worse) with horror films. He creates an unforgettable picture of a man losing everything — including his self respect, but is unable to understand why. Had Peter Cushing been a bigger name, an Academy nomination surely would have been his.

In a strangely prophetic scene, as he walks with Deborah Kerr, he tells her that his future includes a possible OBE (Order of the British Empire) and knighthood. The first has already come true.

Sadly, *The End of the Affair* did little to boost his film career. He was still quite active in television (nine plays 1954–55) but only appeared in three films in the next two years.

Notes

1. Quentin Falk, *Travels in Greeneland.*
2. Ibid.
3. Gene D. Phillips, *Graham Greene: The Films of His Fiction.*
4. Columbia press book.

Alexander the Great
(1955)

Credits and Cast

Released May 1956 (U.K.), 161/141 minutes; Technicolor; Cinemascope; Released through United Artists; Filmed in Spain. Director, producer, screenplay: Robert Rossen; Music: Mano Nascimbene; Director of photograhy: Robert Krasker; Editor: Ralph Kempler; Set design: Andre Andrejen; Costumes: David Folkes; Set dresser: Dario Simoni; Makeup: David Aylott; Hairdresser: Gordon Bond; Special effects: Cliff Richardson; Technical adviser: Prince Peter of Greece.

Richard Burton (Alexander), Fredric March (Philip), Claire Bloom (Barsine), Harry Andrews (Darius), Stanley Baker (Attalus), Niall MacGinnis (Parmenio), Peter Cushing (Memnon), Michael Hordern (Demosthenes), Barry Jones (Aristotle), Marisa DeLeza (Eurydice), Gustavo Rojo (Cleitus), Ruben Rojo (Philatas), William Squire (Aeshines), Helmut Dantine (Nectanebus), Friedrich Ledeber (Antipater), Peter Wyngarde (Pausanis), Virgilio Texeira (Ptolemy), Teresa Del Rio (Roxana), Julio Pena (Arsites), Jose Nieto (Spithridates), Danielle Darrieux (Olympias).

Peter Cushing as General Memnon in *Alexander the Great*.

Synopsis

It is 365 B.C. Demosthenes (Michael Hordern), a powerful Greek orator, has been denouncing Macedonia's King Philip (Fredric March) who has been mercilessly attacking Greece. Day by day his forces move closer to Athens.

A victory at Olynthus is celebrated drunkenly by the Macedonians, with Philip's vicious General Attalus (Stanley Baker) thirsty for more blood.

That night Philip learns of the birth of his son — Alexander. Olympias (Danielle Darrieux) believes her child to be a god.

A rumor spreads that the Egyptian Nectanebus (Helmut Dantine) is the actual father, and Philip rushes home to his wife with murder on his mind. His friend Parmenio (Niall MacGinnis) persuades him not to murder the Egyptian. Olympias now despises her husband and plans to raise Alexander to become more powerful than his father.

Alexander's (Richard Burton) education from Aristotle (Barry Jones) is cut short when the youth is appointed regent by his father. As the conquest of Greece continues, Alexander saves Philip's life at the battle of Chaeronea. Greece soon falls to the might of the Macedonians.

During the peace negotiations, Alexander meets Barsine (Claire Bloom), the wife of Memnon (Peter Cushing), an Athenian general. The two are mutually attracted.

Meanwhile, Philip had divorced Olympias, who arranges his murder at a religious festival. Now twenty years old, Alexander becomes king. He leads a massive army across the Hellespont and wins a huge victory at Granicus. Memnon, now an exile, is killed in the battle. Barsine is taken hostage and she and Alexander become lovers.

Before a battle against King Darius (Harry Andrews), Alexander solves the legendary problem of the Gordian knot by shearing it in half with the thrust of his sword. The legend says that he who unties the knot will rule Asia.

Alexander feels that it is his calling to spread Greek culture and to unite East and West, which he thinks excuses the carnage he creates. In doing so, he conquers Persia and, despite his love for Barsine, marries Princess Roxana (Teresa Del Rio).

After conquering most of the known world, Alexander is felled by an illness and dies at age thirty-two. His lieutenants fight each other for control of his empire.

Commentary

> *Peopled with a Cast of Thousands! In Preparation for Over a Decade! So Mighty It Staggers the Imagination!*

Sound familiar? The mid–1950s to the mid–1960s produced many epics, including *Ben Hur* (1959), *Spartacus* (1960), and *Lord Jim* (1964), starring such heroic types as Charlton Heston, Kirk Douglas, and Peter O'Toole.

As primarily a classically trained stage actor, Richard Burton was, perhaps, a bit out of his element in his role as Alexander — a role for which

Richard Burton, as Alexander, strikes a heroic pose.

he supposedly had little respect. At his best in smaller films like *The Spy Who Came in from the Cold* (1966), he seems uncomfortable and out of place—much like he seemed in *Cleopatra* (1963).

Director Robert Rossen was clearly fascinated with the character of Alexander and his world. He devoted years to researching the man and the legends that grew around him and was determined to bring the epic story down to a human level. He succeeded to some degree, but the film was advertised as a "mighty epic," and an epic it was.

Despite all the research and attempts to downplay its proportions, *Alexander the Great* remains somewhat undistinguishable from other epics of the period (which is to say that the film is quite good, considering the others in its class).

Reviewers noted Rossen's lofty goal. *The London Times* (May 21, 1956) felt that "Mr. Rossen's object has clearly been to avoid excessive heroics and to furnish a sombre historical document." Hollis Alpert in the *Saturday Review* (March 3) opined that "the acting is several cuts above the level usually associated with this kind of movie."

Peter Cushing's inclusion in the international cast was a big boost to his film career. *Alexander the Great* was his twelfth film, but only his fifth since returning to England. He was a hot young talent at this time, having performed excellently in *The End of the Affair* and winning several Best Actor awards for his television work.[1]

He was identified in a *New York Times* review (April 24) as "playing several Shakespearian roles at the Old Vic." "Memnon is played with saturnine inscrutability by Mr. Peter Cushing," according to *The Times*.

Peter Cushing realls the role in this way: "As the Athenian General Memnon ... having taken a fond farewell of my wife, played by Claire Bloom, I rode a horse, bareback, to be slaughtered in the battle of Granicus by Richard Burton's legions."[2]

Cushing's athletic background again served him well, as the role required a great deal of physical ability and stamina. Although he often discusses his horseback riding as "at my peril," he is really quite an accomplished rider and appears very natural in the saddle (or in this case, riding bareback).

In a film of this size and scope, simply moving the cast and crew provided Robert Rossen with problems similar to those encountered by Alexander in moving his troops. Transporting everyone across Spain involved the use of 14 cars, 9 buses, 2 trailers, 20 trucks, 5 vans, 2 ambulances, 1 jeep, 9 portable dressing rooms, and 1 water tank truck.[3] Props included 5,000 bows and arrows, 1,000 shields, 5,000 spears, 50 chariots, 2,000 suits of armor, and 300 horses. Wearing, riding, and firing this mass of equipment were over 6,000 extras.[4]

Equally staggering is the amount of print advertising — an estimated 300 million individual magazines and newspaper ads. Proving that movie tie-in merchandizing didn't begin with *Star Wars* (1976), *Alexander the Great* boasted connections with Burma-Bibas neckties, Wohl shoes, American Airlines, Sally Victor hats, Gemex watches, Cecil Chapman fashions, and Shields jewelry.[5]

In addition to this film, Peter Cushing was quite busy on television during 1955, appearing in "Richard of Bordeaux," "The Browning Version," "The Moment," and "The Creature." Cushing later appeared in the film version of television's "The Creature" in Hammer's 1957 production of *The Abominable Snowman of the Himalayas*.

Notes

1. The National Television Award 1953, 1954, sponsored by the *Daily Mail*, and the Guild of Television Producers and Directors 1955, Best Performance for 1984.
2. Cushing, *Past Forgetting.*
3. United Artists press book.
4. Ibid.
5. Ibid.

Magic Fire
(1955)

Credits and Cast

Released April 1956; 95 minutes; Tru color; Presented by Herbert Yates; A William Dieterle production; Released by Republic; Filmed in Bavaria. Director and producer: William Dieterle; Screenplay: Benita Harding, E. A. Dupont, David Chantler; Based on Harding's novel; Director of photography: Ernest Haller; Music: Richard Wagner, conducted by Erich W. Korngold; Art director: Robert Herlit; Sound: Frank Dyke; Choreography: Taijanan Grover; Opera scenes: Rudolf Hartmann.

Alan Badel (Richard Wagner), Yvonne De Carlo (Minna), Carlos Thompson (Liszt), Rita Gam (Cosima), Valentina Cortese (Mathilde), Peter Cushing (Wesendonk), Frederick Valk (Von Moll), Gerhard Reidman (Ludwig), Eric Schumann (Von Buelow), Robert Freytag (Roeckel), Charles Regner (Mayerbeer).

Synopsis

> *For your birthday present, allow me to secure the continuance of your work.* — Otto Wesendonk.

Outspoken German composer Richard Wagner (Alan Badel) marries Minna (Yvonne De Carlo), despite her disapproval of her radical political views. A major talent, Wagner has difficulty getting his work performed because he lacks a sponsor. His abrasive personality and antigovernment stance continue to hold him back.

He seeks — and gets — support from several established musicians, including Franz Liszt (Carlos Thompson). However, his political activism continues and causes a split with Minna. He is soon in danger of being arrested and, through the efforts of Liszt and his daughter Cosima (Rita

Otto Wesendonk (Peter Cushing) might not be smiling if he knew about Wagner's (Alan Badel) affair with his wife (Valentina Cortese) in *Magic Fire*.

Gam), he leaves Germany. Now an exile, he finds asylum at the Swiss estate of Otto Wesendonk (Peter Cushing) and his wife Mathilde (Valentina Cortese).

Wagner foolishly is drawn into an affair with his host's wife which ends when Minna arrives unexpectedly. When his liaison with Mathilde is exposed by Minna, Wagner is confronted by Otto. The composer is ordered off the estate.

While in Venice, Wagner is pardoned by King Ludwig (Gerhard Reidman), but a scandal erupts linking him with the now married Cosima. Wagner returns to Venice in disgrace.

There, after a violent argument with Cosima's outraged father, Wagner suffers a heart attack and dies. His music, however, has been performed and lives on after his death.

Commentary

Although hardly Peter Cushing's fault, this is an incredibly boring film and is practically unwatchable. Despite a capable cast and director (William Dieterle directed the 1939 *Hunchback of Notre Dame*), the film never seems to get started.

Peter Cushing's appearance in the film is difficult to place in context. He had, by this time, established himself as film actor with featured roles in *The Black Knight* (1954), *The End of the Affair* (1954), and *Alexander the Great* (1955). Why he would have been chosen for (or accepted) such a small part is anyone's guess. His time on-screen totals only minutes and he is photographed only in medium shots—no close-ups. When one considers that he was but one film away from stardom with *The Curse of Frankenstein* (1956), this film seems out of place.

The film itself looks something like a gaudy postcard, despite the obvious money spent on period costumes and location shooting. Perhaps the best thing about the film is its music—a fortunate ocurrence in a biography of a composer. The opera scenes were staged by Professor Rudolf Hartmann of Munich, with ballet choreography by Iatjana Gsousty.

The title is explained in the following line: "The Magic Fire that Sparked the Genius of Composer Richard Wagner Was the Women in His Life."

Peter Cushing (quite understandably) has commented very little on his appearance, mentioning only the "heavy Gothic and Baroque architecture of Munich"[1] in a list of his cinematic travels.

He would return to Bavaria in 1977 to film *Hitler's Son* with even worse results—at least *Magic Fire* was released.

Critical response to *Magic Fire* was not positive. Robert Kass in *Catholic World* called it "romanticized slush . . . overloaded with pretentiousness and bad acting." The *Motion Picture Herald* (May 2, 1956) called it "hardly of the stuff that great dramas are spun."

Note

1. Cushing, *An Autobiography*.

Time Without Pity
(1956)

Credits and Cast

Released May 1956 (U.K.); 88 minutes; Black and white; A Harlequin Production; Released through Eros (U.K.), Astor (U.S.). Director: Joseph Losey; Producers: John Arnold, Anthony Simmons; Executive producer: Leon Clore; Screenplay: Ben Barzman; Music: Tristan Carey; Music supervisor: Marcus Dods; Director of photography: Freddie Francis; Production design: Reece Pemberton; Art director: Bernard Sanon: Editor: Alan Osbiston.

Michael Redgrave (David Graham), Ann Todd (Mrs. Stanford), Leo McKern (Stanford), Peter Cushing (Jeremy Clayton), Alec McCowen (Alec Graham), Renee Houston (Mrs. Harker), Paul Daneman (Brian Stanford), Lois Maxwell (Vicky Harper), Richard Wordsworth (Maxwell), George Devine (Barnes), Joan Plowright (Agnes Cole), Ernest Clark (Under Secretary), Peter Copley (Padre), Richard Leech (Bartender), Hugh Moxey (Prison Governor), Julian Somers (Warden), John Chandos (Journalist), Dickie Henderson, Jr. (Comedian).

Synopsis

> *You've got to understand something, Graham. It happens every-*
> *time there is to be an execution. They get dozens of last-minute*
> *alibis—even confessions. It's as I told you this morning—only*
> *some concrete evidence—something tangible.*—Jeremy Clayton

David Graham (Michael Redgrave), an alcoholic author, is recovering in a Canadian sanatorium when he learns of his son's murder conviction in London. Although estranged from Alec (Alec McCowen) for years, Graham decides to fly to London. His help will be, perhaps, too late. Alec is to be hanged in twenty-four hours.

Jeremy Clayton (Peter Cushing), Alec's lawyer, meets Graham at the airport and briefs him on the trial and the victim—Alec's lover, Jenny. Armed with this information, his visits Jenny's sister Agnes (Joan Plowright) and becomes convinced from her responses that some evidence has been overlooked—and that Alec is innocent.

Graham next encounters the Stanford family. Alec was friendly with Brian (Paul Daneman) since college and was often a guest in their opulent apartment. Robert (Leo McKern) is a wealthy car manufacturer given to rages and mistreating his wife Honor (Ann Todd). More interesting is that the murder took place in the Stanford apartment.

Brian confides to Graham that Robert is not his real father—he is adopted. He is hesitant to reveal the possible value of a note written by Robert. It was mistakenly sent to Graham, stuck in a magazine that Brian thoughtfully posted to David in Canada every month. Graham has not seen it and calls Montreal to trace the magazine's whereabouts.

Complicating the family problems are Robert's frequent mistresses— including Vicky (Lois Maxwell), his recently promoted secretary. Graham suspects something but, due to his constant fog of withdrawal, is unable to piece things together.

A visit to Alec in prison is arranged by Clayton, who informs Graham that Stanford is paying his fee. Alec refuses to see his father and a priest (Peter Copley) tells Graham that Alec has accepted his fate.

Graham begins to collapse under the strain and weakens, getting drunk in a pub. Honor finds him there and takes him to the apartment,

David Graham (Michael Redgrave) and Jeremy Clayton (Peter Cushing) run out of time in *Time Without Pity*.

where he learns the contents of the note. Robert wrote it, threatening suicide the day after Jenny's murder. Brian also intimates there was an affair between his stepmother and Alec.

Through his alcoholic haze, Graham begins to suspect Stanford, despite realizing that Robert was with Vicky—all night—when Jenny was murdered. A visit to the Home Office is arranged by Clayton, but to no avail. The secretary (Ernest Clark) is unsympathetic to his request for a delay of execution.

A second visit to Agnes solves the puzzle—Jenny had recently been beaten by a wealthy man she had been seeing behind Alec's back. Graham rushes to Vicky who admits that she was not with Stanford the night of the murder, but had been promoted as payment to supply an alibi if needed. Clayton tells Graham that all this means nothing—what is needed to save Alec is something concrete.

Graham finds Stanford at the test track and follows him into his office. Stanford confesses his guilt—he "lost control"—but feels safe as Graham has no proof. Pulling out a gun he stole from Stanford's apartment, Graham holds Stanford at bay and phones Clayton, telling him that

Stanford is about to kill him. Graham allows Stanford to take the gun from him, then attacks, forcing Stanford to kill him.

Brian and Honor enter the office to find Stanford bent over Graham's corpse. Brian phones Clayton to get in touch with the Home Office.

Commentary

Time Without Pity was released in America after *The Curse of Frankenstein* and Peter Cushing's starring role as the baron was played up in the film's publicity. He was not yet considered a "horror star," and his role as Frankenstein was just another part well played. This situation would not last long and, with the exception of a short run of nonhorror parts in the early 1960s, he would soon be locked in — or out.

American director Joseph Losey was living and working in England — but not by choice. A target of the McCarthy witch-hunt for communists, he sought refuge in England after being blacklisted in Hollywood. *Time Without Pity* was the first British film on which his name would appear — his first two films billed him under an alias.[1]

Time Without Pity was photographed by Freddie Francis, soon to be an Academy Award winner for *Sons and Lovers* (1960). He would eventually become a director in the 1960s and would direct Peter Cushing eight times beginning with *The Evil of Frankenstein* (1963).

Joseph Losey enhanced the complex but compelling story with many interesting touches. While in a drunken stupor on a subway train, Michael Redgrave holds on to a leather grip which looks like a hangman's noose.

Losey was, however, less than generous with Peter Cushing's character. While obviously not a lead role, Jeremy Clayton is very important to the plot, yet is seen only in extremely short scenes. In one he speaks but a single line. In two others he is heard over the telephone, but not seen on screen. Cushing makes the most of his one big scene in which he unwittingly sends Michael Redgrave to his death.

Although well done in all areas, *Time Without Pity* was unable to find an audience, despite positive reviews. Perhaps filmgoers of the 1950s were not willing to accept a neglectful, alcoholic father as a hero. Also, the film was simply too depressing to attract a mass audience. The less than subtle plea against capital punishment may not have helped much, either.

Michael Redgrave carries the film with an excellent, low-key portrayal as the anguished father and is literally in every scene. Unfortunately, Leo McKern as Stanford is a bit over the top and should have been spotted early on by the police. Interestingly, Peter Cushing is billed above Leo McKern on the American poster and third behind Michael Redgrave and Ann Todd, despite his relatively minor role.

The Times (March 15, 1957) stated, "The film does not woo the audience's attention with the graces of subtlety, it compels it with a baleful eye and a bludgeon." Variety (April 17) felt that "Peter Cushing . . . top(s) a fine supporting team." The Evening Standard (March 26) praised the film: "as a thriller, it is first rate. It has been made with that patience in detail that gives such British films . . . a note of chilling authenticity."

For the first time since his television career began, Peter Cushing was absent from the small screen during this year. He did, however, continue his stage work with The Silver Whistle.

Note

1. Katz, The Film Encyclopedia.

The Curse of Frankenstein
(1956)

Credits and Cast

Released May 1957 (U.K.); 83 minutes; Warner color; A Hammer Film Production; Released through Warner Brothers; Filmed at Bray Studios, England. Director: Terence Fisher; Producer: Anthony Hinds; Executive producer: Michael Carreras; Associate producer: Anthony Nelson-Keys; Screenplay: Jimmy Sangster; Based on the novel by Mary W. Shelley; Music: James Bernard; Music supervisor: John Hollingsworth; Director of photography: Jack Asher; Production design: Bernard Robinson; Art director: Ted Marshall; Editor: James Needs; Production manager: Don Weeks; Sound recordist: Jock May; Camera operator: Len Harris; Assistant director: Robert Lynn; Continuity: Doreen Soan; Makeup: Phil Leakey; Hairdresser: Henry Montash; Wardrobe: Molly Arbuthnot.

Peter Cushing (Baron Victor Frankenstein), Hazel Court (Elizabeth), Robert Urquhart (Paul Krempe), Christopher Lee (The Creature), Valerie Gaunt (Justine), Noel Hood (Aunt Sophia), Melvyn Hayes (Young Victor), Sally Walsh (Young Elizabeth), Paul Hardtmuth (Professor Bernstein), Fred Johnson (Grandfather), Claude Kingston (Small Boy), Alex Gallier (Priest), Patrick Troughton (Kurt), Michael Mulcaster (Warder), Andrew Leigh (Burgomaster), Anne Blake (Burgomaster's Wife).

Synopsis

The Curse of Frankenstein will haunt you forever!—Warner Brothers publicity

Baron Victor Frankenstein (Peter Cushing), awaiting execution for murder, relates this story to a priest (Alex Gallier) in his prison cell.

Orphaned as a teenager, Victor (Melvyn Hayes) has inherited the family wealth and hires Paul Krempe (Robert Urquhart) as his tutor. Their aimless researches take form and lead them into a study of life and death.

After restoring a dead puppy to life, Victor (now Cushing) proposed that they create a man—perfect mentally and physically—from parts of the dead. Paul reluctantly agrees, but is concerned about Victor's blindness to possible consequences.

Their work is interrupted by the arrival of Elizabeth (Hazel Court), Victor's cousin, promised to him in marriage. Paul decides the experiment must now end, but Victor refuses. He continues to assemble organs and limbs for his Creature, now lacking only a brain.

When elderly Professor Bernstein (Paul Hardtmuth) visits the engaged couple, Victor pushes him to his death off a balcony. As he removes the professor's brain in the family crypt, it is damaged in a struggle with Paul.

Since Paul has completely withdrawn his help but continues to live at the Frankenstein chateau to protect Elizabeth, Victor forges on alone. However, the apparatus for giving life was constructed for dual operation. While Victor attempts to blackmail Paul into reconsidering, the Creature (Christopher Lee) is unexpectedly brought to life by a lightning bolt. When Victor investigates a crashing sound in the laboratory, he is choked by the hideous being. Paul knocks it unconscious with a chair and then, assisted by Victor, straps it to a table. Paul begs Victor to destroy the Creature, but he refuses.

The Creature escapes into the forest where, after killing a blind man (Fred Johnson) and his grandson (Claude Kingston), it is shot and killed by Paul. Victor, furious at Paul's action, buries the Creature in the woods. Feeling that Elizabeth is now safe, Paul leaves the chateau, parting bitterly with his former friend.

Victor restores the Creature to life and uses it to murder Justine (Valerie Gaunt), a maid attempting to blackmail him into marriage.

When Paul returns for the wedding, Victor shows him the Creature. Disgusted and horrified, Paul rushes out to report Victor to the authorities with the baron in pursuit.

The neglected Elizabeth sees her chance to investigate the forbidden laboratory, entering just after the Creature breaks free of its chains. It observes her through a skylight and startles her with a noise. She goes to the roof to investigate.

Arguing below, Victor and Paul see the Creature on the roof. As Paul goes to the village for help, Victor runs to the roof. The Creature closes in on Elizabeth from behind, and Victor shoots wildly, accidentally hitting

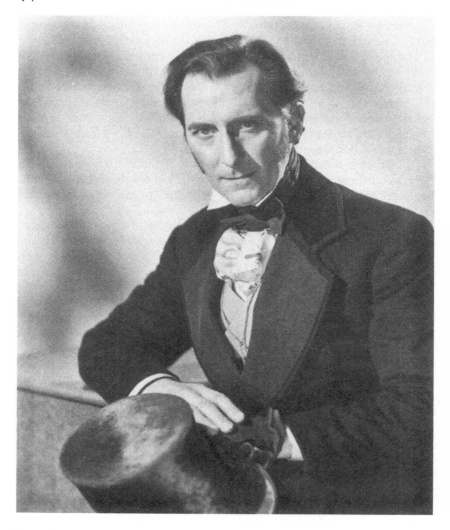

Peter Cushing in his most famous role as the baron in Hammer's *The Curse of Frankenstein*.

Elizabeth. As the maddened Creature approaches, the baron sets it ablaze with a kerosene lamp. It falls through the skylight into an acid vat, destroying any evidence of its existence.

After concluding his story, Victor is visited in his cell by Paul, who has come with Elizabeth. Paul denies the Creature's existence and, since he is the only living person other than Victor to have seen it, the baron is forced to accept full responsibility for the murders. As Paul and

Elizabeth leave the prison, Victor is led toward the guillotine. Victor watches as its blade rises.

Commentary

By 1956 the so-called classic horror film was dead. The traditional monsters of folklore and literature had been replaced by ones from outer space and had little pathos or humanity. A departure from this trend was a low-budget British film of 1955, *The Quatermass Experiment* (U.S. title; *The Creeping Unknown*), which featured a recognizably human monster. The film's international success led its producer—Hammer Films—to produce their own version of Mary Shelley's 1818 novel *Frankenstein*.

Although the novel was in the public domain, the Universal Studios' version (1931) and its many sequels were copyrighted. Hammer producer Anthony Hinds remarked that "Universal was waiting in the wings with a lawsuit."[1] This caused Hammer to revamp the entire approach to the subject, beginning with the title character.

The Curse of Frankenstein was Peter Cushing's most important film to that point and, while not his best, remains the one that made him famous worldwide. Until this film, his career lacked focus and direction. Despite good performances and reviews, he was still an unknown to most moviegoers. His greatest success was in television, and his performance in the 1954 BBC production of *1984* brought him to Hammer's attention.

"I had seen [the original *Frankenstein*] and thought it was splendid, so when I heard that Hammer was going into production with a coloured remake, I asked [my agent] to suggest me for the part of the Baron."[2] Cushing is being, perhaps, a bit modest.

Anthony Hinds recalled things differently. "Never were any other actors considered. Cushing was one of Britain's first real television stars . . . and whatever he was in would empty all the pubs and bring people home to their TV sets. We wanted him and we got him."[3]

As the baron, Cushing seized the part and made it his own, his surface charm hiding a callous ruthlessness that made him far more chilling than his pathetic creature. Due to his expert acting, Frankenstein is the most fascinating character in horror films. With the focus of the film on the baron and not his monster, the Hammer version was entirely different from the Universal original. In fact, the films are so dissimilar that any comparisons are pointless. Relaxed censorship, changing acting styles, and color photography make them distant cousins. One of the few things the two films share is having almost nothing to do with the Shelley novel. Jimmy Sangster's script was as much of a departure from the source novel as the original Boris Karloff film had been.

Hazel Court has the distinction of not only being Peter Cushing's first film leading lady — she is also the only actress to have starred with Peter Cushing, Christopher Lee, Boris Karloff, Vincent Price, and Peter Lorre. Her fine acting in *The Curse of Frankenstein* is often overlooked. She gives a believable performance as the confused — and finally angered — Elizabeth, and adds more to the film than beauty. Court shared her thoughts on Peter Cushing with the authors.

> If you told me in 1956 that someone in 1991 would be interested in the film, my reaction would have been total amazement!
>
> I had seen Peter on the London stage and thought him marvelous. They said he was going to be the new Olivier. When he did the Frankenstein film a few years later, his career went in a different direction.
>
> He was a very kind man — so gentle. . . . He also had an aura of mystery — a side you never quite got to. He was really born out of his time. With his beautiful manners and movements, he was a man of the nineteenth century.
>
> It's amazing how actors often put down the films that made them famous. Peter did not do this, and neither do I. These films are the highlights of my life, and I'm proud to have made them.

If the little girl playing Elizabeth as a child looks like excellent casting, it was. The child was Hazel Court's daughter, Sally Walsh.

Christopher Lee's interpretation of the Creature suffers in comparison to Boris Karloff's, but one must remember that they are playing completely different characters with different functions in their respective films. Phil Leakey's makeup for Lee, while inferior to Jack Pierce's masterpiece for Karloff, is just right within the film's framework.

Lee stated in his club journal[4] that the film "was the start of a very deep friendship between myself and Peter Cushing, whom I found to be a person of exceptional character and deep understanding. I would certainly liked to have played some of Peter Cushing's parts, notably Baron Frankenstein — but only once."

The physical aspects of the film are excellent, starting a tradition of outstanding set design and costuming that Hammer would continue into the 1970s. Hazel Court recalls that her beautiful dresses were "actually part of a real Victorian wardrobe that had [been] handed down over the years."

Immediately upon its British release in May 1957, the film was an unqualified success with audiences. The critics, as might be expected, weren't so sure.

C. A. Lejune, in *The Observer* (London, May 5), gave the most negative of the British reviews. "I should rank *The Curse of Frankenstein* among the half dozen most repulsive films I have encountered." Oddly, this perceptive critic was unable to follow the film's simple plot. "[Mr.

Sangster] takes as his central character Victor, son of the celebrated Baron Frankenstein. . . . He employs Papa's formulae [?] and wealth in the evolution of a creature."

Unfortunately, this level of criticism set the pattern that others would willingly follow and would haunt the stars, director, and studio for years to come.

American Bosley Crowther (*New York Times*, August 8) also missed the point, calling the film a "routine horror film which makes no particular attempt to do anything more important than scare you with corpses and blood. In the role of the Baron, Peter Cushing likewise does a conventional job."

Jim O'Connor (*The New York Journal*, August 7) seems to have seen the right film. "Despite its melodramatic title, it is an ably acted picture. . . . I think top laurels should go to Peter Cushing, who enacts the role of Baron Victor Frankenstein without overacting. You could almost hear the nerves snapping in the audience."

Variety (August 7) felt that "Peter Cushing gets every inch of drama from the leading role, making almost believable the ambitious urge and diabolical accomplishment."

Despite the mixed reviews, audiences worldwide loved it and still do. At its time, and for many years after, it was the most profitable film (based on its cost) ever made by a British studio. With the excesses of the 1970s and 1980s, the film now seems almost tame, and someone seeing it today for the first time might wonder what all the fuss was about.

Director Terence Fisher — a man often unfairly condemned — could hardly be bettered in his straightforward telling of the tale. An unpretentious man, Fisher always referred to himself as a "working director." Hazel Court remembers him as "a kind, thoughtful man, unconcerned with self-promotion. One always felt safe with Terry."

Due to the film's considerable success, the path of both Peter Cushing's career and of the horror film in general were changed forever. Of Cushing's remaining seventy-six films, over fifty would be somehow connected to horror fantasy. Does he mind? Apparently not. "I do the parts now that I think the audiences want to see me doing," he says. "Who wants to see me do Hamlet? Very few. But millions want to see me as Frankenstein, so that's the one I do."[5]

Peter Cushing's career since *The Curse of Frankenstein* will forever be associated with a studio, a director, and an actor. It is impossible to consider Cushing without recalling Hammer Films, Terence Fisher, and Christopher Lee. Since these three will be mentioned often in the pages to come, perhaps a brief survey is in order.

Hammer Film Productions can trace its origins to Exclusive Films, formed in the mid–1930s by Will Hinds and Enrique Carreras. Hinds was a successful London jeweler who appeared on the stage as Will Hammer; and Carreras owned a chain of cinemas called the Blue Hall. Their first production was *The Private Life of Henry the Ninth* (1935), a comedy; more prophetic was *The Mystery of the Mary Celeste* (1936) with Bela Lugosi. Enrique's son James (later Sir James) joined the partners in 1939, followed by his own son Michael in 1943; Will's son Anthony soon followed.

After a short run of four films, production was halted due to World War II. The studio was reborn as Hammer Film Productions in November 1947. The first film was *River Patrol*, a forty-six-minute police thriller.

During the early 1950s Hammer developed a few practices that would prove to be successful. They often made films based on a presold concept, such as a popular radio or television series. To gain an American audience, they would often star a fading but still well-known American actor. In 1951 Hammer struck the first U.S.-U.K. coproduction deal with Robert Lippert Productions which ensured an American release.

The typical Hammer film of the period was a black and white thriller. Even at this stage, their films had a quality that belied their low production costs. Much of this was achieved by a 1951 move to Bray Studios. When Hammer left Bray after *Frankenstein Created Woman/The Mummy's Shroud* (1966) much of the company's charm was left behind.

Another reason for Hammer's high quality was its ability to assemble a talented team of writers, directors, composers, and set designers (Jimmy Sangster, Terence Fisher, James Bernard, Bernard Robinson) to work on film after film. Bray's small size was also a plus—only one film at a time could be produced, guaranteeing everyone's concentration and best effort.

Like Peter Cushing, director Terence Fisher was also synonymous with Hammer Studios. He directed his first film for the company in 1951 (*The Last Page*) and his last in 1972 (*Frankenstein and the Monster from Hell*).

After the unexpected international success of *The Curse of Frankenstein*, Hammer began to concentrate on Gothic horror. Far from a nonprofit organization, Hammer strove to give the public what it wanted. Despite unwarranted adverse criticism (or, perhaps, due to it), Hammer hit the theaters with more of the same by reaching into the vaults and resurrecting more ancient horrors. Other than those starring Peter Cushing, the list includes *The Man Who Could Cheat Death* (1959), *The Two Faces of Dr. Jekyll* (1960), *The Curse of the Werewolf* (1961), and *The Phantom of the Opera* (1962). These, like the Peter Cushing films, were notable for their excellent casts, high production values, attention to detail, intriguing variations on old themes, and eye-popping color.

Despite Hammer's reputation as a horror factory during this period, the company was actually quite diversified, producing war drama (*Yesterday's Enemy*, 1959), social comment (*Never Take Sweets from a Stranger*, 1960), comedy (*A Weekend with Lulu*, 1960), and costume adventure (*Pirates of Blood River*, 1962).

A variation on the company's Gothic horrors was an unrelated series of black and white thrillers, including *Taste of Fear* (1961) and *Paranoiac* (1962).

By the mid–1960s Hammer was producing sequels to its own originals, and the once novel formula began to wear a bit thin. Although a few good films loomed in the future, it was really over by the decade's end. An ill-conceived attempt to update Dracula (*Dracula A.D. 1972*), coupled with a new emphasis on sex and violence and lack of imagination, showed that Hammer, perhaps, had outstayed its welcome.

In 1968 Hammer was given the Queen's Award for Industry for the company contribution to the British economy. What Hammer really deserved was fair evaluation from the critics and a very loud thankyou for producing the finest Gothic fantasies ever made.

Producer-director-writer Michael Carreras sums up Hammer in this way: "I don't have any pretensions about our films but I think they're good within the areas we lay down. The one thing we never do is make a shoddy film. [We] give the people who go and see a Hammer film a respectable hour and a half. ... I think that one of the reasons our horror films certainly became leaders in the market was that they were always beautifully photographed, the sets were always extremely believable. They've never been shoddy productions."[6]

Equally unpretentious was director Terence Fisher. "I was just a hack director," he said, "who was asked to direct their pictures. I work from emotion and intuition and as far as people are concerned who want to analyze my work — well, a director shouldn't speak for his films, they speak for themselves."[7]

He was born February 23, 1904, in Maida Vale, London, England. His first job was as a seaman. Fisher entered the film industry in 1932 as "the oldest clapper boy in the business."[8] In 1946, as an editor for the Rank Studio, he entered a school for aspiring directors. His first film as a director was *Colonel Bogey*, released the following year.

Terence Fisher joined Hammer in 1951 and directed eleven films of varying interest and quality until his "accidental" assignment on *The Curse of Frankenstein*. "We weren't influenced at all by the old Universal horror films when we started ours. I didn't screen them or refer to them at all. I was uninterested in them. I started from scratch."[9]

After the back-to-back success of *The Curse of Frankenstein* and *Horror of Dracula*, Fisher found himself in much the same situation as Peter Cushing and dealt with it in the same way—"I make what I'm offered. I make them as well as I can." He rode the crest of the horror cycle he had helped to create with beautifully crafted films like *The Man Who Could Cheat Death* (1959) and *The Curse of the Werewolf* (1961). It all seemingly ended after the inexplicable failure of his excellent *Phantom of the Opera* (1962) with Herbert Lom. For the next few years he seemed lost, doing films he had little feeling for and with tepid results. With *The Gorgon* (1964) he made the first step in his comeback which he solidified with *Dracula — Prince of Darkness* (1965) and *The Devil Rides Out* (1968).

A victim of two car accidents, Terence Fisher began to slow down and, after *The Devil Rides Out*, directed only two films — both Frankensteins starring Peter Cushing. He spent the last eight years of his life in forced inactivity, passing away on June 18, 1980.

One of Fisher's greatest talents was as he put it, "a good visual sense within the frame." His best films have a distinctive style that is all his own; described by Harry Ringel as "staging the action in planes rather than cross cutting time and time again."[10]

Terence Fisher was immediately maligned for *The Curse of Frankenstein* by both mainstream critics and horror fans stuck in the 1930s. Attacking the explicit gore of his films, they overlooked what really made them work — his concentration on character and emotion and his forsaking of Germanic symbolism for realism.

Most of this initial (and oft repeated) criticism can now be seen as absurd. One that has always amused the authors has been Fisher's labeling as a "pedestrian" director. This noncomment was first made by Carlos Clarens[11] and has been parroted ever since by many who never seem able to define it.

His strength as a storyteller permeates his films, allowing the script and the actors — not flashy attention-calling effects — to carry the film. Can it be coincidence that most of Peter Cushing's best performances were directed by Terence Fisher?

With his honesty, sincerity, and lack of pretention, it's easy to see why Terence Fisher embraced Peter Cushing as his favorite actor — directing him thirteen times — and how the two talented men complemented each other's skill.

Peter Cushing and Christopher Lee are associated so closely in the minds of film goers that it's difficult to *not* think "and Christopher Lee" when hearing the name Peter Cushing. In all, they appeared together twenty-two times, with the majority of their pairings legitimate costarring ventures. They were the perfect match, with Peter Cushing's mental intensity paired with Christopher Lee's physical presence. Strangely, due the nature of their casting, they actually spent relatively little time onscreen together.

Sharing his birthday with Vincent Price (and one day after Peter

Cushing), Christopher Frank Caradini Lee was born May 27, 1922. He traces his family history to Emperor Charlemagne (see *Nothing but the Night*) and the Borgias. His father was a military man, and Christopher continued the family tradition during World War II as a fighter pilot and intelligence officer.

After the war Lee was introduced by a cousin to Filippo del Giudia, the head of Two Cities Films, a division of Rank. Several weeks later he appeared in his first film, *The Corridor of Mirrors* (1947).

Unfortunately, for the next decade things weren't quite so easy. His commanding 6′ 4″ height and unusual good looks made him difficult to cast. Oddly, these characteristics would eventually be his greatest asset.

It was, in fact, his height that attracted Hammer's attention for the role of the Creature in *The Curse of Frankenstein*. Although Lee had appeared in *Hamlet* (sort of) and *Moulin Rouge*, he and Peter Cushing never actually met until the Frankenstein film. According to John Brosnan, "At the time, it was just another part and Lee did not attach any importance to the film."[12]

It was in his second Hammer film with Peter Cushing that Christopher Lee made his mark. *Horror of Dracula* (1957) more or less defined his career, but, strangely, the next several years found him in mainly supporting roles for Hammer (*Two Faces of Dr. Jekyll*, 1960) and others (*Beat Girl*, 1960).

By this time Christopher Lee had more or less abandoned England for the continent where he was given starring roles (including Sherlock Holmes) in generally poor films. Part of his difficulty may have been caused by his reluctance to repeat his Dracula role for fear of being typecast. John Brosnan comments, "To be perfectly frank, Dracula is one role that Lee has really excelled at. He is a competent actor, but in many parts he has seemed rather inflexible."[13]

After returning to the role in *Dracula — Prince of Darkness* (1965), Christopher Lee hit his stride and would star as *Rasputin — The Mad Monk* (1965) and in *The Devil Rides Out* (1968). However, by the decade's end, Lee was voicing his displeasure wih his horror image and began to appear in mainstream productions like *The Private Life of Sherlock Holmes* (1970), *The Three Musketeers* (1973), and *The Man with the Golden Gun* (1974).

Since his last Hammer film (*To the Devil — A Daughter*, 1976) and his last appearance with Peter Cushing (*Arabian Adventure*, 1978), Christopher Lee has kept busy in a variety of roles in films and on television. He seems to have gotten his wish by breaking free of his Dracula image, but one wonders if it has been worth it.

At his best—which was quite often—there is really no one like Christopher Lee. His Dracula will never be equaled, and the presence and audience sympathy he brought to *The Mummy* is stunning. The list goes on.

Despite his image as being rather aloof and impersonal, his friend Peter Cushing has found him to be quite the opposite. "Christopher has a delicious sense of humour and wit, plus a deep personal kindness. Some are awed when first meeting him in person, but they should know that beneath his outward aloofness and dignity lies a very *human* being; sensitive, warm, and oft-time suffering from nerves which he goes to great length to conceal."[14]

Peter Cushing and Christopher Lee occupy a special place in screen history and will be watched and enjoyed long after many bigger stars are forgotten. Together with Terence Fisher and Hammer, they created, at their best, a body of work that will never be equaled.

Notes

1. "Hammer: The Studio That Dripped Blood," BBC Television, 1987.
2. Cushing, *An Autobiography.*
3. Anthony Hinds, interview by Bruce Hallenbeck, *Fangoria* 74.
4. Christopher Lee International Club, Doreen Hazel, President.
5. John Brosnan, *The Horror People.*
6. Ibid.
7. Ibid.
8. Ibid.
9. Ibid.
10. Harry Ringel, "Terence Fisher—The Human Side," *Cinefantastique* 4, no. 3.
11. Carlos Clarens, *An Illustrated History of the Horror Film.*
12. Brosnan, *The Horror People.*
13. Ibid.
14. Ibid.

The Abominable Snowman
of the Himalayas
(1957)

Credits and Cast

Released November 1957 (U.S.); 83 minutes; Black and white; A Hammer Production; Released through 20th Century–Fox (U.S.) and Warner Brothers (U.K.); Filmed at Bray and Elstree Studios, England, and on location in France. Director: Val Guest; Producer: Aubrey Baring; Executive producer: Michael Carreras; Associate producer: Anthony Nelson-Keys; Story and screenplay: Nigel Kneale; Based on his television play "The Creature"; Music: Humphrey Searle; Music supervisor:

John Hollingsworth; Director of photography: Arthur Grant; Production design: Bernard Robinson; Art director: Ted Marshall; Editor: Bill Lenny; Production manager: Don Weeks; Sound recordist: Jock May; Camera operator: Len Harris; Associate director: Robert Lynn; Continuity: Doreen Soan; Dress designer: Beatrice Dawson; Makeup: Phil Leakey; Hairdresser: Henry Montash; Wardrobe: Molly Arbuthnot. Title in U.K., *The Abominable Snowman.*

Forrest Tucker (Tom Friend), Peter Cushing (Dr. John Rollason), Maureen Connell (Helen Rollason), Richard Wattis (Peter Fox), Robert Brown (Edward Shelley), Michael Brill (Andrey McNee), Wolfe Morris (Kusang), Arnold Marle (Lama), Anthony Chin (Majordomo).

Synopsis

There is no Yeti!—Lama

Nestled somewhere in the forbidding mountains of the Himalayas is a Tibetan monastery where botanist Dr. John Rollason (Peter Cushing) and his assistant Peter Fox (Richard Wattis) study some of the region's unusual plant life, graciously supplied by the ruling lama (Arnold Marle). During their conversation the Lama, with uncanny insight, informs Rollason that he knows an expedition will be arriving shortly and that they are not members of Rollason's botanical foundation. The lama questions Rollason as to their real purpose, but John's responses are evasive. John, however, knows that the team, led by Tom Friend (Forrest Tucker) has come in search of the legendary Yeti—the Abominable Snowman of the mountains—a creature whose existence has for centuries remained a mystery and perhaps a carefully guarded secret as well. Rollason intends to go with the expedition to the very peaks of the mountains to look for evidence of the elusive Yeti. Though his wife, Helen (Maureen Connell) tries desperately to discourage him from going, Rollason departs with the small expeditionary force.

The expedition team soon learns that their mountain climb will be both steep and treacherous—with constant threats of an avalanche or a fatal fall along the snow- and ice-covered passage. That night, finding shelter in a climber's hut, Tom Friend questions Rollason on his knowledge of the Yeti legends. John believes that the creatures have developed on a parallel evolutionary line similar to that of humans and apes. However, because they have remained evasive for so many centuries, John suspects that they have developed into a mentally superior race of beings. He also speculates that they may even be far superior to man and are merely waiting for mankind to finally destroy itself before coming out of hiding to claim the earth for themselves.

Peter Cushing as John Rollason in Hammer's *The Abominable Snowman of the Himalayas.*

Suspicious of the unusual equipment Friend's party has stored along the route on a previous climb (cages, traps, and ammunition), John is able to get Friend to admit the real reason for the expedition. Friend plans to capture a live specimen for commercial exploitation, justifying his motives by claiming that he is only trying to satisfy man's insatiable thirst for the strange and the unknown.

The next day one of the men, Andrey McNee (Michael Brill), a Scottish photographer, is caught in one of Edward Shelley's (Robert Brown) traps, which have been set along the route to catch the creature. While recuperating in his tent, McNee and the expedition's guide, Kusang (Wolfe Morris), see one of the creatures who has broken into the camp. Kusang and McNee flee the campsite and McNee falls to his death off a cliff.

Shelley, who has been on guard duty, shoots and kills one of the creatures. Friend, who is still convinced that he can capture a live Yeti, talks Shelley into volunteering to be the bait for his trap. Covering the roof of one of the nearby supply caves with a steel wire net, Shelley acts as a decoy. Standing guard outside the cave, Friend and Rollason find their sight obscured by the arrival of a sudden blizzard. One of the creatures is momentarily trapped in the cave but escapes before the men arrive. Shelley, however, is found dead from shock.

Later Friend, who believes he hears Shelley calling to him, runs out into the night. He fires several shots trying to determine Shelley's whereabouts, and his irrational act causes a massive avalanche which buries Friend beneath tons of snow. Now only Rollason remains alive. As he waits in the cave for morning, he is suddenly confronted by two of the creatures. Before passing into unconsciousness, he finds himself staring into the face of a creature whose eyes reflect peace, ageless wisdom, and great sadness.

Helen and Fox, who have come in search of the team after Kusang's return to the monastery, find Rollason at the base of the mountain suffering from extreme frostbite and shock. They fail to notice the huge footprints in the snow. Later, a recovered Rollason denies ever having seen any proof of the Yeti's existence.

Commentary

In 1955 Peter Cushing played Dr. John Rollason in the BBC television production of "The Creature," based on a play by Nigel Kneale. He was to repeat his character when in 1957 Hammer Films began production on *The Abominable Snowman* (U.S. title: *The Abominable Snowman of the Himalayas*). Val Guest, who had previously directed the enormously popular *Quatermass* films for Hammer (*The Quatermass Experiment*— U.S. title *The Creeping Unknown*, 1955, and *Quatermass II*—U.S. title *Enemy from Space*, 1957), was set to direct. Forrest Tucker received top billing in the film, replacing Stanley Baker who played the role of Tom Friend, the big game hunter and leader of the expedition, in the British television production.

Interiors and village shots were done at Bray and Elstree Studios, with location shooting done in the Pyrenees Mountains of France and Spain. Peter, Val Guest, some extras and a small camera crew were dispatched for the exterior shots of the climb. In an interview with David Soren, Peter told Soren that Forrest Tucker had a prior commitment so a double was used in his place. "I stopped every once in a while and looked around," Peter said. "Nobody else in the group did anything at all because none of them were actors."[1]

Cushing believed the film had great atmosphere but confessed that it was the first time he had to disagree with the director on a point. In an interview with Steve Swires, Peter said, "At the end of the movie the Yeti saved me and I was discovered in a frost-bitten condition by my wife. To achieve that effect, they had an airplane propeller blowing the 'ice' at me. Val Guest . . . wanted me to keep my eyes open. I said: 'Dear boy, it is physically impossible. Let me wear contact lenses, at least. If you don't believe me, come here and try it yourself.' He took one look at what I was going through and said: 'On second thought, I agree with you.' So I was able to keep my eyes closed."[2]

Val Guest, who wasn't at all happy with the way the film turned out, citing its low budget and limited locations for his dissatisfaction, remembered his association with Cushing fondly and with a touch of amusement.[3] Guest also had this to say about Cushing: "Peter Cushing is a great, great actor and a good personal friend. Sadly, that was the only picture I've every worked with him on and we had a lot of laughs doing it. Peter is a great one with props. . . . He would go and mull over a part and figure out all the props he could use and he never told you about them. They were just part of his character." Guest, also cites a particular scene where he was surprised at Cushing's sudden change of approach:

> I'll never forget one scene where the High Lama had given him [Cushing] the Yeti tooth and we rehearsed it with him looking at the tooth and studying it. . . . We went into the take and Peter brought out a nail file and scratched the tooth to see what consistency it was. Then he took out a tape measure and measured it. . . . We were in hysterics because we knew of his work with props. We got it on the first take because I knew we'd never last through another one without collapsing . . . it was the first any of us knew he had the props with him. That was typical of Peter. We used to call him Peter "props" Cushing.[4]

Forrest Tucker also concurred with his director on Cushing's serious approach to his character. It seemed that Cushing always had questions regarding the authenticity of what he was asked to do in the script. Tucker cites the following examples:

> Peter . . . is a terribly meticulous man. He had to know [if he took] his mittens off at this altitude, how long could he have his hands out . . . before they would be frost bitten. And can you actually light a butane lamp here or could a man logically smoke at this altitude, light fire. . . . I used to kid the [bleep] out of him. You know, I'd say, "Pete, I'm gonna [bleep] smoke a cigarette at nine thousand feet and I'll find a way to get this bastard lit, now you watch me."

However, kidding aside, Tucker had to admit that though Peter was the film's greatest critic, he was probably its savior too:

> I think more than anyone else, [Peter was] responsible for the fact that this show had this enormous authenticity. . . . Oh, he does months and months of research on everything he does. . . . He's a very valuable asset to a producer . . . he can save you thousands of dollars . . . because [of] what he's gonna do himself. Even such things as what we carried in our pack . . . cause you know, our prop men, they'd throw three cans of Spam in there!. . . It was a very exciting experience for me to watch an actor work that hard in . . . other areas of making a film.[5]

Some film critics were dissatisfied with the film's subtle handling of the Yeti's on-screen appearance but as Peter explained to Steve Swires, "it was extremely effective. The original idea was that you saw the great big footprint and then the great shadow but you never actually saw the Yeti because no one has . . . so to leave it to the imagination was the intention. Just to show the eyes was quite a brilliant thought."[6] It seems some even thought the director used Peter's eyes for the Yeti, but Peter was quick to state for the record, "Actually, they used a very well-known Irish actor who had marvelous sad eyes."

Critical reviews of the film were generally good, though *The Times* (August 26, 1957) started off by saying that "The performances of a cast headed by Forrest Tucker and Peter Cushing were . . . to a large extent wasted . . . for once an engaging monster is neither bombed, roasted nor electrocuted. . . . I salute 'the Abominable Snowman.'" *Variety* reviewer "Whit" (November 6, 1957) stated: "lensed largely in the Pyrenees which provides realistic backgrounds of which director Val Guest takes fine advantage. He generates plenty of suspense . . . Forrest Tucker and Peter Cushing . . . give substance to their roles. . . . Photography . . . is interesting and . . . tight editing . . . and score are additional assets." Tuesday's edition of the *Christian Science Monitor* (December 24, 1957) gave the film a nice Christmas gift that year when it said, "A taut adventure with Science Fiction added. . . . Character contrasts in the film are nicely emphasized and it is made with a subtlety that leaves room for imagination. . . . Anticlimax comes in most Science Fiction stories with the actual appearance of the monster. The director Val Guest has conquered the problem by withholding confirmation until almost the end of the picture. Then he makes it a moment of curiosity mingled with awe."

Notes

1. Peter Cushing, interview with David Soren, *Gore Creatures* 18.
2. Peter Cushing, interview with Steven Swires, *Famous Monsters of Filmland* 146.
3. Val Guest, interview with Philip Nutman, *Fangoria* 49.
4. Val Guest, interview, *Little Shoppe of Horrors* 7.
5. Forrest Tucker, interview with David Aquino and George Stover, *Black Oracle* 8.
6. Cushing, interview, *Famous Monsters of Filmland* 146.

Violent Playground
(1957)

Credits and Cast

Released April 1957; 108 minutes; Black and white; Released through Rank (U.K.); Filmed at Pinewood Studios, England, and on location in Liverpool. Director: Val Guest; Producer: Michael Relph; Executive producer: Earl St. John; Screenplay: James Kennaway; Director of photography: Reg Wyer; Music: Phillip Green; Art director: Maurice Carter; Editor: Arthur Stevens; Camera operator: David Harcourt; Makeup: Alec Garfath.

Stanley Baker (Truman), Anne Heywood (Cathie), David McCallum (Johnny), Peter Cushing (Priest), John Slater (Sergeant Walker), Clifford Evans (Heaven), Moultrie Kelsall (Superintendent), George A. Cooper (Inspector), Brona Boland (Mary), Fergal Boland (Patrick), Michael Chow (Alexander), Tsai Chin (Primrose), Sean Lynch (Slick), Bernice Swanson (Meg).

Synopsis

In the midst of a series of unexplained fires in Liverpool, Detective Truman (Stanley Baker) is transferred to Juvenile Liaison. His difficult job is to prevent young children in trouble from becoming criminals.

When the Baker twins (Fergal and Brona Boland) are caught stealing from a store, Truman takes them home where he meets their troubled older brother Johnny (David McCallum). Truman gets little help from their attractive older sister Cathie (Anne Heywood) who regards the detective with disdain.

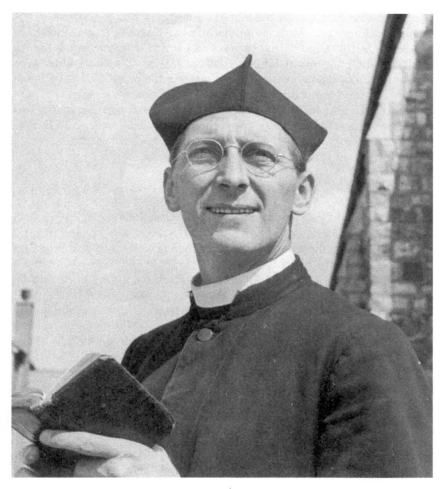

Peter Cushing as a caring priest in *Violent Playground*.

Attracted to Cathie and suspicious of Johnny, Truman continues to visit the Bakers. His presence makes Johnny nervous and he consults his priest (Peter Cushing) for advice. When the two are startled by Truman's sudden appearance, Johnny runs off. The padre explains to Truman that, as a child, Johnny was involved in a fire — and could be involved in the current rash of arson.

Johnny starts a fire in a hotel in return for once being evicted, but is caught at the scene. He jumps out of a window and steals a laundry truck, running over the Chinese boy who was driving it. After his escape, a friend gives him a machine gun.

On the run, he spends the night in a school, but is discovered by the teacher and her class. In desperation, he holds them hostage — including the twins. Surrounded by the police and parents, Johnny begins to lose control. When the priest climbs a ladder to the classroom window to reason with Johnny, he pushes it away causing the priest to fall and break his arm. In the confusion, Johnny panics and shoots a child.

Cathie is sent in by the police and manages to get Johnny to surrender. As the police take him away, the priest gently explains to Cathie that Johnny's example might save others from a life of crime.

Commentary

When asked by a character in *The Wild One* (1954) what he is rebelling at, motorcycle hoodlum Marlon Brando replied, "What have you got?" This pretty well summed up the spirit of teenagers as they would be portrayed on-screen during the decade.

The 1950s were, in both America and England, a time of increasing alienation, dissatisfaction, and rebellion. World War II and its troubled aftermath would change forever many attitudes and beliefs previously held sacred.

In the United States violence often erupted in urban schools to the loud accompaniment of rock and roll. Evan Hunter's novel, *The Blackboard Jungle*, filmed brilliantly in 1955 with Glenn Ford, Sidney Poitier, and Vic Morrow, accurately portrayed the deteriorating situation. Incredibly, the film contained a disclaimer that situations depicted in the film were rare!

James Dean provided a dictionary definiton of teenage alienation in Nicholas Ray's *Rebel Without a Cause* (1955) and Elvis Presley was final proof to adults that their worst nightmare had come true.

England was having its own problems. A postwar depression, decaying urban areas, and a dissatisfaction with class distinctions caused a similar situation. For the first time, British teenagers were viewed as potential menaces.

Violent Playground was one of the first British films to address this change in the social order and, as such, opened itself up to a different level of criticism. *The Times* (March 3, 1958) chose to review the film as a social comment rather than a thriller, finding it "a film which sets out with such self avowed high purposes [but] degenerates into something that is basically dishonest, since the real issues are evaded. The ineffectual priest, to whose platitudes not even Mr. Peter Cushing can give weight . . . [has] no reality."

The key words in this review, for our purposes, are "not even." They indicate the high regard in which Peter Cushing was held even before he reached international stardom. This praise was probably based mainly on his award-winning television work.

Variety (January 22, 1958) was more impressed with the film, possibly because of viewing the actual situation from a distance. The review referred to the "human and literate screenplay," and called it "an absorbing film. There are a number of very credible performances, including . . . Peter Cushing."

Sandwiched between *The Abominable Snowman of the Himalayas* and *Horror of Dracula*, this was the last straight film Peter Cushing would appear in before becoming generally known as a horror star. After *Violent Playground*, straight roles certainly came his way, but were often overlooked by critics who chose to label him as Frankenstein.

Although his screen time was limited, Cushing, as usual, managed to make his presence felt and his kindly, concerned manner gave the film its moral tone. His attempt to enter the classroom by ladder, in the hands of the lesser actor, could have come off as senseless heroics, but the scene is believable and a highlight of the film.

Star Stanley Baker turns in his usual excellent performance as Truman — a man certainly torn by his sense of duty and his personal feelings. He and Peter Cushing were seeing a lot of each other during this period by also appearing in *Alexander the Great* and the BBC production of *The Abominable Snowman* (titled "The Creature").

David McCallum, who would eventually — and briefly — find his niche in the television series "The Man from U.N.C.L.E." is fine as the troubled Johnny and ably projects the young man's confusion.

If the events in the film seem to be based on fact, it's because the juvenile unit depicted is based on one actually instituted in Liverpool. A Rank publicity handout explains:

> In 1949, the Chief Constable of Liverpool, taking action against a growing wave of juvenile crime, instituted the Juvenile Liaison Officer's Scheme.
> These Officers dealt with children under seventeen years of age who have committed a minor offense . . . who have never come to the notice of the law before.
> At their direction, the child is not brought to court, but is taken under the care and guidance of the JLOS.
> Over 92% of the children handled in this way have not committed a second crime.

By the time *Violent Playground* opened at London's Marble Arch Odeon, it had gone through several title changes — from the original *Violent Playground*, to *Children of the Street*, and back again.

Peter Cushing was absent from the stage in 1957—his theatrical career was to include only three more roles. He continued his television work that year with "Home at Seven" and "Gaslight."

Horror of Dracula
(1957)

Credits and Cast

Released May 1958; 82 minutes; Technicolor; A Hammer Film Production; Released through Universal; Filmed at Bray Studios, England. Director: Terence Fisher; Producer: Anthony Hinds; Executive producer: Michael Carreras; Associate producer: Anthony Nelson-Keys; Screenplay: Jimmy Sangster; Based on the novel *Dracula* by Bram Stoker; Production manager: Don Weeks; Assistant director: Robert Lynn; Continuity: Doreen Dearnaley; Director of photography: Jack Asher, B.S.C.; Camera operator: Len Harris; Sound mixer: Jock May; Art director: Bernard Robinson; Stills cameraman: Tom Edwards; Supervising editor: James Needs; Editor: Bill Lenny; Makeup: Phil Leakey; Makeup assistant: Roy Ashton; Hairdresser: Henry Montash; Wardrobe: Molly Arbuthnot; Musical director: John Hollingsworth; Music composer: James Bernard; Special effects: Sidney Pearson. Title in U.K., *Dracula*.

Peter Cushing (Dr. Van Helsing), Michael Gough (Arthur Holmwood), Melissa Stribling (Mina Holmwood), Christopher Lee (Count Dracula), Carol Marsh (Lucy Holmwood), John Van Eyssen (Jonathan Harker), Miles Malleson (Marx, the Undertaker), Valerie Gaunt (Vampire Woman), Geoffrey Bayldon (Porter), Paul Cole (Lad), Janina Faye (Tanya), Olga Dickie (Gerda), Barbara Archer (Inga), Charles Lloyd Pack (Dr. Seward), George Merritt (Policeman), George Woodbridge (Innkeeper), George Benson (Frontier Official), Guy Mills (Coach Driver), Dick Morgan (Driver's Companion), John Mossman (Hearse Driver), Also with Judith Nelmes, William Sherwood, Stedwell Fulcher, and Humphrey Kent.

Synopsis

Jonathan Harker (John Van Eyssen), an assistant to Dr. Van Helsing (Peter Cushing) and a vampire hunter, journeys to Castle Dracula under the guise of a librarian to destroy the vampire king. He is unsuccessful and is, in turn, transformed into one of the undead.

Dr. Van Helsing investigates his disappearance and, finding his colleague and friend in the vampiric state, releases Jonathan's soul. Dracula (Christopher Lee), however, has fled the castle and Van Helsing follows his trail.

Stopping to visit Arthur and Mina Holmwood (Michael Gough and

Melissa Stribling), Harker's fiancée's family, he tells them of Jonathan's death. While offering his sympathies to Harker's fiancée, Lucy Holmwood (Carol Marsh), whom Van Helsing has been told is ill, he discovers that she too has become a victim of Dracula. Enlisting the aid of Arthur Holmwood, they are able to release her from her torment.

Van Helsing and Holmwood then try to determine Dracula's new hiding place, unaware that he has now made Mina his bride and has found refuge in the cellar of Holmwood's house. When Van Helsing discovers this, he confronts the vampire. Dracula abducts Mina and returns with her to his castle. Arthur and the vampire hunter pursue them and Van Helsing battles the nosferatu — eventually destroying him and saving Mina.

Commentary

When the moviegoing public of 1958 sat in their theater seats awaiting the opening credits for Hammer's latest foray into the supernatural, they were thoroughly unprepared for what was later to be described by many as a cinematic event. *Horror of Dracula* was unlike any of its predecessors. It shook off many of the previously held taboos and showed us in living technicolor just what it was really like to come face to face with terror. Like its sister film, *Curse of Frankenstein, Horror of Dracula* broke new ground and, although critics were guarded and in some cases openly hostile in their reviews, the audience didn't care; they loved it! Horror movies would never be the same again.

Devotees of the genre have often pondered the question as to why Hammer films were so successful. Certainly color had a great appeal. More gore, violence, and sex was another popular argument. But when one comes right down to it, there was the obvious — dedication. Hammer wanted to make good, quality motion pictures, films which the general moviegoing public would enjoy going to see and which were "updated" for more modern tastes. This sense of devotion to their product extended not only among the top executives but to the writers, directors, production people, and, most of all, the actors themselves. They all took their assignments seriously and tried to do the best they could. It showed!

The players chosen for *Horror of Dracula* were exceptional. Christopher Lee, whose features were totally masked by heavy makeup as the creature in *The Curse of Frankenstein*, proved to be just as frightening at times without it as when he wore the bloodshot eye contact lenses and fangs for his role as the vampire count. The thought that beneath those handsome, aristocratic features lurked a terrible creature whose thirst for human blood had to be satiated and that the monster beneath the facade could appear at any moment kept audiences riveted in anticipation.

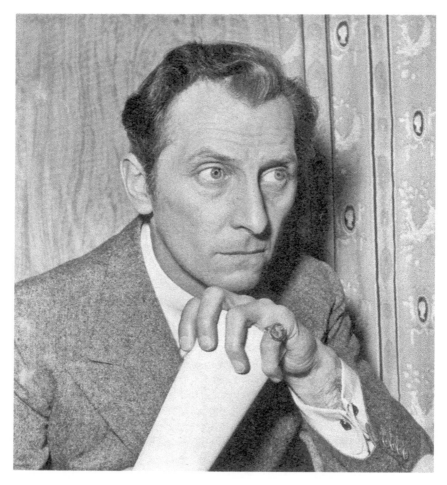

A pensive Peter Cushing (Dr. Van Helsing) faces the press at the premiere of *Horror of Dracula* in London 1958.

However, it was the casting of Peter Cushing as Dr. Van Helsing that proved to be the most inspiring of all. Here was a performer who could be even more relentless and aggressive than Lee's Dracula, creating a new hero for fantasy film fans that would last for generations. "Cushing showed himself to be an opponent worthy of the evil count's mettle. A deeply sincere man, [Cushing] once said that he fervently believed that the reason the kind of horror films in which he was involved had found such favor with the public was because they were about the eternal conflict between good and evil; something he thought that was too often dismissed in the other arts in contemporary days," noted author Tom Hutchinson.[1]

When Peter took on the role of Van Helsing, his vision of the character was quite different in some ways from Edward Van Sloan's interpretation in Universal's 1931 version of *Dracula*.

> I read the book [*Dracula* by Bram Stoker] when I knew I was going to play the character . . . and discovered that Stoker had described him as a little old Dutchman with a bald head and sporting a small beard. Therefore, all the production team got together and decided that it would be better to inject more vigor into the character. So I played the part more or less as myself. But with the overwhelming success that Hammer had had with *Curse of Frankenstein*, they decided that Christopher's name and mine clicked together and they decided to cast Chris as Dracula and myself as his rather fanatical pursuer, Van Helsing.[2]

Although Cushing through his modesty felt this was the only reason why Hammer decided he should take the role, many felt that it was because he was such an extraordinary actor that no one else could have brought to the part the vitality and sincerity that Peter was able to convey. "Peter Cushing is to the film's dynamic concept as Edward Van Sloan was to the more slowly-paced version. Wise beyond his years, Cushing possesses not only Van Sloan's mental ability of competing with Dracula, but the physical agility and strength . . . as well. And, like Van Sloan, Cushing's manner and precise voice is convincing enough to make the existence of vampires believable to even the most skeptical."[3]

Once production had begun, Peter would also prove to be as valuable behind the cameras as he was in front of them. Some of the key scenes in the film that also proved to be the most exciting were the results of Cushing's input. "In the original script," Cushing explained to Ron Borst, "Van Helsing was sort of like a salesman for crucifixes. He was pulling them out of every pocket. He was giving them to children to protect themselves, and putting them in coffins and so on. At the end of the film, he pulled out another one, so I asked if we couldn't do something exciting instead. I remembered seeing a film years ago called *Berkeley Square* (1933) in which Leslie Howard was thought of as being the Devil by this frightened little man who suddenly grabbed two big candlesticks and made a sign of the cross with them. I remembered that this had impressed me enormously. I suggested the run along the refectory table to jump onto the curtains and hit Dracula square in the face with the sunlight. He would, of course, be trapped. Then I could come along like a hero, grab the two candlesticks and make the cross with them in his face. They agreed . . . I think it was quite an effective ending to that picture."[4]

This is quite true, for the ending of *Horror of Dracula* was one of the most memorable in horror film history. Very few films after it would make as lasting an impression. Seeing Dracula literally crumble to dust before our wide-opened eyes lived long after the film's end.

Peter could also go to lengths to prove a point, as in the scene where Van Helsing discovers Dracula's coffin, which had been hidden in the Holmwoods' cellar, and is confronted by Dracula. "Van Helsing's movements in this scene were directly attributable to Cushing who had asked Fisher [the director] if he might make a jump over the bannister instead of running around to the steps. The director replied that he shouldn't perform such a potentially dangerous stunt. However, when the scene was filmed, Cushing went ahead with the leap on his own accord and accomplished it perfectly in a single take."[5]

There is also the scene where Van Helsing, in a wild coach chase, pursues Dracula back to his castle. "The coach scenes were filmed just after dawn one morning on an almost deserted country road. . . . Cushing, who refused to have a double for the scenes, had been practicing the drive for two days and admitted at the time that he was having enormous fun."[6]

It is quite a rarity when an actor and his director have a good working relationship on a film. Many times it's more a battle of wits than a cooperative arrangement. Terence Fisher had the wisdom to listen to input and made changes whenever he felt that the film would benefit. One cannot help but feel that to a certain extent this is yet another reason why *Horror of Dracula* worked so well.

Fisher had this to say about his friend in a 1974 interview with Gary Parfitt.

> Peter Cushing and I met for the first time as actor and film director in 1956 when Hammer decided to make a new version of *Frankenstein*. This was closely followed by *Dracula* in 1957 and laid the foundation of the so-called Hammer Horror Cycle. This association has been for me deeply satisfying both professionally and personally. Apart from his acknowledged high standing as an actor, he brings to every part he plays a wonderful integrity of approach which results in a deep and studied understanding of the character he is portraying. This comes across strongly to the audience in all his films and makes him, I believe, as being more than a highly professional actor. He absorbs himself in all the details of the production he is working on and unselfishly contributes many ideas that are for the good of the film as a whole.[7]

Horror of Dracula premiered in New York on Thursday, May 29, 1958, at the Mayfair Theater. Both Christopher Lee and Peter Cushing were flown over from England to attend the opening and were on hand in the lobby of the theater to sign autographs. Each patron was also given complimentary copies of the pocketbook edition of *Dracula* as well as soft drinks which were appropriately called "courage cocktails."[8]

Critiques of the film included *Cue* (May 24, 1958), which noted, "The production is most elaborate, and the performances are vigorous, sincere, and filled with conviction." *British Monthly Film Bulletin* reported, "Peter

Cushing is cooly scientific . . . the Jack Asher photography [is] full of forboding atmosphere. Directed by Terence Fisher with immense flair." Dorothy Masters of the *New York Daily News* (May 29, 1958) remarked that "unlike most of Hollywood's quickies, *Horror of Dracula* has allocated time, thought and talent to an enterprise which successfully recaptures the aura and patina of yesterday's middle Europe . . . some of the photography is good enough to frame. . . . All performances are good and many of the special effects are electrifying." *The Times* advised, "Its purpose is to tell a ghost story, and all the trappings of the cinema are used to this end. . . . Mr. Peter Cushing, as the one who carries on the battle against the monster, is suitably tight-lipped and resolved. . . . Altogether this is a horrific film, and sometimes a crude film, but by no means an unimpressive piece of . . . story-telling." "Gills" of *Variety* (May 7, 1958) wrote that *Horror of Dracula* had "Gore aplenty . . . a serious approach to the macabre theme that adds up to lots of tension and suspense. . . . Screenplay has ably preserved the sanguinary aspects of the novel. . . . Eerie atmosphere is accented by physical values and Bernard Robinson's art direction. . . . Peter Cushing is impressive as the painstaking scientist-doctor who solves the mystery." The *New York Herald Tribune* (G.G., May 29, 1958) warned, "If you find the sight of blood abhorrent, this picture is not for you. If the children are likely to take it seriously and become frightened, keep them at home. For the rest of the viewers, there will be shocks and jolts aplenty. . . . The cast play their roles straight and capably, giving the impression that they believe every line." *Motion Picture Exhibitor* (May 14, 1958) noted, "The use of Technicolor has transformed what could have been an ordinary horror film into one of vivid terror where the blood drips realistically, the shadows are eerier, the gloom deeper, and the atmosphere maddening. Horror is presented here as it has rarely been pictured before, and audiences will indeed have to be strong to bear up."

Notices for *Horror of Dracula* seemed to unilaterally reflect the raw emotional impact the film had had not only on critics and audiences but the motion picture industry as well. However, whether they praised or condemned it, whether they were insightful enough to recognize the up-and-coming trend Hammer Films was establishing or not, both *Curse of Frankenstein* and *Horror of Dracula* were directly responsible for the significant changes filmmakers would make, both in their approach and execution, of many of the world's fantasy films for years to follow.

Notes

1. Tom Hutchinson, *Horror and Fantasy in the Movies.*
2. Peter Cushing, interview in *Little Shoppe of Horrors* 4.

3. Ron Borst, "The Vampire in the Cinema," *Photon* 18.
4. Ron Borst, "The Horror of Dracula," *Photon* 27.
5. Ibid.
6. Ibid.
7. Gary Parfitt, *The Films of Peter Cushing.*
8. Melvin Maddocks, *Christian Science Monitor,* May 29, 1958.

The Revenge of Frankenstein
(1958)

Credits and Cast

Released August 1958 (U.K.), June 1958 (U.S.); 91 minutes; Technicolor; A Hammer Film Production; Released through Columbia; Filmed at Bray Studios, England. Director: Terence Fisher; Producer: Anthony Hinds; Associate producer: Anthony Nelson-Keys; Executive producer: Michael Carreras; Screenplay: Jimmy Sangster; Additonal dialogue: H. Huford Janes; Music: Leonard Salzedo; Conductor: Muir Mathieson; Director of photography: Jack Asher; Production design: Bernard Robinson; Supervising editor: James Needs; Editor: Alfred Cox; Sound recordist: Jock May; Production manager: Don Weeks; Camera: Len Harris; Makeup: Phil Leakey; Hairstyles: Henry Montash; Continuity: Doreen Dearnaley; Wardrobe: Rosemary Burrows; Working Title: "Blood of Frankenstein."

Peter Cushing ("Dr. Victor Stein"), Francis Matthews (Dr. Hans Kleve), Eunice Gayson (Margaret), Michael Gwynn ("Karl"), John Welsh (Dr. Bergman), Lionel Jeffries (Fritz), Oscar Quitak (Karl), Richard Wordsworth (Up Patient), Charles Lloyd Pack (President), John Stuart (Inspector), Arnold Diamond (Malke), Margery Cresley (Countess), Anna Walmsley (Vera), George Woodbridge (Janitor), Michael Ripper (Kurt), Ian Whittaker (Boy), Avril Leslie (Girl), Michael Mulcaster (Tattoo).

Synopsis

> If the brain hadn't been damaged, my work would have been hailed as the greatest scientific achievement of all time.... I swore I would have my revenge. They will never get rid of me. — Dr. Stein

Baron Victor Frankenstein (Peter Cushing), convicted of several murders he claims were committed by a being he created, is led to the guillotine. A priest and a crippled guard (Oscar Quitak) lead him to the scaffold. As the priest reads from the Bible, the guard and executioner exchange a glance. The blade rises.

Fritz (Lionel Jeffries) and Kurt (Michael Ripper) drunkenly discuss robbing a grave for money — the grave of an executed prisoner. When they

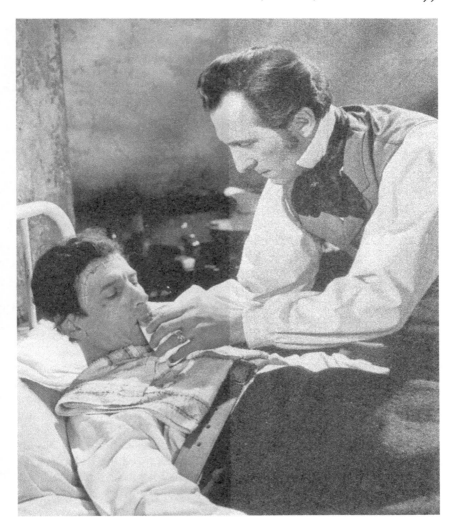

Karl (Michael Gwynn) being tended to by his creator in Hammer's *The Revenge of Frankenstein.*

open the coffin, the body is that of a priest! The baron and the cripple emerge from the shadows.

Three years later in Carlsbruck, the medical council discusses a certain Dr. Stein, who not only refuses to join but is also stealing their best patients. The president (Charles Lloyd Pack), Dr. Hans Kleve (Francis Matthews), and Dr. Bergman (John Welsh) decide to confront him at his charity clinic for the poor.

At the clinic, their arrival is announced by an obnoxious up patient (Richard Wordsworth). Dr. Stein arranges to meet them in the ward — a foul-smelling hell filled with recent and future amputees. He refuses the invitation to join the council and diagnoses another amputation — this time for an infected arm.

After the surgery he returns to his office where Dr. Kleve awaits. Hans has recognized him as the baron and promises to exchange his silence for medical knowledge. Dr. Stein reluctantly agrees.

The pair go to Dr. Stein's secret laboratory where an incredible operation is to take place. Karl, the crippled guard, is to receive a new, perfect body to complete the bargain made in prison. The body is an artificial one, made from the limbs of the poor.

A complication arises when Margaret (Eunice Gayson), whose father is an official, arrives at the clinic to do volunteer work. Karl becomes infatuated when they meet briefly in the office.

That night the operation begins. Karl's brain is removed and placed into the artificial body which is then brought to life by an electric shock. As Karl (now Michael Gwynn) recuperates, Dr. Stein feeds raw meat to Otto, a chimp given the brain of an orangutan.

Karl is taken to an attic room at the clinic under the unseen observation of the up patient. As he listens at the door, there is a shriek from within.

A week later the bandages are removed, revealing a normal-looking man with a forehead scar. Dr. Stein tests his reactions and, well pleased, leaves. Hans, in an effort to keep Karl's mind active, tells him of his future as an object of scientific curiosity. Karl is repelled at the thought of still being a freak.

Margaret learns of the special patient and, given the key by the up patient, visits Karl. She does not, of course, recognize him. After inviting him to her estate when he is well, she loosens his binding straps. Down in the office, a chance remark from the up patient startles Hans as he recalls that chimps are vegetarians.

Dr. Stein explains that, after the transplant, Otto injured his brain and turned cannibal. Since Karl is also aware of this, Dr. Stein assumes he will take care that it does not happen to him. Hans is then shown an exact double of Dr. Stein — again created from the bodies of his patients.

Karl removes his straps and, while dressing, glimpses his perfect body in a mirror. He returns to his "birthplace" to destroy his old body. After burning it, he is discovered by the janitor (George Woodbridge), who savagely beats him. After a vicious blow to the head, Karl strangles his attacker. He stares at the corpse and, after glancing at Otto eating raw meat, looks back at the body. He drools.

Dr. Stein and Hans discover Karl's escape and track him as far as the lab. Margaret finds Karl in her stable and, since he is terrified of Dr. Stein, goes to Hans instead. Karl's body is slowly changing, twisting back to its original shape. That night in the park Karl savagely attacks a young girl. There is blood on his lips.

The elite of Carlsbruck are attending a musical evening at Margaret's family estate. Dr. Stein confronts her in the drawing room but she does not know Karl's whereabouts. Suddenly, Karl crashes through a window, staggers to his creator, and shouts, "Frankenstein! Help me." He dies at Dr. Stein's feet.

Word of the incident spreads through Carlsbruck. The Medical Council has the baron's grave exhumed and learns the truth. The charity patients riot and savagely beat their mutilator. Hans spirits him, near death, to the laboratory and, following his orders, removes his brain. Hans takes the artificial body from its tank.

At the London office of Dr. Franck, Hans watches as the doctor greets a patient. Dr. Franck's forehead is lightly scarred.

Commentary

"Cushing Is New Karloff" screamed a headline in the *New York Daily News*. And indeed he was. When *The Revenge of Frankenstein* opened at Brooklyn's Fabian Fox in June 1958, *Horror of Dracula* was still playing in over 100 theaters in the New York metropolitan area. After only 4 horror films, Peter Cushing's image was cast.

As with most films that develop into a series, *The Curse of Frankenstein* was not intended to start one. But, just in case, the baron survived even though his creature didn't. This would set the stage for the series — a concentration on the baron and not his monsters.

Asked what parallels existed between his Frankenstein films and the vintage 1931 Universal version, director Terence Fisher said, "I wouldn't dream of comparing them. His [director James Whale's] was probably a greater achievement in that it was the first."[1] And, despite the bleating of contemporary critics, *The Revenge of Frankenstein* was probably no more violent in 1958 than *The Bride of Frankenstein* was in 1935.

As in the Universal series, the first two Hammer films are the only two with a direct and noncontrived link. *The Revenge of Frankenstein* literally begins where *The Curse of Frankenstein* ends. When watched back to back, they blend perfectly.

Peter Cushing is even better than in his original outing as the baron. He was given a far more interesting and unusual script, along with a quirky sense of humor. He also has a moral ambiguity lacking in most horror film heroes. Frankenstein seems genuinely concerned about Karl — in both bodies. While interested in his own ends, he also wants the operation to succeed for Karl's sake. His work at the charity hospital, while supplying him with limbs, also benefits many patients beneath the dignity of the Medical Council.

Screenwriter Jimmy Sangster created a truly disturbing character in Karl—a "monster" only because the film requires one. Karl simply wants to be like everyone else, and the look of joy on his face when he catches a glimpse of his new body in a mirror is perfectly realized. Michael Gwynn's performance is excellent but strangely overlooked by both critics and fans.

Sangster also makes points about class distinctions in Carlsbruck— the idle rich and the diseased poor. These two worlds are brought start- lingly together when Karl crashes through the window and dies, begging for help, at the baron's feet.

Producer Anthony Hinds had this to say about his star: "I have never worked with a more pains-taking actor. Cushing goes to the most extraor- dinary lengths to insure that everything he does is strictly authentic and it's because he's such a stickler for accuracy and authenticity that he brings such a complete conviction to his Frankenstein role."[2]

Francis Matthews, who matches Peter Cushing's excellence and sin- cerity in his role as Hans, shared his memories of Cushing with the authors. They offer a fascinating view of Peter Cushing in and out of char- acter.

> Peter had scored a personal success in the remakes of *Frankenstein* and *Dracula* and, although he had been a well-known and respected televi- sion actor, he had now crossed boundaries and was suddenly very "bank- able."
>
> Nevertheless, he made me feel instantly at home with him on the set and extended the warmth of his friendship which helped us to form one of the happiest working relationships I have ever experienced. We were on the screen together throughout most of the picture, with me, of course, a few steps to the rear.
>
> On the set, during the long lighting breaks, we both did *The Times* crossword to see who could finish first and there was a great deal of cheating. The crossword finished or abandoned, we played, day after day, a game called "Battleships" to which Peter introduced me. It involved shouting out numbers and mouthing the sounds of exploding shells. The sight of two grown men doing this who were about to transplant the brain of a dwarf into a monster didn't seem to faze anyone.
>
> It certainly didn't faze Peter who, the moment the camera began to roll, switched into the total absorption in his role that is the hallmark of a true professional. He was unerringly sharp, keen and stimulating to work with. Courteous and considerate, I never saw him angry with any- one. His laughter was a tonic that made the working days fly by.
>
> One scene in which I was removing Peter's brain into a new body

involved the use of a sheep's brain, about which Peter said, "I hope you're not all trying to tell me something."

I would sometimes give him a lift if we finished work at the same time. I would call in to see not only his extraordinary collection of toy soldiers, but most of all his wife, a lovely and tender woman whose devotion to Peter was equalled by his to her. She was the moving force and center of his life and when she died the light went out of Peter's eyes.

But the light was still there when we attended the premiere of *Revenge* together. We sat side by side both reasonably content with the results of our labors until the moment when, with Frankenstein killed, I have the awesome job of resurrecting him. Gazing up at the new body, suspended in a glass casing, I say, "Pray God I have the skill to do this." The cinema literally exploded with laughter, not quite what was intended, and I buried my head in my hands. Peter leant over, close to my ear, and simply said, "Wrong."[3]

Filled with bits of black humor, the film is unique and is, arguably, the best of the Hammer series. The acting, photography, costumes, and set design have rarely been bettered by any horror film — or straight film, for that matter. In fact, it is so well done, even many critics liked it.

The Times (September 1, 1958) felt that Peter Cushing had created a "suavely sinister character." Frank Quinn in the *New York Daily Mirror* (June 17) called it "less a shocker than the previous outing. Partially robbing it of its horror is the sympathetic personality of its ... monster." *Variety* (June 18) went farther. "A high-grade horror film, gory enough to give adults a squeamish second thought and a thoroughly unpleasant one.... Production is a rich one. The settings, the costumes, and other physical aspects are on the level of any top productions.... Screenplay is well-plotted, peopled with interesting characters aided by good performances."

Not everyone, however, was pleased. *The Observer* (August 31) was offended that "Peter Cushing, who can be an actor of parts when he so chooses, again demeans himself by playing the hero.... A crude sort of entertainment for a crude sort of audience."

By the time that *The Revenge of Frankenstein* was in general release, a reaction against horror films began in both England and the United States. In addition to the Peter Cushing/Hammer product, films like *I Was a Teenage Werewolf* (1957), *Attack of the Crab Monsters* (1957), and *Blood of the Vampire* (1958) had certain reactionary groups convinced that the end of Western civilization was near.

Petitions to Parliament to curb the production of horror films had, fortunately, little or no effect. Nor did letters of outrage to *The Times*. The first mention of organized protest against horror appeared in 1958. The floodgates opened in 1960, with negative articles on March 30, July 5, and November 30. The tone of all this is represented by Parliament requiring the Council of Kinematograph Renters Society (October 6, 1958) to submit rough layouts of horror film posters to local watchdog committees to prevent offending public taste.

The onslaught of adverse critical comment directed at both Hammer and American International (which was described as having the same status in the American film industry as the man hired to sweep behind the elephants in a circus parade) also had little or no effect.[4] Hammer's Michael Carreras actually appreciated these reviews. "In general," he stated, "those sort of criticisms are highly exploitable."[5]

Like rock and roll, horror films have always benefitted from a less than respectable image. Carreras continues: "When the National Film Theatre . . . gave us a two week season I was horrified. I thought if they made us respectable it would ruin our whole image."[6]

The real question here is — are films like *The Revenge of Frankenstein* harmful? Do acts of explicit violence on screen cause acts of real violence? Naturally, both sides of this question have their supporters.

Producer Anthony Hinds: "To the sceptics who peer at me superciliously and demand to know why I make pictures like *Dracula* and *Frankenstein*, I answer that it is my job—I do it for the money. And to those who depict me as the exploiter of the basest of human tastes and desires for the sake of profit, the answer is equally simple: I don't drive the public into the cinemas. They go because they want to go, but only when there is something they want to see."[7]

Peter Cushing agrees that this type of film is harmless and fulfills a need for the average person. "I think horror films are marvelous. To me, a real *horror* film is something like *The Godfather* or films about the war. These are things that *have* happened to people and *do* happen, but basically "horror" pictures are fantasies that take people out of themselves. They can laugh at them if they want to, as long as they enjoy them."[8]

Cushing stated to the authors that, in his opinion, "violence that is similar to that in everyday life is, perhaps, harmful to certain viewers, but scenes depicted in our films are not those likely to be copied."

To be fair, it should be pointed out that it is only natural that people connected with making this kind of film would deem it harmless. Many would—and do—disagree. Perhaps it is a matter of limits. To the authors, that limit might have been reached during the 1980s with a concentration on ghastly murder for its own sake without a thought given to characterization. It is difficult for us to believe that anyone is actually harmed by watching a Peter Cushing film.

The period settings and supernatural creatures distance the viewer from everyday reality, making it ludicrous to think of someone leaving *Horror of Dracula* to suck someone's blood. Anyone sick enough to engage in activities like that would be set off by practically anything, and it's hardly reasonable to blame aberrant behavior of that level on a movie.

However, recent trends in the horror film—which have absolutely nothing to do with Peter Cushing's type of film—might be another thing altogether. It's difficult to say how much is too much. Critics of *The Revenge of Frankenstein* thought that—compared to the Karloff films of the 1930s—the film was over the limit. Now, many of us think the slasher films of the 1980s have gone too far.

One sure thing among all this uncertainty is that each generation needs *more* to shock it. Perhaps one day we will look back on the 1980s splatter films as examples of cinematic restraint.

Notes

1. Harry Ringel, "Terence Fisher—The Human Side," *Cinefantastique* 4, no. 3.
2. Columbia Press book.
3. Ringel, "Terence Fisher—The Human Side," *Cinefantastique* 4, no. 3.
4. Brosnan, *The Horror People*.
5. Ibid.
6. Ibid.
7. Hammer publicity release.
8. Brosnan, *The Horror People*.

John Paul Jones
(1958)

Credits and Cast

Released November 1959; 126 minutes; Technicolor; Technirama; A Samuel Bronston Production; Released through Warner Brothers. Director: John Farrow; Producer: Samuel Bronston; Screenplay: John Farrow, Jesse Lasky, Jr.; Music: Max Steiner; Director of photography: Michel Kelber; Editor: Eda Warren; Art director: Franz Bachelin; Costumes: Phyllis Dalton; Special effects: Roscoe S. Cline; Makeup: Neville Smallwood.

Robert Stack (John Paul Jones), Marisa Pavan (Aimée de Tellison), Charles Coburn (Benjamin Franklin), Erin O'Brien (Dorothea Danders), Macdonald Carey (Patrick Henry), Jean Pierre Aumont (King Louis XVI), David Farrer (John Wilkes), Peter Cushing (Captain Pearson), Susana Canales (Marie Antoinette), Jorge Riviere (Russian Chamberlain), Tom Brannum (Peter Wooley), Bruce Cabot (Gunner Lowrie), Basil Sidney (Sir William Young), John Crawford (George Washington), Felix de Pomes (French Chamberlain), Thomas Gomez (Esek Hopkins), and Bette Davis as Catherine the Great.

Synopsis

> *I have not yet begun to fight.* — John Paul Jones to Captain Pearson.

In 1743 a young Scottish sea captain (Robert Stack) accidentally kills a mutinous sailor off the Tobago coast. Fearing for his safety, he escapes to America, calling himself John Paul Jones. He falls in love with Dorothea (Erin O'Brien), a member of a wealthy and respected family, but is spurned because of his lowly social standing. Dejected, he returns to the sea as an officer in the Continental Navy.

Although he distinguishes himself in the War for Independence against England, political maneuvering deprives him of his command. Disgusted with this reversal, he meets General Washington (John Crawford) at the Valley Forge encampment to resign. The general convinces him to accept a more difficult assignment — to sail through the British blockade to deliver an important message to Benjamin Franklin (Charles Coburn) in Paris.

After meeting with Franklin, Jones meets and falls in love with Aimée (Marisa Pavan) and receives political support from Marie Antoinette (Susana Canales) who supplies him with a new ship — the *Bonhomme Richard*.

In a 1779 battle against the *Serapis* commanded by Captain Pearson (Peter Cushing), Jones wins a major victory, which leads to the eventual defeat of the British navy. Impressed with Pearson's courage, Jones does not, as is customary, accept his sword in surrender.

Jones suffers other personal setbacks, however; Aimée declines to marry him due to his lack of position, and his views on American sea power are rejected at the conclusion of the Revolution.

He travels to Russia to help Catherine the Great (Bette Davis) defeat her enemies on the Black Sea. After a great victory he returns, ill and exhausted, to Paris where he dies.

Commentary

Filmed in the middle of Hammer's first run of horror films, *John Paul Jones* was (along with *Violent Playground*) a rare step outside the fantasy genre for Peter Cushing during the late 1950s. While it is interesting that he should be given guest star billing in a "straight" film at this time, his part was small and went unnoticed by most critics.

His segment was filmed in Spain before his appearance as Sherlock Holmes in *The Hound of the Baskervilles*, and could have been a turning

Captain Pearson surrenders to John Paul Jones (Robert Stack).

point in his career. Although fast becoming associated with horror films, he had actually only appeared in four of them. Had his role led to other straight parts, his career could have gone in a very different direction. However, his next four films were *The Hound of the Baskervilles, Mania, The Mummy,* and *The Brides of Dracula.*

Both star Robert Stack and director John Farrow had naval experience in World War II. This sense of authenticity was further enhanced by adviser Alan Villiers who, in 1957, sailed a replica of the *Mayflower* from England to Plymouth, Massachusetts. A search by Captain Villiers uncovered two ancient hulls of sailing ships used to haul fruit between Spain and France. With different riggings and cosmetic changes, they represented the *Bonhomme Richard* and *Serapis.*[1]

Filming a sea battle, according to Peter Cushing, is not much different from actually being in one. "To give the impression of gunshot hitting planks and bulwarks, small charges of gunpowder were placed in strategic positions all over the decks. At given moments they were detonated electrically by the special effects department, but in the fury of mock battle with so much noise and action, plus other things to think about, it was extremely difficult to remember exactly where these explosions occurred, so we had to leave our safety solely in the hands of those splendid experts, and to their credit, we all emerged from those dangerous skirmishes unscathed."[2]

Peter Cushing made the most of his short screen time, looking magnificent in his British navy uniform and giving dignity to Captain Pearson's hard fought defeat.

Robert Stack is fine as Jones, but to a modern audience he seems a bit out of place after being associated with *The Untouchables, Airplane!,* and other tough-guy roles (and parodies of same!) The film's one jarring note is Bette Davis' walk-on as Catherine the Great, late in the proceedings.

Released the same year as *Ben Hur, John Paul Jones* may have helped to usher in a wave of epic productions in the early 1960s, including *Spartacus* (1960) and *El Cid* (1961). Compared to most historical sagas, it is fairly true to its subject and its attention to detail cannot be faulted. The *New York Herald Tribune* (June 17, 1959) felt that "the first film portrait of the great sea hero is a beautiful one." *Time* (June 29) called it "A full color saga of the sea on which the movie makers have lavished $4,000,000 and infinite care." *Variety* (June 17) was unimpressed, commenting, "big, long, slow historical picture," while the *Los Angeles Examiner* (March) praised its "excellent cast including members of the Old Vic Co. like ... Peter Cushing."

Notes

1. Warner Brothers publicity.
2. Cushing, *Past Forgetting.*

The Hound of the Baskervilles
(1958)

Credits and Cast

Released May 1959 (U.K.); 84 minutes; Technicolor; A Hammer Film Production; Released through United Artists; Filmed at Bray Studios, England. Director: Terence Fisher; Producer: Anthony Hinds; Executive producer: Michael Carreras; Associate producer: Anthony Nelson-Keys; Screenplay: Peter Bryan; Based on Sir Arthur Conan Doyle's novel; Music: James Bernard; Music Supervisor: John Hollingsworth; Director of photography: Jack Asher; Editor: Alfred Cox; Supervising editor: James Needs; Production manager: Don Weeks; Sound recordist: Jock May; Camera operator: Len Harris; Continuity: Doreen Soan; Costumes: Molly Arbuthnot; Hairdresser: Henry Montash; Makeup: Roy Ashton.

Peter Cushing (Sherlock Holmes), Andre Morell (Dr. Watson), Christopher Lee (Sir Henry Baskerville), Marla Landi (Cecile), David Oxley (Sir Hugo Baskerville), Francis De Wolff (Dr. Mortimer), Ewen Solon (Stapleton), John Le Mesurier (Barrymore), Miles Malleson (Bishop Frankland), Sam Kydd (Perkins), Helen Goss (Mrs. Barrymore), Judi Moyens (Servant Girl), Dave Birks (Servant), Michael Mulcaster (Selden), Michael Hawkins (Lord Caphill), Ian Hewitson (Lord Kingsblood), Elizabeth Dott (Mrs. Goodlippe).

Synopsis

> *There is more evil around us here than I have ever encountered*
> *before.* — Sherlock Holmes

In the Baker Street rooms of Sherlock Holmes (Peter Cushing) and Dr. Watson (Andre Morell), Dr. Mortimer (Francis De Wolff) relates the legend of the Hound of the Baskervilles.

One hundred years earlier, Sir Hugo Baskerville (David Oxley) — a notorious libertine — kidnapped a servant girl (Judi Moyens). Enraged when she escaped, he set his pack of hounds upon her trail, with himself in close pursuit. Finding her in a ruined abbey on the moor, he stabbed her. Moments later, he was savagely killed by a monstrous hound. Since that day, the male heir of each generation has been a victim of an unexplainable death — the curse of the Hound.

Sir Henry Baskerville (Christopher Lee) — the remaining heir to the fortune — has just arrived in London. Dr. Mortimer fears for Sir Henry's life, since the baronet's uncle, Sir Charles, died under mysterious circumstances. His body, found near the abbey, was surrounded by the footprints of a gigantic hound.

Although put off by Dr. Mortimer's manner, Holmes agrees to take the case — provisionally. He and Watson meet Sir Henry at the Northumberland Hotel and find the baronet more concerned over the loss of a boot than the curse. While discussing the possible dangers of his going to Baskerville Hall, Sir Henry is attacked by a tarantula secreted in a boot. Like his uncle, Sir Henry has a weak heart and only Holmes' quick action saves him from a potentially lethal bite. Sir Henry insists on going to the Hall but, due to heavy commitments in London, Holmes cannot accompany him. To Watson's great delight, Holmes sends the doctor in his place.

When they arrive at Baskerville Hall, several disconcerting facts obscure the case. Dr. Mortimer, while outwardly helpful, benefited greatly from Sir Charles' will. Selden (Michael Mulcaster), a convicted murderer, has escaped from nearby Dartmoor Prison. Mysteriously missing from the staircase is a portrait of Sir Hugo; and the Barrymores (John Le Mesurier and Helen Goss), the family servants, are behaving oddly.

While walking on the moor, Watson is mistaken for Sir Henry by Stapleton (Ewen Solon), a farmer with a surly manner and a disfigured hand. He warns Watson to stay on the path and avoid the deadly Grimpen Mire. Continuing on his walk, Watson startles Stapleton's daughter Cecile (Marla Landi) who runs from him straight into the swamp. While chasing her, Watson nearly drowns. When the Stapletons return Watson to the Hall, Sir Henry meets Cecile and becomes infatuated with her.

That night Sir Henry is awakened by the sound of a woman sobbing. When he and Watson investigate, they notice a light on the moor. Against Holmes' warning to avoid the moor, they search for the light and are accosted by Selden. During the ensuing chase, Sir Henry is terrified by a demonic howl and suffers a mild attack. Watson sends for Dr. Mortimer to attend to Sir Henry and then returns to the moor.

Searching the abbey, Watson is shocked to find Holmes, who has been on the scene since the beginning as an unseen observer. As they talk, a man—presumably Sir Henry—is brutally killed by the Hound. Holmes covers the corpse with his cloak as he and Watson return to the Hall for assistance. Upon their arrival, they find Sir Henry.

Holmes deduces that the body is Selden, mysteriously clad in a suit of Sir Henry's. The next morning Holmes and Watson go to retrieve the body and find it has gone. They follow a trail of blood to the abbey and discover Selden's body, mutilated by Sir Hugo's dagger.

Back at the Hall, Holmes confronts the Barrymores with his knowledge that Selden was Mrs. Barrymore's brother. She confesses that she is aiding him with food and clothing—hence Sir Henry's suit.

Holmes visits Bishop Frankland (Miles Malleson), a noted entomologist who has "lost a tarantula." The slightly dotty bishop mistakes Holmes for an optical technician who has come to repair his telescope. Despite the bishop's inability to focus on reality, Holmes does learn that the tarantula in London was indeed stolen from him. After Holmes leaves, the bishop spies Sir Henry on the moor through his recently repaired telescope.

Sir Henry has called on Cecile, who confides that she hates life on the moor and wants only to return to her native Spain. As they embrace, Sir Henry is startled by Stapleton who invites him and his two "friends" to dinner that evening.

Traveling by carriage, Holmes and Watson discuss the case. Even Sir Henry is a suspect in Sir Charles' death for, as Holmes points out, £1 million is a great temptation. A chance remark by Watson, who refers to the monster as the "Hound of Hell," causes Holmes to investigate an abandoned tin mine under Stapleton's farm as a possible lair of the Hound.

While Watson and Perkins (Sam Kydd)—the Baskerville groom—wait above, Holmes, Mortimer, and Stapleton explore the mine. Holmes discovers what he has been seeking—a freshly gnawed beef bone—when a

The screen's finest Sherlock Holmes — Peter Cushing in Hammer's *The Hound of the Baskervilles.*

bone-chilling howl echoes through the tunnel. Without warning, a railroad car smashes into a support, burying Holmes in the rubble.

After a search proves fruitless, Holmes is found sitting in the cart, complaining of being cold, hungry, and having injured his leg. He sardonically requests that they return to the Hall.

While nursing his injury, he and Watson discover that Sir Hugo's dagger is missing from where Holmes had secreted it in a dresser drawer.

When Sir Henry informs him of the invitation to dinner, Holmes rudely dismisses both his host and the meal. As Sir Henry storms out to meet Cecile, who is waiting downstairs, Watson admonishes Holmes' behavior. Holmes springs into action—he was purposely rude to send Sir Henry off without them. Sir Henry is to die tonight.

Pausing on the staircase, Watson asks Holmes what he has learned about the missing portrait. Holmes reveals that the painting showed Sir Hugo's deformed hand—linking him as an ancestor of Stapleton.

Stapleton, an illegitimate descendant of Sir Hugo, waits at the abbey for Sir Henry's arrival—baited by Cecile. When the couple arrives, Sir Henry's advances are ended by a slap and a horrifying revelation. Cecile also lured Sir Charles to his death—a fate awaiting Sir Henry. His death will leave the Stapletons as heirs to the Hall.

Holmes and Watson, hiding nearby, glimpse the gigantic Hound as it leaps on Sir Henry. Watson shoots Stapleton as Holmes wounds the Hound. Maddened, it mauls the fallen Stapleton before Holmes kills it with a volley of shots. In the confusion, Cecile escapes, only to drown in the Mire. Shaken, Sir Henry is made to look at the dead beast—the curse of the Hound has been lifted.

Back at Baker Street, Holmes receives the missing portrait—and a generous check—from Sir Henry. When Watson inquires as to when he realized the true nature of the case, Holmes replies that the missing boot "put him on the scent."

Commentary

The Hound of the Baskervilles was, financially, a relative failure for Hammer Films and any existing plans for a Sherlock Holmes series starring Peter Cushing were dropped. This is unfortunate, for the film contains one of Cushing's best performances and is excellent in practically all areas.

"Many people had said [I] ought to play Sherlock Holmes," Cushing recalls, "and when I was offered the part I was absolutely thrilled. It's a marvelous opportunity when you've got so much detail to base your character on."[1]

His preparation for the role was even more exhaustive than usual due to his interest in the character since childhood. As an owner of some of the original Strand magazine publications of the stories, he had ample time to study the Sidney Paget illustrations and based his appearance on them.

Part of his preparation was to insist on the proper clothing and accessories used by Holmes. The popular image of the detective in deerstalker cap and Inverness cloak is a long way from Holmes' typical London attire. One bit of preparation, however, was accidental. When Peter Cushing appeared on the first day of shooting, producer Anthony Hinds commented on his dedication to have lost weight for the part. "I'm afraid I hadn't been as conscientious as all that," admits Cushing. "It was Spain what done it! I'd been out there filming *John Paul Jones* [1959] and a mild bout of dysentery had fined me down."[2]

The role of Sherlock Holmes is a personal favorite of Peter Cushing's. "It's a very difficult part to play," he said, "because he's so . . . he goes up and down like a yo-yo. You've got to be awfully careful when you play a part like that that it doesn't become annoying to the audience. To have played that character is, I think, an answer to most actors' dreams."[3]

He has often said that, to many people, he is better known as Holmes than Frankenstein due to his frequent appearances as the detective over the next twenty-five years.

In 1968 he starred in a sixteen-episode BBC television production of Holmes stories that included a two-part (July 7 and 14) adaptation of *The Hound of the Baskervilles.* The cast included Nigel Stock as Watson and Gary Raymond as Sir Henry. Peter Cushing played Holmes again in the 1984 Tyburn production for television, "Masks of Death," from an original story by Anthony Hinds. Costarring were old friend John Mills as Watson and Anton Diffring as the villain. Of Cushing's performance, *The Observer* noted that he "still brings great dignity and subtlety to the role."

Peter Cushing turned down an opportunity to play Holmes in the 1975 Broadway production of *Crucifer of Blood.* As he explained in a letter (July 11, 1975) to the authors, "The part of Sherlock Holmes was originally offered to me, but I'm afraid the theatre is a thing of the past as far as I'm concerned." He was also forced to withdraw from a second Tyburn production of *The Abbot's Cry* due to illness.

The Times (August 7, 1958) announced the beginning of production on *The Hound of the Baskervilles* but, at that point, Dr. Watson had not yet been cast. Peter Cushing seems to have been the only choice for Holmes, despite fellow cast member Christopher Lee's better physical match. Cushing's casting indicates Hammer's view of who was the studio star.

The final casting of Andre Morell as Watson could not have been better. He is the screen's finest Watson due to the decision to play the part as Sir Arthur Conan Doyle wrote it. Morell commented, "Conan Doyle, after all, felt that Watson was a doctor and not an idiot as he was often made out to be."[4] Peter Cushing was more than pleased with his frequent costar's casting. "Andre Morell," he mused, "well, you can't go much better, can you?"[5]

The supporting cast is also excellent. Christopher Lee, in a requested change of pace role, made the most of a blandly written part and makes Sir Henry somewhat more than just a standard hero. As Sir Hugo, David Oxley creates as evil a character as one could bear in his short screen time.

Peter Cushing played a major role in the casting of Marla Landi as Cecile. Having seen her in the film version of Graham Green's *Across the Bridge* (1957), he alerted Anthony Hinds who, after seeing the film, cast her without a test.

As one would expect in a late 1950s Hammer production, the physical aspects are beyond reproach. The costumes, sets, and technicolor photography are beautiful and make one wonder what standards are used by the Motion Picture Academy when handing out their awards. James Bernard's score (lifting a segment from *Horror of Dracula*) adds to the tension and quality of the production.

Director Terence Fisher, who drew such excellent performances from his human actors, was badly let down by Colonel as the hound. The dog's appearance is simply not eerie enough and is quite a disappointment after the careful eighty-minute buildup. Peter Cushing describes an interesting idea that failed. "The production team, endeavouring to create an illusion of the dog's massive proportions, hit upon the idea of employing three young boys corresponding in relative size to Andre Morell, Christopher Lee and myself. . . . On the following day the rushes were viewed and disappointment deflated all concerned. We saw three small boys dressed up as if playing a game of charades, foggy toy scenery, and a wet, hungry dog in the middle."[6]

This failure aside, *The Hound of the Baskervilles* is arguably the finest version of the classic story (with heavy competition from the 1939 Basil Rathbone version and the Granada television production with Jeremy Brett). *The Times* (March 30, 1959) felt that the film "can be forgiven for not following . . . the book faithfully, but some other omissions, distortions and additions are harder to understand. Holmes is a difficult part to play, but Mr. Peter Cushing makes an interesting attempt." The *New York Herald Tribune* (July 4) said, "Peter Cushing is a forceful and eager Sherlock Holmes." *Variety* (April 1) found, "It is difficult to fault the performance of Peter Cushing." The London *Daily Mirror* (March 30) enthused that, "Peter Cushing is a splendid Holmes." *Newsweek* went one better: "a living, breathing Holmes — the best yet."

Perhaps the best compliment of all comes from Jeremy Brett, who has won recent and highly deserved praise as Holmes. Brett generously allowed that "Peter Cushing was marvelous."[7]

Despite the fact that Sherlock Holmes is missing for a great period of time, *The Hound of Baskervilles* is probably the favorite among the sixty tales and is easily the most often filmed. The authors do not intend to enter a rather pointless debate as to which version is the best, but there can be little argument that the finalists would be the Hammer version, the 1939 20th Century–Fox–Basil Rathbone version, and the BBC-Granada television film with Jeremy Brett.

All three have their strong and weak points, and it might be said that, for the best version, one should return to the novel. Sir Arthur Conan Doyle had tired of his hero and, seemingly, killed him off in a short story entitled *The Final Problem* (1893). Public outrage forced the contrite author to bring the detective back in *The Hound of the Baskervilles* (1901), which, conveniently, took place prior to *The Final Problem*. With its fascinating mixture of great characters, detection, and Gothic menace, it has been a favorite ever since.

The Basil Rathbone version of 1939 is generally regarded as the best version of the story, as well as the best Holmes film, and for good reason. It's an excellent example of the best of Hollywood filmmaking in an exceptionally creative year. Rathbone is faultless as Sherlock Holmes and shows why he was considered Hollywood's top character actor. It is no wonder that his is the image most readily conjured as Holmes. He was to repeat the performance, with gradually diminishing results, until 1946. While it's easy to criticize some of his "modernized" Universal Holmes efforts, his acting in *The Hound of the Baskervilles* is as legendary as the beast.

On close inspection, though, the film is not without flaws. Top-billed Richard Greene is just adequate as Sir Henry. Lionel Atwill is more than a bit stiff as Mortimer, and then there is Nigel Bruce as Watson.

The film's strong climax makes up for some unnecessary dragging in the middle — especially a ridiculous seance that appears nowhere in the novel. Perhaps the weakest point is the flashback to Sir Hugo. Filmed through the blurred pages of the "manuscript" and accompanied by a totally out of place musical score, it nowhere approaches the sense of menace and evil of the Peter Cushing version.

The BBC-Granada film is a very literal translation of the novel, with each performance, set, and costume absolute perfection. Its only defect (to our taste) is that, for some reason, it lacks the sense of supernatural mystery one has come to expect from the tale.

As previously mentioned, the Peter Cushing version isn't perfect either. The film would have been greatly improved with some exterior shots of London, and is not helped by extraneous nonsense like the "sacrificial dagger" and the poorly conceived climax. The three lead actors, as a group, are probably the strongest casting ever and this alone elevates the film to an exceptionally high level.

Which film is the best? Take your pick. As for the worst, there can be little doubt that the 1972 made-for-television fiasco is a prime contender. Stewart Granger was horrendously miscast as Holmes, and things went downhill from there.

There have been countless other versions, notably in 1921 (a U.K. film directed by Maurice Elvy with Ellie Norwood), in 1932 (a U.K. film directed by Gareth Gundrey with Robert Rendel), and a 1980s British television film with the excellent Ian Richardson.

It would take an entire book to deal with the exploits of the great detective, and highly recommended is *Holmes of the Movies* by David S. Davies. The foreword is by Peter Cushing.

Notes

1. David Stuart Davies, *Holmes of the Movies.*
2. Cushing, *Past Forgetting.*
3. "Peter Cushing—A One-Way Ticket to Hollywood," BBC Television, 1989.
4. Davies, *Holmes of the Movies.*
5. "Peter Cushing—A One-Way Ticket to Hollywood."
6. Cushing, *Past Forgetting.*
7. Peter Haining, *The TV Sherlock Holmes.*

Mania
(1959)

Credits and Cast

Released February 1960 (U.K.), January 1961 (U.S.); 97 minutes; 74 minutes (U.S. 1965 version); Black and white; Cinemascope; A Triad Production; Released through Regal International (U.K.) and Joseph Harris–Sig Shore, Valiant (U.S.); Rereleased (1965) by Pacemaker Pictures. Director: John Gilling; Producers: Robert S. Baker, Monty Berman; Screenplay: John Gilling, Leon Griffiths; Based on a story by John Gilling; Music: Stanley Black; Editor: Jack Slade; Director of photography: Monty Berman; Art direction: John Elphick. Title in U.K. *Flesh and the Fiends*; also released as *Psycho Killers* (U.S.); rereleased 1965 as *The Fiendish Ghouls* (U.S.).

Peter Cushing (Dr. Robert Knox), June Laverick (Martha), Donald Pleasence (Willie Hare), Dermot Walsh (Dr. Mitchell), Renee Houston (Helen Burke), George Rose (Willie Burke), Billie Whitelaw (Mary Paterson), John Cairney (Chris Jackson), Melvyn Hayes (Daft Jamie), June Powell (Maggie O'Hara), Geoffrey Tyrrell (Old Davey), Beckett Bould (Old Angus), George Bishop (Blind Man), Philip Leaver (Dr. Elliott), George Woodbridge (Dr. Ferguson), John Rae (Reverend Lincoln), Andrew Faulds (Inspector McCulloch), Esma Cannon (Aggie), Raf de la Torre (Baxter), Michael Balfour (Drunken Sailor), George Street (Barman), Michael Mulcaster (Undertaker), Jack McNaughton (Stallholder).

Synopsis

> *Ah yes, Parliament! With 500 walking corpses there, you'd think*
> *they could spare one!*—Dr. Robert Knox

As the director of a medical academy, Dr. Robert Knox (Peter Cushing), an anatomist in nineteenth-century Edinburgh believes that nothing should deter the study of the human body for the potential betterment of medical science. Because it is illegal to obtain bodies for research unless they are those of condemned criminals, Knox is forced to deal with grave robbers. Eventually he forms an association with two men, Burke and Hare (George Rose and Donald Pleasence) who would one day become infamous in the annals of criminology.

Discovering that there is a lot of money to be made in providing doctors with corpses for study and that the fresher the body the more money paid for it, Burke and Hare decide to take the process one step farther—they turn to murder to keep the academy well supplied with "subjects." However, in their greed, they make some fatal mistakes when they murder a prostitute, Mary Paterson (Billie Whitelaw), her boyfriend and academy student, Chris Jackson (John Cairney), and a village simpleton, Daft Jamie (Melvyn Hayes). All three victims were physically healthy, young, and well known in the community.

When one of the townspeople witnesses Jamie's murder, she informs the police. Suspecting that Dr. Knox is collaborating with Burke and Hare, the police go to the academy and find Jamie's body being prepped for study. Although Knox is not charged with collusion, he has many enemies in the medical council who try to use his association with the grave robbers to discredit him and close the academy.

Burke is put on trial for murder. Hare turns king's evidence to save himself. Found guilty, Burke is hanged. Hare is released by the police but is met by some of the townspeople who exact their own form of justice and he is blinded.

Knox continues his lectures at the academy. Though he is never implicated in the murders and is exonerated by the medical council, he is broken in spirit. Knox is now hated and feared by the people of Edinburgh who had once respected him and his efforts to turn out knowledgeable, competent doctors.

> I will continue to teach anatomy—using the best specimens available—
> to turn out doctors who will replace quacks!
> Dr. Robert Knox

The lighter side(?) of Dr. Knox in *Mania*.

Commentary

Peter Cushing, Billie Whitelaw, Donald Pleasence and George
Rose were the stars in my picture and I don't think I have ever
worked with a finer cast. — John Gilling, Director[1]

There are few genre pictures which truly deserve to be tagged "horror" films. *Mania*, however, is one of them. John Gilling's screenplay, based on the infamous exploits of bodysnatchers-murderers Burke and Hare and their fatal association with Scottish anatomist Dr. Robert Knox is horrifying because, in this case, all three men were real "monsters" and the story is based on fact.[2]

Gilling's script is a character study of the contrasts and startling similarities of his three main subjects — Willie Burke, Willie Hare, and Dr. Knox. Though Burke and Hare's murder spree is motivated solely by monetary greed, Dr. Knox willingly lends himself as an accomplice to satisfy his own personal obsession — the illicit procurement of bodies for anatomical research by the medical students he teaches; bodies that were otherwise denied him by law. Feeling himself justified by his overall goal — that of molding his students into qualified doctors of medicine — Knox permits his procurers to continue their nefarious activities without bringing them to justice.

The film asks its audience to decide whether or not the end justified the means. Who was the more guilty? Burke and Hare, who resorted to murder to keep physicians well supplied? The doctors who paid them for the bodies of their victims? Or British law, which denied doctors the legal use of human cadavers for study, thus forcing the medical profession to deal with grave robbers and, eventually, killers?

Producers Robert S. Baker and Monty Berman, who had formed Triad Productions with Gilling in order to make the film, assembled a remarkable, highly skilled cast and crew. *Mania* proves that an excellent film can be produced on a limited budget if all concerned believe in the worthiness of the project.

Mania is rich in mood and atmosphere — two essential elements for this type of picture. Berman's photography (in black and white), sets, and decor all blend to help recreate realistic backdrops of the era and add immeasurably to the general tone of the piece.

The entire cast is uniformly excellent. However, Donald Pleasence, George Rose (as Hare and Burke, respectively), Billie Whitelaw (Mary Paterson), and Peter Cushing (as Knox) are all exceptional performers. Peter Cushing, who based his character Victor Frankenstein in part on the historical Dr. Knox, plays the anatomist with the same single-minded, detached, and sardonic attitude that made Frankenstein such a powerful and frightening study. Knox, like Frankenstein, feels himself above the laws of man (in the latter case, above God's laws as well), in that by breaching those cumbersome precepts he is able to continue his work for the eventual good of mankind. Knox's blatant arrogance and definace of the rules might be forgiven in a film performance but such traits in a real-life situation would prove a little harder to accept by contemporaries in any era. Though the real Dr. Knox's career ended in disgrace, Gilling's screenplay allowed him to continue teaching to standing room only lecture halls while Burke was being led to the gallows and Hare faced the wrath of an outraged mob.

There are many familiar faces in *Mania* who also appeared in other Cushing films. Donald Pleasence, as the sociopath William Hare, also appeared in *The Risk* (1959), *From Beyond the Grave* (1973), *Trial by Combat* (1976), *Land of the Minotaur* (1975), and *The Uncanny* (1976), as well as the 1954 BBC television production of *1984*. Renee Houston, Burke and Hare's landlady and coconspirator, also worked in *Time Without Pity* (1956) and in *Legend of the Werewolf* (1974). Although best known to genre fans as the demonic nanny in *The Omen* (1976), Billie Whitelaw also appeared with Peter in *The Devil's Agent* (1962) and "A Tale of Two Cities," the Hallmark Hall of Fame–CBS television production originally broadcast in 1980.

Melvyn Hayes, who played the young Victor Frankenstein in Hammer's production of *The Curse of Frankenstein* (1956) would work again with Peter twenty-two years later in *Touch of the Sun* (1978). Another Hammer character actor, George Woodbridge, worked on three other Cushing-Hammer films, *Horror of Dracula* (1957), *The Revenge of Frankenstein* (1958), and *The Mummy* (1959). Michael Mulcaster, who had a minor role in *Mania* as an undertaker, can also be seen in *The Curse of Frankenstein* (1956) and *The Hound of the Baskervilles* (1959).

Mania was very well received by critics. *The Times* (February 8, 1960) noted that it was "a horrific story ... at pains to emphasize its more ghastly aspects ... a competent piece of work, concisely written with tension, dramatically sustained and well acted in both major and minor parts. The director, Mr. John Gilling, has a feeling for the period and is well-supported by Mr. Peter Cushing as Dr. Knox, a sarcastic and autocratic figure, whose only interest lies in the pursuit of anotomical knowledge." *Picturegoer* asked the question, "When will horror film merchants realize that its the unseen terror that is the most spine chilling?" And in *Variety* "Rich" (February 10, 1960) reported that "This latest version of the story about ... Knox ... and Burke and Hare ... is competently filmed, has some very good performances.... There are one or two strong-meat scenes, but it should go down well ... with the big, varied audiences that go for this sort of fare.... Peter Cushing, playing Knox, is an expert in this sort of fare. He knows that any parody is fatal and so he plays the part with ... straight-forward sincerity, dignity and authority.... John Gilling has directed conscientiously and makes a good point in his contrast of the academic atmosphere with that of the evil sleaziness of the 19th century Edinburgh's slums, brothels and taverns. Cushing's scenes in the lecture hall, his bitter exchanges with the medical tribunal, the roistering sequences in the inn and the brothel and the final near-lynching scenes all come off fairly well."

Notes

1. John Gilling, *Little Shoppe of Horrors* 4.
2. John Gilling wrote 60 screenplays and directed 26 films. He died at the age 74 in 1985.

The Mummy
(1959)

Credits and Cast

Released December 1959; 88 minutes; Technicolor; A Hammer Film Production; Released through Universal International (U.S.) and Rank (U.K.); Filmed at Bray Studios, England. Director: Terence Fisher; Producer: Michael Carreras; Screenplay: Jimmy Sangster; Story based on the screenplay "The Mummy" by John L. Balderston, based on a story by Nina Wilcox Putnam and Richard Schayer; Director of photography: Jack Asher; Production designer: Bernard Robinson; Music: Frank Reizenstein; Editors: James Needs, Alfred Cox; Associate producer: Anthony Nelson-Keys; Music director: John Hollingsworth; Additional scenes supervisor: Andrew Lowe; Production manager: Don Weeks; Assistant directors: John Peverall, Tom Walls; Makeup: Roy Ashton; Costumes: Molly Arbuthnot; Masks: Margaret Carter (Robinson); Camera operator: Lee Harris; Sound recordist: Jock May; Hair stylist: Henry Montash.

Peter Cushing (John Banning), Christopher Lee (Kharis), Yvonne Furneaux (Isobel/Ananka), Eddie Byrne (Inspector Mulrooney), Felix Aylmer (Stephen Banning), Raymond Huntley (Joseph Whemple), George Pastell (Mehemet), George Woodbridge (Police Constable), John Stuart (Coroner), Harold Goodwin (Pat), Dennis Shaw (Mike), Michael Ripper (Poacher), Gerald Lawson (Irish Customer), Willoughby Gray (Dr. Reilly), David Browning (Police Sergeant), Frank Sieman (Bill), Stanley Meadows (Attendant), Frank Singuineau (Head Porter).

Synopsis

He who robs the graves of Egypt–DIES! — Mehemet

While on an archaeological expedition in Egypt, Stephen Banning (Felix Aylmer), his son John (Peter Cushing), and fellow archaeologist, Joseph Whemple (Raymond Huntley) discover the 4,000-year-old tomb of a high priestess — the Princess Ananka (Yvonne Furneaux) — a find Stephen Banning has been searching for all his life. While taking inventory of the tomb's priceless treasures, the elder Banning finds the sacred "scroll of life." Having ignored the warnings of a mysterious Egyptian, Mehemet

(George Pastell), and the curse that would befall anyone who dared to desecrate the ancient tombs of the country, Banning translates the scroll and goes mad when he is confronted with the tomb's guardian — the living mummy, Kharis (Christopher Lee). The expedition is forced to return to England and Stephen Banning is committed to an asylum.

Some years later John and his wife, Isobel (Yvonne Furneaux) are summoned to the asylum where John is warned by his father that death awaits all of them at the hands of the mummy. John doesn't believe his father, who he assumes is incurably insane.

The next day Stephen Banning is found murdered. After a formal inquest regarding his father's mysterious death, John goes over his father's papers in search of any clues that might lead him to the murderer's identity. He finds the legend concerning the Princess Ananka who had died on a pilgrimage to the sacred city of Amtak. The legend also tells the story of Kharis who was buried alive to guard the high priestess because he dared to love her and was caught trying to bring her back from the dead using the powers of the scroll. However, what John does not learn from his father's notes is that the Egyptian Mehemet has followed the expedition to England with the mummy. Using the sacred scroll, Mehemet has resurrected the monster and intends to use Kharis as the instrument of death for the remaining expedition members.

Later that night John's uncle, Joseph Whemple, is murdered by the mummy when it breaks into the Banning house. John shoots at it several times but to no effect. After describing the extraordinary circumstances to Police Inspector Mulrooney (Eddie Byrne), the officer is naturally suspicious and goes off in search of a more "human" killer.

The mummy returns to kill John but is thwarted in the attempt when it sees Isobel, who bears more than a striking resemblance to Princess Ananka. The mummy leaves without fulfilling its task. When Mehemet learns that John is still alive, he again sends the mummy to destroy the desecrater. However, this time Mehemet follows Kharis to Banning's home. When he sees that Kharis is hesitant to kill John because of Isobel, Mehemet orders the mummy to kill her. Kharis turns on his master and murders him. The mummy then abducts Isobel after taking the sacred scroll from Mehemet's body. John and the police pursue them into the swamps where Isobel manages to free herself from Kharis. But the mummy cannot escape the murky waters of the quicksand-like bog and sinks into its bottomless depths — still holding the "scroll of life" tightly in his grip.

Commentary

Comparisons would be pointless. Obviously the technical advances in movie-making since the ... 30's give the latter productions

Cushing in a publicity shot for Hammer's *The Mummy*.

*certain advantages over the originals, but as films, they should be
judged on their own merits.* —Peter Cushing

*It's difficult to talk about Peter without being overly sentimental,
which he would hate. . . . Peter is truly one of the really good people I've ever met. He's played all these evil, wicked characters but
he's completely the opposite of that. A truly superb actor, with a
marvelous sense of humor.* —Christopher Lee[1]

It seemed inevitable that Hammer Films would follow their enormously successful interpretations of Frankenstein and Dracula with an adaptation of *The Mummy*. However, although the 1932 Universal version was based on a story by Nina Wilcox Putnam and Richard Schayer, Hammer's script, twenty-seven years later, by Jimmy Sangster, took many of the best elements from the entire Universal Mummy series for its newest rendering. The result was an exciting, beautifully crafted, and in many ways, a far superior version than its prototype.

No one could find fault with Boris Karloff's marvelous performance in the original. However, Jack Pierce's makeup and the film's excellent lighting effects added much to Karloff's overall terrifying countenance. Christopher Lee, on the other hand, constricted as he was in pounds and pounds of bandages throughout the film, spoke volumes with his towering height and sad, expressive eyes. Whereas Karloff's Imhotep was played as an evil, calculating monstrosity, Lee's Kharis gave us a frightening, yet tragic, monster who was once a man—a man who paid the ultimate price for his forbidden love. Viewers are constantly reminded of his punishment and the hopelessness of his situation by the continued presence of his mummy trappings.

When Kharis gazes upon Isobel Banning (Yvonne Furneaux), who bears a striking resemblance to his beloved Ananka, we are painfully cognizant of the fact that the ensuing centuries have not diminished Kharis' all too human desires and the bitter results of what he had dared to do in the name of love.

In developing his two key figures, Sangster gave Kharis and John Banning similar character profiles. Both man and monster have a physical disability which correspondingly inhibits their mobility. Banning breaks his leg just prior to the opening of Ananka's tomb. Due to the lack of proper medical care at the time, Banning's leg is stiff and he has a noticeable limp. Kharis' movements are greatly restricted due to the tight-fitting burial bandages that surround his legs and body.

Banning and Kharis are also emotional cripples. Although separated by centuries in life, both men allowed their chosen professions to take precedence in their youth, preventing them from leading otherwise normal existences.

Due to his sacrilegious act, Kharis was cursed for all eternity when he profaned the tomb of the Princess Ananka. Similarly, John Banning and the entire archaeological team were also cursed when, over 4,000 years later, they too invaded the high priestess' resting place.

Both Kharis and Banning go to excessive lengths to try to prove their love for others. Kharis risks his career, and eventually his life, for the woman he loves. John Banning constantly tries to prove his love and loyalty to his father who, like Kharis' Ananka, accepts his unselfish devotion as his due and not necessarily something which has to be reciprocated. Not even death will keep these men from their obsessive goals. Consequently, both men are faced with the ruination of their respective lives.

Banning and Kharis were both attracted to the same type of woman. At first, Kharis wants to destroy Banning because he has violated Ananka's tomb. The creature becomes even more volatile when he discovers that Banning's wife, Isobel, is the image of Kharis' princess. Banning has won the woman of Kharis' desire and reason for his subsequent damnation.

Ironically, John Banning, who has devoted his life to the study of a long dead civilization, finds himself the potential victim of it. Kharis attempts to restore the princess using the sacred scroll of life. In a cruel turn of events he becomes the instrument of death for anyone who attempts to resurrect Ananka from her burial place. The story forms a bridge in time drawing both men toward their eventual fates.

In what has to be one of Terence Fisher's finest works, his tender directorial hand is evident throughout the production. Despite the subject matter's limited range, Fisher was brilliantly successful in weaving the film's main antagonists (Mehemet, played by George Pastell, and the mummy) amid the rather bizarre love quartet (John and Isobel Banning, Ananka and Kharis) that consequently came into play as a result of modern man's curiosity and irreverent meddling with the past. Fisher's living tapestry is vivid with color and deft in composition.

All aspects of the film, both on the acting and technical side, were superbly handled. Frank Reizenstein's music score was both sensitive and appropriate. Roy Ashton's mummy makeup was, in a word, astounding. Molly Arbuthnot's costumes and Bernard Robinson's sets were equally breathtaking.

Peter Cushing gives one of his best performances in this picture. The role of John Banning seemed tailor-made for Peter, allowing him a much wider range than many of his previous screen performances. As expected, Cushing took full advantage of the part, widening the role's possibilities and adding new dimensions to an already well-developed character.

Surprisingly, most critical reviews for *The Mummy* were on the negative side. *The Observer* (September 27, 1959) referred to it as "a sockdolager of a horror film, compounded of well-tried ingredients plus an Egyptological knowhow that should make budding Champollions of the entire youth of the nation."[2]

The *New York Herald Tribune* (Paul V. Beckley, December 17, 1959) called the film "Pretentious.... Doesn't seem to be quite certain whether it means to be a suspense picture or a romantic episode of ancient Egypt.... If the bulk of the film is more promise than fulfillment one must admit that the climax is properly frantic." Even in *Variety* "Whit" (July 15, 1959) gave the picture a lukewarm response, referring to *The Mummy* as a "Mild horror film, well-produced. . . . Premise is fairly well developed while offering little of actual newness to plot. . . . Yarn carries the type of action expected, and while chiller aspects aren't too pronounced they're sufficient for those who want to find them. . . . Cushing delivers handily."

Howard Thompson of the *New York Times* (December 17, 1959) thought *The Mummy* "Should have been better. . . . Woodenly directed. . . . For a superior version of a nearly identical horror yarn, with a little style and imagination, catch the 1932 version now floating around on television. This one just lumbers."[3]

More positive evaluations came from *The Times* (September 28, 1959) which thought that "Hammer Films . . . made the most distinguished . . . of English horror films . . . partly by the employment of excellent actors. The cast of their present film . . . contains the familiar Mr. Peter Cushing." *Films and Filming* (1959) begrudgingly felt it had "enough gloss to satisfy its undemanding customers and enough thrills to keep them halfway to the edge of their seats."

In August 1959 Peter also worked in the stage production of William Fairchild's play, *The Sound of Murder.* Presented at the Aldwych Theatre in London, former American Peter Cushing Club member Rukmani Singh Devi managed to see one of Cushing's performances during the three months he starred in the play. Devi provided members with her impressions of the performance.

> Charles Norbury is a successful author who lives in a capacious Surrey cottage. He bides his time dictating marvelous slosh for children's books into a tape-recorder and making his wife's life a misery. For Charles Norbury is also a vindictive scoundrel. The play is full of contrasts. Seemingly affable people caught in a dire situation. Prosaic furnishings in a house filled with bitterness. The dialogue contrasts the innocuous banalities of Norbury's writings with his odious personal observations.
>
> Peter Cushing played Charles Norbury . . . Elizabeth Sellars [portrayed] the long-suffering wife; Terence Longdon, her admirer, and Patricia Jessel is Norbury's secretary.
>
> Every play needs a central factor; perhaps a figure to dominate the action, on whom the other characters focus their attention. That figure was Mr. Cushing, the agent of Miss Sellar's suffering and the object of Mr. Longdon's ministrations, in this case, murder. Mr. Longdon plots to kill Norbury and is blackmailed by Miss Jessel.
>
> Obviously, the catalyst to such events must be unredemptive and Peter Cushing was just the person to make Charles Norbury as sadistic as necessary. . . . He has the power to turn each of his features into a malign asset. The narrowing of his eyes radiating an intense glow. The slightest flaring of his nostrils. A smile so coldly sinister as to belie its perfection. And once again that voice: subtle, deft, but registering new inflections of malice. He succeeded in engaging everyone's disdain.

Notes

1. Lawrence French, "The Christopher Lee Interview," part 2, *Fangoria* 2.
2. Jean-François Champollion (1790–1832), French Egyptologist who deciphered the hieroglyphics of the Rosetta stone.
3. It seems the *New York Times'* counterpart had an entirely different viewpoint when he reviewed Karloff's version back in 1932. This critic noted that "most of *The Mummy* is costume melodrama for the children."

The Risk
(1959)

Credits and Cast

Released 1960; 81 minutes; Black and white; A Boulting Brothers Production; Released through British Lion (U.K.), Kingsley International (U.S.). Directors and producers: John and Roy Boulting; Screenplay: Nigel Balchin; Dialogue: Jeffrey Dell, Roy Boulting; Director of photography: Max Greene; Camera: Peter Allwork; Makeup: Freddy Williamson; Music: Chopin and Schriabin, arranged by John Wilkes; Editor: John Jympson; Sound: George Stephenson; Scenic artist: Alan Evans; Assistant director: Basil Rabin; Production manager: Philip Shipway; Title in U.K. *Suspect.*

Tony Britton (Bob Marriott), Virginia Maskell (Lucy Byrne), Peter Cushing (Professor Sewell), Ian Bannen (Alan Andrews), Raymond Huntley (Sir George Gatling), Thorley Walters (Mr. Prince), Donald Pleasence (Mr. Brown), Spike Milligan (Arthur), Kenneth Griffith (Dr. Shole), Robert Bruce (Levers), Anthony Booth (Parkin), Basil Dignam (Dr. Childs), Brian Oulton (Director), Sam Kydd (Slater), John Payne (Iverson), Margaret Lacey (Secretary), Bruce Wightman (Phil), Ian Wilson (Pin-Table Man), Murray Melvin (Teddy Boy), Geoffrey Bayldon (Rosson), Andre Chanse (Heller).

Synopsis

> *M.I.5 — Confidential from the Prime Minister's Office, Whitehall*
> *London.* — Security stamp of the Official Secrets' Act.

A research team led by Professor Sewell (Peter Cushing) and made up of Bob Marriott (Tony Britton), Lucy Byrne (Virginia Maskell), and Dr. Shole (Kenneth Griffith) has discovered a germ that could end bubonic and typhus epidemics. However, in the wrong hands, the discovery could be used for germ warfare.

With this in mind, the Authority — a highly secret government organization — blocks the team's plan to publish their findings. By envoking the

Official Secrets Act, the team is legally "gagged." Government guards are stationed throughout the laboratory complex and even Professor Sewell needs a pass to enter. Although the research team desperately wants to publish their findings, there is little choice but to comply.

Lucy introduces Bob to her ex-fiancé, Alan Andrews (Ian Bannen). Alan was severely injured during the war, losing an arm. He holds the Authority responsible for the destruction of both his arm and his life. Despite having Lucy standing between them, the two men develop an uneasy friendship, with their hatred of the Authority as their bond.

Bob is soon introduced by Alan to a Mr. Brown (Donald Pleasence), a "publisher" who claims that he can get around the gag order and print the team's findings. Bob stupidly falls for the deception engineered by Alan, who plans to commit suicide once the material is safely in enemy hands — his final revenge against the Authority.

Professor Sewell, noticing Bob's unusual behavior, suspects something is wrong. He manages to stop him before the exchange is made, preventing Bob from committing his act of innocent treachery.

Commentary

This well done, low-budget film was a relatively important one for Peter Cushing. Despite his just completed run of horror films, his casting indicates that, at least for thinking producers, he was not just a horror star. Unlike Bela Lugosi before him, and Peter's contemporary Christopher Lee, Cushing was never completely identified with horror roles until fairly late in his career. As the press book publicity drove home, "He's had a succession of starring roles in horror films like *The Curse of Frankenstein*, but this week, he loses the 'horror' tag."

The Boulting twins (John and Roy), a producer-director team, first achieved success with thrillers like *Seven Days to Noon* (1950). Cowritten by Hammer music composer James Bernard — for which he won an Academy Award — the film concerned a scientist (Barry Jones) at odds with the government over the use of nuclear weapons. After a string of comedies (*I'm All Right, Jack,* and *Man in the Cocked Hat,* both in 1959), they returned to the type of film that had initially brought them fame.

Using techniques also employed by Alfred Hitchcock in *Psycho* (1960), the Boultings attempted to create a feature film by using television production methods. They had just finished a film ahead of schedule and had time remaining on their studio rental. Not wishing to waste studio time, they hired a cast and crew, and had a screenplay written (based on an existing novel). The production began after Christmas 1959 and was completed the second week of January. Production time was cut to a bare minimum by using a limited number of sets and nearby areas for location

A director's eye view of Peter Cushing and Raymond Huntley on the set of *The Risk*.

filming.[1] The extremely low budget and hurried schedule do not show due to the intriguing story and excellent cast.

Wearing a mustache and bow tie, Peter Cushing was convincingly professor-like. After a string of roles playing dominant characters, Professor Sewell was a refreshing change of pace and allowed Cushing to display more range than his recent roles had permitted.

Playing a key role as the embittered traitor was Ian Bannen. He had become popular in comedy roles in the late 1950s (*The Man in the Cocked Hat*, 1959), and *The Risk* also provided a change in his career direction. After his excellent performance, Bannen continued with heavy drama, notably in *The Hill* (1965) and *The Offence* (1971).

Ian Bannen recalled for the authors a rather unusual picture of Peter Cushing ... blowing his lines! "I remember him having a hard time on his first day of shooting," said Bannen. "I recall some excitement as he stumbled nervously through a scene twenty-eight times! Roy (Boulting) could be a shock to the system occasionally. I bumped into Peter many years later when we were working on different films at the same studio and he was as nice and as charming as ever."

The film was well received critically, but, sadly, it seems to have all but vanished with no video release and extremely sparse showings on television. The *New York Times* (September 25, 1961) found *The Risk* "An unusual spy drama . . . crisp and exciting." The *New York Daily News* (September 27) called it "suspenseful and exciting." In agreement was the *New York Journal* (September 27): "The British have a way with spy stories and *The Risk* is a good example. Tense and taut."

Peter Cushing's lone television appearance for the year was as a guest on "Down You Go."

Note

1. British Lion publicity.

The Brides of Dracula
(1960)

Credits and Cast

Released September 1960; 85 minutes; Technicolor; A Hammer Film Production; Released through Universal International; Filmed at Bray Studios, England. Director: Terence Fisher; Producer: Anthony Hinds; Executive producer: Michael Carreras; Associate producer: Anthony Nelson-Keys; Screenplay: Jimmy Sangster, Peter Bryan, Edward Percy; Director of photography: Jack Asher; Music composed by Malcolm Williamson; Music supervisor: John Hollingsworth; Production designer: Bernard Robinson; Art director: Thomas Goswell; Editors: James Needs, Alfred Cox; Special effects: Syd Pearson; Camera operator: Len Harris; Assistant director: John Peverell; Sound recordist: Jock May; Sound editor: James Groom; Makeup: Roy Ashton; Costumes: Molly Arbuthnot; Continuity: Tilly Day; Hairdresser: Frieda Steiger.

Peter Cushing (Dr. Van Helsing), David Peel (Baron Meinster), Yvonne Monlaur (Marianne Danielle), Martita Hunt (Baroness Meinster), Freda Jackson (Greta), Miles Malleson (Dr. Tobler), Henry Oscar (Herr Lang), Mona Washbourne (Frau Lang), Andree Melly (Gina), Victor Brooks (Hans), Fred Johnson (Priest), Michael Ripper (Coach Driver), Norman Pierce (Innkeeper), Vera Cook (Innkeeper's Wife), Marie Devereux (Village Girl), Harold Scott (Severin).

Synopsis

Only God has no fear.—Dr. Van Helsing

Marianne Danielle (Yvonne Monlaur) is en route by coach to the Lang Academy at Badstein where she is to assume a teaching post. Stopping at a village inn, Marianne is abandoned by the coach driver (Michael Ripper) and meets the Baroness Meinster (Martita Hunt) who offers her shelter for the night and transportation to the academy the next morning.

That evening at the Meinster's chateau, Marianne learns that the baroness' son (David Peel) is being kept prisoner and releases him — unwittingly freeing a vampire. Marianne flees from the castle and is found by Dr. Van Helsing (Peter Cushing), who had been summoned by a local priest (Fred Johnson) to investigate some inexplicable disappearances and deaths in the region.

Escorting Marianne to the academy, Van Helsing follows some leads that take him to the Meinster chateau where he finds that the baroness herself has been made one of the undead by her own son. Van Helsing frees her soul. Baron Meinster visits Marianne at the academy and when he proposes marriage, she accepts.

Van Helsing returns to the school when he learns that one of the teachers, Gina (Andree Melly), has been found dead. Examining the body, the doctor finds the telltale signs of the vampire. Marianne tells Van Helsing of her upcoming marriage to the baron.

After witnessing Gina's "rebirth" as one of the undead, Marianne is abducted by the baron and taken to his lair — an old windmill. Van Helsing confronts the vampire and when the baron threatens to make Marianne one of the undead, the two battle for her soul. Van Helsing ultimately destroys Baron Meinster by trapping the vampire outside the windmill, using its blades to form the sign of the cross. Trapped in the shadow of the holy symbol, the vampire cannot escape the upcoming dawn and the lethal rays of the morning sun.

Commentary

After the phenomenal box office success of *Horror of Dracula*, Hammer was anxious to follow it with another Dracula vehicle for its superstar, Christopher Lee. However, Lee, fearful of being typecast in the role that had brought him international recognition as it had done for Bela Lugosi in Universal's 1931 version, steadfastly refused to reprise his role as the count for Hammer, a conviction that he would adhere to fervently until 1965 when he once again starred as Dracula in *Dracula — Prince of Darkness*. As a result of Lee's rejection, Hammer executives, still hoping to draw back into theaters the prior film's massive worldwide audience, had to scramble to find another actor to fill Lee's cape. Their final choice for the film would prove to be quite controversial. In fact, so much of the

Peter Cushing is the quintessential Dr. Van Helsing in *The Brides of Dracula*.

production was steeped in setbacks that Hammer might have been wise to have entitled their film, "The *Curse* of Dracula."

According to various sources, there were originally three different scripts under consideration at the time. Aside from Christopher Lee's refusal, another reason for the difficulties surrounding the film's production delay seems to stem from its star, Peter Cushing.

Although Peter was most anxious to recreate his Van Helsing character since it was so well received by audiences in the prototype, he was not happy with the way his character was being represented in the finale of Hammer's latest screenplay. In short, he insisted on a rewrite. Evidently, according to Anthony Hinds, the film's producer, Peter became quite agitated over it: "Peter Cushing . . . just wouldn't tolerate anything that he thought was second best and used to nag me if he thought I was taking the easy way out of a difficulty, and quite rightly."[1]

Michael Carreras, the executive producer, agreed, adding, "I have seen Peter Cushing get slightly disturbed, to put it mildly. He would become icy cold and you could feel it. But I never saw him do it without good reason. Whomever he did it to would have to admit that they deserved it. And the moment the situation was over, it was over. He never held a grudge."[2]

One can hardly fault Cushing's passionate response with regard to the character as presented in the original script. Having already established his role in *Horror of Dracula* as a highly knowledgeable, God-fearing, and fearless vampire hunter, in this latest adaptation Van Helsing can only be described as misinformed and irreverent. For example, the climax of this script has Van Helsing resorting to occultism to achieve his ends. The professor draws a pentacle on the floor of the windmill, placing himself and Marianne within the safety of its mystical confines and out of the vampire's reach. It also has him reading an incantation from an ancient book of rituals to call forth the powers of darkness in the form of bats to destroy the vampire. These methods are totally out of character for Professor Van Helsing, whose previous tools of the trade were strictly stakes, crosses, bibles, and holy water. It is no wonder Cushing was so adamant against these drastic changes in Van Helsing's basic character profile.[3]

The cast members were all quite impressive in their roles. David Peel, a Royal Academy of Dramatic Art alumnus, also appeared in productions for the Shakespeare Memorial Theatre from 1945 to 1949, and worked not only in several films in supporting roles but also on the London and New York stages before appearing in his first starring role for Hammer.

What was unique about the casting of Peel as Christopher Lee's successor was the fact that he was to become the screen's first blond male vampire. Christopher Lee's dark and demonic, sensual and savage vampire count was in direct contrast to Peel's light, and therefore more deceptively, angelic look.

Peel handled his role energetically and with just enough subdued menace to make his character both believable and entertaining. Some horror fans, however, were openly hostile toward his interpretation at the time. Having felt cheated by the absence of Lee in the role and its misleading title, some of them launched a smear campaign against Peel (he was alleged to have been a homosexual—a taboo subject back then). Time, though, has since changed their opinion of the picture and Peel's performance in it. Today it is valued as the classic it was all along. Unfortunately, after appearing in *The Brides of Dracula*, Peel retired from films and started a career in real estate, and later, the antique business. He passed away in 1982 at the age of sixty-two.

Other supporting cast members were equally effective. Of special note was Freda Jackson as the maniacal nanny, Greta. Her cackles alone were worth the price of admission! Miles Malleson as the hypochondriacal Dr. Tobler and Michael Ripper, another Hammer cornerstone, were also enjoyable in their supporting roles and brought to the film their own unique style.

However, it is the subtlety of Peter Cushing's performance that really makes this one of the best of Hammer's entire vampire series. Cushing's Van Helsing, more than any other actor's portrayal of this character, is more in keeping with the true essence of Bram Stoker's vision. He is a kind, caring man, one who is deeply dedicated to the people with whom his work has brought him into contact. He is the real Professor Van Helsing of Stoker's conception. Killing vampires and ridding the world of evil is secondary to him. His belief in God and the triumph of good over evil is never questioned. It is taken for granted and gives him the strength he needs to tread where those of a lesser conscience might hesitate. Peter brings all this and more to his character and because he truly believes in these qualities himself, it comes off more than convincingly in his portrayal. Cushing is the quintessential Abraham Van Helsing.

On the production side of *The Brides of Dracula*, all aspects of the film were top-notch. Set designer Bernard Robinson created magnificent backdrops for the players, especially the brooding Chateau Meinster. Gothic in the highest sense of the word, its grandeur lulled the viewer into a false sense of security for the underlying decadence of its strange inhabitants. Equally impressive was the windmill he designed for the film's finale. Like the chateau, it too played an intricate and dramatic part in the picture. The closing shots of the structure in its fiery brilliance—its blades in the form of a gigantic Maltese Cross against the predawn sky—helped create one of the most dramatic and exciting climaxes ever seen in the genre.

Malcom Williamson's score for the film, one of three he had done for Hammer (*Crescendo* and *Horror of Frankenstein* both filmed in 1970), beautifully framed the moody, mysterious, and desolate facets of the picture's gothic theme. Williamson would also score two other Cushing works, *Nothing but the Night* and "Masks of Death" (a television Sherlock Holmes film) for other studios.

In an interview Williamson told the author that he had met Peter Cushing several times. "To meet him is to love him," Williamson said. "He is very dedicated ... one of the noblest souls in the acting profession. He's taken a paternal attitude toward out-of-work actors. There are a great many kindnesses he does in films as well as in the theatre that are generally not known at all. He is so thoroughly professional, and who could name all the films whose dialogue he has elevated through the mere clarity of his diction."[4]

Terence Fisher's direction of the film has been called by some critics as "understated" and that he employed "shifting moods to elicit tension."[5] Others say it was fast paced and still others say it was "a near copy of its predecessor, *Horror of Dracula*, from a technical standpoint."[6] But all seem to agree that Fisher was in his element with this particular film and whether or not viewers missed Christopher Lee's presence, the film stands on its own as one of Fisher's best for Hammer.

Fisher not only enjoyed a working relationsip with Peter Cushing but a personal one as well. They were good friends for years. "Peter ... is one of the happiest associations that I could possibly imagine both professionally and personally. There is the most tremendous integrity in his performance, ... preparation and thought about his roles. Tremendously constructive in his ideas ... I think with Peter we have a kind of rapport.... We can almost read each other's thoughts which I've never experienced with anybody else. Personally, he has all the qualities of what I would call a gentleman and a very dear friend."[7]

Although critics' reviews were mixed, the *People* publication called it, "a well-made shocker which doesn't pretend to do anything but make you shudder." *The Times* (July 7, 1960) reported: "A film that gives fair warning that it is a horror film at least abides by the rules of the game ... there are some handsome sets ... the cast is too good for its material." *The Observer* (July 10, 1960) was negative about the film, saying, "ludicrous monstrosity following a spoor of technicolor blood, which leads farther and farther still away from the force, pity and near-dignity of Bram Stoker's original novel." The *New York Herald Tribune* (Judith Crist, September 6, 1960) also was critical, saying, "Blood and thunder mishmash ... not one new thrill has been added to the original Dracula film.... Dabs of Freud and/or Tennessee Williams help not at all.... The acting matches the mediocrity of the script and even the most devoted aficionados of the cult will find this depiction thereof at best a bore." The *New York Times* (Bosley Crowther, September 6, 1960) predictably called it "Another repetition of the standard tale of the vampire bugaboo who likes to sink his oversized dentures into the necks of pretty girls. There is nothing new or imaginative about it." In *Variety* "Holl" (May 18, 1960) called it "a technically well-made film embellished with color.... Terence Fisher's direction treats the proceedings seriously and avoids ludicrous moments.... Technical aspects are fine."

Notes

1. Letter Column, *Little Shoppe of Horrors* 9.
2. Michael Carreras, interview with Anthony Timpone, "The Fall of Hammer," *Fangoria* 63.
3. Oscar A. Martinez and Bob Sheridan, "The Evolution of *The Brides of Dracula,*" *Little Shoppe of Horrors* 6.
4. Malcolm Willamson, interview with Sam Irvin, *Little Shoppe of Horrors* 10.
5. Alain Silver and James Ursini, *The Vampire Film.*
6. Gary D. Dorst, "Dracula in Retrospect," *Little Shoppe of Horrors* 4.
7. Gary R. Parfitt, "The Fruitation of Terence Fisher," *Little Shoppe of Horrors* 3.

Trouble in the Sky
(1960)

Credits and Cast

Released 1960 (U.K.), March 1961 (U.S.); 92 minutes (76 minutes, U.S.); Black and white; A Bryanston–British Lion Production; Released through British Lion International (U.K.) and Universal International (U.S.). Director: Charles Frend; Producer: Aubrey Baring; Screenplay: Robert Westerby; Additional dialogue by Jeffrey Dell; Based on a novel by David Beaty; Director of photography: Arthur Grant; Music composed and conducted by Gerald Schurmann; Art director: Wilfred Shingleton; Editor: Max Benedict; Sound: John Cox, Peter Dukelow, Buster Ambler; Production manager: Jack Rix; Assistant director: Basil Rabin; Makeup: Freddie Williamson; Hairdresser: Anne Box; Wardrobe: Bill Walsh. Title in U.K. *Cone of Silence.*

Michael Craig (Captain Dallas), Peter Cushing (Captain Judd), Bernard Lee (Captain Gort), Elizabeth Seal (Charlotte Gort), George Sanders (Sir Arnold Hobbes), Andre Morell (Captain Manningham), Gordon Jackson (Captain Bateson), Charles Tingwell (Captain Braddock), Noel Willman (Nigel Pickering), Delphi Lawrence (Joyce Mitchell), Marne Maitland (Mr. Robinson), William Abney (First Officer), Jack Hedley (First Officer), Simon Lack (Navigator), Charles Mylne (Steward), Howard Pays (Steward), Ballard Berkeley (Commissioner), Charles Lloyd Pack (Commissioner), Homi Bode (Controller), Anthony Newlands (Controller), Hedger Wallace (Navigator).

Synopsis

When veteran British pilot Captain George Gort's (Bernard Lee) jet plane crashes on takeoff, he is accused of pilot error and is found guilty by a court of inquiry. However, because of his previously untarnished record, his pilot's license is not revoked.

Captain Dallas (Michael Craig) berates Captain Judd (Peter Cushing) in *Trouble in the Sky*.

Gort's daughter, Charlotte (Elizabeth Seal) is convinced of her father's innocence and seeks the help of examiner Captain Dallas (Michael Craig) to investigate, and hopefully vindicate, her father. Tragedy strikes soon after, however, when Captain Gort is killed in a similar plane crash.

Captain Dallas doubles his efforts. During a second inquiry he proves that one of the plane's designers, Nigel Pickering (Noel Willman) had deliberately withheld information concerning a known defect in the take-off apparatus — which Pickering had been secretly trying to perfect.

The court clears Captain Gort of all charges. Charlotte and Dallas are finally able to clear the captain's good name and reputation.

Commentary

Perhaps only those suffering from aerophobia might be pleased to know that *Trouble in the Sky* is a rarely seen Cushing film that had a limited Universal release back in 1961 and has since apparently disappeared.

However, during its release, the film did gather some very favorable reviews, despite some sixteen minutes of trimming from its original running time (ninety-two minutes) by Universal prior to its distribution in America.

The film was directed by Charles Frend, who had begun his motion picture career as a film editor in 1931. Frend had worked on a few Hitchcock films, including *Secret Agent* and *Sabotage* (both in 1936), as well as other equally prestigious motion pictures such as *A Yank at Oxford* (1938), *Goodbye Mr. Chips* (1939), and *Major Barbara* (1941) before assuming the director's chair in the early 1940s.

Producer Aubrey Baring assembled a highly proficient cast and crew who strove to make the film as realistic as possible. Their combined efforts seemed to have achieved the desired effect because the film was praised as being both "accurate and authentic" by a spokesman of the International Federation of Airline Pilots who had been invited to a special screening of the film prior to its official release.[1]

In his autobiography, *Past Forgetting*, Peter Cushing recalled that he was required to learn the mechanics of flying from an airline pilot instructor who sat him in a simulated cockpit and attempted to teach him the rudimentary exigencies of a trained airline pilot. Unfortunately, or fortunately, Peter "never got his wings," as he put it. Somehow the thought of Dr. Frankenstein himself at the controls of a jumbo jet is a bit too frightening to contemplate!

Reviews for the film included "Rich" in *Variety* (May 18, 1960), who commented that *Trouble in the Sky* was a "Well-made drama. . . . Craig as the training officer and Peter Cushing, convinced of [Bernard] Lee's guilt, provide sound contrasting acting. . . . Charles Frend has directed with complete sureness of touch and flying effects. This plus slick lensing add greatly to the authenticity of the film." Eugene Archer of the *New York Times* in his July 13, 1961, commentary said,

> Give a British cast an aviation drama to enact, with characters displaying calm fortitude when faced by mechanical disaster, and it is only logical to expect an admirably underplayed performance . . . they give this quiet, compact study of the unheroic death of a veteran commercial pilot a dramatic interest beyond its modest pretensions. . . . Andre Morell as the airline boss and Peter Cushing as a backseat flier comport themselves with commendable reserve.

Bob Salmaggi of the *New York Herald Tribune* (July 13, 1961) advised that what was "notable about this British import are the incisive performances of Bernard Lee and the reliable George Sanders. Elizabeth Seal, Michael Craig and Peter Cushing lend able support . . . it will easily hold your interest." *The Observer* in its April 24, 1960, critique reported that

"The unassuming British film called *Cone of Silence* by director Charles Frend is a cautionary tale for pilots of jet airlines. . . . The acting is quiet and rather above average."

Among Peter's costars in the film, Bernard Lee (Captain Gort), known to millions of fans worldwide for his portrayal of "M" in the popular James Bond series, also worked with Cushing in *Fury at Smuggler's Bay* (1961), *Dr. Terror's House of Horrors* (1964), and *Frankenstein and the Monster from Hell* (1972). Another player, Gordon Jackson (Captain Bateson) also appeared with Cushing in the British television–Tyburn Production of "Masks of Death" (1984). Charles Lloyd Pack is a familar face from Hammer's *Horror of Dracula* (1957) and *The Revenge of Frankenstein* (1958). Anthony Newlands can also be seen in AIP's *Scream and Scream Again* (1969).

Note

1. Universal International publicity manual.

The Sword of Sherwood Forest
(1960)

Credits and Cast

Released 1961; 80 minutes; Technicolor; Megascope; A Hammer-Yeoman Production; Released through Columbia; Filmed at Bray Studios, England, and County Wicklow, Republic of Ireland. Director: Terence Fisher; Producers: Sidney Cole, Richard Greene; Executive producer: Michael Carreras; Screenplay: Alan Hackney; Music: Alun Hoddinott; Musical director: John Hollingsworth; Director of photography: Ken Hodges; Editor: James Needs; Production managers: Don Weeks (England), Ronald Liles (Ireland); Art director: John Stoll; Camera: Richard Bayley; Makeup: Gerald Fletcher; Hairdresser: Hilda Fox; Wardrobe: John McCorry; Continuity: Pauline Wise, Dot Foreman; Horsemaster: Ivor Collin.

Richard Greene (Robin Hood), Peter Cushing (Sheriff of Nottingham), Richard Pasco (Newark), Sarah Branch (Marion), Niall MacGinnis (Friar Tuck), Nigel Green (Little John), Dennis Lotis (Alan a'Dale), Jack Gwillim (Archbishop of Canterbury), Oliver Reed (Melton), Edwin Richfield (Sheriff's Lieutenant), Vanda Godsell (Prioress), Brian Rawlinson (Falconer), Patrick Crean (Ollerton), Derren Nesbitt (Martin), Reginald Hearne (Man at Arms), Jack Cooper (Archer), Adam Kean (Retford), Desmond Llewellyn (Traveler), Charles Lamb (Old Bowyer), Aiden Grennell (Outlaw), James Neylin (Roger).

Synopsis

He was no coward. — Said of the Sheriff by the Earl of Newark
after his murder.

Outlaws Robin Hood (Richard Greene) and Little John (Nigel Green)
find a badly wounded man in Sherwood Forest. After tending to the man,
Robin discovers the beautiful Marion (Sarah Branch) who is swimming
nearby. She pretends to be repelled by Robin but leaves a note inviting
him to meet her at the Owl Inn.

Little John suspects a trap and is proven correct when Robin meets
not only Marion but also the Sheriff of Nottingham (Peter Cushing), who
offers Robin a pardon if he will turn over the wounded man. Robin refuses
and, to Marion's disgust, the sheriff's men try to capture the outlaw whom
she tried to help.

Back at camp, the wounded man mumbles a warning of "danger at
Bawtry" and dies. The sheriff, who has invaded the forest, captures one
of Robin's men and has him murdered after forcing him to betray the
camp's location.

Robin visits Friar Tuck (Niall MacGinnis) to advise him of the situation. There he meets a group of men led by the Earl of Newark (Richard
Pasco). Robin, a stranger to Newark, impresses him with his skill as an
archer by killing Melton's (Oliver Reed) falcon in flight. Newark hires
Robin to kill a man, as yet unnamed.

At Bawtry, the sheriff tries to claim an estate for Newark. The earl
plans to build a fortress in defiance of the king's law. The sheriff's attempt
is blocked by the Archbishop of Canterbury (Jack Gwillim) who opposes
Newark and is, in fact, Robin's unnamed target. Marion, seeking justice
for Robin's men, joins the archbishop on the road back to London.

On the road they are attacked by Newark's men disguised as outlaws.
Robin and Little John repel the attack and the intended victims take
refuge in a priory run, unknown to them, by Newark's cousin (Vanda
Godsell).

When the sheriff objects to Newark's plan to murder the pair in the
priory, he is brutally stabbed in the back by Melton. Newark and his men
attack the priory and are met by the Sherwood outlaws. Newark dies on
Robin's sword, ending the conspiracy.

The danger past, Robin and Marion return to Sherwood to marry.

Commentary

Despite a good cast and production values typical of Hammer films
during this period, *The Sword of Sherwood Forest* is a disappointment.

The Sheriff of Nottingham in Hammer's *The Sword of Sherwood Forest*.

Although the subject matter was a natural for Hammer, the film is slow and boring. Comparisons to the 1938 classic *The Adventures of Robin Hood* with Errol Flynn would be unkind.

Star and coproducer Richard Greene, at age forty-two, was physically beyond the role and is certainly no match for the twenty-nine-year-old Flynn. Greene's performance is fine in the nonaction scenes, but action is what Robin Hood is all about.

Director Terence Fisher must also share the blame. While his gothic fantasies are among the best ever made, his ventures outside this area are less than distinguished. This was no exception. Although he and Richard Greene had worked on the "Adventures of Robin Hood" television series in the 1950s, Fisher "never felt very deeply about the character."[1] The fact that Greene supposedly saw Robin as an allegorical figure[2] does not come across in the film (possibly for the best). Fisher was unable to stage any convincing action scenes—the battles seem to be in slow motion. The location photography in County Wickham, Ireland, is beautiful, but the director seems lost without Bernard Robinson's set design from the Frankenstein-Dracula series.

Peter Cushing, however, has nothing to be ashamed of. He heads a fine supporting cast and makes the sheriff one of his more memorable villains. His role more or less equates with Basil Rathbone's in the 1938 version as Sir Guy of Grisbourne, since the sheriff (Melville Cooper) was an ineffectual character at best. He fills Rathbone's boots (again) excellently.

As usual, Peter Cushing was outstanding in scenes involving physical prowess, and is one of the few actors in the cast that looks comfortable handling a sword or riding a horse. He described the latter activity as "riding at my peril,"[3] but it does not show.

His treachery is mixed with a gentle voice and sincere demeanor which keeps the viewers—even though they know his true intentions—off balance. His stabbing by Oliver Reed is one of the film's few surprises—certainly a departure from the expected "duel to the death" with Robin. Reed, by the way, delivers a performance difficult to define. His simpering voice and attitude are ridiculous and it's hard to believe that he is the same actor who was so convincing in *Curse of the Werewolf* (1960).

The Sword of Sherwood Forest may or may not have been intended to kick off a series. If it was, killing the sheriff was certainly a foolish idea. The film died at the box office, anyway, and is rarely seen on television. With the 1938 version readily available, that is quite understandable.

Variety (January 11, 1961) felt that "Peter Cushing plays the Sheriff, the way the Sheriff should be played." The *New York Times* (January 26) stated, "Peter Cushing, Richard Pasco, and Jack Gwillim are excellent."

Notes

1. *The Halls of Horror* 22, July 1978.
2. Ibid.
3. Cushing, *Past Forgetting*.

The Hellfire Club
(1960)

Credits and Cast

Released September 1963 (U.S.), March 1961 (U.K.); 93 minutes; Eastman color (U.K.), black and white (U.S.); A New World Production; Released through Regal International (U.K.) and Embassy (U.S.). Directors and producers: Robert S. Baker, Monty Berman; Screenplay: Leon Griffiths, Jimmy Sangster; Based on a story by Jimmy Sangster; Camera: Robert S. Baker, Monty Berman; Music composed by Clifton Parker; Music conducted by Muir Mathieson; Played by Sinfonia of London; Art direction: Ray Simon; Editor: Fred Wilson; Sound: Bill Daniels.

Keith Michell (Jason), Kai Fischer (Yvonne), Andrienne Corri (Isabel), Peter Arne (Thomas), David Lodge (Timothy), Bill Owen (Martin), Peter Cushing (Merryweather), Francis Matthews (Sir Hugh), Desmond Walter Ellis (Lord Chorley), Denis Shaw (Sir Richard), Tutte Lemkow (Higgins), Peter Howell (Earl of Chatham), Bernard Hunter (Marquis de Beauville), Michael Balfour (John the Juggler), Miles Malleson (Judge), Jean Lodge (Lady Netherden), Andrew Faulds (Lord Netherden), Martin Stephens (Jason as a Boy), Rupert Osborne (Thomas as a Boy), Skip Martin (Joey the Dwarf).

Synopsis

> *You will observe the Highwayman on his way to the gallows? One of my less fortunate clients.* — Mr. Merryweather, Solicitor

England 1752. Two young boys, Thomas (Rupert Osborne) and Jason (Martin Stephens), curious about the secret late-night activities of Jason's father, Lord Netherden (Andrew Faulds) and his companions, bear witness to the wickedness of the infamous Hellfire Club. Later, Jason is soundly beaten by his sire for his indiscretion.

Vowing that her immoral husband will never touch the child again, Lady Netherden (Jean Lodge) flees with her son but is killed en route when their carriage careens down a hillside. Jason is saved by the coach driver, Timothy (David Lodge), who becomes the child's guardian. Together, they escape to Holland where they join a troupe of circus performers in a traveling carnival. Jason's father, believing at the time that both his wife and son were killed in the accident, names his nephew, Thomas, as his heir.

Fifteen years later, Jason (Keith Michell) receives word of his father's death and learns that his cousin, Thomas (Peter Arne) has usurped the title as well as becoming the new president of the Hellfire Club. Jason vows to reclaim his inheritance and to expose the nefarious members of the club.

Jason visits the Netherden's family solicitor, Mr. Merryweather (Peter Cushing). Merryweather informs Jason that Lord Netherden had always harbored a suspicion that his son was still alive. Merryweather learned that Lord Netherden had supposedly written a letter to him indicating this possibility. The letter — for unknown reasons — had never arrived, but Merryweather is certain that a copy exists and might be found somewhere at the Netherden's estate. Jason also learns that some highly placed officials in the British government are also interested in seeing the Hellfire Club disbanded as a result of intelligence reports that placed certain members in collusion with the French. Jason agrees to return to Netherden Hall, where he is hired as a groom, and finds the letter that proves his claim. But Thomas later implicates Jason in the murder of Timothy, whom Thomas' henchmen had killed, and Jason is sent to prison to await execution. Jason's circus friends come to his rescue and free him. Jason returns to Netherden Hall posing as a French courier and, after duelling with his cousin, kills him.

Though he is successful in proving his claim and exonerating himself of Timothy's murder, as well as ending the existence of the club, the new Earl of Netherden prefers the company of his circus friends. Leaving his inheritance in Merryweather's care, Jason returns to the carefree life of a carnival acrobat.

Commentary

Peter Cushing's rapid-fire delivery and seemingly boundless energy, along with Keith Michell's acrobatic swordplay are the only significant moments in this otherwise unimpressive, unoriginal entry.

In their attempt to make a family movie, the producers eliminated all the best historical elements that might have made *The Hellfire Club* vastly more interesting. One doubts the British government during this period in history would have devoted so much time and energy in an attempt to disband an organization that the film basically depicted as a group of overgrown Boy Scouts caught red-handed with their older brothers' girlie magazines!

Though British prints were in Eastman color, Embassy Pictures released all its U.S. films in black and white. This also heavily detracted from the costume drama's appeal.

As is usually the case with many British B-features, sets, locations, costumes, and especially the cast came to the rescue in this production. *The Hellfire Club* assembled another competent group of players which, coincidentally, also included several actors who had appearances in other Cushing films. Adrienne Corri, who plays Isabel, also appeared in *Madhouse* (1973). *Francis Matthews (Sir Hugh), a Hammer veteran, costarred in The Revenge of Frankenstein (1958)*. Another Hammer luminary, Miles Malleson (the Judge), had parts in *Horror of Dracula* (1957), *The Hound of Baskervilles* (1958), *The Brides of Dracula* (1960), and *Fury at Smuggler's Bay* (1961). David Lodge (Timothy), also had featured roles in *Night Creatures* (1962), *Corruption* (1968), *Scream and Scream Again* (1969), and *Bloodsuckers* (1969). Michael Balfour (John the Juggler) can be spotted in *Mania* (1959) and *Moulin Rouge* (1952). Jean Lodge (Lady Neterden) worked in *The Black Knight* (1954). Andrew Faulds (Lord Netherden) had an appearance in *Mania* (1959), and Tutte Lemkow (Higgins) had a supporting role in *Moulin Rouge* (1952).

Robert S. Baker's direction was both crisp and well paced. However, Leon Griffiths and Jimmy Sangster's screenplay proved too predictable to sustain any interest. All technical credits were up to par as was Clifton Parker's music score, which was appropriately effective.

Reviews of *The Hellfire Club* include the *New York Herald Tribune's* Robert Salmaggi (October 10, 1963), who wrote, "What might have been an intriguing look at the notorious 'Hellfire Club' of merry old England turns out to be nothing more than a routine derring-do melodrama.... What went on in those Hellfire caves would make Fanny Hill blush. The film simply plays up the club as a background.... But the orgies are strickly for grandma!"

Jeffrey Richards wrote, "While including glimpses of some disappointing tame orgies, [the film] centers on the attempts of the Prime Minister ... to suppress the Club, which contains a group of dissident aristocrats who are threatening the throne. The script orchestrates all the time-honoured ingredients ... and gives us an archetypal hero.... Keith Michell tackles his heroics with obvious enthusiasm and considerable attack ... Peter Arne contributes a splendidly urbane and soft-spoken villain, and Peter Cushing steals scenes effortlessly as a pedantic snuff-taking, twinkly-eyed lawyer."[1]

Note

1. Jeffrey Richards, *Swordsmen of the Screen*.

The Devil's Agent
(1961)

Credits and Cast

Released 1961 (Germany), 1962 (U.S.), June 1964 (U.K.); 77 minutes, Black and white; A Criterion-Constantin Production; Filmed in Dublin, Ireland. Director: John Paddy Carstairs; Producer: Emmet Dalton; Screenplay: John Paddy Carstairs, Robert Westerly; Based on a novel by Hans Habe; Director of photography: Gerald Gibbs; Music: Philip Green; Pianist: Clive Lithgoe; Editor: Tom Simpson; Art director: Tony Inglis; Production manager: Victor Lyndon; Sound: Liam Savrin.

Peter Van Eyck (Droste), Marianne Koch (Nora), Macdonald Carey (Mr. Smith), Christopher Lee (Baron Von Staub), Billie Whitelaw (Piroska), David Knight (Father Zomabary), Marius Goring (General Greenhahn), Helen Cherry (Countess Cosimano), Colon Gordon (Count Dezsepaluy), Niall MacGinnis (Vass), Eric Pohlman (Bloch), Peter Vaughn (Chief of Police), Jeremy Bulloch (Johnny), Peter Cushing (role deleted).

Synopsis

> The Devil's Agent . . . *selling treachery to the highest bidder!*—
> British Lion Publicity

Double agent George Droste (Peter Van Eyck) is a spy not due to any political motivations—he is in it strictly for the money. Through an old friend, Baron Von Staub (Christopher Lee), he is introduced to the high living that such work can provide and does not plan to give it up easily. His sole redeeming factor is his desire to provide for his son Johnny (Jeremy Bulloch).

Through a series of adventures in Eastern Europe, he becomes relatively wealthy and falls in love with Nora (Marianne Koch), an escapee from communist Hungary. She is, at first, unaware of his true nature.

After playing many different sides against each other, Droste feels that it is time to get out and start a new life with Nora. However, she has learned the truth. After promising to care for Johnny after Droste is killed, she leaves him.

Commentary

No, you didn't miss Peter Cushing's name in the synopsis. *The Devil's Agent* is definitely an oddity in his career—his scenes were cut before the film's release! Although Cushing continues to list the film among his credits, he has no memory of his role or why it was cut. Since the film also featured his frequent costar Christopher Lee, Cushing's mysterious disappearance is even more unfortunate.

Due to the episodic structure of *The Devil's Agent*, it would not have been difficult to cut out Peter Cushing's (or anyone else's) scenes to keep the running time down. However, since Peter Cushing was the best known name in the cast, why him?

Apparently the production was a rather haphazard one. Christopher Lee recalls that he never encountered Peter Cushing during the filming and that it "staggered from crisis to crisis as if it were never certain whether the money would be coming for the next reel."[1] Under conditions like these, anything can happen.

Critic Leslie Halliwell thought the film was a mélange of "scrappy cold war adventures which look as though they were originally intended as episodes in a TV serial."

Note

1. Christopher Lee, *Tall, Dark, and Gruesome.*

The Naked Edge
(1961)

Credits and Cast

Released July 1961 (U.S.); 99 minutes; Black and white; A Pennebaker-Baroda Production; Released through United Artists; Filmed at Elstree Studios, England. Director: Michael Anderson; Producers: Walter Seltzer, George Glass; Executive producer: Marlon Brando, Sr.; Screenplay: Joseph Stefano; Based on the novel *First Train to Babylon*, by Max Ehrlich; Photographer: Edwin Hillier; Editor: Gordon Pilkington; Musical score: William Alwyn; Conductor: Muir Mathieson; Played by Sinfonia of London; Art director: Carmen Dillon; Sound recorder: Norman Coggs; Assistant director: Peter Bolton; Assistant producer: Jock McGregor; Production supervisor: Billy Kirby.

Gary Cooper (George Radcliffe), Deborah Kerr (Martha Radcliffe), Eric Portman (Jeremy Clay), Diane Cilento (Mrs. Heath), Hermione Gingold (Lilly Harris), Peter Cushing (Mr. Wrack), Michael Wilding (Morris Brooke), Ronald Howard (Mr. Claridge), Ray McAnally (Donald Heath), Sandor Eles (Manfridi), Wilfrid Lawson (Mr. Pom), Helen Cherry (Miss Osborne), Joyce Carey (Victoria Hicks), Diane Clare (Betty), Frederick Leister (Judge), Martin Boddey (Jason Roote), Peter Wayn (Chauffeur).

Synopsis

> *Only the man who wrote* Psycho *could jolt you like this.* — United
> Artists publicity

Businessman Jason Roote (Martin Boddey) is stabbed by an unidentified man in the doorway of his office.

At the Old Bailey Court along the Thames, Roote's employee George Radcliffe (Gary Cooper) sweats nervously as he awaits his turn on the stand. The prosecutor, Mr. Wrack (Peter Cushing), smugly, and rather flamboyantly, questions him about his past association with Roote, his working overtime the night of the murder, and his knowledge of £60,000 being delivered that evening.

Wrack leads Radcliffe to condemn the accused Donald Heath (Ray McAnally), which is fairly easy considering the evidence against him.

Roote entered Radcliffe's office that evening and, after some small talk, returned to his office. Moments later, he screamed. Radcliffe glimpsed Heath — carrying a bundle — running out. With the help of a police officer, Radcliffe apprehended Heath. Mr. Claridge (Ronald Howard), Heath's attorney, questions Radcliffe about the £60,000. No, Heath was not holding it when arrested. In fact, it was never recovered.

While the jury deliberates, Radcliffe is approached by businessman Morris Brooke (Michael Wilding) and they finalize a proposal. In court the jury convicts Heath, mostly on Radcliffe's testimony.

Upon leaving the court with his wife Martha (Deborah Kerr), he shows her a property he and Brooke plan to purchase and develop. Suddenly, he spots a man who was in the courtroom observing them. Jeremy Clay (Eric Portman), a retired attorney, accuses George of perjury, and hints at worse.

Radcliffe later explains to Martha that he can afford the new venture due to his stock investments. He made, he tells her, "a killing."

Six years pass, and Radcliffe is now a wealthy businessman. His life, however, is shattered by the recovery of a mailbag stolen in a train robbery six years ago. All the recovered mail has been forwarded to its intended recipients — including Radcliffe. Martha has opened the letter. It's a blackmail threat from Clay. Since no action was taken by Clay after six years, Martha initially dismisses the letter. But there is the missing money and George's sudden wealth.

The Radcliffes' relationship begins to deteriorate as George suspects Martha of suspecting him. Martha begins to interpret George's every action as one of guilt and deceit. She begins to investigate on her own, reading old newspaper articles, seeking out Heath's still faithful wife (Diane Cilento), and even contacts Clay.

Clay convinces Martha that he is telling the truth, and she confronts her husband with her belief.

Radcliffe angrily leaves the house with a veiled threat against Clay. As Martha prepares for her bath, she is stalked by a shadowy figure — George. He has returned, and suggests that she take a sleeping pill.

In the bathroom Martha sobbingly calls to George, but is suddenly seized and has her mouth taped shut. Clay holds her, with George's straight razor clenched in his teeth. As George sits in his study, Clay confesses to Martha as he prepares to slit her wrists in the tub. George hears her muffled scream and after a brutal fight subdues Clay, saving Martha's life and their marriage.

As they go downstairs to let in the police, Clay — wielding the razor — charges maniacally at them but falls to his death.

Commentary

Remembered mainly as superstar Gary Cooper's last film, *The Naked Edge* has been unjustly criticized as a poor way for his career to end.

Actually, Cooper should have been praised for a rare "stretch" in his rather unsympathetic character performance — a refreshing change from his standard good guy stint. Although few could have been surprised at Radcliffe's eventual innocence, Cooper is very convincing and keeps one off balance. "The problem," he said, "is to play on the innocent side and still bring out to the audience the circumstances that seem to make me guilty."[1]

Cooper died shortly after completing the film, but gives the audience his best effort. Strangely, he was almost killed while filming the scene along the Thames. A faulty heater in his dressing room exploded shortly after he had left.[2]

The publicity stressed the somewhat shaky relationship of *The Naked Edge* to *Psycho* (1960) — they share the same scriptwriter, Joseph Stefano. One wonders what Robert Bloch's reaction to the publicity blurb (quoted in the synopsis) might have been.

Peter Cushing's role was a small one, but gave him the opportunity to act one on one with Gary Cooper — a personal favorite. Cushing makes the most of his screen time — photographed mostly in close-ups — and delivers a sly, insinuating performance. Totally lacking in sympathy, Mr. Wrack seems more interested in his performance in court than in finding the truth. His playing with his robe and glasses accentuate his theatrical approach to justice.

Cushing was reunited with another of his favorites, Deborah Kerr. She thought highly of Peter Cushing and regretted that this was their last film together. He returned the compliment by describing Kerr to the authors as "a most charming and gracious lady and a superb actress."

While no classic, *The Naked Edge* is more than competent and manages quite a few suspenseful moments (although, naturally, nothing like *Psycho*). Moodily photographed in black and white by Edwin Hillier, this well-acted film deserved better than it got. The public simply was not interested in Gary Cooper cast out of his typical part, and his tragic death did little to help the film.

The National Board of Review named it as being among the year's ten best. *Variety* (July 5, 1961) called it "neatly constructed, thoroughly professional." *Time* felt it to be "a waste of a good man."

Film Quarterly (Fall 1961) objected — quite rightly — to the advertising campaign linking *The Naked Edge* to *Psycho*. "The resemblance to *Psycho* claimed by the posters is limited to the horrific use of a bathroom and a stairway. The pace is neatly accelerated. There is one watery dissolve and negatives frame two flashbacks (if their purpose is to cast doubt on the reliability of the scenes they frame, they are successful), but most of the cutting is quick and often shocking." One (slight) link to *Psycho* that might have been mentioned is the similarity of their opening credits.

The *Washington Post* (July 28) showed some initiative in its review by Richard L. Coe. "Despite what others have written about this essay as unworthy of his film finale, I disagree. It's a good role of its kind and Coop kept it spinning all the way."

Dilys Powell, in *The Sunday Times* (London, undated) took the short view. "I am left regretting that Gary Cooper ... should have ended his career with a film so absurd."

Notes

1. United Artists publicity handout.
2. Ibid.

Fury at Smuggler's Bay
(1961)

Credits and Cast

Released April 1961 (U.K.); 97 minutes; Eastman color (U.K.) PanaScope (U.S.); A Mijo Production; Released by Regal (U.K.), Embassy (U.S.); Filmed at Twickenham Studios, London, and on location in Ireland. Director, Producer, Screenplay,

Story: John Gilling; Associate producer: John Gossage; Executive producers: Joe Vegoda, Michael Green; Music: Harold Geller; Director of photography: Harry Waxman; Production supervisor: Fred A. Swann; Editor: John V. Smith; Wardrobe: Phyllis Dalton; Presented in U.S.A. by Joseph E. Levine.

Peter Cushing (Trevenyan), John Fraser (Christopher), Michelle Mercier (Louise), Bernard Lee (Black John), June Thornburn (Jenny), William Franklyn (The Captain), George Coulouris (Lejeune), Liz Fraser (Betty), Katherine Kath (Maman), Jouma, Miles Malleson (Duke of Avon), Christopher Carlos (The Tiger), Thomas Duggin (Red Friars), Maitland Moss (Tom), Humphrey Heathcote (Roger), Bob Simmons (Carlos), James Liggat (Sergeant), Alfred Pim (Jasper), Ken Buckle (The Fox).

Synopsis

> *"You remember the whip you used on me back when I was servant?"* — Black John
> *"Take care I don't use it again!"* — The Squire

In late eighteenth-century England, harsh taxation has caused smuggling in some districts to become accepted as an almost legitimate activity. However, some have gone too far. These are the Wreckers — cutthroats who lure ships into dangerous waters with false lights. The ships are destroyed, the cargo stolen, and the crew murdered.

When Squire Trevenyan (Peter Cushing) returns to London to his coastal district, he is less than pleased. Smuggling is on the rise, and his son Christopher (John Fraser) is involved with Louise (Michelle Mercier), the daughter of a suspected smuggler. Her father Lejeune (George Coulouris) is typical of the district — a basically law-abiding citizen who supplements his meager income by accepting smuggled goods.

But the Wreckers are the squire's real problem. Despite ample evidence against Black John (Bernard Lee) as being their leader, Trevenyan fails to act, causing a rift between himself and Christopher. The squire seems more intent on prosecuting the relatively harmless Lejeune and plans to secure military assistance. The captain (William Franklyn), a mysterious highwayman, learns of the squire's plan and intercepts the coach en route to the duke (Miles Malleson) and robs Trevenyan and Christopher. Finally arriving at the duke's estate, they are promised military aid.

When they reach home, Christopher immediately warns Lejeune of his impending arrest. When he spots the Wreckers about to strike, Christopher intervenes and, in self defense, kills one of Black John's men. After telling his father about the killing, Christopher is disgusted. His father seems protective of Black John and insists that Christopher leave

Christopher (John Fraser) argues with his father the squire (Peter Cushing) over the death of a Wrecker in *Fury at Smuggler's Bay*.

immediately for London to avoid prosecution. After giving his sister Jenny (June Thornburn) a letter of farewell for Louise, he boards a coach for London.

After his departure the duke's soldiers strike and Lejeune and others are arrested. Largely on the false testimony of Black John, Lejeune is convicted and sentenced to deportation, further securing the Wreckers' position. Louise contacts Christopher, who immediately returns.

Lejeune sends Louise to meet the captain, whom her father once saved from death. On the way she is assaulted by Black John but protected by the captain who subdues and humiliates the ruffian.

Mad with rage, Black John barges into the squire's home and demands the removal of the troops—and reveals his hold on Trevenyan. Christopher is illegitimate, and, if this were revealed, it would ruin both father and son.

The captain intercepts Christopher's coach and holds him against the squire's release of Lejeune. Pushed too far, the squire confronts Black John, but fails to move him. When he returns home, Trevenyan tells Jenny the truth, but still signs the order for Lejeune's deportation.

At the captain's camp Christopher strikes a bargain—they will duel, with Christopher's life as the prize. Through a combination of skill and luck, Christopher wins the duel and the captain's respect.

The captain rescues Lejeune as he is to board a ship for Australia. After a fierce battle with the Wreckers, Christopher — in disguise — joins their depleted ranks. Thinking Christopher was killed in the battle, the squire orders in more troops to kill Black John and every one of his men. When Trevenyan realizes that his son has infiltrated the Wreckers, he rushes to save him.

During the frenzied battle, the squire dies shielding Christopher from Black John who is, in turn, killed by the captain.

Now the squire, Christopher offers the captain either a pardon or a head start. He chooses the latter.

Commentary

As a child, Peter Cushing was a fan of westerns in general and cowboy Tom Mix in particular. As a young man in Hollywood he actually met his childhood hero and even witnessed the legendary cowpoke's signature on a contract. As an actor he never appeared in a western, but he came close.

Peter Cushing describes *Fury at Smuggler's Bay* as "a sort of English cowboy picture set in the nineteenth century. The scenario contained all the traditional ingredients: lots of shootin', the inevitable brawl in a saloon, a *High Noon* confrontation between duellists . . . and the cavalry charging to the rescue in the nick of time."[1] With a change of accents and scenery, the film would indeed play as a western.

Aided by a fine cast and beautiful location photography (near Fishguard, Ireland), *Fury at Smuggler's Bay* is an enjoyable action film that supplied Peter Cushing with a well-written, nonhorror part — the type of role he seemed to be seeking in the early 1960s.

As Squire Trevenyan, he is a government official, in contrast to his typical "lone wolf" casting. Another departure from his standard role is that he has two children. One of them is illegitimate and he is being blackmailed for his indiscretion — a very un–Cushing–like situation!

For his death scene at the film's climax, Peter Cushing adds much more to the traditional "dying in your loved one's arms" scene by playing it entirely with his eyes. His expert acting did not escape the notice of Christopher Lee. When the film played on British television in the late 1980s, Lee telephoned his long-time costar. "You rode the horse very well, dear fellow," he said, "and the expression on your face when you died was exactly the same as when you were told what your salary for the film was going to be."[2]

Pressbook publicity described Peter Cushing as "the man voted England's top TV Actor of the Year for three consecutive years." Since this was almost a decade after the fact, it seems like an attempt to play down his Hammer image and give the film a more mainstream appeal.

Prominently featured in the cast was Bernard Lee, cast against type as a scruffy villain. As the somewhat standard handsome young hero, John Fraser is more than adequate and displays his athletic skills in a well-staged sword fight with William Franklyn. The latter almost steals the film as the mysterious captain—a character worthy of his own film.

Writer-director John Gilling does his usual fine job in both departments. Gilling was very active in British low-budget horror adventure films of the period and had previously directed Peter Cushing in *Mania* (1959).

The film was not widely released in the United States and, for some unknown reason, the American prints are in black and white. The authors had the opportunity to see a British print in Eastman color which, obviously, enhanced the beautiful scenery and well-executed costumes and sets.

Critical appraisal was also limited. Leslie Halliwell found it a "watchable, then forgettable variation on *Jamaica Inn*."[3] Jeffrey Richards enjoyed its "plentiful, fast moving action sequences. There is a high quality cast who give of their best, particularly Peter Cushing."[4]

The *New York Daily News* (December 12, 1963) reported that "Peter (usually Sherlock Holmes) Cushing is its grim star, squire of the village, too. Young men in the 8–13 group will think this is keen stuff." The *New York Herald Tribune* (January 1, 1964) dismissed the film with, "Ho, hum! John Gilling directed this dreary costume drama from his own screenplay."

Notes

1. Cushing, *Past Forgetting.*
2. Ibid.
3. Leslie Halliwell, *Halliwell's Film Guide.*
4. Richards, *Swordsmen of the Screen.*

Cash on Demand
(1961)

Credits and Cast

Released 1961 (U.S.), October 1963 (U.K.); 66 minutes; Black and white; A Hammer-Woodpecker Production; Released through British Lion (U.K.), Columbia

(U.S.); Filmed at Bray Studios, England. Director: Quentin Lawrence; Producer: Anthony Nelson-Keys; Executive producer: Michael Carreras; Screenplay: David Chantler, Lewis Greifer; Based on Jacques Gillies' play *The Gold Inside*; Music: Wilfrid Josephs; Music Supervisor: John Hollingsworth; Director of photography: Arthur Grant; Production Design: Bernard Robinson; Art director; Don Mingaye; Editors: James Needs, Eric Boyd-Perkins; Production Manger: Clifford Parkes; Sound recordist: Jock May; Sound Editor: Alban Streeter; Camera operator: Len Harris; Assistant director: John Peverall; Continuity: Tilly Day; Makeup: Roy Ashton; Wardrobe: Molly Arbuthnot, Rosemary Burrows.

Peter Cushing (Fordyce), Andre Morell (Colonel Hepburn), Richard Vernon (Pearson), Barry Lowe (Harvill), Norman Bird (Sanderson), Edith Sharpe (Miss Pringle), Charles Morgan (Collins), Kevin Stoney (Detective Mason), Alan Haywood (Kane), Lois Daine (Sally), Vera Cook (Mrs. Fordyce), Gareth Tandy (Tommy), Fred Stone (Window Cleaner).

Synopsis

> *How to rob a bank ... and get away with it?* — Columbia poster blurb

Mr. Fordyce (Peter Cushing) is the manager of a small provincial bank. He is universally disliked by his employees due to his stern, inflexible personality and his all too frequent habit of becoming nasty and arrogant when challenged.

This particular Christmas, he is even worse. Fordyce has instigated a new efficiency program at the bank that is driving the employees to distraction. However, they are looking forward to the annual Christmas party despite their superior's cold, humorless attitude. Then, Colonel Hepburn (Andre Morell) enters the bank.

The colonel—a smooth-talking, well-dressed, intimidating type—announces that he is an insurance investigator and wishes to inspect the vaults for a security check. Incredibly, Fordyce—apparently intimidated by the colonel—fails to follow one of his own dictates by not phoning London to confirm Hepburn's credentials. Flustered by the colonel's commanding presence, Fordyce takes him to the vaults.

Hepburn is not a colonel, nor is he an insurance investigator. He is, in fact, a criminal. Hepburn informs Fordyce that his wife (Vera Cook) and son Tommy (Gareth Tandy) are being held hostage by an accomplice and will be ... damaged ... if Fordyce does not comply with his demands. What Hepburn wants is the £93,000 in the vault.

The colonel seems almost as fascinated by Fordyce's miserable personality as he is by the loot and observes with considerable interest the interplay of emotions and attitudes toward the manager by his employees.

Never one to show any warmth toward his employees – or expect any from them – Fordyce must now put his family's lives in their hands. He begs them not to interfere in the robbery and pleads with them to actually aid the colonel.

Unknown to Fordyce, Pearson (Richard Vernon), one of Fordyce's favorite targets, has taken it upon himself to follow the check-up procedure that the manager has so blithely ignored. After leaving the bank, Hepburn is now the target of the police.

This sad, humiliating experience has actually been beneficial to Fordyce, as he now has faced his many personality flaws and he vows to change them. As Fordyce basks in his newfound humanity, Hepburn, captured a few miles away, is in police custody.

Commentary

While this may seem to be an unusual film for both Peter Cushing and Hammer to become involved in, *Cash on Demand* fit well into what both the actor and the studio required at the time.

As previously mentioned, it is fairly obvious that by 1961 Peter Cushing had grown a bit weary of Gothic horror (and why not?) and was seeking roles outside the restrictions of the genre. After appearing in Hammer's *The Brides of Dracula* (1960), he acted in six straight nonhorror films before *Cash on Demand* and three more following it. The string was finally broken with Hammer's *The Evil of Frankenstein* (1963).

Cash on Demand also satisfied Hammer's requirements by securing Peter Cushing's services for a role perfectly suited to his talents. In addition to *Cash on Demand*, Hammer's 1961 production schedule included one horror film (*Terror of the Tongs*), two comedies, two thrillers, and an adventure film. All but *Terror of the Tongs* were in black and white. Based on a television play ("The Gold Inside") by Jacques Gillies, *Cash on Demand* was a return to Hammer's policy of adapting television and radio programs for the screen.

Although released in America early in 1962, *Cash on Demand* was not released in England until October 1963. This was probably due to its short running time (less than seventy minutes), and it found itself in support of other, probably less worthy, films. This is also what happened in the United States when *Cash on Demand* was paired with *Walk on the Wild Side*.

After its opening at Brooklyn's Fabian Fox, *Cash on Demand* received favorable, if not rave, reviews in the New York press.

The *New York Post* (April 19, 1962) called it a "Raffles-type crook film from England, makes captivating and diverting fare. *Cash* is an obviously

Bank manager Fordyce's life unravels in Hammer's *Cash on Demand*.

inexpensive movie in black and white nicely played by Peter Cushing and Andre Morell. Director Quentin Lawrence deftly handles the screenplay."

The *New York Tribune* (April 17) noted the film's similarity to *A Christmas Carol*: "It is the Christmas season and several Bob Cratchits in the outer office are a-thrill about the impending office party." The similarity to Dicken's classic does not end there, either. Mr. Fordyce and Scrooge share many personality flaws, and both become human due to a horrifying experience that causes them to examine themselves and their relationships with others.

Bosley Crowther's *New York Times* (May 11) review called the movie a "neat, unpretentious little British film ... providing a few engaging moments of suspense and some modest exchanges of humor between Mr. Morell who is casual and dry, and Peter Cushing who is pinch faced and nervous as the cornered bank manager.... It might help, with a bag of popcorn, to put the bad taste of *Walk on the Wild Side* out of your mouth."

The *New York Daily News* (April 19) found it "easy to take because of competent acting, humor, and accelerated direction."

Question: If the film was so well praised, why has it seemingly vanished? The authors — despite years of fruitless searching of television listings — have never found a broadcast showing. Our only viewing of the film was in the late 1970s, courtesy of a private collector of 16mm films. Again, its short running time and black and white photography worked against it. This is unfortunate, for it contains two outstanding performances by two excellent actors.

Peter Cushing described his role as Fordyce thus: "I don't mean he's evil, he is simply a man who lacks charity and warmth. In his office, as manager of the bank, he is stern and forbidding. He derives smug satisfaction from holding the threat of dismissal over his staff. This, then, is the man who suddenly finds himself the center of a drama that rocks him to the core and alters his life."[1] Cushing made the most of the opportunity to play a realistic, complex character and turned in one of his best performances.

Andre Morell also shines in what is essentially a two-character film. The two actors' professional association dated back to the BBC production of "1984" (1954) and covered five films, peaking with *The Hound of the Baskervilles*. Morell had a varied career, appearing in both low-budget horror (*Plague of the Zombies*, 1966, and *The Giant Behemoth*, 1959) as well as top-level prestige pictures like *Bridge on the River Kwai* (1957) and *Ben Hur* (1959).

Morell brought to all his roles a commanding authority due, possibly, to his experiences in World War II as a major in a Welsh Division. He often played military men, notably in *Camp on Blood Island* (1958). This talented, underrated actor died, at age sixty-nine, in 1978.

Due to the two lead performances and crafty similarity to *A Christmas Carol*, this is one "lost" film that certainly deserves to be found and given a fair chance to attract an audience.

Note

1. Columbia press book.

Night Creatures
(1962)

Credits and Cast

Released June 1962; 81 minutes; Eastman color (U.S.), Technicolor (U.K.); A Ham-mer-Major Film Production; Released through Universal International (U.S.) and Rank (U.K.); Filmed at Bray Studios, England. Director: Peter Graham Scott; Pro-ducer: John Temple-Smith; Screenplay: John Elder (Anthony Hinds); Additional Dialogue: Barbara S. Harper; Director of photography: Arthur Grant; Editors: James Needs, Eric Boyd-Perkins; Production manager: Don Weeks; Music: Don Banks; Conducted by Philip Martell; Assistant directors: John Peverall, Peter Medak; Art direction: Bernard Robinson, Don Mingaye; Special effects: Les Bowie; Sound: Jock May; Makeup: Roy Ashton; Hair stylist: Frieda Steiger; Ward-robe: Molly Arbuthnot. Title in U.K. *Captain Clegg.*

Peter Cushing (Captain Clegg/Dr. Blyss), Yvonne Romain (Imogene), Patrick Allen (Captain Collier), Oliver Reed (Harry Crabtree), Michael Ripper (Mipps), Martin Benson (Rash), David Lodge (Bosun), Derek Francis (Squire), Daphine An-derson (Mrs. Rash), Milton Reid (Mulatto), Jack MacGowran (Frightened Man), Peter Halliday (Jack Pott), Terry Scully (Dick Tate), Sydney Bromley (Tom Ketch), Rupert Osborne (Gerry), Gordon Rollings (Wurzel), Bob Head (Peg-Leg), Colin Douglas (Pirate Bosun).

Synopsis

> *Why did you flinch when I touched your arm?* — Captain Collier
> *It wasn't my arm, Captain, you trod on my foot!* — Dr. Blyss

In late eighteenth century England, the notorious pirate, Captain Clegg (Peter Cushing) fakes his own death and, under a new alias as Dr. Blyss (Peter Cushing), takes up residency as the vicar of the small village of Dymchurch. However, the village is not the sleepy little town it appears to be to outsiders. In reality it is a cover for a group of expirates and villagers turned smugglers who are led by the vicar himself. Under assumed identities the vicar and his men defy the king's import duties and smuggle in goods from other countries to be sold tax free.

In order to keep their true identities secret and to avoid having their hidden stores discovered, they ride out to meet the ships in disguise. They are the "Marsh Phantoms." These eerie spectral figures are so greatly feared that the local townsfolk refuse to go anywhere near the places they have been seen.

When an informant from the village is reported missing by the king's revenue men, Captain Collier (Patrick Allen) and his men investigate. At first they find nothing out of the ordinary. However, among Collier's men

Peter Cushing as Dr. Blyss in Hammer's *Night Creatures*.

is a mulatto (Milton Reid). Collier had rescued him from a deserted island where he had been left to die, his tongue having been cut out by Captain Clegg. When the mulatto sees Dr. Blyss, he goes wild and tries to murder the vicar. Collier grows suspicious.

Always one step ahead of the revenue men, the smugglers try to carry on their trade. After one of them is shot while posing as a lookout and is later revealed to be Harry Crabtree (Oliver Reed) the town squire's son, Collier and his men confront the vicar in his church.

Collier tries to solicit the help of the villagers to round up the other smugglers. When Blyss reminds them of the prosperity that the village has enjoyed from the profits of the runners' trade, the people side with the vicar.

Blyss tries to escape in the ensuing mêlée, but is shot in the back by one of the king's men. Mipps (Michael Ripper), one of the smugglers posing as a coffin-maker (and a former pirate under Clegg), rescues the vicar and takes him to his shop. In the shop the mulatto, who has been in hiding there, harpoons Dr. Blyss. Mipps, in turn, kills the mulatto, and carries his dead captain to be buried in the same grave where Captain Clegg was supposedly buried sixteen years before.

Commentary

Strongly based on the 1936 Gainsborough production, *Dr. Syn*, John Elder's screenplay generally succeeds in its attempt to recreate all the romance and adventure of eighteenth-century England. While Britain's monarch was continuing to have his troubles with the colonies and France, there was a revolution of sorts going on in his own country. Many Englishmen, especially the poor citizens, resented the king's harsh taxation on imported goods. As a result, small pockets of resistance sprung up all over the land in the form of smugglers. Under the cover of darkness, these brave souls dodged the king's revenue men to bring in duty free goods.

It has been said that Hammer's *Night Creatures* takes historic license at times. If it has, it has only done so for the sake of dramatic effect. Scenes involving the Marsh Phantoms are indeed memorable and exciting. The vicar and his followers are able to establish an almost immediate rapport with the audience.

The film's approximately $200,000 budget was put to amazingly good use by its director, Peter Graham Scott, and his more than competent technical team. Though interiors were shot at Bray Studios, to save costs, Scott relied on the picturesque villages of nearby Denham and Bray for location filming. Denham, a small village about twenty miles away from the studios, was transformed, with the addition of about a ton of topsoil to cover road asphalt, into Dymchurch. Black Park made a convincing Romney Marsh, thanks to Les Bowie's magnificent matte paintings. And even an old church, awaiting the wrecking ball, was not overlooked and was converted into the Vicar Blyss' house of worship.[1]

In addition to Les Bowie's special effects and Bernard Robinson's effective set designs, performances all around were also impressive. *Night Creatures'* star, in his dual role as Captain Clegg and Dr. Blyss, afforded Peter Cushing a marvelous opportunity to portray two very distinct and equally diverse characters. One is the tyrannical Captain Clegg—pirate and cutthroat. The other is the meek and benevolent reverend of the parish of Dymchurch, Dr. Blyss—who is also the brains behind a well-organized and profitable smuggling ring. He is a sort of Robin Hood in clerical robes who, though he tries to hide his dark past, has in essence traded the high seas for a new career as a land pirate.

With his well-known passion for authenticity, Peter Cushing sought out the vicar of Bray when he learned that he was to conduct the wedding ceremony between his daughter, Imogene (Yvonne Romain)[2] and Harry Crabtree (Oliver Reed)[3] in the film. The vicar kindly coached the actor in the actual marriage service.[4]

Cushing has some delightful interplays with Patrick Allen (Captain Collier) during the course of the film. Though Peter's character, Dr. Blyss, always managed to win the upper hand, Allen must be credited for being quite capable of holding his own against the formidable vicar.

Another actor who deserves an acknowledgment is Michael Ripper (Mipps). His performance here proves the scope of his previously untapped talents. A severely underrated actor whom Hammer primarily wasted in bit parts and for comic relief in the past, Ripper is allowed a rare platform upon which to showcase his dramatic capabilities in *Night Creatures.*

Although the script is slow in spots this, fortunately, does not in any way detract from the overall potency of the film. Director Peter Graham Scott's grasp of the historic aspects of the period and the basic character of the people who lived in those bygone times is a major asset. He never allows his actors to revert back into a twentieth-century state of mind and utilizes their diversified talents to the best advantage throughout.

Scott, who has known Peter Cushing for more than thirty-five years, kindly offered to share some of his memories of this long and happy association.

> I first met Peter in the mid 1950s when I was producing live television plays and he had had a tremendous success as Winston Smith in George Orwell's *1984*, directed by Rudolph Cartier.... We had several talks about possible television plays, but none materialized. However, in 1959 my wife and I were having a new house built, and I was offered a financially rewarding film, as director, based on Russell Thorndyke's novel, *Doctor Syn*, and I approached Peter to play the lead along with Oliver Reed and Yvonne Romain. John Temple-Smith discovered that although he had paid the Rank Organization a large sum for what he thought were the complete film rights, all he had bought was the right to re-make a Gaumont British version ... and the Walt Disney Organization had secured the original rights to the novel.

This is how the film came to be known as *Captain Clegg* or *Night Creatures*. John and I enlisted Peter's help to re-write the script to keep the basic idea of a vicar in Napoleonic times, living in the Romney Marshes, who was the organizer of a liquor smuggling organization by night, without breaching Disney's copyright. During this period, I got to know Peter and his wife well and to admire his classical mind and gift for creating plot and dialogue. It was this that gave his performances such distinction in the various Hammer films. He prepared his character very thoroughly before shooting and I remember one morning when he turned up at a church, which was to be the scene of the final climax of the film, when the Revenue Men come to arrest the vicar. During the night, Peter had re-written his sermon to remind the villagers that when he had arrived in the village they were starving under bitter taxation and he had brought them prosperity and a good life. It was beautifully phrased and Peter delivered it superbly in one take.

I never worked with Peter after this film . . . but I always remember Peter's enormous enthusiasm, energy and awareness of what he was doing. I saw him again last year (1989) at the funeral of our mutual agent, John Redway, and was pleased to see that he seemed in the best of health.

His relationship with his wife, Helen, was interesting; they had no children and when she died he felt her loss very strongly. In a way she was more of a mother figure to him. I am sure you will also know about his massive collection of toy soldiers with which he fought the great battles of history.

Notable critical reviews of *Night Creatures* include "Pit" in *Variety* (May 9, 1962) who wrote, "Pure escapism, of course, but notable is that the Hammer imprimatur has come to certify solid values in all production departments, and there's no mystery why these films rate audience allegiance . . . the histronics are generally convincing, especially Peter Cushing as the pirate-cum-vicar. . . . Peter Graham Scott's direction is savvy and the range of technical credits are all on the plus side." Joseph Morgenstern in the *New York Herald Tribune* (September 20, 1962) reported that "Peter Cushing as the bootlegging parson, Patrick Allen . . . and Michael Ripper . . . all perform well." And *The Times* in its June 8, 1962, review wrote that "while Mr. Peter Cushing, as the benign vicar with a past who captains the smugglers' side and Mr. Patrick Allen as the . . . naval captain, engage in their battle of wits, *Captain Clegg* is acceptable enough."

Notes

1. Keith Dudley, "Dr. Syn to Dr. Blyss and Capt. Clegg," *Little Shoppe of Horrors* 9.

2. Romain, born in France in 1938, had a sporadic career in films. Among her

credits was *Curse of the Werewolf* (1961) for Hammer, in which she played Oliver Reed's mother. Yvonne married British composer Leslie Bricusse, who won an Oscar in 1967 for his title song from *Doctor Dolittle* entitled "Talk to the Animals."

3. Reed costarred in two other films with Peter Cushing, *Sword of Sherwood Forest* (1960) and *Touch of the Sun* (1978). He was once described by Peter as "A young man with a burning desire to succeed," and so he did, achieving widespread fame during his long career. The nephew of director Sir Carol Reed, Oliver Reed had his autobiography entitled *Reed All About Me* published in 1981.

4. Universal International publicity release.

The Man Who Finally Died
(1962)

Credits and Cast

Released December 1962 (U.K.); 100 minutes; Black and white; Dyalascope; A Magna Production; Released through British Lion (U.K.), Goldstone (U.S.); Filmed at Shepperton Studios, and on location in Germany and Surrey, England. Director: Quentin Lawrence; Producer: Norman Williams; Screenplay: Lewis Greifer (from his story), Louis Marks; Music: Philip Green; Director of photography: Stephen Dade; Editor: John Jympson; Camera: John Winbolt; Art director: Scott MacGregor; Production manager: John Pellat; Sound: William Bulkley; Continuity: Gladys Goldsmith; Makeup: Freddie Williamson; Hairdresser: Doris Pollard; Wardrobe: Jackie Cummins.

Stanley Baker (Joe Newman), Peter Cushing (Von Brecht), Mai Zetterling (Lisa), Eric Portman (Hofmeister), Niall MacGinnis (Brenner), Nigel Green (Hirsch), Barbara Everest (Martha), Georgina Ward (Maria), Harold Scott (Professor), James Ottoway (Rahn), Alfred Burke (Heinrich), Mela White (Helga), Maya Sorell (Minna), Brian Wilde (Cemetary Superintendent), Frank Sremann (Hotel Clerk), Danny Grover (Karel), Martin Boddey (First Policeman), Anthony Sheppard (Second Policeman), Ivor Slater (Ambulance Driver), Larry Taylor (Ernst), John Longden (Munch), Miriam Pritchett (Fat Lady).

Synopsis

> The mystery of the century explodes! — Goldstone publicity

Kurt Deutsch is being laid to rest in Konigsbaden, Bavaria. However, in London, his son Joe Newman (Stanley Baker) takes a phone call from ... Kurt Deutsch.

Joe has lived in London for over twenty years, since the start of World War II. He has always thought that his father died in 1943. He leaves immediately for Germany and learns Kurt has been a prisoner of war in

Stanley Baker and Peter Cushing make a startling discovery in *The Man Who Finally Died.*

Russia for eighteen years and, after an escape back to Germany, lived at the home of Dr. Von Brecht (Peter Cushing). Also, he has remarried a young woman named Lisa (Mai Zetterling), now his widow.

Joe is told that his father is now truly dead. Von Brecht explains that Kurt was the victim of a stroke. But the London phone call is unexplained—as also are Lisa's nervousness, Von Brecht's evasive answers and Police Inspector Hofmeister's (Eric Portman) lack of cooperation. The only thing Joe is sure of is that all three would like him to leave as soon as possible.

One mystery is soon solved. The phone call was placed by Brenner (Niall MacGinnis), an insurance investigator who wanted to get Joe quickly to Germany. Brenner thinks that Deutsch is still alive and that his "death" is an attempt at an insurance fraud.

At the funeral was a lone mourner, Maria (Georgina Ward). She is a refugee from a displaced persons camp run by Von Brecht. Her father died the same day as Deutsch.

Joe demands an exhumation, assuming that his father's coffin will be empty, but it does contain a corpse. His only remaining lead takes him to Von Brecht's house.

That night Joe breaks in and finds an elderly man in the attic. As he moves to embrace the man he assumes to be his father, he is attacked by Hofmeister.

Joe learns from Hofmeister that there is indeed a plot. An important scientist had switched identities with Kurt Deutsch, and Hofmeister planned to kidnap the man and take him to the East. Armed with this knowledge, Joe is able to prevent the kidnapping—which would have been disastrous to the West—and get the scientist safely out of Germany.

Commentary

The Man Who Finally Died was a final change of pace role for Peter Cushing before returning to Hammer's Frankenstein series. During the period 1960–62 Cushing appeared in ten films, with only one (*The Brides of Dracula*, 1960) a true horror film.

"People will always think of me as sort of monsterish with teeth and blood dripping from every eyeball," he explained. "Of course ... I brought it upon myself ... and I got identified with the Monster when really in every [film] I was a blushing hero. After all, Frankenstein was really a nice fellow who went a bit wrong."[1]

After finishing *The Man Who Finally Died*, he would appear in fifty-seven more films, with only a handful that were not in the horror–science fiction–fantasy genre. This film, then, marked the end of his brief hiatus from horror roles and the start of an almost unbroken run of them for the next twenty-three years.

"I played quite a good chap, really, although I still go around with a gun in my hand. I have no doubt people will remember me in this picture as the villain," he lamented with much truth.[2]

During location filming in Richmond, Surrey, the crew set up a mock cemetery in a park with permission from the local government. As a scene was being filmed of an exhumation, a passerby was outraged at this desecration of consecrated ground for a movie. He stormed off promising to report the incident to his Burial Board superiors.[3]

Peter Cushing described a follow-up to the film as "the easiest job I ever had!"[4] A clip from *The Man Who Finally Died* was incorporated with actor Griff Rhys Jones for a commercial for Holstein Pils. In the clip, Cushing is seated in a chair. Rhys Jones, at a fireplace, is commenting on the product as Peter Cushing attempts to lure him to the basement. When this fails, he (actually a double) pulls a lever, opening a trapdoor!

The film itself was a low-key spy drama—a type of entertainment on its way out due to Ian Fleming's *Dr. No* (1962) which spawned the James Bond series. As such, the film was lost in the shuffle. Since it was filmed in black and white, it is hardly ever shown on television and could be considered a lost film until it (hopefully) reappears in video form.

Critic Leslie Halliwell called the film a "Busy adaptation of a TV serial which might have been more pacily developed and better explained."

Notes

1. Goldstone press book.
2. Ibid.
3. Cushing, *Past Forgetting*.
4. Ibid.

The Evil of Frankenstein
(1963)

Credits and Cast

Released April 1964; 84 minutes; Eastman color; A Hammer Film Production; Released through Universal (U.S.) and Rank (U.K.); Filmed at Bray Studios, England. Director: Freddie Francis; Producer: Anthony Hinds; Screenplay: John Elder (Anthony Hinds); Music: Don Banks; Music supervisor: John Hollingsworth; Director of photography: John Wilcox; Art director: Don Mingaye; Production manager: Don Weeks; Editor: James Needs; Sound recordist: Ken Rawkins; Camera operator: Ronnie Maasz; Assistant director: Bill Cartlidge; Continuity: Pauline Harlow; Makeup: Roy Ashton; Hairdresser: Frieda Steiger; Special effects: Les Bowie.

Peter Cushing (Baron Frankenstein), Peter Woodthorpe (Zoltan), Sandor Eles (Hans), Duncan Lamont (Chief of Police), Katy Wild (Beggar Girl), David Hutcheson (Burgomaster), Caron Gardner (Burgomaster's Wife), Tony Arpino (Body Snatcher), James Maxwell (Priest), Alister Williamson (Landlord), Frank Forsyth (Manservant), Kenneth Cove (Cure), Michele Scott (Little Girl), Howard Goorney (Drunk), Anthony Blackshaw (Burly Constable), David Conville (Young Constable), Timothy Bateson (Hypnotized Man), and Kiwi Kingston (The Creature).

Synopsis

> *Cut out his heart?* — Body Snatcher
> *Why not? He has no further use for it.* — The Baron

A body snatcher (Tony Arpino) steals a corpse and delivers it to the secluded laboratory of Baron Frankenstein (Peter Cushing). As the baron —

Peter Cushing back as the baron in Hammer's *The Evil of Frankenstein*.

assisted by young Hans (Sandor Eles) — removes the heart, the experiment is interrupted by an outraged priest (James Maxwell) who destroys the apparatus.

The baron and Hans flee to Frankenstein's long abandoned chateau in Karlstadt. The pair slip unnoticed through the town due to the yearly carnival. When they reach the chateau, the baron finds his treasures looted.

Depressed and angry, he tells Hans about the Creature (Kiwi Kingston) he had created there years before.

The Creature, after being taught some rudiments of human behavior, escaped and killed a flock of sheep. Found by the angry villagers, it was shot and, with the baron in pursuit, fled into the mountains to fall to its death.

The baron and Hans decide to attend the carnival in disguise. At a tavern, Frankenstein notices the burgomaster (David Hutcheson) wearing his stolen ring. He foolishly demands the burgomaster's arrest, and is forced again to flee. The pair find refuge in the wagon of Zoltan (Peter Woodthorpe), a traveling hypnotist.

Frankenstein and Hans escape from the town by crossing the mountains and are joined by a mute beggar girl (Katy Wild) who was mistreated by the villagers. When a storm approaches, they find shelter in a cave where they discover the body of the Creature, preserved in a glacier.

They transport it back to the chateau and the baron revives its body but not its mind—the brain is dormant. Frankenstein decides that the brain requires a direct shock. Zoltan is recruited and accepts the challenge and succeeds—too well. The Creature is now under his hypnotic spell and will obey only him. He plans to exhibit the Creature and the baron is forced, for now, to agree.

Zoltan has other plans that he does not reveal—to use the Creature to rob the village and punish officials who had forced him out of town. The Creature goes too far and kills the burgomaster and a policeman.

The baron discovers Zoltan's plot and throws him bodily from the chateau. Mad with rage, the hypnotist returns and orders the Creature to kill Frankenstein, who forces it back with fire. Confused and terrified, it kills Zoltan with a spear.

The chief of police (Duncan Lamont) deduces that the baron is responsible for the deaths and arrests him at the chateau.

Frankenstein escapes and returns to the chateau to find the Creature out of control—it has drunk several bottles of brandy. Stupified, it mistakenly drinks a bottle of chloroform and, in a rage, sets the laboratory ablaze. The baron tries to lead it to safety, but the chateau explodes into a ball of fire as Hans and the beggar girl watch in horror.

Commentary

The Evil of Frankenstein was a false step in a film series that took very few of them. It seems out of place in the Hammer series due to its "Universal-style" monster and plot devices. Peter Cushing starred in two startlingly original Frankenstein films that were the antithesis of the Universal films and had created an entirely new concept of the story. This came to a grinding halt with *The Evil of Frankenstein*. The film is slow, boring, and almost impossible to enjoy.

Releasing through Universal gave Hammer the opportunity to use the Karloff-type makeup denied them in the first two films. Having the Karloff makeup, however, is of little value if you don't have Boris Karloff. What Hammer had was Kiwi Kingston.

At 6' 5" and 238 pounds, Kiwi Kingston was certainly a physically impressive choice as the Creature. A wrestler and horseman, the New Zealander had little experience to prepare him for this (or any) role.[1] However, considering the poorly developed part, no experience was really necessary. He is no worse than Glenn Strange when Universal reduced the monster character to a breathing prop, but he's not very good, either.

Freddie Francis' direction is flat and lacks the flair and sense of period detail that Terence Fisher brought to the series. The cliché-ridden, multiple revenge plot, which was creaking with age in the 1940s, was a far cry from the innovative scripting of Jimmy Sangster in the first two films. Producer Anthony Hinds (writing as John Elder) had just written an excellent script for *Kiss of the Vampire* (1962) but seems to have run out of ideas. With composer James Bernard and set designer Bernard Robinson also missing, the film seems to be the work of Hammer's second team.

Although he gives his usual professional and spirited performance, Peter Cushing cannot save the film. At times, a bit of self-parody seems to creep into his performance, especially in a scene in which he escapes from the burgomaster's bedroom. The asides he delivers to Caron Gardner (as the burgomaster's wife) are totally out of place and seem like an attempt to inject a James Bond–like quality into the character. Peter Cushing stated to the authors that "Baron Frankenstein really cannot be developed beyond Mary Shelley's original conception, but the demands of each script bring out various aspects of his character." One doubts, however, that Shelley would recognize her hero in this film.

The supporting cast is the weakest of the series. Sandor Eles is no more than adequate as the young assistant, and Katy Wild can do little as the mute beggar girl. Peter Woodthorpe hams outrageously as Zoltan but is at least amusing.

One of the many things that helps sink the film is a lack of connection to *The Revenge of Frankenstein*. When last seen, the Baron was practicing in London. How he ended up in Central Europe is anyone's guess. There was also no attempt to follow the idea of the baron's brain in a new body. The Creature bears no resemblance to anything else in Frankenstein's laboratory—before or since. After a six-year wait, fans expected and deserved more.

Contemporary reviews were, interestingly, split. Genre publications were unfavorable in their comments, while mainstream reviews were kinder. Typical of the negative, fan-oriented reviews was *Castle of Frankenstein* (number 24): "So what has Hammer proven? Not much, except that a kind of quality identified with most of their films is evincing signs of vanishing. . . . We've never seen Peter looking more bored or distressed. The ending, of course, leaves room to speculate . . . a sequel, though we hope not if it is planned as ineptly as this disappointing rehash."

Variety (April 22, 1964) felt that "Cushing plays the Baron with his usual seriousness, avoiding a disastrous tongue-in-cheek attitude and he is the main prop in the proceedings." *The Times* (April 16) said the film "has its moments. . . . One or two of the actors get quite out of control but Mr. Peter Cushing is, as ever, authoritative as the idealistic, misunderstood Baron Frankenstein. . . . The script by Mr. John Elder is engagingly aware of its own absurdity."

When the film was sold to NBC television for a prime time airing in America, new footage had to be shot to pad its length for the two-hour time slot. Fortunately, none of this footage involved Peter Cushing and only succeeded in making the discomfort of watching *The Evil of Frankenstein* last a bit longer. These ineffective scenes were directed by Irving J. Moore.

Note

1. Universal press book.

The Gorgon
(1964)

Credits and Cast

Released October 1964 (U.K.) 83 minutes; Eastman color; A Hammer Film Production; Released through Columbia; Filmed at Bray Studios, England. Director: Terence Fisher; Producer: Anthony Nelson-Keys; Screenplay: John Gilling; Based on J. Llewellyn Devine's story; Music: James Bernard; Music supervisor: John Hollingsworth; Director of photography: Michael Reed; Editor: James Needs; Camera: Cece Cooney; Production manager: Don Weeks; Production design: Bernard Robinson; Art director: Don Mingaye; Sound: Roy Hyde; Makeup: Roy Ashton; Special effects: Syd Pearson; Wardrobe: Rosemary Burrows; Hairstyles: Frieda Steiger; Fight arranger: Peter Diamond; Assistant director: Bert Batt; Continuity: Pauline Harlow.

Peter Cushing (Dr. Namaroff), Christopher Lee (Meister), Barbara Shelley (Carla), Richard Pasco (Paul), Michael Goodliffe (Professor Heitz), Patrick Troughton (Kanof), Jack Watson (Ratoff), Jeremy Longhurst (Bruno), Sally Nesbitt (Nurse), Prudence Hyman (The Gorgon), Toni Gilpin (Sacha); Redmond Phillips (Hans); Joyce Hemson (Martha).

Synopsis

> *It never ceases to amaze me that the most noble work of God — the human brain — is also the most revolting to the human eye.* — Professor Namaroff

Central Europe, 1910. Vandorf, a police state, is the scene of a series of inexplicable murders in which the victims are turned to stone.

Sacha (Toni Gilpin) tells her lover Bruno (Jeremy Longhurst) that she is pregnant with his child. When his response is less than positive, she runs into the night to become the next victim. The prime suspect, Bruno, is found hanged. A biased court rules murder-suicide.

His father, Professor Heitz (Michael Goodliffe), disagrees and proposes to remain in Vandorf until he learns the truth. His questioning leads him to a hospital run by Dr. Namaroff (Peter Cushing), a brain specialist Heitz met in college. When Heitz mentions his suspicions involving Megera, Namaroff terminates the discussion. Megera was a Gorgon — a creature of mythology whose horrible face can turn a human to stone.

Heitz moves into his son's cottage with his old servant Hans (Redmond Phillips), but angry villagers soon set it ablaze. Fearing for his life, Heitz contacts his friend Professor Meister (Christopher Lee) who is also his son Paul's (Richard Pasco) teacher at the university. Paul takes the next train to Vandorf.

A strange sound attracts Heitz and draws him from the cottage toward the Castle Borski — a place of terror in the area. There, in the musty castle, he sees something. Dumbfounded, he staggers back to the cottage. Heitz dismisses Hans and, while outlining his suspicions in a letter to Paul, dies. His body has turned to stone.

When Paul arrives and learns of his father's death, he visits Namaroff and is rudely dismissed. However, he gains the sympathy of Namaroff's beautiful nurse Carla (Barbara Shelley). She and Namaroff have an undefined but unsettling relationship.

Carla later visits Paul at the cottage and secretly reads his father's letter which she later recites to a sombre Namaroff. The hospital warden Ratoff (Jack Watson) interrupts to report the escape of Martha (Joyce Hemson), a violent inmate. Namaroff reveals to Carla that Megera does exist and occasionally takes over the body of a human being.

Dr. Namaroff shows Paul (Richard Pasco) the result of glimpsing the gorgon in Hammer's *The Gorgon*.

Paul investigates the same sinister sound that lured his father to his death, but is saved by glimpsing the horror in a reflecting pool. He awakens five days later — aged ten years — in Namaroff's hospital. Shaken, but determined to destroy the creature, Paul returns with Carla to the cottage. Namaroff instructs Ratoff to follow Carla. There is a full moon.

Under that moon, Paul exhumes the stone-like body of his father while Carla silently watches. Later, she confides to Paul that, while Namaroff is in love with her, she is terrified of him. Paul promises to take her with him when the mystery is solved, but Carla fears it will be too late.

As Professor Meister arrives at the cottage, Namaroff, at the hospital, removes Martha's brain. She died soon after her capture by Ratoff. Carla had assumed that Martha was the chief suspect. She now fears something far worse.

Paul and Meister visit the chief of police (Patrick Troughton) and the professor threatens him into revealing that Carla arrived in Vandorf as an amnesiac just prior to the first murder.

Carla meets with Paul at Castle Borski to tell him she will go with him, but it must be now. He declines and she runs off. When he follows, Ratoff attempts to kill him, but is dispatched by Meister.

The professor has decided, after studying records stolen from the hospital, that Carla becomes an amnesiac during the period of the full moon. During this period, her body is entered by the spirit of Megera.

Paul and Carla finally come to an understanding—she will leave immediately and he will follow when the case is closed.

While Carla is hiding upstairs, Namaroff and the police enter the cottage. She leaves through a window while they argue downstairs with Meister.

Paul cables Leipzig, where Carla is to arrive by train. There is no trace of her. Paul goes to the Castle Borski as the full moon rises.

Waiting for him in the shadows is Namaroff, who attacks him with a sword. As they struggle, the Gorgon (Prudence Hyman) appears at the top of the staircase. Namaroff dies in an attempt to behead her. The creature traps Paul against a mirror as Meister silently approaches from behind. He beheads her—too late to save Paul, who dies sobbing as he. watches the monster's face turn back to Carla.

Commentary

After a period of five years, Hammer Films finally saw fit to reunite stars Peter Cushing and Christopher Lee with director Terence Fisher. This trio had revitalized not only the horror film but the entire British film industry with their remakes of *Frankenstein* and *Dracula*. However, after *The Mummy* (1959), their triple collaboration ended.

During this hiatus, Peter Cushing appeared in only two horror films and concentrated on drama and costume adventure. Christopher Lee drifted into sleazy exploitation (*Beat Girl*, 1960), pirate adventure (*Pirates of Blood River*, 1962), and European horrors (*Night Is the Phantom*, 1963). After the inexplicable failure of his excellent *Phantom of the Opera* (1962), Terence Fisher found himself assigned nonsense like *The Horror of It All* (1964).

The Gorgon, then, was a return to form and got all three back on the path (for better or worse) they had seemingly left in 1959. The remainder of the 1960s would find the two actors together in six more films, and both would continue playing their trademark horror characters. At the decade's end, Terence Fisher would direct perhaps his best film (*Frankenstein Must Be Destroyed* 1969).

Compared to Peter Cushing's initial run of Gothic horrors, *The Gorgon* is something of a letdown. It does, however, deserve consideration for doing something different in a genre that too often repeats itself.

First, Peter Cushing and Christopher Lee seem to have switched roles. Cushing is cold, calculating, and aloof while Lee is quite charming—certainly a reversal of their standard casting. Namaroff is one of Peter Cushing's few roles that alienates the audience. "I played an evil man," said Cushing, "although to be fair, even this character had a secret reason for behaving as he did."[1]

Also, Hammer finally came up with a new monster and not a copy of Universal's (or their own). While certainly no match for Dracula, the change was welcome.

Barbara Shelley, who portrayed the title character (or did she?), revealed to interviewer Al Taylor she has "very happy memories of [*The Gorgon*], and also one big regret. It is true that when the Gorgon actually appeared it was another actress made up to look like the Gorgon, and the reason is because of makeup difficulties. If I was needed on the set as Karla [sic], . . . it would [have taken] one and a half to two hours to switch from the Gorgon to Karla, or even longer the other way."[2]

She also recalled Peter Cushing's "impish sense of humor. He loves cartoons, especially Sylvester the Cat. Peter does a marvelous impression of Sylvester which can always be relied upon to make Chris Lee laugh."[3]

This and other shortcuts involving the monster considerably reduced the film's impact. The scenes involving the Gorgon should have been the film's highlight but are in fact the weakest, and prevent the film from being truly outstanding. The Gorgon's headful of writhing snakes was just beyond makeup man Roy Ashton and effects man Syd Pearson and the result is laughable. This totally destroys the climax that Terence Fisher had so skillfully built to. It's unfortunate that the effects did not match the acting, atmosphere, and set design.

The Gorgon was released as a double feature with Hammer's inferior *Curse of the Mummy's Tomb* in some American markets, and this gave the publicity department of Columbia Pictures an opportunity to develop a ludicrous promotional campaign. The press book urged theater owners to present patrons with "Black Stamps" that may (or not) be traded in at a "local soda fountain" or to win (unspecified) merchandise at a local store.

This type of childish advertising did little to promote the true nature of the film, which was certainly more adult than the black stamps would lead one to believe. What the campaign may have accomplished was to prevent the film's real audience from seeing it.

Peter Cushing was fairly active in television in 1964, appearing on "Late Night Line Up," "The Caves of Steel," and "Julius Caesar" (as Cassius) in the BBC series, *Spread of the Eagle*.

Notes

1. Peter Cushing, *Tales of a Monster Hunter.*
2. Richard Klemensen, *Little Shoppe of Horrors 7.*
3. Ibid.

Dr. Terror's House of Horrors
(1964)

Credits and Cast

Released March 1965 (U.S.), February 1965 (U.K.); 98 minutes; Technicolor and Techniscope; An Amicus Production; Released through Regal Films International (U.K.) and Paramount (U.S.); Filmed at Shepperton Studios, England. Director: Freddie Francis; Producers: Max J. Rosenberg, Milton Subotsky; Screenplay: Milton Subotsky; Director of Photography: Alan Hume; Editor: Thelma Connell; Music: Tubby Hayes; Played by the Tubby Hayes Quintet and the Russ Henderson Steel Band; Songs: Kenny Lynch; Choreography: Bosco Holder; Art director: Bill Constable; Production manager: Ted Wallis; Special effects: Ted Samuels; Makeup: Roy Ashton; Hairdresser: Frieda Steiger; Wardrobe supervisor: Bridget Sellers.

Peter Cushing (Dr. Schreck), Christopher Lee (Franklyn Marsh), Roy Castle (Biff Bailey), Donald Sutherland (Bob Carroll), Neil McCallum (Jim Dawson), Alan Freeman (Bill Rogers), Max Adrian (Dr. Blake), Edward Underdown (Tod), Ursula Howells (Dierdre), Bernard Lee (Hopkins), Peter Madden (Caleb), Katy Wild (Valda), Anne Bell (Ann Rogers), Sarah Nicholls (Carol Rogers), Jeremy Kemp (Drake), Kenny Lynch (Sammy Coin), Harold Lang (Shine), Thomas Baptiste (Dambala), Tubby Hayes Quintet (Bailey's Band), Michael Gough (Eric Landor), Isla Blair (Pretty Girl), Jennifer Jayne (Nicolle), Al Mulock (Detective), Christopher Carlos (Vrim), George Mossman (Pony and Trap Driver), Russ Henderson Steel Band (Themselves), Hedger Wallace (Surgeon), Judy Cornwall (Nurse), Faith Kent (Lady in Art Gallery), Brian Hankins (First Male Friend), John Martin (Second Male Friend), Kenneth Kove (Third Male Friend), Walter Sparrow (Second Ambulance Man), Frank Forsyth (Toastmaster), Frank Barry (Johnny Ellis), Irene Richmond (Mrs. Ellis), Laurie Leigh (Nurse), Tauros (Werewolf), James (Simian Artist).

Synopsis

> There is within each of us a twin destiny — the natural and the
> supernatural. The cards are attracted to the supernatural part of
> our destiny.... The strange, the weird, the unknown, the terrify-
> ing.... This deck can forewarn us. I call it, my House of Hor-
> rors. — Dr. Schreck

Five men, all strangers to each other, board a train for a town named Bradford and, just before the train departs, they are joined by a very mysterious looking man named Dr. Schreck (Peter Cushing). During the ride, Dr. Schreck's traveling case falls open and a deck of tarot cards tumbles to the floor of the car. Curious, the men ask the doctor about the cards and he offers to tell them their fortunes:

Werewolf: Passenger Jim Dawson (Neil McCallum), an architect, will be sent to his ancestral home to discuss some alterations with the new owner, Dierdre Biddulph (Ursula Howells). Dawson, however, will die as a result of an ancient family curse, which manifests itself in the form of a werewolf. The werewolf will turn out to be Mrs. Biddulph.

Creeping Vine: Passenger Bill Rogers (Alan Freeman) will return from a vacation with his wife and daughter and will find a new addition in their garden. The intruder is a climbing vine with an almost human intelligence that will not only murder a research botanist, Drake (Jeremy Kemp), whom Rogers has sought for help in destroying the growing menace, but will eventually engulf Rogers' home and trap him and his family within it.

Voodoo: Passenger Biff Bailey (Roy Castle), a jazz musician, will journey to the West Indies and will make the grave mistake of stealing music from a ritual dance he witnesses. The voodoo god Dambala (Thomas Baptiste) himself will follow Biff and will not let him escape vengenace for the sacrilege.

Disembodied Hand: Passenger Franklyn Marsh (Christopher Lee), an art critic, will eventually drive an artist, Eric Landor (Michael Gough), to commit suicide. The artist, however, will exact retribution in the form of his disembodied hand—the hand Marsh severed when he deliberately ran over Landor with his car. The severed hand will continue to haunt Marsh until he has an automobile accident which results in his going blind.

Vampire: Passenger Bob Carroll (Donald Sutherland), a doctor, will return to his New England hometown with his bride, Nicolle (Jennifer Jayne), and will make the horrifying discovery that his wife is a vampire! Encouraged by a colleague, Dr. Blake (Max Adrian), to destroy her, Bob will find that Dr. Blake has ulterior motives in mind. Bob is arrested by the police for his wife's murder. Dr. Blake reveals that the town was too small for two doctors ... and for two vampires!

Their fortunes now told, the five passengers suddenly realize that none of them have any future. They are convinced the train is going to crash. Instead, the train pulls into a deserted station. Their relief is only temporary, however, for they discover that the train has already crashed and that Dr. Schreck is, in reality, the Grim Reaper!

Death awaits you in the Amicus Production, *Dr. Terror's House of Horrors.*

Commentary

Approximately four years after the release of their first full length fantasy film *Horror Hotel* (U.K. release was titled *City of the Dead,* 1959), producers Max Rosenberg and Milton Subotsky began work on a horror film anthology that would make their newly formed film company, Amicus, a serious rival for Hammer's previously held monopoly in the British genre film trade. That film was *Dr. Terror's House of Horrors.*

"I had always admired *Dead of Night* (1945) and thought the time was ripe for another film like it," said Subotsky. "Max had a dreadful time obtaining financing . . . and we nearly stopped shooting the film after the first two weeks. Our British co-financier, Joe Vegoda, came to the rescue with additional investment after part of the American financing was withdrawn. The film was an enormous success everywhere."[1]

Boosted by the appearance of both Peter Cushing and Christopher Lee, the film was rich in atmosphere. The time was indeed ripe for an anthology of this type and would prove to be Amicus' most popular and profitable of film formats. By linking four or five short stories within the framework of a basic premise, it presented audiences with a variety of themes. If one or two of the stories were weak, usually the others made up for the temporary lapse rather than have the entire film fail on the basis of a single story line.

Dr. Terror's House of Horrors, like all of the Amicus film compilations, is a dark fairy tale, and like all fairy tales there is a message or moral to the story. In this instance, Dr. Schreck (Peter Cushing), portrays the Angel of Death who has come to collect five souls. Each of the men gathered in the railway coach has a grim future, as played out by Schreck's deck of tarot cards. Each man's life has only one possible conclusion, the certainty of death. As with all living beings, the final card will always be the same. However, what comes to each in the hereafter is up to the individual while he or she still lives. If one lives an evil life, one's death will be just as tragic. Life is a card game and one can hold a winning or losing hand, but it is death who always holds the final trump card.

Dr. Terror's House of Horrors was a very well-produced film on all levels and cast performances were uniformly good. Of particular note was the exemplary interpretation of Christopher Lee as the terrorized art critic, Franklyn Marsh. Though Peter Cushing was cast in the linking story, he was in fine form and easily managed to rivet audience attention with his mysterious and frightening character, although his on-screen time was limited.

Roy Castle, Peter's costar in the film, who would later make two other films with Cushing (*Dr. Who and the Daleks* in 1965 and *Legend of the Werewolf* in 1974), fondly remembers his initial meeting with Peter on the set. "The first time I filmed with Peter Cushing was in the film with the late-viewing title of *Dr. Terror's House of Horrors*. A young and eager actor in the same film was a Canadian 'bean pole' called Donald Sutherland. I was also an eager young actor!! What went wrong? My first scene was sitting opposite P.C. in a railway carriage. He was the bearer of most distressing news (the Grim Reaper). He was extremely aware of the set lighting and used it very professionally. He was wearing a wide-brimmed hat which cast a shadow over his eyes. As he delivered his spine-chilling lines which ended in the word "Death," he spoke from a shaded face until that last word when he gauged the shadow to slowly move up his face, and at exactly the 'zing' moment, the light revealed his piercing water blue eyes! I knew I was in the company of a great actor."

Michael Gough, who also costarred in *Horror of Dracula* (1957) and *The Skull* (1965), related an amusing incident on the set: "I had to introduce my mother to Peter Cushing. We were sharing a dressing room and I couldn't remember Peter's name! I couldn't remember my mother's name either — she had just remarried!"[2]

Reviews of the film included *The Times* (February 18, 1965) which noted it was "Another occasion for uncritical pleasure. . . . The writer, Mr. Milton Subotsky, has hit on a convenient formula. . . . None of it is very original but at least each of the episodes is short enough not to pall. . . . Mr. Freddie Francis directs with efficiency which once or twice . . . rises to real inspiration." "Rich" in *Variety* (March 10, 1965) said, "Five short horror episodes, thinly linked, provide a usefully chilly package deal which will offer audiences several mild shudders and quite a lot of amusement. . . . The cast, headed by experienced horror practitioners, such as Peter Cushing . . . sensibly play it straight. . . . Helmed by Freddie Francis . . . the film has good production values and several imaginative directing touches."

New York Daily News reporter Ann Guarino gave the picture 3½ stars in her June 19, 1965, review saying, "Horror fans are in for a treat in the English Technicolor production of *Dr. Terror's House of Horrors* . . . they get not one chilling story but 5 episodes. . . . . Skillful direction by Freddie Francis keeps suspense high throughout and though the stories are only predictions, the results are scary. Acting is tops . . . Peter Cushing appears properly mysterious as the fortune teller. . . . The movie reaches a logical conclusion, but it is not for the faint-hearted."

Robert Salmaggi of the *New York Herald Tribune* (June 17, 1965) called the film "a cleverly contrived *Science Fiction* shocker made up of five distinct parts ala *Dead of Night*." He also stated "that each scary adventure will keep you watching, sitting on the edge of your seats one second, laughing the next (there are some deft touches of humor) and all in all, nicely entertained. Peter Cushing, Michael Gough . . . are just some of the very competent actors peopling this polished, well done, package."

Notes

1. Milton Subotsky, interview, *Little Shoppe of Horrors* 2.
2. Michael Gough, interview with Juanita Elefante-Gordon, *Fangoria* 84.

She
(1964)

Credits and Cast

Released April 1965; 104 minutes; Metrocolor and Cinemascope; A Seven Arts–Hammer Film Production; Released through MGM (U.S.) and Pathé-Warner (U.K.); Filmed at MGM-EMI Studios, Elstree, England, and on location in Israel. Director: Robert Day; Producer: Michael Carreras; Associate producer: Aida Young; Screenplay: David T. Chantler; Based on the novel *She* by H. Rider Haggard; Director of photography: Harry Waxman, B.S.C.; Art director: Robert Jones; Supervising editor: James Needs; Production manager: R. L. M. Davidson; Assistant to producer: Ian Lewis; Assistant director: Bruce Sharman; Camera operator; Ernest Day; Editor: Eric Boyd-Perkins; Music composed by James Bernard; Musical supervisor: Philip Martell; Sound recordist: Claude Hitchcock; Sound editors: Jim Groom, Vernon Messenger, Roy Hyde; Continuity: Eileen Head; Makeup: John O'Gorman; Hair stylist: Eileen Warwick; Wardrobe: Jackie Cummins; Assistant art director: Don Mingaye; Research: Andrew Low; Special effects: George Blackwell; Special process: Bowie Films Ltd.; Special effects makeup: Roy Ashton; Construction manager: Arthur Banks; Location manager: Yoske Hausdorf; RCA sound system; Recording director: A. W. Lumkin; Choreography: Cristyne Lawson; Costumes for Miss Andress: Carl Toms.

Ursula Andress (Ayesha), Peter Cushing (Major Horace L. Holly), Bernard Cribbins (Job), John Richardson (Leo Vincey), Christopher Lee (Billali), Rosenda Monteros (Ustane), Andre Morell (Haumeid), John Maxim (Guard Captain), Soraya, Julie Mendez, Lisa Peake (Nightclub Dancers), Cherry Larman, Bula Coleman (Handmaidens), Oo-Bla-Da Dancers.

Synopsis

> *Blimey! They just don't make them like that anymore, sir!* — Job
> to Major Holly

Palestine 1918. At the close of World War I three exsoldiers and comrades, Major Horace L. Holly (Peter Cushing), his valet, Job (Bernard Cribbins), and Leo Vincey (John Richardson), are not looking forward to returning to England and their former dull lives — especially after years of fighting and sampling the excitement and history of the Middle East. Mindful of their future prospects, the men indulge themselves at a local cabaret. While they are enjoying the entertainment, Leo sees an attractive young woman, whose name he later learns is Ustane (Rosenda Monteros), enter the night club. He makes her acquaintance and after a time the two leave together. Walking along a darkened street, Leo is attacked and knocked unconscious. He later reawakens in a strange room where he meets Ayesha (Ursula Andress), an exquisitely beautiful and equally

Ustane (Rosenda Monteros) and Major Holly (Peter Cushing) check their bearings in the Hammer adaptation of H. Rider Haggard's *She.*

mysterious woman with whom he instantly falls in love. She tells him that her city lies near a place called "The Mountains of the Moon"—across the desert and many days' journey from Jerusalem. Ayesha gives Leo a ring and a map and tells him that if he follows her there, she will grant him everything he desires: power, wealth, glory—and herself. Leo agrees to join her and returns to his friends with the map and ring.

Major Holly, who before the war was a professor of archaeology, immediately recognizes the ring as the insignia of the high priest of Isis, some 2,000 years old. He recalls the legend about a group of Egyptians who were banished for killing a high priest named Killikrates. Later they built a secret city somewhere in the mountains—the lost city of Kuma—the very place indicated on the map Ayesha gave to Leo. Holly is most eager to join Leo since such a discovery would be, for him, a crowning achievement. The three men gather supplies and set out for the mountains.

The journey is a very hard and dangerous one, and eventually the elements, as well as an attack by Arab bandits, claim Leo's strength and he collapses. Ustane, who had been following them at a discreet distance, rushes to Leo's side and helps him to recover. She leads the men to her village near Kuma. When the primitive natives see Leo's face, they are greatly disturbed. Their leader, Haumeid (Andre Morell), Ustane's father, explains that Leo is the image of Killikrates. He shows Holly the medallion he wears which bears a cameo of Killikrates and Holly sees that the likeness is striking. Meanwhile, the natives, fearful of Leo's presence, are about to sacrifice him to their god when Ayesha's high priest, Billali (Christopher Lee), and her guards arrive to stop them. Leo and his friends are taken to the sacred city of Kuma to meet its queen, Ayesha, and under Ustane's care, Leo recovers. Later he is summoned to Ayesha's chambers, and once again he is overwhelmed by her beauty. Ayesha tells Leo that he is Killikrates reborn and that she is an immortal being, having bathed in the fires of the Eternal Flame—a secret revealed to her by an old mystic whom she had come upon in the desert during her banishment for murder—the murder of her lover, Killikrates. She has mourned for many centuries but was sure that one day her love would return to her, and now he has—reincarnated as Leo Vincey. Ayesha shows Leo the secret chamber that houses the Eternal Flame and promises that when the time is right, they will bathe in the cool flames of immortality.

Ustane, who is in love with Leo, knows that she cannot compete with the queen and comes to Leo's rooms to say goodbye. Leo kisses her and their embrace is seen by Ayesha, whose jealousy over a similar scene 2,000 years ago led to Killikrates' death. Ayesha orders that Ustane is to be executed. Leo tries to intervene but Ayesha offers him a choice, her own death or Ustane's. Leo cannot kill Ayesha and surrenders to her will. Due to their meddling, Holly and Job are banished from the city.

Later, Ustane's ashes are given to her father, Haumeid. In a fit of rage, Haumeid and the natives revolt against the queen and her minions. Major Holly and Job rush back to the city to try to save Leo. Ayesha tells Leo that the time has come to enter the flame. Billali, who has always sought immortality for himself as his due for faithfully serving the queen, challenges Leo. They fight and Billali is killed. Before Holly and Job can get to him, Leo and Ayesha enter the flames. Leo is made an immortal. Ayesha, however, inexplicably begins to age and soon crumbles to dust. Holly tells Leo that he believes one can only utilize the powers of the Eternal Flame once, and that to enter the fires a second time would reverse its effects. Leo tells Holly that he longs for the day when the flames will once again cool so that he too can undue his fate. As it was with Ayesha, it is now Leo who waits.

Commentary

We spent two weeks in Israel where it was so hot the moisture just went out of us. We had to keep eating salt all the time. Filming had to begin at 4 o'clock in the morning because by half-past three in the afternoon the cameras started to melt!—Peter Cushing[1]

I had to ride a camel. Now that is a mode of transport I do not recommend to the uninitiated, especially when that capricious quadruped takes it into its mulish head to sit down and/or get up, which was all too often in my experience. (If you are ever in contact with one, be warned—get nowhere near its breath!)—Peter Cushing[2]

Hammer's 1964 version of *She*, based on H. Rider Haggard's novel (first published in 1886—selling well over 83 million copies in 44 languages) was actually the fifth time the story had been adapted for the screen.[3]

According to press information released by Pathé-Warner (the U.K. distributors for the film), producer Michael Carreras and director Robert Day opted to shoot the exteriors in Israel (site of another Haggard novel, *King Solomon's Mines*) instead of in Africa, where Haggard's *She* originally took place. Day found the perfect site—the Negev Desert and the legendary mountains of the ancient king's mines—which he felt were necessary to recreate the mysterious and awesome atmosphere of *She*. Interiors were completed back in England at Elstree Studios, whose sound stages were transformed into "the giant caves, the massive main chamber of the lost city of Kuma, the exotic volcanic gardens, the cliff caves of the Amahagger warriors and the Arab night club in Jerusalem."

In an article for *ABC Film Review* (March 1965), author John Doran accompanied cast and crew during the film's shoot in southern Israel. Every morning six huge army trucks, loaded with the unit's equipment, would depart from their hotel in Eilat (a small but modern town with a population of about 12,000) for the desert. "We arrived at the first location after a drive of 90 hair-raising minutes," Doran reported. "The one road out of Eilat—little more than a narrow strip of tar over the undulating sand—provided the Israeli drivers with great sport. Whenever they met a truck coming in the opposite direction, the drive developed into a 'chicken' run, with the first one off the road a 'cissy.'"

According to Doran, after the equipment was set up, rehearsals would normally begin around 8:00 A.M. However, by then, the sun had already changed the sky from "early morning blue to off white ... to scorch the film-makers." Makeup had to be constantly checked and the makeup crew were forever applying "a fine spray of moisture to the artist's faces. This had to be done, not for their comfort, but to ensure that they appeared to be sweating when they came to film the scene. No one shows visible signs of perspiration in the Negev. It's too hot!"

Although the intense heat was dangerous enough, it was not the only threat to the cast and crew. Doran remembered one unscheduled break in the shoot. "It occurred when one of the technicians put up a huge umbrella and a large black scorpion fell to the ground. Immediately it froze — its venomous tail raised to strike. A heavy Israeli boot was raised and fell, and the threat was removed. 'No need to worry about the black scorpions,' said the local. 'Their bite only make you very bad. It's the yellow one you watch out for. If they bite — you dead!'" It was a typical day's outing and all for the sake of about three and one half minutes of film!

She, although badly dated even in 1965 when the Hammer film was originally released, still holds some minor interest and appeal for today's audiences. Interiors were on the skimpy side, but costumes, special effects, and makeup were all assets to the production. James Bernard's score for *She* was beautifully arranged and Harry Waxman's photography was also a plus.

With a superior cast that included Cushing, Andre Morell, and Christopher Lee, this version would have fared far worse if not for their combined talents. Though all three merely play second fiddle to the story's lovers, it's worth watching for Lee's duel to the death and Cushing's attempt at belly dancing! Ursula Andress and John Richardson, as the film's eternal lovers, are compatible in only one respect — the woodiness of their performances. Though they just barely manage to get by, it's more than obvious that both were hired merely for their stunning looks and, in the former's case, the fact that Andress was still bankable due to her appearance in the phenomenally successful James Bond film, *Dr. No* (1962).

Director Robert Day, whose work included five Tarzan movies and who would also be directing Peter in his 1967 television appearance in "The Avengers" ("Return of the Cybernauts"), was able to carry the film adequately, even though David T. Chantler's screenplay had about as many peaks and valleys as the mountains of the moon itself. Day handles the action scenes well, but otherwise the script and subject matter only hamper him.[4]

As expected, most critics went for the film's throat in their reviews. *Time* (September 17, 1965) claimed that "*She* is for children, television addicts and those who relish cinema clichés. . . . Miss Andress . . . with the help of a makeup man has to demonstrate at the fadeout what a 2,000-year-old woman really looks like. She doesn't look a day over 1,500." The *Christian Science Monitor* (F.H.G., August 19, 1965) felt that "Peter Cushing and Bernard Cribbins [were] livelier and more sympathetic as his [Richardson's] loyal fortune-hunting friends. . . . The fantastic story keeps tripping over its own logic, but plods ahead with stony-faced insistence on its own grandeur." The *Saturday Review* (May 8, 1965) called it "a curious compote of *King Solomon's Mines* and *Lost Horizon.*" The *British Monthly Film Bulletin* referred to the film as "a flat and uninspired affair." *The*

New Yorker (Brendan Gill, September 11, 1965) was critical of director Day, saying, "The picture, which features rich color and bargain-basement dialogue, has been directed by Robert Day in a style that is nearly as old as the princess and every bit as tiresome." *Variety* (April 21, 1965) was a little kinder, reporting that "Current . . . filming of Haggard's fantasy adds color and widescreen to special effects, all of which help overcome a basic plot no film scripter has yet licked . . . boasts lively direction and good per-formances. . . . Production values save the day, with crowd scenes and palace pomp worthy of far more expensive films . . . art direction . . . cameraman . . . and . . . costumer can all take a bow." However, the *New York Times* (Bosley Crowther, September 2, 1965) gave *She* its most scath-ing review, stating that it was "ridiculously old-fashioned . . . everything about the picture . . . looks old and distinctly unmodern. It lacks style, sophistication, humor, sense and, above all, a reason for being since it isn't even as good . . . as the last remake of *She* done . . . in 1935. Peter Cushing and Bernard Cribbins are foolish as his [Richardson's] veddy English friends . . . screenplay and the direction of Robert Day are as fustian as such can be." And Kathleen Carroll of the *New York Daily News* gave *She* only 2½ stars saying, "Cushing is by far the best for his cynical attitude towards this nonsense."

Notes

1. Mike Nunn, "The Nicer Side of Peter Cushing," (source unknown).
2. Cushing, *Past Forgetting*.
3. *She* was originally filmed in 1908 (this version, however, lasted only 5 minutes!) It was filmed again in 1910 (in a 9-minute version). In 1925 a British ver-sion was filmed, starring Betty Blyth, and in 1935 RKO filmed *She* in Hollywood with Helen Gahagan in the lead role.
4. Robert Day directed Gordon Scott in *Tarzan the Magnificent* (1960); Jock Mahoney in *Tarzan's Three Challenges* (1963); and Mike Henry in *Tarzan and the Valley of Gold* (1966), *Tarzan and the Great River* (1967), and *Tarzan and the Jungle Boy* (1968). Day also directed Boris Karloff in two films in the 1950s: *The Haunted Strangler* (1958) and *Corridors of Blood* (1958), which also starred Christopher Lee.

Dr. Who and the Daleks
(1965)

Credits and Cast

Released June 1965 (U.K.), May 1966 (U.S.); 83 minutes (U.K.), 85 minutes (U.S.); Technicolor; Techniscope; An AARU Production; Released through Regal Films and British Lion (U.K.), and Continental–Walter Reade–Sterling (U.S.); Filmed at Shepperton Studios, England. Director: Gordon Flemyng; Producers: Milton Subotsky, Max J. Rosenberg; Executive producer: Joe Vegoda; Screenplay: Milton Subotsky; Based on the BBC television series by Terry Nation; Director of photography: John Wilcox; Music composed and conducted by Malcolm Lockyer; Electronic music: Barry Gray; Art direction: Bill Constable; Set decorations: Scott Slimon; Editor: Oswald Hafenrichter; Sound: Buster Ambler; Special effects: Ted Samuels; Makeup: Jill Carpenter; Hairstyles: Henry Montash; Wardrobe: Jackie Cummins; Production manager: Ted Lloyd; Assistant director: Anthony Waye.

Peter Cushing (Dr. Who), Roy Castle (Ian Chesterton), Jennie Linden (Barbara), Roberta Tovey (Susan), Barrie Ingham (Alydon), Geoffrey Toone (Temmosus), Mark Petersen (Elyon), John Bown (Antodus), Michael Coles (Ganatus), Yvonne Antrobus (Dyoni).

Synopsis

While giving his granddaughter's boyfriend, Ian Chesterton (Roy Castle), a brief tour of the TARDIS (Time and Relative Dimensions in Space), a time machine camouflaged as a British police call box, Dr. Who (Peter Cushing) and his granddaughters Susan (Roberta Tovey) and Barbara (Jennie Linden) are accidentally transported to an unknown planet in another time when Ian inadvertently sets the time machine in motion.

As a result of a neutron bomb war many years ago, the planet has been reduced to a petrified world where plants and animals crumble to dust when touched. The only inhabitants are two divergent species of beings—the Thals, a peaceful race of humanoids, and the Daleks, non-humanoid creatures who, because of the toxic atmosphere, must live encased in metal, robotic bodies. The Daleks, who are the reciprocal enemies of the Thals, capture Dr. Who and his group. They plan to use them in their plot to destroy the Thals, becoming the sole masters of their planet.

Utilizing Susan as their emissary, the Daleks send her to the Thals' encampment in search of the drug the Thals have developed to make them immune to the poisonous air. Since the doctor and the others are affected by the air quality, Susan manages to gain the Thals' confidence and is given the antidote. The Daleks, however, hope that they can adapt the drug to use on themselves so that they can finally be free from their restrictive armor cases. When the drug fails to give them immunity, the Daleks decide to set off another neutron bomb, this time to hopefully destroy the remaining Thals. Dr. Who and his associates manage to escape from the city, and joining forces with the Thals, help them to overthrow the Daleks' despotic rule.

THE WILDEST SPACE ADVENTURE ON...OR OFF THE EARTH !

Half Men...Half Machines... "THE DALEKS" rule a scorched planet with an iron hand— and they plot to rule the Universe!

WALTER READE-STERLING presents

"Dr. WHO AND THE DALEKS"

Starring
PETER CUSHING · ROY CASTLE · JENNIE LINDEN · ROBERTA TOVEY
Executive Producer JOE VEGODA · Producers MILTON SUBOTSKY and MAX J. ROSENBERG · Director GORDON FLEMYNG
Screenplay by MILTON SUBOTSKY · From the Original BBC-TV Serial by TERRY NATION · A LION INTERNATIONAL FILM
TECHNISCOPE° and TECHNICOLOR° CONTINENTAL

T H E A T R E

Leaving the planet in the Thals' care, Dr. Who, his granddaughters, and Ian return to earth but because the TARDIS isn't functioning up to par, they arrive about 2,000 years too soon!

Commentary

> It seems a shame Bill [William Hartnell] isn't doing the film because he's so good in the part. I remember how I felt when they were casting for the film 1984. I was so keen to repeat my TV role, but they gave it to Edmond O'Brien instead. All part of life's ups and downs. — Peter Cushing[1]

AARU Production's screen version of the immensely popular British television hero and his archenemies the Daleks had originated in the fertile mind of author Terry Nation. Milton Subotsky's screenplay was an adaptation of Nation's seven-episode serial, "The Dead Planet," which first appeared in its televised version on November 23, 1963. The Daleks would go on to appear in ten more serials (sixty-six episodes in all) before the BBC eventually dropped them from the series.[2]

According to press releases from AARU, the Daleks were described as "a gelatinous mass of intensified brain power which was the product of mutations after radiation fall-out. They had developed a cone-shaped shell from which to operate . . . . The robot's power was seemingly limitless with its capacity of directing rays that could either kill or paralyze, depending on the mood of the living brain embedded in its interior. Generated by electricity conducted through metal floors, the Daleks were able to glide through their custom-made city bent on destroying any other form of life."

However, though it appeared that these alien creatures were quite formidable, Dr. Who, the exiled Time lord, could be trusted to come up with more than a few tricks of his own with which to combat the evil Daleks and any other malevolent force in the universe. As one of a race of superintelligent, scientifically minded humanoids, Dr. Who uses his vast intellect in lieu of more visceral emotions to eventually defeat the Daleks each and every time.

Producers Subotsky and Rosenberg were confident that their screen adaptation would heighten overseas audience interest in the good doctor and might, in turn, result in a series of spinoffs. When *Dr. Who and the Daleks* failed at U.S. box offices, Subotsky blamed it solely on poor distribution. This may, to an extent, be true but perhaps the primary reasons were more attributable to the AARU production itself and the fact that the British television series never took off in America.

Dr. Who and the Daleks' austere budget, script redundancy, and prosaic production values were the film's main drawbacks. The Daleks themselves were another big flaw. More sophisticated audiences probably could not help but compare the robotic aliens to rather ornate salt and pepper shakers. Also, one had to chuckle over what the film described as its futuristic alien gadgetry and which turned out to be nothing more than cardboard computer paneled walls and lava lamps! The film's dialogue was geared to the most elementary of literacy levels that even Saturday matinee crowds would have found insulting. The musical score by Malcolm Lockyer and Barry Gray was in a word, dreadful!

It was, without a doubt, in Peter Cushing's favor that he managed to wade through all this muck and mire and still give an energetic performance. Although portrayed as a kindly, compassionate figure, Cushing's Dr. Who was a little too clichéd in the absent-minded professor mode to suit the tastes of most American audiences.

To a minor extent, Cushing did have his work cut out for him right from the beginning. In an interview with Mike Munn for his article entitled, "The Nicer Side of Peter Cushing," Cushing revealed his biggest handicap. "The difficulty with playing Dr. Who on the screen," Peter explained, "was that one couldn't expect everyone in the world to know about him and his TARDIS and the television series. So we decided to play him simply as a professor who has invented this machine that travels through time and space and I created my own character out of that idea, realizing that a lot of people in Britain might be disappointed. Actually, most people weren't."

While it is true that *Dr. Who and the Daleks* did place in Britain's top twenty box office hits of 1965, it wasn't due to the critical notices the film received. "Rich" in *Variety* (July 7, 1965) referred to the film as "A slice of sci-fi for beginners. . . . A few more thrills and a rather more edged script would have made *Dr. Who* a shade more acceptable. . . . Gordon Flemying has played his direction straight. . . . [However] his chore would have been helped if the screenplay had had a little more bite and inventiveness. Peter Cushing plays Dr. Who with amiable gravity. . . . It will be interesting to see how [*Daleks*] stands up to stiffer Yank 'sci fi' competition." *The Times* (June 24, 1965) astutely pointed out that "The technical advantages of the cinema over the television only show up the shoddiness of the sets and the dialogue . . . is too feeble even to be funny."

Peter Cushing had not made any stage appearances since 1959 due to his heavy schedule of motion picture and television work. However, he did manage one theatrical appearance in a comedy written by Ben Travers. The play was *Thark!* which opened in the West End of London at the Garrick Theatre and was directed by Ray Cooney.

A former member of the American Peter Cushing Club, Rukmani

Singh Devi, attended one of Cushing's performances and gave members her own personal account of the experience: "a stylish flat of the 1920s peopled by cavorting flappers, jealous matrons and unsuccessful lotharios; and later a sombre Norfolk seat complete with thunder, lightning and an old family retainer named 'Death.' An Englishman's home is his castle and both these 'castles' belong to Sir Hector Benbow [Peter Cushing]. *Thark!* is the starkly descriptive name of the Benbow's manor house. Most of the action involves fiancées and wives who are suspicious of the fiancés'/ husbands' intentions towards third parties. And all to no avail. For the men, though caught in compromising situations, are innocent of all but the most meager intentions. *Thark!* is a farce . . . the result is a well-tempered look at preposterous zanies. The dialogue lacks the sophistication of Noel Coward and the actor is therefore more pressed to create the necessary color and spirit. If you've never seen Mr. Cushing in a comedy, you've missed a delight. Watching him turn into a flustered inciter of reprisals one sees true inspiration. The dishevelled hair and wild glance of someone who lives in a nonsensical universe—and realises it."[3]

In between his film and theatrical commitments, Peter also made a guest star appearance on "The Bernard Cribbins Show," a British television variety show hosted by Cushing's costar and friend from *She*. Cribbins would also appear the following year, along with Peter, in AARU's Dr. Who–Daleks sequel, *Daleks Invasion Earth 2150 A.D.*

Notes

1. Dick Tatham, "Peter the Great," *My Weekly*, August 23, 1969.
2. Although AARU is, in reality, Amicus, the picture was released under this pseudonym due solely to the insistence of the film's financial backer.
3. *The American Peter Cushing Club Journal* 5.

The Skull
(1965)

Credits and Cast

Released August 1965; 83 minutes; Technicolor; An Amicus Production; Released through Paramount (U.S.); Filmed at Shepperton Studios, England, and on location. Director: Freddie Francis; Producers: Milton Subotsky, Max J. Rosenberg; Screenplay: Milton Subotsky; Based on *The Skull of the Marquis de Sade* by Robert Bloch; Director of photography: John Wilcox; Editor: O. Hofferstein; Production design: Bill Constable, Scott Sliman; Music: Elisabeth Lutyens; Special effects: Ted Samuels.

Peter Cushing (Christopher Maitland), Christopher Lee (Sir Matthew Phillips), Jill Bennett (Jane Maitland), Patrick Wymark (Anthony Marco), George Coulouris (Dr. Londe), Nigel Green (Police Inspector Wilson), Peter Woodthorpe (Mr. Travers), Michael Gough (Auctioneer), April Olrich (French Girl), Anna Palk (Maid), Maurice Good (Phrenologist), Frank Forsyth (Judge), Patrick Magee (Police Surgeon), Paul Stockman (First Guard), Geoffrey Cheshire (Second Guard), Jack Silk (Driver), George Hilsdon (Policeman).

Synopsis

In a wild, long-abandoned graveyard in early nineteenth-century France, a phrenologist (Maurice Good) has paid grave robbers to open the coffin of the infamous Marquis de Sade. Decapitating the corpse, he returns to his home and places the head in acid to remove any remaining skin on the skull. Since the phrenologist's field is the study of human character and mental capacity based on skull development, he hopes to unravel some of the mystery surrounding the marquis' evil behavior. The phrenologist's study of the skull, however, is short-lived. His body is found by his mistress (April Olrich) floating in a bathtub with his throat cut. Soon after, she too is murdered by a friend of the late phrenologist, Dr. Londe (George Coulouris). The skull disappears.

The story picks up in present-day England where fellow collectors of the occult, Sir Matthew Phillips (Christopher Lee) and Christopher Maitland (Peter Cushing), vie for unique collectibles at an auction. Maitland notices that his friend, Sir Matthew, is behaving oddly, but before he can determine the cause, he is approached by a dealer, Anthony Marco (Patrick Wymark) who informs him that he has some items of interest to the collector.

Later that night, Marco brings a book, bound in human skin, and sells it to Maitland. The book is a biography of the Marquis de Sade. Maitland's interest in the marquis is piqued. Marco returns the next evening with the actual skull of the marquis, but Maitland is skeptical of its authenticity. He meets with his friend, Sir Matthew, who tells him the skull is not only authentic but still possessed of the demon spirit that had once taken possession of the marquis—which might explain the fact that the marquis was thought to be insane by his contemporaries. Sir Matthew cautions Maitland against obtaining the skull as it was once in his collection and he was relieved when it was stolen. Sir Matthew believes the skull to be pure evil and that it will possess whoever owns it, especially during the cycle of the new moon when it is at the height of its powers.

Maitland heeds Sir Matthew's advice at first, but soon becomes more and more obsessed with the skull. He begins to have all too real nightmares. In one dream he actually finds himself at Marco's apartment—

On the set of *The Skull*. Left to right: Patrick Wymark, Peter Cushing, director Freddie Francis, Nigel Green (standing), and Patrick Magee.

as if the skull were drawing him there to possess it. Eventually, Maitland goes to buy it but instead finds Marco dead — his throat cut. Maitland calls the police but hides the skull in a hall closet of the apartment building. When he returns later, he is confronted by the landlord who tries to blackmail him. Maitland murders him and leaves with the skull.

Slowly he too is becoming possessed by the demon that inhabits the skull. But when it tries to have Maitland kill his wife (Jill Bennett), he manages to overcome the demon's hold on his mind. Demanding that a sacrifice be made, the skull takes Maitland's life instead for his disobedience.

Commentary

> *Other things I have learnt how to do in the line of duty include snooker ... my contestant being Christopher Lee, who came to a sticky end on the green baize amongst an assortment of colored balls. I'd turned rather beastly and hit him over the head with something hard (a statue?) ... but I don't think it was because I was losing the frame.* — Peter Cushing[1]

The Skull was Amicus' next production after *Dr. Terror's House of Horrors.* However, instead of the latter film's multistory theme, which had proved enormously successful with audiences, Milton Subotsky (producer and screenplay writer on the film) adapted Robert Bloch's eight-page short story "The Skull of the Marquis de Sade" into a full length feature with a single storyline. Subotsky revealed that this picture fulfilled a longtime ambition: "I read Robert Bloch's . . . story . . . and saw that it could be turned into the kind of film I had always dreamed about—a film with almost no dialogue. The picture was made on a very low budget. It's a fantastic film and, I think, will someday be considered a horror classic."[2]

Filmed at Shepperton Studios, most of the movie was shot on one composite set which consisted of five rooms and a hallway. Although the picture was criticized for its sometimes dark and murky photography, art director Bill Constable explained the reasons for this, "I knew that the Skull had to move about, that it was white or light ivory, and I had therefore to keep the walls dark. I had black-painted woodwork everywhere and dark blue wallpaper so that we could see it at any time."[3]

Constable's concepts are nicely executed and give the skull an almost three-dimensional look without the use of special photographic equipment. Bill Constable also had to improvise on a scene which involved Peter Cushing during the film's dream sequence: "In one scene Peter Cushing was trapped in a small room with the walls closing in on him. The 'walls' had to be built in trucks and pushed in. My biggest worry was that the crew pushing them in wouldn't stop in time!"[4]

Most of the film's technical aspects are correspondingly impressive. Freddie Francis' direction is very good. However, the film could have benefited from some tighter editing. In an effort to build suspense, certain key scenes tend to drag on too long. On the whole, though, *The Skull* is one of the genre's better productions of the 1960s.

Freddie Francis gave a little more insight into his participation in the film. "I think I can say in all modesty that most touches and gimmicks . . . have been all my own work. . . . The idea of shooting through the Skull was my idea. . . . In fact I operated the camera on those shots. I had an Aeroflex which I was holding in my hands with the Skull mounted on the front. I was wearing roller skates and was being pushed about as if I was moving and chasing Peter Cushing. . . . [It has been said that] it must have been hard for Peter to play to this skull mask. In actual fact, of course, when one considers the number of things Peter has to do merely playing to the camera, it probably was, in a sense, rather easier for him to have the . . . thing he was playing to actually there to play at."[5]

The film's greatest asset was its marvelous cast which included Christopher Lee, Patrick Wymark, Nigel Green, Jill Bennett, Michael Gough, and Patrick Magee—even though the latter four have very brief appearances. *The Skull*, however, is Peter's film and gives him an ideal opportunity upon which to build his character, Christopher Maitland.

Like some avid collectors, Maitland is obsessed with his hobby. *The Skull* merely plays upon the more bizarre slants of this pastime by turning a mild-mannered, civilized man into a man possessed.

The Skull also presents an interesting concept. While focusing on the historical Marquis de Sade, it attempts to theorize that perhaps de Sade himself was possessed by a demon spirit — justifying the reason for his cruel and perverse behavior. This angle comes off very convincingly in the film.

Milton Subotsky put it quite simply when he said, "A true horror film is the story of man versus the unknown. Sometimes the unknown wins, sometimes the man."[6] In *The Skull*, man, unfortunately, loses.

Some of the critical reviews of *The Skull* included: *Variety* ("Mosk," August 4, 1965), "classy shudder film . . . script is sound except for dragging in some scenes for effect only. . . . The right ascetic approach is given by Peter Cushing as the determined collector." *British Monthly Film Bulletin*, in its review wrote, "directed by Freddie Francis with an individual flair which far outstrips the standard gimmicks of the genre."

In 1965 at the Third Trieste Fantascience Film Festival author Robert Bloch was given an award for his short story, "The Skull of the Marquis de Sade."

Notes

1. Cushing, *Past Forgetting.*
2. Milton Subotsky, interview, *Little Shoppe of Horrors* 2.
3. Paramount press book manual for *The Skull*, 1965.
4. Paramount press book.
5. Freddie Francis, interview, *Little Shoppe of Horrors* 2. Francis would use the same technique in *The Creeping Flesh* (1972)—shooting through the eye socket in the skeleton's face.
6. Milton Subotsky, *Shriek* 2, October 1965. London: The House of Horror.

Island of Terror
(1966)

Credits and Cast

Released June 1966; 89 minutes; Eastman color; A Planet Production; Released through Universal; Filmed at Pinewood Studios, London. Director: Terence Fisher; Producer: Tom Blakeley; Executive producers: Richard Gordon, Gerald A.

Fernback; Screenplay: Edward Andrew Mann, Allan Ramsen; Director of photography: Reg Wyer; Art director: John St. John Earl; Editor: Thelma Connell; Production manager: Roy Baird; Camera: Frank Drake; Continuity: Kay Mander; Sound: Bob McPhee; Wardrobe: Rosemary Burrows; Makeup: Binty Phillips; Hairdresser: Stella Rivers; Special effects makeup: Billy Partleton; Special effects: John St. John Earl, Michael Albrechtson.

Peter Cushing (Dr. Stanley), Edward Judd (Dr. West), Carole Gray (Toni), Eddie Byrne (Dr. Landers), Sam Kydd (Constable Harris), Niall MacGinnis (Campbell), James Caffrey (Argyle), Liam Gaffney (Bellows), Roger Heathcote (Donley), Keith Bell (Halsey), Shay Gorman (Morton), Peter Forbes-Robinson (Dr. Phillips), Richard Bidlake (Carson), Joyce Hemson (Mrs. Bellows), Edward Ogden (Pilot).

Synopsis

> *Watch it boy, or I'll sue you for malpractice.* — Dr. Stanley to Dr. West, soon after having his hand amputated with an axe.

A new shipment of chemicals is brought to Dr. Phillips' (Peter Forbes-Robinson) cancer research center on a remote island off the Irish coast. The doctor is somewhat of a recluse and several of the island's leading citizens — Dr. Landers (Eddie Byrne), Constable Harris (Sam Kydd), and Mr. Campbell (Nial MacGinnis) are uncertain of his actual work. They also bemoan the island's lack of a telephone system and the once-a-week-only ship from the mainland.

At his research center Dr. Phillips decides to go ahead with a new experiment without confirmation from similar centers in Rome, New York, and Tokyo. There is an explosion.

Ian Bellows (Liam Gaffney), out walking, investigates a strange electronic sound coming from a cave. He enters the cave and screams.

His wife (Joyce Hemson), concerned by his lateness, asks Harris to search for him. He finds Ian's body — or is it? — in the cave, totally devoid of bone structure. The constable reports his findings to a skeptical Dr. Landers who decides, after seeing the body, that a specialist is needed.

Dr. Stanley (Peter Cushing), a London pathologist, agrees to help. He contacts Dr. West (Edward Judd), a bone specialist, to join the investigation. West's girlfriend Toni (Carole Gray) wrangles her way by securing her father's helicopter for the return trip to the island. Their consensus, after an autopsy, is that Ian was attacked by an enzyme that consumes human bones.

The three doctors drive to the center to secure Dr. Phillips' help, but find that he is beyond theirs. He — and the rest of his staff — are in the same state as Ian Bellows. Stanley gathers Phillips' notes and learns that he was trying to create an organism that would devour cancer cells.

Dr. Stanley is about to lose his hand but not his resolve in *Island of Terror*.

Harris; looking for Dr. Landers, just misses them at the center. While investigating the horror there, Harris is attacked by a snake-like appendage.

With Toni, the doctors return to the center to find Harris dead and are attacked by the creatures that have mutated from Phillips' experiment. Landers is killed while attacking one with an axe. Stanley leads West and Toni to safety as the creatures divide in half.

Stanley and West explain the situation to Campbell, who informs the doctors that animals have been dying in the same manner as the humans. At a town meeting Campbell informs the panic-stricken islanders of the danger and plans an attack.

Guns, fire, and explosives have little or no effect, and each passing moment brings the creatures closer to dividing. A dead creature is discovered and Stanley decides that it had eaten a radiation-poisoned dog. He plans to return to the center for Strontium 90 and inject the remaining cattle, which have become the creature's main food supply.

He and West secure the radioactive material but, as Stanley loads it into the car, he is seized around the wrist by a tentacle. West, unable to free him, chops off Stanley's hand with an axe.

Stanley survives the grisly amputation, but is now virtually useless in fighting the creatures. The islanders huddle together, waiting to see if Stanley's theory is correct. After an agonizing delay, the creatures begin feeding on the cattle, and, after an equally agonizing delay, begin to die.

In Tokyo a lab technician enters a cancer research laboratory and, soon after hearing a strange electronic sound, screams.

Commentary

Island of Terror was the first of two similar science fiction films starring Peter Cushing, directed by Terence Fisher, and produced by Planet Films. Both are concerned with an isolated community placed in peril by a seemingly unstoppable alien force. In Island of Terror the danger comes from a botched experiment. The enemy in Night of the Big Heat (1967) is from space. Neither are terribly convincing as destructive forces and both films rely more on their casts than on special effects.

While neither film is representative of the best work of the actors or director, Island of Terror is the better of the pair and is an enjoyable effort from all concerned.

Executive producer Richard Gordon has a rich tradition in the horror-science fiction field and is perhaps the only producer to have worked with Bela Lugosi, Boris Karloff, Christopher Lee, and Peter Cushing. Gordon was behind two of Boris Karloff's finest post–1940s films—Corridors of Blood and The Haunted Strangler (both 1958). Interviewed by Tom Weaver, he revealed that "Island of Terror came to me when Gerry Fernback sent me a screenplay called The Night the Silicates Came. I read it and really thought it was one of the best finished science ficton/horror screenplays that I'd read for a very long time. I thought Island of Terror turned out well—in fact, even when I look at it now, I must say that for a picture of its era it worked extremely well."[1]

He also served as executive producer on a cofeature, The Projected Man. Budgetary problems caused him to devote more time on this film than he had intended, pulling him away from Island of Terror. As a result, he could not spend as much time working with Peter Cushing and Terence Fisher as he would have liked. He described Cushing to the authors as "an excellent, highly professional actor and a very nice man. I'm sorry that I didn't have the opportunity to work with him again."

Peter Cushing's performance as Dr. Stanley is very amusing and is a departure from the more straight-laced, serious characters with which he is usually associated. Dr. Stanley is something of a "character" and is not above the occasional wisecrack aside—even at the expense of his amputated hand. Early in the film he makes a joke while riding in a car and quickly glances at the others for their approval. It is a small moment, but typical of the detail that Cushing invests in his characters. This bit of business establishes Stanley as, perhaps, not as sure of himself as he seems and gives him a vulnerability that a lesser actor could never have conveyed.

Unfortunately, Terence Fisher's direction is a bit limp, and in no way approaches his excellent work with Peter Cushing at Hammer. Author Harry Ringel said that Fisher replaced "Bernard Robinson's planned ornateness with indifferent location shooting. Thematically, [the Planet films] fall victim to the subordination of character to concept trap which science fiction so often sets, and which Fisher had worked so hard to avoid in his horror movies."[2]

The supporting cast is adequate, with only Carole Gray seeming out of place. Her character does nothing for the film. She is there simply because it was assumed that the audience required an attractive woman (which she is). The plot contrivance of her father owning a helicopter is absurd and, once on the island, she is quickly reduced to the standard female in distress.

The creatures seem sadly ineffective in 1991 due to the giant strides in special effects over the past two decades, but they were acceptable by the standards of the mid-1960s. According to Richard Gordon, they were moved "mostly with wires, being pulled along the ground — there was no stop motion photography or anything like that."[3]

Concerning his amputation scene, Peter Cushing told the authors: "I think it's a pity to let audiences know how special effects are achieved in films — it spoils the illusion. In any case in this particular instance, it was really done by the editing, and when I was handless in the scene that followed the amputation, I had a jacket with one sleeve just a little longer than the other which helped to give the impression of a foreshortened arm."

As in many low-budget films of this type, *Island of Terror* works best when no special effects are used and the tension is built through the writing, direction, and acting. The real suspense stems from the character's isolation and vulnerability.

Variety (March 22, 1967) stated, "Peter Cushing, whose performances in this type of role are always above average, is properly brusque and has a wryly objective point of view. He also varies between heroism and cowardice, creating a character with natural, not exaggerated fears and hesitations."

Peter Cushing was fairly inactive during 1966 and, other than his limited film work, appeared in only one television production, "Monica."

Notes

1. Tom Weaver, *Interviews with B Science Fiction and Horror Movie Makers.*
2. Harry Ringel, *Cinefantastique* 4, no. 3.
3. Weaver, *Interviews with B Science Fiction and Horror Movie Makers.*

Daleks Invasion Earth 2150 A.D.
(1966)

Credits and Cast

Released July 1966 (U.K.), June 1967 (U.S.); 84 minutes; Technicolor, Techniscope; An AARU Production; Released through British Lion (U.K.), and Continental–Walter Reade–Sterling (U.S.); Filmed at Shepperton Studios, England. Director: Gordon Flemyng; Producers: Max J. Rosenberg, Milton Subotsky; Executive producer: Joe Vegoda; Screenplay: Milton Subotsky; Based on the BBC television series by Terry Nation; Additional dialogue: David Whittaker; Director of photography: John Wilcox; Music composed and conducted by Bill McGuffie; Electronic music by Barry Gray; Editor: Ann Chegwidden; Art direction: George Provis; Set decorations: Maurice Pelling; Special effects: Ted Samuels; Sound: John Cox, Buster Ambler; Wardrobe: Jackie Cummins; Makeup: Bunty Phillips; Hairstyles: Bobbie Smith; Production manager: Ted Wallis; Assistant director: Anthony Waye.

Peter Cushing (Dr. Who), Bernard Cribbins (Tom Campbell), Ray Brooks (David), Andrew Keir (Wyler), Roberta Tovey (Susan), Jill Curzon (Louise), Roger Avon (Wells), Keith Marsh (Conway), Geoffrey Cheshire (Roboman), Steve Peters (Leader Roboman); Philip Madoc (Brockley), Eddie Powell (Thompson), Godfrey Quigley (Dortmun), Tony Reynolds (Man on Bicycle), Bernard Spear (Man with Carrier Bag), Sheila Steafel (Young Woman), Eileen Way (Old Woman), Kenneth Watson (Craddock), John Wreford (Robber), Robert Jewell (Leader Dalek Operator).

Synopsis

> *Obey motorized dustbins? We'll see about that!* — Resistance
> Fighter Dortmun

In an attempt to report a burglary in progress, London constable Tom Campbell (Bernard Cribbins) stumbles into a police call box only to find that he has entered Dr. Who's (Peter Cushing) time and space machine (TARDIS) instead. Along with the doctor are his niece, Louise (Jill Curzon) and his granddaughter, Susan (Roberta Tovey). Together they journey to the year A.D. 2150 but they find that the earth has been taken over by Dr. Who's archenemies, the Daleks. The Daleks have enslaved many of the inhabitants and plan to blast out the metallic core of the planet with a bomb in order to use the earth like a giant spaceship to return to their galaxy.

Joining forces with local resistance fighters David (Ray Brooks) and Wyler (Andrew Keir), Dr. Who and his wards travel to a mining site controlled by the Daleks. With the help of the miners, Dr. Who devises a way to deflect the bomb just enough to cause the powerful magnetic force of the earth's core to suck down the metallic, robotic Daleks and reinstate humans as the sole masters of the planet.

Dr. Who and the girls return Tom to his time moments before the burglary. Tom thwarts the robbers. Driving them in their own getaway car to the local police station, Tom fantasizes about the promotion he will receive as a result of the arrests.

Commentary

Milton Subotsky and Max Rosenberg's follow-up to *Dr. Who and the Daleks*, produced a year later, was also based on one of Terry Nation's previously televised six-part serials entitled "World's End." Once again, Subotsky scripted the film version relying heavily on Nation's teleplays as his source.

Although box office receipts for *Dr. Who and the Daleks* were not good, AARU went ahead with the proposed sequel and budgeted it at $286,000. Unfortunately, this sequel also failed to attract interest in overseas markets. As a result, a proposed third Dr. Who film was abandoned.

Of the two films, *Daleks Invasion Earth 2150 A.D.* was the superior effort. Acting was good overall. Cushing's character was played with noticeably less eccentricity, placing it more in keeping with the doctor's original television personality.

Though scripting was upgraded in an attempt to entice a more intellectual audience, and more action scenes were added to hopefully appease younger viewers, some scenes dragged on much too long and the comedic bits failed to elicit the desired effect.

Set in the year A.D. 2150, London still contained some throwbacks to the mid-twentieth century. Clothing and automobiles from the 1960s were visible in scenes, detracting somewhat from the overall set design but they were not altogether obtrusive.

The special effects fared much better in this film. The Daleks' space-

Peter Cushing as the Time Lord, Dr. Who, in Amicus' *Daleks Invasion Earth 2150 A.D.*

craft was well designed and effective. Spaceship hardware was also grades higher than the cardboard sets of the initial entry.

Direction in both films was competent if not exactly trend-setting. However, Gordon Flemying did seem to have a firmer grasp of his subject in this sequel. As a result, *Daleks Invasion Earth 2150 A.D.* moved along far more smoothly and credibly.

"Rich" in his *Variety* review (August 10, 1966) felt it was "a little too advanced for the main core of Daleks followers.... Ted Samuels ... pulled off a lively job with the special effects and the Daleks' themselves.... It is ... decked out with impressive scientific jargon.... Peter Cushing as the professor plays it with the necessary seriousness.... But it is the clever way in which the cone-like Daleks are moved and juggled that gives the film its main kick. It is well-lensed in technicolor by John Wilcox. Bill McGuffie's score is occasionally over-heavy on the ear but other credits, such as editing ... artwork and sound are efficient." *The Times* (July 21, 1966) was far less obliging in its critique. "The second cinematic excursion of the Daleks shows little advance on the first.... The filming of all this is technically elementary.... The cast, headed by the long-suffering much ill-used Peter Cushing, seem able, unsurprisingly to drum up no conviction whatever in anything they are called on to do. Grownups may enjoy it but most children have more sense."

An interesting postscript to *Daleks Invasion Earth 2150 A.D.* occurred in October 1974 when Shepperton Studios held a props auction of some notable film memorabilia. Among the items up for bid was a ten-feet-high sponge rubber Triffid from Steve Sekely's *Day of the Triffids* (1962); eight flying fortresses from Steve McQueen's *The War Lover* (1962); and the Daleks' spaceship model (whose diameter was described as being the size of a large dining room table). The latter was eventually sold to one of the special effects people who had worked on Stanley Kubrick's *2001: A Space Odyssey* for approximately $300.

Frankenstein Created Woman
(1967)

Credits and Cast

Released June 1967 (U.K.), March 1967 (U.S.); 86 minutes; Technicolor; A Hammer Film Production; Released through Pathé-Warner (U.K.), 20th Century–Fox (U.S.); Filmed at Bray Studios, England. Director: Terence Fisher; Producer: Anthony Nelson-Keys; Screenplay: John Elder; Music: James Bernard; Musical supervisor: Philip Martell; Director of photography: Arthur Grant; Editor: James Needs; Camera: Moray Grant; Production design: Bernard Robinson; Art director: Don Mingaye; Production manager: Ian Levy; Wardrobe: Rosemary Burrows; Hairstyles: Frieda Steiger; Special effects: Les Bowie.

Peter Cushing (The Baron), Susan Denberg (Christina), Thorley Walters (Dr. Hertz), Robert Morris (Hans), Peter Blythe (Anton), Barry Warren (Karl), Derek Fowlds (Johann), Alan MacNaughton (Kleve), Peter Madden (Inspector), Kevin

Flood (Jailer), Philip Ray (Mayor), Ivan Beavis (Landlord), Colin Jeavons (Priest), Bartlett Mullins (Bystander), Alec Mango (Spokesman), Duncan Lamont (The Prisoner).

Synopsis

> *For one hour my body had died and yet my soul remained. Now why? Where was it? Was it trapped within me? Could it be trapped forever?* — Baron Frankenstein

A laughing, drunken prisoner (Duncan Lamont) is executed by guillotine before the horrified eyes of his yong son Hans (Stuart Middleton), who is hiding nearby. The boy runs off.

The years pass. Hans (now Robert Morris) runs past the rotting guillotine to the home of Dr. Hertz (Thorley Walters). The pair are assisting Baron Frankenstein (Peter Cushing) in an experiment to trap the soul after death. The baron, frozen into a state approaching hibernation, survives and his soul is trapped within his body, although he is not sure why.

To celebrate their success, the trio decide on champagne. Hans is sent — without money — to the village cafe, wearing Hertz's coat against the evening chill. At the cafe he meets the landlord's daughter, Christina (Susan Denberg), who is crippled and facially deformed. Her father Kleve (Alan McNaughton) disapproves of their friendship because of Hans' father and treats the young man with contempt. He agrees, however, to trade one bottle of champagne for Hertz's coat.

Before Hans can leave, three young dandies enter the cafe demanding wine. The most obnoxious of the trio is Anton (Peter Blythe) who insists that Christina serve them. Karl (Barry Warren) and Johann (Derek Fowlds) share the "joke."

Christina accidentally spills wine on Anton who angrily pushes her aside. Hans knocks him to the floor as Karl and Johann join the fight. Out of control, Hans slashes Anton's forehead and is subdued by Kleve and several policemen. Furious, Hans threatens to kill the landlord. After calming down, Hans agrees to come in the next day and clean up.

After Hans leaves, the baron and Hertz arrive and, seeing the destruction, guess the worst. They claim their champagne and Hertz treats Anton's wound for the price of a meal.

Alone in her room, Christina sits at her mirror and stares at her deformity. Hans enters through her window to apologize for losing his temper. When she tells him that she is leaving the next day for another operation, he replies that her appearance does not matter. She turns down the lamp and they embrace.

Singing in the rain? Susan Denberg (as Christina) and her creator in Hammer's *Frankenstein Created Woman*.

The dandies leave the cafe drunk and crudely "serenade" Christina with an insulting song. They decide to return to the now closed cafe to continue drinking. Kleve, who has forgotten his house key, returns and discovers the break-in. The dandies panic and kill him.

Early the next morning Christina leaves on the coach, unaware of her father's murder. Hans is later arrested for the crime based on his threats and the overcoat found on the floor.

The real reason for his arrest comes out in court, as the prosecutor (Peter Madden) presses Hans hard about his father's crimes. Called to the stand as a witness for Hans, the baron makes a mockery of the state's case. But Hans, who could free himself by saying that he spent the night with Christina, refuses to soil her reputation. He is convicted and is to be guillotined, like his father, at dawn.

The baron plans to preserve Hans' soul by having Hertz obtain his body for a short time after the execution. Hertz gets the cooperation of the jailer (Kevin Flood) with a blackmail threat. Once the soul is trapped in the laboratory apparatus, the baron will place it in the first available body.

The next morning Hans is executed as Christina rides past in the coach. Heartbroken, she throws herself into a nearby river and drowns. Soon after Hans' body is delivered to Hertz, Christina is pulled from the river. The villagers bring her body to Hertz, but there is nothing he can do. The baron, however, sees this as an ideal opportunity — he will place Hans' soul into Christina's body.

Christina is reborn as a stunning beauty with no memory of her past. However, Hans' soul soon begins to dominate. One night she creeps out of the house and goes to the village where she meets, seduces, and kills Anton. The next night she does the same to Karl, who writes the name "Hans" with his own blood.

Suspecting that the baron is somehow behind the killings, the villagers storm Hertz's home. The baron suggests that Hans' body be exhumed to prove that he is truly dead. When the coffin is opened, the corpse is found to be headless.

Christina sits before the head which instructs her to kill Johann for the final vengeance. As he attempts to flee the village, Christina meets him on the coach. She seduces him and suggests they picnic in the forest.

As the baron races after the coach, Christina reveals her identity to Johann before she stabs him. Frankenstein arrives too late to save Johann, but pleads with Christina to have mercy on herself. Despite his pleas, the distraught creature throws herself into a torrential river and, for the second time, drowns.

Defeated, the baron turns and walks away.

Commentary

Despite a central idea that is fairly ridiculous, *Frankenstein Created Woman* is an enjoyable entry in the Hammer series and was a giant step upward from its predecessor. It could be considered the midpoint in the series in quality.

Author Bob Sheridan reported that "Christopher Lee, who had played both the creature in *The Curse of Frankenstein* and the tile role in *Dracula*, refused to repeat either characterization, causing Hammer to cancel both *Revenge of Dracula*, and *And Then . . . Frankenstein Made Woman*."[1] If this is the case, Hammer had been toying with the idea as early as 1958 and Lee's refusal to repeat his Creature led to the superior *The Revenge of Frankenstein* as the first sequel.

Frankenstein Created Woman is often unfairly compared to Universal's classic *Bride of Frankenstein* (1935). The two films have, literally, nothing in common and any comparison is pointless. *Frankenstein Created*

Woman is just about as far from the Universal concept as it is possible to go.

Unlike the rest of the Hammer series, the focus is not on laboratory horrors but on the twisted social structure of the fairy tale–like village. Prejudice is everywhere. Hans is convicted of the murder mostly because his father was a murderer. Christina is an outcast because of her appearance — even her father seems ashamed of her. The three young villains regard anyone beneath their social position with contempt.

Like the film, the baron is more restrained than usual. The script allows Peter Cushing to show more warmth and humor than we've come to expect from the character, and, by adding these touches, he comes as close to a hero as possible. He kills no one, tries to help the unfortunate Christina, and appears almost benign when compared to the trio of hoodlums. Linking his character to the previous *The Evil of Frankenstein* (1963) are his burned hands and his burning desire to succeed. Cushing described his feelings about the baron by saying, "Frankenstein is not evil, but a man obsessed by what he is trying to achieve by any means that will justify the ends."[2]

In his fourth outing as the baron, Peter Cushing delivers his usual excellent performance. It was perhaps at this point of his career that he began being taken for granted by most fans and critics and was becoming a victim of his own high standards. It was simply *expected* that he would be good. A highlight is the courtroom scene in which he delivers some devastating put downs — verbal and visual — to the unfortunate prosecutor (Peter Madden).

The supporting cast is also excellent. Thorley Walters' kindly, bumbling Dr. Hertz reminds one of Nigel Bruce's Dr. Watson, and his relationship with the baron has more than a whiff of Baker Street. Walters shared his feelings about Peter Cushing with the authors: "Peter Cushing is an old and dear friend. I even regard him as close friend, but he was always a very private man and, like myself, a highly professional one. I remember only happy memories in my personal and professional association with him."

Austrian born Susan Denberg is something of a mystery to horror fans. She moved to England at age eighteen, joined the Bluebell Dance Troupe, and traveled to Las Vegas where she was spotted by a Hollywood talent agent. She posed for *Playboy*, appeared in *An American Dream* (1966) and, after her fine performance as Christina, vanished from films.

Variety praised *Frankenstein Created Woman* (March 15, 1967) as a "technically excellent programmer. . . . Cushing could walk through the Frankenstein part blindfolded by now, but he still treats it seriously as though he were playing Hamlet. The cast is uniformly superior to the roles they're 'playing.'" *The London Times* (May 18, 1967) felt that "script writer John Elder and director Terence Fisher have a nice sense of the balance between horror and absurdity and the film has the courage of its lunatic convictions."

The film was released as a double feature in some markets with *The Mummy's Shroud.*

Announced for 1967 production was an intriguing Hammer project, *Blood of the Foreign Legion* to be produced by Anthony Hinds and scripted by Peter Bryan. Peter Cushing was set to star in the "tense, adult adventure" describing the last days of the French Foreign Legion. It was never begun.[3]

Notes

1. Glen Davies, "The Unfilmed Hammer," *Little Shoppe of Horrors.*
2. Alan Frank, "The Life and Times of Peter Cushing," *The House of Hammer* 18.
3. Davies, "The Unfilmed Hammer," *Little Shoppe of Horrors.*

Some May Live
(1967)

Credits and Cast

Released 1967; 89 minutes, 105 minutes; Technicolor; A Krasne Production; Released through Butcher's Film Service (U.K.) and RKO (U.S.); U.S. release to television; Filmed at Twickenham Studios, England, and on location. Director: Vernon Sewell; Producers: Philip Krasne, Clive Sharp; Screenplay: David T. Chantler; Director of photography: Ray Parslow; Music: Cyril Ornadel; Editor: Gordon Pilkington; Production design: George Lack; Alternate title: *In Saigon, Some May Live.*

Joseph Cotten (Colonel Woodward), Martha Hyer (Kate Meredith), Peter Cushing (John Meredith), John Ronane (Captain Thomas), David Spenser (Inspector Sung), Alec Mango (Du Crai), Walter Brown (Major Matthews), Kim Smith (Allan Meredith), Burnell Tucker (Lawrence).

Synopsis

The story takes place during the early years of the Vietnam conflict. Kate Meredith (Martha Hyer) has been living in Saigon with her British foreign correspondant husband, John Meredith (Peter Cushing) and their young son, Allan (Kim Smith). Kate works as a decoder for U.S.-Allied army intelligence. She is also a Communist spy who has been providing her husband with vital information. He in turn has been relaying these reports to the Viet Cong.

When a top secret visit by a U.S. senator is interrupted by an attempted assassination, Colonel Woodward (Joseph Cotten), a high-level official in army intelligence, suspects that an inside leak was responsible.

Kate has been tortured by guilt over her duplicity. Disenchanted with her marriage to John, who had forced her into providing him with these reports, she has also been having an affair with Captain Thomas (John Ronane), Woodward's assistant. When a secret message is received concerning a delay in a planned U.S.–Allied invasion, Kate confronts Woodward and admits her guilt. Kate tells him that her husband is a spy and that he has been awaiting this particular piece of information before permanently returning to China.

Woodward offers Kate an alternative if she is willing to relay false intelligence data to her husband. Kate agrees to cooperate in order to save her son, even though she knows John will be executed by the Communists when the information proves inaccurate.

Shortly after John's departure, Kate is visited by her husband's superior, Du Crai (Alec Mango). When he tries to force Kate and her son to leave with him and join John in China, Kate attacks Du Crai and renders him unconscious. Thomas, who had been ordered to keep Kate under surveillance, tries to help her. He kills Du Crai and leaves the body on the side of a road, making it look as if Du Crai had been the victim of a hit-and-run accident.

The Vietnamese police find Du Crai's body and Kate is subsequently interrogated by Police Inspector Sung (David Spenser), who knows Du Crai was involved with John Meredith. Rather than admit she is a spy, she tells Inspector Sung that she and Du Crai were lovers and that they quarreled. In order to save Thomas, her son, and the U.S. war effort, Kate confesses to Du Crai's murder.

Commentary

Unfortunately, *Some May Live* will never be listed in the annals of the greatest war-intrigue motion pictures of all time. While probably one of the earliest examples of anti–Vietnam war sentiment — innovative in that it was done prior to the all-out attack movements of the 1970s — the picture uneasily vacillates between the "red menace" scare tactics of some 1950s' films while trying to make a case for the human side of war. It attempts to point out that in any war, innocent civilians will be unwittingly caught up in the conflict and that, as a result, many will be forced to take

Some May Live, but this film died. Martha Hyer and Peter Cushing as Communist agents.

sides, question personal loyalties, and otherwise make some supreme sacrifices that, under normal circumstances, they would never have been forced to make. If all this sounds like it has been done before, it has, and in many cases, a lot better. *Some May Live* waves a flag, but it's at half mast.

This mildly interesting spy thriller is stagy, relying too heavily on dialogue. There is virtually no action and no suspense. It's dull, dull, *dull!*

After several boring minutes of opening voice-over narrative (which makes absolutely no sense) and some lovely scenic location photography of Asian river junks, troop ships, and shoreside hovels, a lone gunman climbs onto a rooftop (which looks suspiciously like a backlot studio trailer) and fires several rounds. However, the camera never reveals what the man was shooting at other than a long shot of what appears to be a blue station wagon! There is no reaction from passersby and traffic moves along unaffected. For all the viewer knows, the sniper could have been skeet-shooting!

Filmed in its entirety at Twickenham Studios, the picture flaunts its meager budget (half of which was wasted on technicolor processing) with cheap-looking sets and seedy, dime-store Chinese bibelots.

Equally puzzling is the cast. Martha Hyer and Peter Cushing give it their best, in spite of the odds, and are assets. Joseph Cotten walks through his scenes without making the slightest of thespian attempts, giving the impression that he made his appearances under protest. And lastly, as Hyer's love interest, is the inconceivable John Ronane! An "actor" who appears to view his craft as if it were a totally alien concept!

The preachy script is both laughable and annoying. The romance is forced and hopelessly inane. When Captain Thomas (Ronane) takes Kate (Hyer) to his apartment (after narrowly escaping the bombing of a local bar), they make love to the strains of background title-song music, distant machine-gun fire, and mortar hits — the only other indication, aside from some stock footage of army troop carriers, that there's a war going on all around them!

Another sore point is the blatant Oriental stereotypes that run amok throughout. From the toothpicks under the fingernails interrogation tactics of the local police on the captured sniper (obviously bamboo was in short supply on the set), to the Charlie Chan wisdom of the police inspector, who deduces that a switchblade knife found on villain Du Crai's body had recently been opened(?), these merely succeed in adding to the film's insipidness.

Vernon Sewell's direction leaves one with the uneasy feeling that he only had a one-week shooting schedule. Most of the scenes seemed to have been done on single takes and only troopers like Cushing manage to give reliable, credible performances despite the film's rushed look. Technical credits are a shade above the mediocre.[1]

Other than Peter Cushing's performance in the first half of the film, *Some May Live* is totally forgettable fluff.

Note

1. *Some May Live* was picked up by RKO in the United States for television distribution only.

Night of the Big Heat
(1967)

Credits and Cast

Released December 10, 1967; 94 minutes; Color; A Planet Production; Filmed at Pinewood Studios, England. Director: Terence Fisher; Producer: Tom Blakeley; Associate producer: Ronald Liles; Screenplay: Ronald Liles; Based on John

Lymington's novel; Director of photography: Reg Wyer; Art director: Alex Vetchinsky; Film editor: Rod Keys; Music composed and conducted by Malcolm Lockyer; Assistant director: Ray Frift; Camera: Frank Drake; Continuity: Joy Mercer;
Wardrobe: Kathleen Moore; Makeup: Geoff Rodway; Hairdresser: Stella Rivers;
Sound: Dudley Messenger; Alternate·title: *Island of the Burning Damned*.

Christopher Lee (Hanson), Patrick Allen (Jeff), Sarah Lawson (Frankie), Jane Mer-
row (Angela), William Lucas (Ken Stanley), Kenneth Cope (Tinker Mason), Jack
Bligh (Ben), Thomas Heathcote (Bob), Sidney Bromley (Tramp), Percy Herbert
(Foster), Anna Turner (Stella), Barry Halliday (Radar Operator); special guest star
Peter Cushing (Dr. Stone).

Synopsis

> *Are you saying that earth has become the subject of a probe carried*
> *out by creatures from another planet?* — Dr. Stone

A small island off the British coast is experiencing an unusual
November — while the mainland temperature is 24 degrees, on the island
it is 90 degrees and rising.

Angela Roberts (Jane Merrow), a secretary, arrives on the island to
work for author Jeff Callum (Patrick Allen). Jeff's wife Frankie (Sarah Lawson) is unaware that the two have had an affair. Jeff is confused as to what
he really wants to come of Angela's return, but welcomes her to her new
position. The threesome will be residing at The Swan — the local inn owned
by the Callums.

One of the guests, Hanson (Christopher Lee), is a source of concern
among the locals — especially Frankie and Dr. Stone (Peter Cushing).
They are puzzled by his odd comings and goings — often with a camera —
and his habit of locking himself in his room. His unnecessary rudeness
does little to endear him to the small community.

When Ben Siddle (Jack Bligh) a shepherd, is found delirious, mumbling about his sheep being killed, Hanson brutally questions the man until
Dr. Stone intervenes.

Other unusual events soon follow. The island's television and radio
sets no longer function, and there is a periodic whirring sound. The temperature continues to rise.

Becoming paranoid, Jeff, Frankie, and Angela suspect an extraterrestrial cause — and Hanson as their agent. When confronted by Jeff, Hanson admits that he fears that the island had been invaded by space creatures. While investigating the strange sound, they find the burned-out remains of a car belonging to Bob (Thomas Heathcote), a friend of the Callums. As the temperature continues to rise, beer bottles explode in the
Swan's bar.

Dr. Stone's temper rises with the temperature in Planet Films' *Night of the Big Heat*.

Bob appears at The Swan, but is not himself. He attacks Angela, who fights him off with a bottle. Subdued by several bar patrons, Bob is held while Dr. Stone is summoned. Before Stone's arrival, Bob escapes and is destroyed by an extraterrestrial force.

Armed only with two-way radios, Stone and Hanson track the creatures. With Hanson based at The Swan, Stone drives his car toward the
suspected landing site of their spacecraft. Kept in touch by the radios,
Stone informs Hanson that his car has stalled and that he will continue
on foot. Hanson, horrified, hears Stone scream.

When Hanson investigates the landing site, he determines that the
creatures are unable to exist at an average earth temperature and are ar-
tificially causing the tremendous increases by the emission of heat from
their bodies. He also learns that the beings can transmit themselves — like
television signals — from their home planet.

Since the creatures are apparently attracted by light energy, Hanson
tells Jeff to turn off all electric lights in the area.

Hanson dies after an abortive attempt to destroy the creatures by fire.
As the creatures advance on Jeff, Frankie, and Angela, a violent storm
breaks. As the torrential rain causes the temperature to drop, the creatures are destroyed and the invasion is ended. Also ended is Jeff's infatua-
tion with Angela, and he and Frankie go on as before.

Commentary

Like *Island of Terror* (1966), this was a science fiction film directed by
Terence Fisher — far from an admirer of or expert in the sci-fi field. "Personally," Fisher once said, "I detest most science fiction films.... The
future holds no interest for me."[1] Perhaps this explains why his science
fiction films are so boring and lack any trace of the style and beauty of his
Gothic fantasies.

Night of the Big Heat best serves as an example of talented people
working in an area in which they are not suited. Due to their many appearances in period costumes, Peter Cushing and Christopher Lee often
look startlingly out of place in modern clothing, and their mannerisms are
far better suited to an earlier time. It simply seems disconcerting to see
Peter Cushing driving a car. While viewing the film, one senses that no one
was particularly interested in, or felt very deeply about, the project.

Given guest star billing, Peter Cushing has quite a bit of screen time,
mostly sitting in Patrick Allen's bar. One can't help wondering why he
doesn't remove his sweat-stained jacket in the stifling heat. Perhaps it was
the writers' method of showing the character's "class."

Christopher Lee recalls, "The film was shot in the depths of the
English winter to show the bare trees and add veracity to the story. The
entire cast wore the flimsiest of clothing and we were covered in artificial
sweat."[2]

Although the two costars and a fine supporting cast deliver adequate performances, the film is just too leisurely written and directed to have any impact. Peter Cushing manages to instill in his stilted lines some urgency (which is more than Christopher Lee does), but even he is unable to lift the film above the mediocre. Author Harry Ringel perhaps put it best: "Not even Peter Cushing could enliven the flattened souls who inhabit Fisher's faintly printed science fiction universe."[3]

The *Los Angeles Times* liked the film, calling it "taut British sci-fi ... a sort of low-budget *Andromeda Strain*." The *Daily Cinema* found it "well-made ... reliable cast make it all quite believable."

Most fans of the stars and director found it to be a waste of time and talent.

Notes

1. Harry Ringel, "Terence Fisher—The Human Side," *Cinefantastique* 4, no. 3.
2. Pohle and Hart, *The Films of Christopher Lee.*
3. Ringel, "Terence Fisher," *Cinefantastique* 4, no. 3.

Torture Garden
(1967)

Credits and Cast

Released April 24, 1968 (U.S.); 93 minutes (100 minutes, U.S. television); Technicolor; An Amicus Production; Released through Columbia (U.S.); Filmed at Shepperton Studios, England. Director: Freddie Francis; Producers: Max J. Rosenberg, Milton Subotsky; Screenplay: Robert Bloch; Based on Robert Bloch's short stories; Director of photography: Norman Warwick; Editor: Peter Elliott; Music: Don Banks, James Bernard; Music conducted by Philip Martell; Piano solo played by Martino Tirimo; Production designer: Bill Constable; Sound: Ken Rolls; Assistant director: Derek Parr; Construction manager: Bill Waldron; Camera grip: Ray Jones; Production supervisor: Ted Wallis; Production manager: Tony Wallis; Camera Operator: David Harcout; Continuity: Barbara Rowlands; Art directors: Don Mingaye, Scott Slimon; Set dresser: Andrew Low; Makeup: Jill Carpenter; Hairdresser: Ann Fordyce; Wardrobe: Evelyn Gibbs.

Jack Palance (Ronald Wyatt), Burgess Meredith (Dr. Diabolo), Beverly Adams (Carla Hayes), Peter Cushing (Lancelot Canning), Barbara Ewing (Dorothy Endicott), Michael Bryant (Colin Williams), Maurice Denham (Colin's Uncle), John Standing (Leo Winston), Robert Hutton (Bruce Benton), John Phillips (Eddie Storm), Michael Ripper (Gordon Roberts), Bernard Kay (Dr. Heim), Catherine Finn (Nurse Parker), Ursula Howells (Miss Chambers), Niall MacGinnis (Doctor),

Timothy Bateson (Fairground Barker), David Bauer (Mike Charles), Nicole Shelby (Millie), Clytie Jessop (Atropos, Goddess of Destiny), Michael Hawkins (Constable), Hedger Wallace (Edgar Allan Poe), with Roy Stevens, James Copeland, Roy Godfrey, Geoffrey Wallace, Norman Claridge, and Barry Low.

Synopsis

> *This is a figure from ancient legend. Atropos, Goddess of Destiny.*
> *In her left hand, the skein of life. In her right, the shears of fate.*
> *Each colored thread represents a human life. And the shears have*
> *the power to cut it short!* —Dr. Diabolo

Five people are lured into a carnival sideshow attraction called "The Torture Garden." Once inside they meet their guide, Dr. Diabolo (Burgess Meredith). With the assistance of a mannequin dressed as a gypsy woman, whom Diabolo refers to as Atropos, the goddess of destiny, Diabolo gives each of his guests a glimpse into their own future. He provides them with a window into the evil nature of each of these men and women — and their fate if they fail to heed his warnings.

Colin Williams (Michael Bryant) murders his uncle (Maurice Denham) for his money, only to find that he, like his uncle before him, becomes the slave to a witch's familiar, a cat with the diabolical name of Belphegor, and possessed of a demon who promises him riches if he will provide it with the sustenance it needs, human heads! At first, Colin complies, but when he is faced with the horror of what he has been forced to do, he refuses to help the demon again. As a result, Colin is caught with the body of one of his victims and is imprisoned. While incarcerated, Belphegor visits Colin in his cell and eats his head in retribution.

Carla Hayes (Beverly Adams), an overly ambitious, would-be starlet, schemes her way into the film business and has an affair with movie idol, Bruce Benton (Robert Hutton) in order to further her career plans. But when she witnesses Benton's murder at the hands of two thugs for gambling debts and then his incredible return to the set the following week, Carla discovers his terrible secret. Benton and others like him — those seemingly immortal stars of the silver screen — have been preserved for all time due to the genius of a surgeon, Dr. Heim (Bernard Kay), who has transferred the brains of "the elite" into synthetic bodies. In order to prevent Carla from revealing this secret to the outside world, she too is made into an automaton — forever young and beautiful — a living doll!

Dorothy Endicott (Barbara Ewing), a magazine reporter, interviews a famous pianist, Leo Winston (John Standing), and they fall in love. However, Leo also loves his music and seems obsessed with his prized grand piano, whom he has named, Euterpe, after the goddess of music. Dorothy soon learns why her fiancé is so enamored of the instrument. It is because the piano is possessed by the spirit of his dead mother—a woman who made it her life's work to see her son become the world's greatest living pianist. When Dorothy threatens to destroy his dedication to the arts, she is murdered by the mother's vengeful spirit.

Ronald Wyatt (Jack Palance), a collector, meets Lancelot Canning (Peter Cushing), who is the premiere collector of the works of author Edgar Allan Poe. Wyatt manages to get an invitation to Canning's home in Maryland, where he is stunned to find that Canning has amassed the ultimate in Poe memorabilia—an accumulation that not only includes previously unpublished works written on twentieth-century paper, but also the resurrected Poe (Hedger Wallace) himself! However, when Wyatt is persuaded by Poe to help him die, Wyatt too is killed in the ensuing fire.

Dr. Diabolo offers to let the fifth visitor, Gordon Roberts (Michael Ripper), see into his own future. However, Roberts, terrified over the prospect, kills Diabolo with the Sibyl's shears. The others all flee the exhibit in horror. But it is revealed that Roberts was Diabolo's assistant and that the "murder" was staged. Diabolo is, in reality, the Devil himself and he invites the audience to learn their own destinies.

Commentary

> We have to think of the substantial American market for our films
> . . and so we always try to include at least two actors who are well-
> known in America. In Torture Garden one was [Jack] Palance
> and the other was Burgess Meredith, who played Dr. Diabolo. . . .
> The picture has done very well over there.—Milton Subotsky,
> Producer[1]

With poor box office returns overseas from their last three releases (all science fiction films: *Daleks Invasion Earth 2150 A.D.*, 1966, *They Came from Beyond Space*, and *The Terrornauts*, both 1967), Amicus returned to fantasy and the multistory format for their next production, *Torture Garden*.

The film was based on four short stories by Robert Bloch: "Enoch," "Terror over Hollywood," "Mr. Steinway," and "The Man Who Collected Poe," all of which had previously been published in genre-related periodicals.[2] Bloch was hired to do the screenplay adaptations of his stories but he was not altogether pleased with the filmed results. Bloch said, "They [Amicus] only did about 60 or 70% of what I had written. There is a general tendency . . . to confuse visual shock with psychological build up and this has become so characteristic you grow to expect it. It's par for the course in this business. . . . There is a longer version [of *Torture Garden*] for television in which there are 12 minutes more of clarification. But even

"The Man Who Collected Poe" is about to add Jack Palance to his collection in *Torture Garden.*

with the additional 12 minutes there are still changes I don't feel are effective."[3]

Initially, producers Rosenberg and Subotsky were considering Christopher Lee to costar with Peter Cushing in the last segment, "The Man Who Collected Poe," but Columbia Pictures had other ideas. Freddie Francis, who had directed Amicus' first anthology, *Dr. Terror's House of Horrors* (1964), clarified this: "Any film I've been on so far, I've always had a quite a lot to do on the casting. . . . When we were doing *Torture Garden,* we were told by Columbia to use Jack Palance and Burgess Meredith."[4] Palance, whose previous film had been a Western, replaced Christopher Lee. Meredith, a Hollywood perennial, who had suddenly found a new audience with his popular portrayal of Penguin in the television series "Batman" (1966–68), substituted his tuxedo for a pair of horns and a pitchfork to play the role of Dr. Diabolo in the linking story.

Torture Garden is entertaining though not one of Amicus' best anthology films overall. Aside from its very weak linking story and farcical episode, "Mr. Steinway" (which concerns a "maternal" piano!), the remaining three segments are thought provoking and imaginative on various levels.

Peter's segment, "The Man Who Collected Poe," is evocative of his earlier film, *The Skull* (also based on a Bloch story). Both center around collectors who are obsessed with their hobby and meet the same fate as a result. Lancelot Canning (Cushing) is a rapacious collector of Edgar Allan Poe memorabilia. However, unlike most bibliophiles, Canning's compilation includes the ultimate in acquisitions — the author himself! Cushing performs extremely well — despite costar Palance's exaggerated portrayal of Ronald Wyatt — and gives the more credible performance. Palance hams it up too much to be taken seriously. Subotsky's initial choice for Wyatt might have elevated the story somewhat. At best it might have made Cushing's job a little easier.

Production properties for *Torture Garden* were generally very good. Cushing's segment, however, seems to have had the lion's share of the film's art direction budget with its opulent Victorian sets and special effects. According to Columbia publicity for the film, an eighty-eight-year-old calligrapher, Tom Maddicks, was hired to give Poe's manuscripts a more authentic look. By employing a formula, which included strong tea, Maddicks was able to yellow or age the manuscripts appropriately.

The portrait of Poe, which held a place of honor in Canning's Maryland home, was reproduced from an authenticated likeness which had originally appeared in William F. Gill's biography of the writer, first published in 1878. Set dresser Andrew Low completed the look with leatherbound books, bric-a-brac and furnishings which included a small drug cabinet, the latter eluding to Poe's known drug addiction.

Critical reviews for *Torture Garden* included *The Times* (John Russell Taylor, November 18, 1967):

> a very superior horror film (no shamefacedness about it this time). The story is by Robert Bloch ... and concerns a fairground charlatan — or is he? — who promises to show his customers the reflection of their own deepest evil desires. The film resolves itself then into four episodes, dealt with very well in suitably contrasted styles by ... director ... Francis. The cast is really excellent.... The end ties all these sequences together neatly and leaves things nicely hanging to tantalize us.

The *Western Daily Press* called the film "Something of a connoisseur's piece." The *New York Times* reviewer Vincent Canby (July 20, 1968) reported that "Freddie Francis ... has become (by default) one of the best and most prolific directors ... in the horror movie genre. His *Torture Garden* ... is a simple-minded forthright horror movie." "Murf" in *Variety* (February 28, 1968) called it a "Good horror programmer ... another of the well-made low-budget chillers from ... Rosenberg and ... Subotsky ... an episodic script in which the situations are developed economically and inventively. The cast is competent.... All credits are good."

As part of Columbia's publicity campaign, participating theaters offered every paying patron a free packet of "Fright Seeds" for their own "Torture Gardens," cautioning patrons to plant these seeds at their own risk! According to Vincent Canby of the *New York Times* (July 20, 1968), who was curious and contacted Columbia, the seeds were actually timothy grass or hay which may ease the minds of all those who still have their packets but were afraid to plant them all these years!

Notes

1. Gwynne Comber, "The Amicus Brain," *Supernatural.*
2. "Enoch" originally appeared in *Bizarre Mystery Magazine* (November 1965); "The Man Who Collected Poe" appeared in *Famous Fantastic Mysteries* (October 1951); "Terror over Hollywood" from *Fantastic Universe Science Fiction* (June 1957); and "Mr. Steinway" first appeared in *Fantastic Mysteries* (April 1954).
3. Robert Bloch, interview with John Stanley, *Castle of Frankenstein 12*. *Torture Garden* was released theatrically with a 93-minute running time. Actually only 7 minutes of footage were added for its television release in the United States.
4. Freddie Francis, interview, *Little Shoppe of Horrors 2*.

Blood Beast Terror
(1967)

Credits and Cast

Released June 1967; Color by Movielab; A Tigon-British Production; Released through Pacemaker; Filmed at Goldhawk Studios, Shepherd's Bush, London. Director: Vernon Sewell; Executive producer: Tony Tenser; Producer: Arnold L. Miller; Screenplay: Peter Bryan; Music: Paul Ferris; Director of photography: Stanley A. Long; Editor: Howard Lanning; Camera operator: Norman Jones; Production manager: Ricky Coward; Art director: Wilfrid Woods; Construction manager: Len Harvey; Set dresser: Frieda Pearson; Makeup: Rosemary M. Peathe; Special effects: Roger Dicken; Hairstyles: Henry Montash; Wardrobe: Marie Feldwick; Continuity: Eve Wilson. Alternate titles: *Vampire-Beast Craves Blood, Death's-Head Vampire.*

Peter Cushing (Inspector Quennell), Robert Flemying (Professor Mallinger), Wanda Ventham (Clare), Vanessa Howard (Meg), David Griffin (William), Glynn A. Edwards (Sergeant Allan), William Wilde (Brightwell), Kevin Stoney (Grainger), John Paul (Warringer), Russell Napier (Landlord), Roy Hudd (Morgue Attendant), Leslie Anderson (Coachman), Robert Cawdron (Constable), Kenneth Collier (James), Beryl Cooke (Housekeeper), Roy Evans (Porter), Joan Ingram (Cook); Simon Cai (Clem).

Synopsis

> *The only time we have a witness to·the murders and he's out of his mind.* — Inspector Quennell

An explorer is being paddled down a jungle river in a canoe. He pulls into shore, enters the jungle, and removes several cocoon-like objects from a tree.

In England a coachman (Leslie Anderson) hears a horrifying cry and stops to investigate. He finds a body completely drained of blood. Overhead, he hears an ominous flapping sound. He looks up, horrified.

Professor Mallinger (Robert Flemying) is teaching a course on insects at his nearby estate when his slide show is interrupted by Inspector Quennell (Peter Cushing), who is continuing his investigation of a student's murder. The professor is not pleased at his arrival.

Sergeant Allen (Glynn Edwards) bursts in to announce the discovery of yet another body on the heath. Still alive, the young man dies as Mallinger attends to his wounds.

The coachman has been found, and is now berserk, raving in his cell about a creature with huge eyes and wings. There have now been six victims — all male.

Quennell investigates the scene and finds some unusual scaly material which he shows to the professor. After listening to Quennell, Mallinger dons a protective mask and enters a locked room in the cellar. There is a hissing shriek.

Mallinger is visited by Brightwell (William Wilde), the explorer, who has brought the specimens he collected in Africa. He meets Clare (Wanda Ventham), the professor's beautiful daughter, who invites him to a party that evening.

The professor is especially interested in the large chrysalis specimens — and is even more interested in creating larger ones in an incubator.

During the party, Clare and Brightwell meet outside and she leads him into the forest for what he assumes will be a seduction. Unseen by both is Quennell, patrolling the grounds, fearing another student's murder. Brightwell is attacked by a horrible creature similar to the one seen by the coachman. Quennell hears his scream but arrives too late. Observed by Mallingers' servant Grainger (Kevin Stoney), Brightwell gurgles the word "death's-head."

The inspector takes the dying man to Mallinger, but to no avail. Incredibly, the professor denies knowing the victim. Quennell is later confused when he learns that Brightwell asked Sergeant Allen for directions to Mallinger's home.

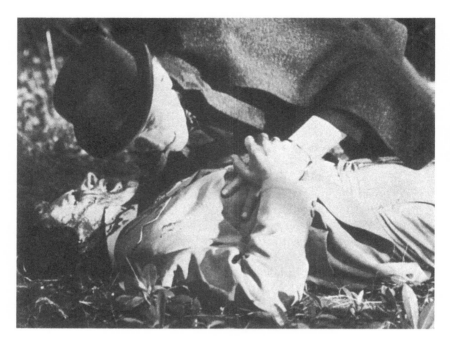

Inspector Quennell finds another victim of the Death's-Head vampire in Tigon's *Blood Beast Terror.*

Upon entering Mallinger's house to question him, Quennell finds Grainger's mutilated body and several skeletal remains. The staff has been dismissed and Mallinger and his daughter have vanished.

The professor has been traced to Waterloo Station in London and from there to the village of Upper Higham. Quennell and his daughter Meg (Vanessa Howard) leave for the village as if on a holiday, with the inspector posing as a banker.

The fugitives have taken refuge at an estate near the village, where Clare begins her seduction of Clem (Simon Cai), the gardener. At the inn Quennell strikes up a friendship with the proprietor (Russell Napier) and Warringer (John Paul), an entomologist on a fishing vacation with his son William (David Griffin). Meg and William, while chasing butterflies, wander on to Mallinger's estate and are ordered off by Clare.

Mallinger has electrically stimulated the huge chrysalis but it needs blood: the blood of a young girl, suggests Clare. She picks up Meg while walking on the road and apologizing for her rudeness, takes her back to the professor. After Mallinger drains some blood and hypnotizes her to forget the experience, she is set free. Clare then seduces Clem, metamorphosing into a huge death's-head moth, and kills him.

At the inn Quennell overhears William discussing a death's-head in his collection and recalls Brightwell's dying words. When William identifies the giant scales that Quennell found at the murder site, the inspector begins to guess the truth.

Mallinger and Clare—his "daughter" that he created as an experiment—argue over his latest creation, a male. Disgusted by his actions, he destroys the male by fire and is attacked by Clare.

Clem's mutilated body is snagged by William's fishing line and brought to the inn where Quennell and the recently arrived Sergeant Allen identify him as another victim of the creature.

Quennell suspects Mallinger as being "Mr. Miles" who lives outside the village and rushes to the estate. William and Meg have gone to see his butterfly collection.

Meg finds the professor's corpse and, panic-stricken, accidentally sets the house on fire. As Quennell saves her from the inferno, William is attacked by Clare who is destroyed by a bonfire, set by Quennell, that attracts her against her will.

Commentary

By the late 1960s many of the horror themes begun ten years previously were beginning to wear thin. The Hammer Frankenstein and Dracula series and the Vincent Price Poe films were just about played out. The 1970s fascination with the occult had not yet begun, leaving low-budget producers groping for a topic—any topic—that had not been done to death. It was this uncertainty as to where the horror film was going that probably led to less than satisfying efforts like *Blood Beast Terror*.

Also known as *Death's-Head Vampire* and *Vampire-Beast Craves Blood*, the film is as awkward as its titles. The very concept of a human-sized, blood-sucking moth is ludicrous and takes one back to Roger Corman's *Wasp Woman* (1960).

Nothing about the film works very well. The Victorian costumes, settings, and color photography are well done, but ten years of Hammer robs them of their novelty. The monster is poorly designed and the film works best when she is off-screen. This is due, one suspects, less to a Val Lewton approach to unseen horror than to a realization that the monster is absurd and the less seen of it the better. She looks, more or less, like something glimpsed in an elementary school Halloween parade.

The script of Peter Bryan (who wrote Hammer's *The Hound of the Baskervilles*) also fails to provide much motivation for Robert Flemying's scientist. To be fair, the film has several running times listed and the version seen by the authors may have had a crucial scene cut. This aside, no intelligent reason is given for Flemying's creation of the creature. The performance of Flemying is rather stiff and too low key for a horror comic like this, and he is unable to fill in gaps left by the script.

In a role originally intended for Basil Rathbone,[1] Peter Cushing shines as Quennell. Cast against type (during this period of his career) as a policeman, he turns in an astonishingly good performance that ranks with his best. What a pity that it should be wasted in such a mediocre film. But then, that's what makes Peter Cushing—well—Peter Cushing.

Inspector Quennell is a well-rounded, human character. Kind and considerate with his daughter, he can be a little testy, especially when his tea is improperly served. "I wish you wouldn't slop it in the saucer!" he snaps at the long-suffering Sergeant Allan. He has problems dealing with his superiors, too.

Unfortunately, his excellent acting is not enough to raise the tired material much higher than to make the film watchable. The indifferent scripting and direction were gradually becoming the norm for the low-budget horror film—a far cry from the previous decade. This unhappy situation would change shortly and Peter Cushing would soon be appearing in some of his best films.

Tigon was a small, independent British production company seeking to get through a crack in the door to the gold already being mined by Hammer, Amicus, and American International. However, after a few attempts (including the excellent *Blood on Satan's Claw*, 1970), Tigon quietly faded from the scene. Even a vehicle featuring Boris Karloff, Christopher Lee, Barbara Steele, and Michael Gough (*Curse of the Crimson Altar*, 1968) failed to excite audiences.

Blood Beast Terror was not widely released or reviewed and is seldom seen on television. It's not hard to see why. A monster film simply needs a better monster than this one provides. In many ways it is similar to Hammer's *The Gorgon* (1969). Critic Leslie Halliwell found it "Unpersuasive and totally idiotic cheapjack horror fare." That seems fairly accurate.

Although little could have been done to improve the film (other than a recasting or rewriting), the unbelievably crude advertising that Pacemaker Pictures saddled it with was no help.

Released as *The Vampire-Beast Craves Blood* in 1969, it was cofeatured with *Curse of the Blood Ghouls* with the following poster ad line "a ravishing Psyco-Fiend with the diabolical power to turn into a Giant Deathshead Vampire feasts on the Blood of her lovers before clawing them to death!"

For those who are interested, the following line advertised the cofeature: "enslave beautiful women through weird ways of love transforming them into Blood Ghoul Vampires to satisfy an insatiable lust." Both pictures Rated G—suggested for general audiences!

Note

1. Michael Weldon, *The Psychotronic Encyclopedia of Film.*

Corruption
(1968)

Credits and Cast

Released December 1968; 90 minutes; Columbia color; A Titan Film Distributors Production; Released through Columbia (U.S. and U.K.); MPAA R; Filmed at Isleworth Studios, England, and on location in London. Director: Robert Hartford-Davis; Producers: Peter Newbrook, Robert Hartford-Davis; Screenplay: Donald Ford, Derek Ford; Director of photography: Peter Newbrook, B.S.C.; Editor: Don Deacon; Music composed and conducted by Bill McGuffie; Production design: Bruce Grimes; Sound: Cyril Collick; First assistant director: Ken Softley; Production supervisor: Robert Sterne; Continuity: Splinters Deason; Set dresser: Hilary Pritchard; Makeup: Biddy Crystal; Special effects: Mike Albrechtsen.

Peter Cushing (Sir John Rowan), Sue Lloyd (Lynn Nolan), Noel Trevarthen (Dr. Stephen Harris), Kate O'Mara (Val Nolan), Diana Ashley (Claire), Victor Baring (Mortuary Attendant), Shirley Stelfox (Girl at the Party), David Lodge (Groper), Anthony Booth (Mike), Wendy Varnals (Terry), Billy Murray (Rik), Vanessa Howard (Girl at the Party), Jan Waters, Valerie Van Ost (Victims), Phillip Manikum, Alexandra Dane (Other Hippies).

Synopsis

Noted surgeon Sir John Rowan (Peter Cushing) attends a party with his fashion model girlfriend and fiancée, Lynn Nolan (Sue Lloyd). Rowan gets into a fight with another guest, Lynn's photographer, when the young man tries to flirt with her. During the struggle, a flood lamp is knocked over and falls on Lynn — disfiguring her face hideously. Feeling personally responsible for the accident, Rowan performs experimental surgery on Lynn, by means of a laser beam and the extract of a pituitary gland he had stolen from a local hospital. The operation proves to be a total success; however, the effects are short-lived.

Determining that the failure was due to the degeneration of the gland tissue used, Rowan is convinced that if he were able to inject her face with fresh tissue, the effects would be more permanent. He is forced to murder a prostitute and, decapitating her, operates once again on Lynn. However, as before, the effects are only temporary. John realizes that he will have to keep on killing young women in order to preserve his love's beauty.

After one of the murders comes to the attention of Rowan's associate, Dr. Stephen Harris (Noel Trevarthen), he suddenly grasps the truth surrounding Lynn's miraculous recoveries. He and girlfriend Val Nolan (Kate O'Mara), Lynn's sister, set out to find Rowan to stop him. They are unaware of the fact that it is Lynn who is responsible for Rowan's obsessive behavior.

Rowan and Lynn, who have retreated to their country home to avoid capture, are confronted by the husband and friends of one of the murder victims. Lynn, by now hopelessly insane, murders the husband and demands that Rowan operate again. She accidentally activates the laser and the machine goes out of control, killing John and his accusers, as well as Dr. Harris and Val. The house catches fire and burns down to the ground, killing Lynn as well.

Sir John awakens from his nightmare and later attends a party with his fiancée, Lynn. During the party, he is introduced to Lynn's photographer friend.

Commentary

Billed as a psychological thriller, this film was promoted in the United States with the following ad line: "*Corruption* is not a woman's picture. Therefore, no woman will be admitted alone to see this super shock film!" This alone should have sounded off warning bells to anyone (male or female) who might have contemplated viewing this film at their local movie palace!

To make matters worse, theater owners were encouraged by Columbia to play up such garish and utterly tasteless gimmicks as having a "for women only" theater entrance, or to employ a man, wearing dark clothes and a top hat, to walk along local streets with a female mannequin's head under one arm and a doctor's bag under the other in an attempt to lure in audiences. Another Columbia brainstorm was to have female mannequin heads hanging by the hair from cinema lobby ceilings.

Gimmicks and clichés not withstanding, the film, released on a double bill in the United States with *Payment in Blood*,[1] suffers from an incredibly bad script, a hideous music score, hack editing, and generally poor directing by Robert Hartford-Davis. Unfortunately, Davis would fare no better the following year with *Bloodsuckers* (1969), and perhaps should have sued to have his name removed from the credits of this film as well.

Peter Cushing, as the guilt-ridden surgeon who is forced into a life of crime, plays the role as straight as possible under the circumstances. However, the entire production seems to be working against him. Its major fault lies in the fact that the script never really makes it clear as to whether

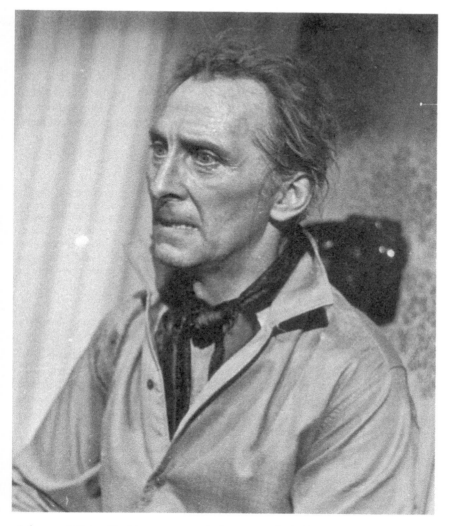

A frenzied Peter Cushing as a twentieth-century Jack the Ripper in Columbia's *Corruption.*

or not Dr. John Rowan is merely clairvoyant or has severe psychological hang-ups. Is the dream-nightmare a case of grotesque Walter Mitty–type fantasy – the type your average mass murderer might have had – or is John actually seeing a glimpse into the future? None of this is ever fully explained, although most viewers would have been put off by what they saw on screen long before any intended symbolism might have taken hold, no matter what the filmmaker's intent.

There is one scene in the film, however, that is quite engrossing. It takes place in Dr. Rowan's home shortly after Lynn's (Sue Lloyd) accident. While pouring over his medical books, Lynn's sister, Val (played very competently by Kate O'Mara) interrupts the physician in his study. Rowan, ridden with guilt and obsessed with finding a cure for his fiancée's disfigurement, verbally lashes out at Val during one point in the scene. Peter is absolutely brilliant here as his frustration builds and finally explodes. It is by far the best scene in the picture and one of Cushing's most memorable.

Peter spoke about his character and the film:

> It was a great idea but the only thing I felt about the picture was that it was repetitive within itself and it had to be, I suppose, because of what the story was about. It was about this man who through an unfortunate accident destroyed the beauty of his dearly beloved and it was his magnificent obsession to bring her face back to normal. But every time the glands he took from the prostitute ran out he had to get some more, so it had to be repetitive. I think with a little more time it could have been made a little more subtle.[2]

According to Columbia's publicity on the film, as with many contemporary horror films, *Corruption* had to be photographed three different ways for Western, European, and Asian markets. Extra quantities of "blood" had to be used, for example, in the Asian version. American and British audiences were shown only the impression of the killings — "a raised knife followed by a shot of a still figure." However, Japanese audiences were shown complete on-screen graphic murder sequences and European versions also contained complete nudity.

Of the cast members who appeared with Peter, Kate O'Mara, an extra in *Night Creatures* (1962), would also star two years later in *The Vampire Lovers* (1970). Valerie Van Ost (the girl on the train), would later be seen in *Bloodsuckers* (1969) and *The Satanic Rites of Dracula* (1973), in supporting roles. Anthony Booth (Mike) had also appeared in *The Risk* (1959).

Among its critical reviews, "Murf," in his *Variety* column (December 11, 1968) called it a

> Fair horror picture ... on a low budget, ... suffered from poor writing, plus often sluggish direction by Robert Hartford-Davis. Two major flaws make the film less than it could have been. First, Sue Lloyd's character, both in writing and acting, vacillates between selfish woman and a woman turned evil by the accident. Second, Cushing's transformation from famed surgeon to killer is fluffed off.... The director at times punches over some genuine suspense, but the pacing and the performances are generally limp ... production credits are okay.

The *Western Daily Press* was more direct in its assessment: "it is an ill-directed, ill-photographed piece of work in excruciatingly bad taste . . . it is, moreover, artistically and morally indefensible, and it is a sad thought that such a film can be made, let alone attract an audience to see it." And, finally, Vincent Canby of the *New York Times* (December 5, 1968) wrote, "*Corruption* is a horror movie in the spare parts category, pituitary glands subdivision. . . . Peter Cushing brings a certain seedy grandeur to his role."

Notes

1. An Italian-made, American Civil War epic starring Edd Byrnes and Guy Madison.
2. Peter Cushing, interview with Chris Knight, *L'incroyable Cinema 6*.

Scream and Scream Again
(1969)

Credits and Cast

Released February 1970; 95 minutes; Color by Movielab; An Amicus Production; Released through American International (U.S.) and Pathé-Warner (U.K.); MPAA M; Filmed at Shepperton Studios and on location in England. Director: Gordon Hessler; Producers: Max J. Rosenberg, Milton Subotsky; Executive producer: Lewis M. Heyward; Screenplay: Christopher Wicking; Based on the novel *The Disoriented Man* by Peter Saxon; Director of photography: John Coquillon; Editor: Peter Elliott; Art director: Bill Constable; Music composed and conducted by Dave Whittaker; Assistant director: Ariel Levy; Production manager: Teresa Bolland; Camera operator: Les Young; Sound: Bert Ross; Music director: Shel Talmy; Songs: "Scream and Scream Again" written by Dominic King, Tim Hayes, "When We Make Love" written by Dominic King; Makeup: Jimmy Evans; Hairdresser: Betty Sherriff; Wardrobe: Evelyn Gibbs; Continuity: Eileen Head.

Vincent Price (Dr. Browning), Christopher Lee (Fremont), Peter Cushing (Benedek), Judy Huxtable (Sylvia), Alfred Marks (Superintendent Bellaver), Michael Gothard (Keith), Anthony Newlands (Ludwig), Marshall Jones (Konratz), Peter Sallis (Schweitz), David Lodge (Detective Inspector Strickland), Uta Levka (Jane), Christopher Matthews (David Sorel), Judi Bloom (Helen Bradford), Clifford Earl (Detective Sergeant Jimmy Joyce), Kenneth Benda (Professor Kingsmill), Yutte Stensgaard (Erika), Julian Holloway (Griffin), Steve Preston (Fryer), Lee Hudson (Matron), Leslie Ewin (Tramp), Kay Adrian (Nurse), Rosalind Elliott (Valerie).

Synopsis

A series of seemingly unrelated murders and disappearances have British police superintendent Bellaver (Alfred Marks) baffled. Some of the brutal killings have all the earmarks of a vampire!

With the help of police pathologist David Sorel (Christopher Matthews) and a police decoy, Helen Bradford (Judi Bloom), the "vampire" (Michael Gothard) is caught. A short time later, while attempting an escape, the vampire is destroyed when he deliberately jumps into a vat of acid housed in a barn on the estate of scientist Dr. Browning (Vincent Price).

The story shifts to the sudden emergence of a new European political movement, whose members have been placed in strategic government positions throughout the continent as well as in the United Kingdom. One of the movement's watchdogs is agent Konratz (Marshall Jones)—a brutal, sadistic killer who victimizes any member who defies or jeopardizes the party's objectives. Konratz is ordered to England by an unknown source.

Believing that Dr. Browning is connected in some way with the killings, Sorel puts the scientist under surveillance and makes a grim discovery. Dr. Browning is creating a race of superhuman beings using body parts from various living victims. However, his new "race" is made up of human-like people who are devoid of any feelings and emotions.

Browning admits that Keith, the vampire, was the result of one of his earlier experiments and that he has since taken steps to correct Keith's particular problem. He is also hopeful that future experiments will result in the complete transformation of the human species, for the betterment of mankind.

Dr. Browning is about to experiment on Sorel's assistant, Bradford, when Konratz interrupts him, claiming that the doctor's experiments are hurting the movement and that he must halt his work for the time being. When Browning resists, Konratz attacks him but Browning overpowers his adversary and throws Konratz into a tub of acid.

Browning's reprieve, however, is only temporary and he is once again interrupted by Fremont (Christopher Lee), a British government official. Like Konratz, Fremont is in reality another of the superhumans whose objective is the peaceful takeover of earth and who echoes Konratz by telling Browning that he is expendable. Using telepathic powers, Fremont forces Browning to commit suicide by drowning himself in the same acid bath where Konratz was destroyed.

Fremont leaves the estate with Sorel and Bradford, but their eventual fates are unknown.

If you blinked you might have missed him. Cushing as Benedek in Amicus' *Scream and Scream Again.*

Commentary

> *I will accept any part — big or small — if I feel my contribution will mean something, and not be a disappointment to those who go to see my performances in particular. Naturally I prefer a large role — because I love work and need to — for many personal reasons apart from the obvious.* — Peter Cushing

While NASA scientists were preparing their trio of astronauts for man's first walk on the moon, Amicus producers Milton Subotsky and Max J. Rosenberg were equally busy preparing movie audiences for yet another alien invasion (of sorts) of earth. Adapting Peter Saxon's science fiction–horror novel *The Disoriented Man* for the screen, production on *Scream and Scream Again* began at Shepperton Studios in the Spring of 1969. Though perhaps not as momentous an occasion as seeing humans cavorting on the lunar surface for the very first time, it was nonetheless an event in its own right. For the first time in fantasy film history, the three "titans of horror," Vincent Price, Christopher Lee, and Peter Cushing, would be appearing together in the same film.

Gordon Hessler, who had previously directed Lee and Price in AIP's *The Oblong Box* (1968), admitted it was executive producer Louis M. Heyward's idea to get all three stars together.[1] However, Hessler also revealed that as a result of Heyward's last-minute decision, there were script problems. The production simply hadn't been designed with them in mind.[2]

Subotsky added, "We wanted the three top horror stars in one film.... I was glad that Cushing and Lee accepted the small roles they had. Perhaps it was a bit of a cheat to advertise them as 'stars' rather than 'guest stars.'"[3]

Not only were viewers cheated by the limited on-screen time of their favorite horror film stars, they were probably just as equally baffled over the film's confusing storyline.

Screenplay writer Chris Wicking spoke about the script's evolution:

> Gordon Hessler didn't like the screenplay. He didn't feel Milton [Subotsky] could deliver what they wanted.... I got a call from Gordon requesting I read the book and then Milton's screenplay. The book gave me goosebumps. Then I read Milton's script, which was totally flat; it was like watching a soufflé dying, it just caved in after awhile.... Gordon and I discussed it at length. He saw the police material as *Coogan's Bluff* country.... The one radical thing we did, which changed what Milton had done and came directly from the book, was take out the blobs from space.... We wanted to do a Don Siegel–style horror film, *Coogan's Bluff* meets *Invasion of the Body Snatchers*, and we needed something stronger than lumps from another planet. So we took the aliens away and implied that Vincent Price's mad doctor character was responsible for the superhuman creatures.... We wanted to investigate science and politics, so we used a lot of material from news headlines, material about transplants and genetic experimentation.[4]

After removing the main thrusts of Saxon's book — which dealt with alien scientists developing a race of superrobots using parts taken from living humans for the express purpose of eventually having these robots conquer the earth — Wicking's own soufflé screenplay turned out more along the lines of an IHOP special! While genetic engineering by our own scientists leaves one with a sour taste, the thought of an alien race of beings tampering with homo sapiens' genes and transplants is even more horrific by virtue of its mere implication. Wicking's script took care of this gaping hole by simply adding a car chase!

Cushing's character, originally Schweitz in Saxon's book, was changed to Benedek for the film. Otherwise, Wicking's screenplay left the character pretty much unchanged (Benedek lived for approximately two pages and then is killed off by a method that can only be described as a "Vulcan neck pinch"!) Both Lee's and Price's characters fared a little better in the film, though the three actors did not have any scenes together.

Scream and Scream Again was released through American International Pictures in the United States and, according to Milton Subotsky, "it made a lot of money." Subotsky also admitted that the story "wasn't all that good." The only reason he could give for the film's success was the fact that it starred the three top horror names and that "it had a good title."⁵

American International Pictures mogul, Samuel Z. Arkoff, described Peter Cushing to the authors as "A competent, highly professional actor," adding that "I never thought of him as a horror star. He lacked the flamboyance of Vincent Price and the diabolical look of Christopher Lee—he was just an excellent actor who somehow got into horror parts." Arkoff believed that Cushing "wasn't a conventional leading man–type and he certainly made the most of being type-cast. It's kind of a shame that it happened, but it did make him a big star."

Arkoff believed that "Cushing's name on a poster meant as much as anyone's—except maybe Vincent Price—when you're talking about getting people to see a horror movie. I would have liked to have used him, but he was in England with Hammer."

Critiques for *Scream and Scream Again* included John Russell Taylor of *The Times* (January 30, 1970), who observed that the film "starts badly, with a lot of seemingly fairly gratuitous unpleasantness and fragments of at least three different plots without any apparent connection. This, at least, should be intriguing, but is only irritating and boring. Little by little though the film pulls itself together ... even if the solution is not particularly satisfactory."

"Rick" of *Variety* (February 11, 1970) wrote that "The logic of Christopher Wicking's screenplay ... has almost as many holes in it as the assorted victims of the action.... Director Gordon Hessler is a low-budget sado-masochistic Hitchcock. Long after *Scream and Scream Again* has emitted its last shrill screech, disquieting nightmare images remain ... very effective, suspensefully developed and gory horror story with spy and sci-fi overtones."

The *New York Times* (Howard Thompson, July 9, 1970) reported that the film "proceeds to unwind British-style, crisply, puzzlingly and with some restraint ... the plot ... begins to loop into a good, tight knot after the director, Gordon Hessler, bears down hard and graphically on a countryside pursuit by the police of a young mod-type killer.... But with the murder of the police inspector..., the picture slouches into standard fare and ends up in still another mad scientist's lair ... it manages to collapse almost triumphantly." And *Films and Filming* remarked that "On one level, it is a thoughtfully efficient computer job."

Vincent Price, however, put it best: "I never knew what it was about.... It was a strange story, a strange movie."⁶

Notes

1. CEO of AIP's European division.
2. Gordon Hessler, interview with Guy Woolsey, *Fangoria* 53.
3. Milton Subotsky, interview, *Little Shoppe of Horrors* 2.
4. Philip Nutman, "Blood from Hammer's Tomb," *Fangoria* 84.
5. Chris Knight, "The Amicus Empire," *Cinefantastique* 2, no. 4.
6. Vincent Price, interview, *Cinefantastique* 19, nos. 1–2.

Bloodsuckers
(1969)

Credits and Cast

Released 1971; 87 minutes; (82 minutes U.S.); Movielab color; A Lucinda-Titan International Production; Released through Chevron (Paragon), A division of Cinecom and Grand National (U.K.); MPAA R; Filmed in England and on location in Cyprus. Director: "Michael Burrowes" (Robert Hartford-Davis); Producers: Peter Newbrook, Robert Hartford-Davis, Graham Harris (*Bloodsuckers*); Screenplay: Julian More; Based on the novel *Doctors Wear Scarlet* by Simon Raven; Director of photography: Desmond Dickinson, B.S.C.; Music composed and conducted by Bobby Richards; Sound: Tony Daive, Denis Whitlock. Title in U.K.: *Incense for the Damned*.

Patrick MacNee (Major Derek Longbow), Peter Cushing (Dr. Walter Goodrich), Johnny Sekka (Robert Kirby), Patrick Mower (Richard Fountain), Madeline Hinde (Penelope Goodrich), Alex Dairon (Tony Seymour), Imogen Hassall (Chriseis Constandinidi), William Mervyn (Honeydew), Edward Woodward (Holmstrom), David Lodge (The Colonel), John Barron (The Diplomat), Valerie Van Ost (Don's Wife), Theo Moreos (The Mayor), Nick Pandelides (Monk Superior), Andreas Potamites (Police Chief), Theodosia Elsethreadon (Old Woman), Christ Elestheriades (The Priest).

Synopsis

> *Richard came to Greece in search of some sort of freedom. To seek his manhood!* — Seymour

> *Oh? Well, they say this climate works wonders for that sort of thing!* — Longbow

Richard Fountain (Patrick Mower), an Oxford don, feeling the pressures of academic life as well as those of his overbearing and dominating provost, Dr. Walter Goodrich (Peter Cushing), who expects him to succeed in his studies as well as marry his only daughter Penelope (Madeline Hinde), flees England for a vacation in Greece.

When Richard fails to return from his extended stay, his friends, Tony Seymour (Alex Dairon), Bob Kirby (Johnny Sekka), and Penelope journey to Greece in search of him. It is there they learn that Richard has fallen victim to a strange cult of perverted socialites, led by an even more mysterious young woman, Chriseis Constandinidi (Imogen Hassall). The group is suspected of practicing the black arts and of being involved in ceremonies which include orgiastic rituals, human sacrifice, and vampirism.

Tony seeks out Derek Longbow (Patrick MacNee), a British embassy official, and discovers that Richard is under suspicion of being an accomplice in the murder of a native woman. He also learns that Chriseis is being investigated in the disappearances and possible ritual murders of other young women in the country. Longbow offers to help Seymour and his companions find Richard and urges him to get Fountain out of the country as soon as possible.

Although Chriseis and her followers are at first elusive, Longbow and the others finally track them down. In a deserted castle high in the mountain regions of the island of Hydra, Longbow, Kirby, and Seymour rescue Richard—found drugged and in a state of semiconsciousness—from Chriseis. However, Chriseis herself manages to escape them. Longbow pursues her across the mountains but is killed in the attempt. Later Chriseis returns to the castle and is discovered by Bob Kirby in the act of drinking Richard's blood. Kirby and the woman struggle and Chriseis is killed.

Near death, Richard is brought back to England by his friends where he eventually recovers. However, the same pressures that drove him to leave Oxford in the first place begin to surface again. Goodrich urges Richard to become engaged to his daughter and personally takes over his social and academic schedules, telling him that if he works hard he stands a good chance of becoming the college's youngest president. Richard suffers a sort of mental breakdown, and imagines that Chriseis has returned from the dead for him. Strange, erotic dreams fill his conscious mind—images of blood sacrifices and other perverted rituals overcome the mental barriers Richard had placed there to try to protect his sanity. During a dinner party at the college, given in his honor, Richard lashes out at the other dons whom he accuses of trying to control his mind as well as the minds of others like him. These "doctors in scarlet" deprive those under their influence of their academic freedoms and, like psychic vampires, suck the very life essence from them. He personally accuses his prospective father-in-law of these underlying perversions. Pandemonium ensues and Richard escapes the gathering with Penelope, whom he takes to his

Richard (Patrick Mower) accuses Dr. Goodrich in Lucinda-Titan's *Bloodsuckers*.

rooms. Kirby and Seymour follow them and when they break into his apartment, they find that Richard has murdered his fiancée by drinking her blood. Kirby pursues Richard out onto the rooftops of the university and Richard accidentally falls to his death — impaled on the spikes of a wrought-iron fence.

As provost of the college, Goodrich maintains the school's reputation by announcing that Richard and Penelope had taken their own lives by mutual consent. Kirby and Seymour, however, make certain that the evil which they believe was responsible for Richard's and Penelope's deaths is once and for all exorcised by driving stakes through their hearts.

Commentary

> *I understand* [Incense for the Dammed] *has been shelved, it not being acceptable to the Censors.* — Peter Cushing (June 1971)

Filmed in 1969, *Bloodsuckers* attempted to bring to the screen an adaptation of British novelist Simon Raven's book, *Doctors Wear Scarlet*.

Raven, at best, could be described as a poor man's Tennessee Williams, and, in more capable hands, the film that resulted from an adaptation might have warranted limited praise. But, truthfully speaking, it is difficult to understand why anyone would want to bother. The novel in and of itself is ponderous and fraught with psychological symbolism that would be extremely difficult to transfer on-screen, even under the auspices of a top-notch production team. Here it turns into a cinematic disaster.

Described as a vampire-horror-adventure film, its designated audience would, naturally, be disappointed. The plot was not conventional, and "traditional" vampires simply did not exist. *Bloodsuckers*, like its original source, attempted to equate the practice of vampirism with human sexual perversion—a psychological disorder practiced by impotent men and frigid women. It also touches on psychic vampirism, the kind practiced, in this case, by intellectuals at the university where Richard teaches. It castigates college dons who suck the mental energies out of others around them. The professors grow stronger while their unsuspecting victims are drained of their own individualism and freedom of personal expression. The film becomes a pointless treatise on the inadequacies of the academic world, personal relationships, and one weak man's descent into his own kind of self-imposed hell. Whatever it is, this was certainly not what the exploitation market—for which the film was eventually geared—expected or wanted to see.

Chevron Pictures sought to draw in audiences for *Bloodsuckers* and its cofeature, the GP rated *Blood Thirst*, with advertising that depicted the fanged, blood-drenched mouths of the undead. Ad lines read: "2 Shiver and Shudder Spine Tinglers! *See* the Terror! *Feel* the Shock! *Live* the Horror!" With come-ons like this, it was as doomed to failure as poor, disturbed Richard Fountain ever was! As it deserved, the film had a limited run and faded into obscurity. Recently, however, it has resurfaced in video format.

According to various sources, *Bloodsuckers* had been held up for approximately two years prior to its release due to internal feuds and lawsuits, in addition to censorship restrictions. The director, Robert Hartford-Davis (*Corruption*, 1968) even had his name removed from the credits in a dispute over the shooting and editing of the film. Then there were battles over the film's ownership. All these tempests seem ludicrous in retrospect, considering the finished product.

Though Cushing's personal participation in *Bloodsuckers* was limited, it was worthwhile. Within the short span of time that Dr. Walter Goodrich—one of Richard's psychic vampires—made his appearance, Peter managed to convey the dominating and overbearing personality of his character with little effort. His performance embodied the worst-case scenario of a prospective in-law that one could possibly imagine.

The rest of the cast, which included Patrick MacNee and Edward

Woodward, was uniformly good, though the material was hardly worth their talents. Technical credits were standard.

Woodward, who very graciously took time away from his busy schedule to respond to the authors' request, had this to say about Cushing: "He is the most loved man in the business — an actor of great integrity and the most delightful companion. You only have to mention his name and a smile appears on the face of all who hear it.

"I can't give you stories or anecdotes — only a warm and loving smile."

Very few critics reviewed the film. Ron Borst (of *Photon* 21) called it "a slow-moving and generally boring little British import. . . . While production values are adequate, the script is flat with heavy-handed direction. Both MacNee and Cushing have relatively minor roles." *Cinefantastique* (Spring 1972) commented, "Unfortunately, except for a few good moments and an exciting climactic roof-top chase . . . director Robert Hartford-Davis cannot sustain audience attention. . . . Performances are good, but Peter Cushing appears only in another one of his 'cameo' appearances." *Cinema/TV Today* gave the film its only favorable notice: "After a slow start, this develops into an adequately exciting, occasionally erotic, out of the ordinary mixture of adventure and horror that may prove too intellectual for the bottom rung of addicts but should compensate for this by keeping the brighter ones more alert and interested than usual. A novel written almost entirely in dialogue with an academic flavour is not the most easy to adapt for the popular market — particularly when the plot is primarily an intellectual exercise for the educated reader who can identify with the posh characters. Decadence is a failing of the upper classes — whoever heard of a decadent dustman?"

Which brings to mind the tale about the decadent regent who paraded through the streets in his latest "finery" to the oohs and ahs of his fellow postulating nobles, when suddenly a peasant child from the crowd of onlookers shouted, "Look! The emperor isn't wearing any clothes!"

Frankenstein Must Be Destroyed
(1969)

Credits and Cast

Released June 1969 (U.K.); 97 minutes; Technicolor; A Hammer Film Production; Released through Warner Brothers; Filmed at MGM/EMI Elstree Studios, England. Director: Terence Fisher; Producer: Anthony Nelson-Keys; Screenplay: Bert Batt, Anthony Nelson-Keys; Music: James Bernard; Music supervisor: Philip Martell; Director of photography: Arthur Grant; Camera: Neil Binney; Editor: Gordon

Hates; Production design: Bernard Robinson; Construction manager: Christopher Neame; Makeup: Eddie Knight; Hairdresser; Pat McDermott; Continuity: Doreen Dearnaley; Sound: Tony Lumkin; Assistant director: Bert Batt.

Peter Cushing (Baron Frankenstein), Veronica Carlson (Anna), Freddie Jones (Professor Richter), Simon Ward (Karl), Thorley Walters (Inspector Frisch), Maxine Audley (Ella Brandt), George Pravda (Brandt), Geoffrey Bayldon (Police Doctor), Colette O'Neil (Mad Woman), Harold Goodwin (Burglar), George Belbin, Norman Shelley, Frank Middlemass, Michael Gover (Guests), Jim Collier (Dr. Heidecke), Alan Surtees, Windsor Davies (Policemen).

Synopsis

> *Excuse me, I didn't know that you were doctors.* — The Baron
> *Doctors? We are not doctors.* — Lodger
> *I beg your pardon. I thought you knew what you were talking about.* — The Baron

Dr. Heidecke (Jim Collier), arriving at his doorway late one night, is beheaded by an unseen man with a sickle.

A seemingly abandoned manor house is ransacked by a burglar (Harold Goodwin). A man, carrying a sinister container, stealthily enters. The thief, startled by a body in a glass case, is further startled by the man — his face hidden behind a loathsome mask. They struggle, and the burglar escapes as Baron Frankenstein (Peter Cushing) peels off his mask in disgust. He dismantles his apparatus, preparing to flee.

The terrified burglar is questioned by the insufferable Inspector Frisch (Thorley Walters) who searches the house. Frankenstein is gone, leaving many questions unanswered.

In Altenburg the baron finds lodging — using the name Fenner — in a beautiful home run by the equally beautiful Anna Spengler (Veronica Carlson). Anna's lover, Karl (Simon Ward), is a doctor at a mental asylum and is treating a colleague of Frankenstein. Dr. Brandt (George Pravda) has been judged hopelessly insane by Dr. Richter (Freddie Jones) — driven mad by his researches. Richter feels that Mrs. Brandt (Maxine Audley) should be told to end her visits.

In Anna's sitting room the baron learns from his fellow lodgers that Brandt is at the asylum. He also learns that Karl is stealing drugs and selling them to support Anna's invalid mother. He blackmails the couple into helping him kidnap Brandt. Karl falls deeper into Frankenstein's grasp when he inadvertently kills an elderly watchman while robbing a medical supply house.

Frankenstein plans to cure Brandt's madness through surgery to learn of a transplant technique Brandt had perfected. During the kidnapping Brandt is injured and suffers a heart attack—he will not survive the planned surgery. Undaunted, the baron kidnaps Dr. Richter and transplants the dying Brandt's brain into Richter's skull.

Frankenstein is spotted on the street by Mrs. Brandt who tracks him to Anna's house. With no options, he takes Mrs. Brandt to the basement where Brandt-Richter is sedated and heavily bandaged. Her "husband" recognizes her through his coma-like state and she is overjoyed that he is alive—and sane. She promises to remain silent.

The baron and his unwilling accomplices leave immediately, taking Brandt-Richter with them. When Mrs. Brandt returns to the house, she finds it empty and contacts the police. In a shed, under the floorboards, is the disfigured corpse of Dr. Brandt.

Frankenstein finds refuge in an abandoned manor house and waits for the moment when he can question his Creature. Karl and Anna plot their escape.

While Anna is tending to the Creature, Karl slips out to hitch the horses. The baron sits, doing nothing, as his custom, sipping coffee.

As Anna enters the basement, the Creature is awake and has removed his bandages. He pathetically shuffles toward her, begging for help.

Meanwhile, the baron has discovered Karl in the stable. The two struggle, and after subduing the younger man, the baron rushes to the basement.

Anna, terrified, has misunderstood the Creature's intentions and stabs him with a scalpel. When the baron arrives, the Creature is gone. When she admits stabbing him, Frankenstein kills her with the scalpel.

The Creature is en route to Brandt's home, where he knows Frankenstein will go to find the transplant notes. Karl has found Anna's body and he, too, knows where to go.

Stealing into Mrs. Brandt's bedroom, the Creature waits, until she has awakened, hidden behind a screen. Sobbing, he explains his horrifying situation. She is, at first, coldly disbelieving—then, even colder, rejects him as a monster.

After allowing her to leave, he prepares for Frankenstein's arrival. Knowing that the baron will enter the study for the notes, he soaks the area with kerosene. When Frankenstein tries to open the door to the study, the Creature hurls a lighted lamp, setting the room ablaze.

As Karl enters the house, the Creature shoots him and he collapses outside. The baron braves the flames and snatches the notes but, while running out, is tackled by Karl.

The Creature pulls them apart, kicks Karl in the face, and hoists the baron to his shoulders. With the baron begging to be released, the Creature reenters the inferno.

"I need her to make coffee." The chauvinistic Baron Frankenstein with Veronica Carlson in Hammer's *Frankenstein Must Be Destroyed.*

Commentary

Director Terence Fisher was very proud of this film, and rightly so. "The two (films) I am most proud of are *Dracula* and *Frankenstein Must Be Destroyed* . . . one which nobody else seems to care for."[1] The film is so ruthless and pessimistic that, unfortunately, he is correct. This aside,

the film is excellent and is argubly Peter Cushing's best horror performance.

Those expecting a Karloff-type film are in for a surprise. The characters are all too real, with few redeeming qualities. The nominal hero is
a cocaine dealer; the heroine accepts his drug dealing since it helps to pay
for her mother's medical expenses; and the baron ... well!

Peter Cushing, in his fifth appearance as Frankenstein, creates as
chilling a character as ever seen on the screen. His evil hidden behind a
mask of civility and elegant clothing, he has lost any trace of humanity
that surfaced in earlier films. Unable to have relationships of his own, he
is bent on destroying those of others. "He's not really an evil man," says
Cushing, "he's a sad man."[2]

Making his starring debut was Simon Ward, who would soon make
his mark as *Young Winston* (1972). Terence Fisher spotted him on a television program and wisely sought the talented young man to play Karl.

In her second starring role was Veronica Carlson—excellent as the be-
leaguered Anna. Carlson shared her memories of the film and Peter Cushing with the authors. "I used to love his pictures as a child—the English
gentleman but sinister underneath. He had an instinct for what audiences
wanted—what his fans wanted to see him in. He was not motivated by
self."

The film went into general release minus a scene that remains controversial even today. As the production neared completion, Sir James
Carreras—owner of the Hammer Company—appeared on the set. According to Carlson, he felt that the film needed a sex scene. "I thought the
world of Jimmy Carreras," she said, "but it was an error."

His idea was to include—after scenes that follow had already been
filmed—a scene in which the baron enters Anna's bedroom and rapes her.
Carlson was opposed to this, as was just about everyone else. However,
she had little choice. "I couldn't refuse to do it. I felt so impotent."

Not surprisingly, Peter Cushing was opposed to it also. "Peter was disgusted with the scene," she recalled, "and he didn't want to do it. He took
me to dinner to discuss the scene. I remember he wore white gloves. I had
a lovely evening, but it didn't make the scene any easier."

"I turned my face from the camera—it was terrible! Terence Fisher
was very understanding, but it was totally embarrassing and humiliating."
However, this new scene was in an unnatural position: "My reactions to
Peter Cushing are false after the scene was inserted—it gives my character no credence and makes me, as an actress, look the fool."

Fortunately for all concerned, the scene was not included in the U.S.
release. It has, however, resurfaced in a print broadcast on the Turner network.

Other memories for Veronica Carlson were more pleasant, especially working with Freddie Jones who, "taught me a great deal by his example. He praised me and gave me confidence – a brilliant actor to play off." This is certainly true – as the victim of the baron's surgery, his "monster" is the most human character in the film. Rounding out the excellent cast was Maxine Audley as Ella Brandt – equally a victim of the baron.

Audley, whose character had every reason to despise Frankenstein, has the opposite feeling toward Peter Cushing. She told the authors of her experiences with him:

> I worked both the highs and lows with him, in that I played in the Olivier/Leigh *Antony and Cleopatra* in which he played, superbly, Lepidus and I, Charmian. It was a joyful season and he was a joyful man to work with. I do not believe he could spell the word "malice."
>
> The less than classy number I did with him was FMBD. It was then I learned something immeasurable about him.
>
> I played a damsel – a slightly mature damsel in the direst distress. My husband was played by that very great actor Freddie Jones. We had to shoot a scene in which Freddie confronted me, having had somewhat primitive surgery from Cushing/Frankenstein....
>
> To survive the morning's shoot, Freddie brought along a modest tot of cognac which we shared, in order to keep our faces straight ... and I learned about Peter.
>
> Peter played the scene with steel, passion, and power that he might have accorded Hamlet. This man, bless his soul, is a supreme professional.
>
> Off screen, he gives one all his considerable love. On screen, he gives his considerable talent. His discipline is tungsten steel. He is special.

The filming was interrupted to present Peter Cushing with an unusual award. The Pipe Smokers Association had voted him Pipe Smoker of the Year (1968) for his portrayal of Sherlock Holmes in the BBC series. Cushing wisely did not reveal that he has never actually smoked a pipe. He simply – and convincingly – uses them as props.

Another interruption occurred when the stars were asked to donate blood by a traveling unit of the National Blood Donors, prompting Peter Cushing to recall an embarrassing moment from the past. "The only time I ever volunteered to give blood was in New York on my way back to England in 1941. I collapsed as I left the hospital and the nurses had to pump two pints back into me."[3]

Most critics were appalled by the violence and were unable to see past it. There were, however, exceptions. The French *Combat* stated, "In the hands of Fisher, Frankenstein becomes a romantic drama with the power of intense emotion." *Variety* (June 11, 1969) rightly applauded Peter Cushing's performance. "There's nothing tongue in cheek about ... the playing of Peter Cushing who gets his effect by an authority which carries along the audience and which he could hardly strengthen even if playing Lear for an Oscar."

The title must have been an unsettling one for Peter Cushing. He revealed to AP writer Phil Thomas that, "When I signed my contract ... I wrote next to my signature "Over my dead body."

Notes

1. Harry Ringel, "Terence Fisher—The Human Side," *Cinefantastique* 4, no. 3.
2. Warner Brothers press book.
3. Ibid.

One More Time
(1969)

Credits and Cast

Released 1970 by United Artists; 93 minutes; Color by DeLuxe; A Chris/Mark Production; Filmed at Shepperton Studios and on location in London and Herefordshire. Director: Jerry Lewis; Producer: Milton Ebbins; Executive producers: Sammy Davis, Jr., Peter Lawford; Screenplay: Michael Pertwee; Director of photography: Ernest W. Steward; Editor: Bill Butler; Production design: Jack Stevens; Music: Les Reed; Production manager: Frank Ernst; Camera: Jimmy Baude, Ronnie Maaz; Sound: Gerry Humphries; Special effects: Terry Witherington; Makeup: George Frost; Hairstyles: Alice Holmes; Wardrobe: Ken Lawton.

Sammy Davis, Jr. (Charlie Salt), Peter Lawford (Chris/Pepper/Lord Sydney), Esther Anderson (Billie), Maggie Wright (Miss Tomkins), Leslie Sand (Inspector Crock), John Wood (Figg), Sydney Arnold (Tombs), Edward Evans (Gordon), Percy Herbert (Mander), Bill Maynard (Jenson), Dudley Sutton (Wilson), Glyn Owen (Dennis), Lucille Soong (Kim Lee), Anthony Nichols (Candler), Allan Cuthbertson (Belton); unbilled: Peter Cushing (Baron Frankenstein) and Christopher Lee (Dracula).

Synopsis

Fined £500 for violations too numerous to mention, penniless nightclub owners Charlie Salt (Sammy Davis, Jr.) and Chris Pepper (Peter Lawford) are forced to make a decision. If they can't pay the fine, they will get six months in prison, much to the delight of their nemesis, Inspector Crock (Leslie Sands). In desperation they turn to Chris' wealthy twin, Lord

Sydney (also Lawford). He promises to pay the fine if the duo promise to leave England.

Not wanting to leave, they decide that the only "sensible" plan is for Chris to impersonate Lord Sydney for a night on the town. The impersonation becomes more permanent when the real lord is found by Chris, murdered. He convinces Charlie and Crock that he is, in fact, Lord Sydney and passes the murdered lord off as Chris.

This proves to be a poor idea when, at Chris' funeral, Mander (Percy Herbert) and Jenson (Bill Maynard) try to murder Lord Sydney . . . er . . . Chris. It seems that Sydney was doing some undercover work investigating diamond smuggling for Interpol — and learned too much.

While hiding out at Pepperworth Castle, Charlie investigates a secret passage leading to a basement and discovers Baron Frankenstein (Peter Cushing) and Count Dracula (Christopher Lee) lurking.

After more near misses — including a pursuit during a fox hunt, the pair set things right and prepare to return to their philandering ways.

Commentary

Both Peter Cushing and Christopher Lee have expressed a mutual (and reciprocated) admiration for the late Sammy Davis, Jr., who was, apparently, a fan of the Hammer horrors.

The mind boggles somewhat at the thought of the "Rat Pack," after a night of doing whatever it was that they did, retiring to Sammy's for a screening of *Horror of Dracula*. Somehow, Peter Cushing and Christopher Lee seem to have little in common with this crowd and one wonders what it was all about. Cushing explains:

> The indefatigable and extraordinarily talented Sammy Davis, Jr., asked me if I'd do him a favor by appearing for a few seconds in his 1969 production *One More Time* which would involve only a morning's work. He had already shown such kindness and hospitality to Helen and me — first night tickets for his show at the Palladium, dinner afterwards at the White Elephant Club, and endless appreciation for the enjoyment my performances had given him. I happily agreed and he took us both out to lunch when my stint was finished. A fortnight later twelve bottles of champagne and a color television set were delivered . . . with a note from Sammy and his director Jerry Lewis. Moreover, when Helen was so ill he sent her a large bouquet of flowers.[1]

The problem here is that Peter Cushing's "gag" appearance as the baron (with Christopher Lee as Dracula) was unbilled and under-publicized. As a result, fans of the two actors had no way of knowing about their favorites' walk-on. This more or less defeats the purpose, since one would imagine most Cushing/Lee admirers would not be standing in line for trash like *One More Time* without the inducement of seeing their heroes. As far as fans of *Salt and Pepper* (1968) (there must be *some*), are concerned, they were probably unimpressed.

To make things even worse, the brief segment in which the two appear is no better than the rest of the film, which is, in a word, terrible. They show up late in the film (*very* late if one is waiting) and are on screen for an instant. Fuzzily photographed and framed by Davis' inane mugging, the scene is embarrassing. To save you the trouble of actually sitting through the film....

Sammy Davis enters a secret passage and descends into a basement, accompanied by a woman's scream. He sees a poorly madeup distant cousin of the Frankenstein monster, who grunts. On a table is an attractive blonde woman. Sammy turns to the camera, expressing some emotion or another, and a hunchback gibbers. The baron, nattily attired as always, intones. "Aha! we have a visitor!" Dracula, raising a glass of blood, asks, "Won't you join our little party?" Sammy runs up the steps....

The rest of the film, minus Peter Cushing and Christopher Lee, is even worse—much worse. It's difficult to see why it was made and who the producers perceived as its audience. It's sad to dwell too long on how films like this actually get released properly throughout the world while other, better films don't get released at all.

One lucrative sidelight is that Christopher Lee continued his association with Sammy Davis for the television movie "Poor Devil" (1973).

Variety (June 3, 1970) was unimpressed with *One More Time,* stating, "Other than the fact that this British made comedy marks the debut of Jerry Lewis as a director of a film in which he does not appear, it has little going for it. The plot, so called, ..." but you already know about that.

Note

1. Cushing *Past Forgetting.*

The Vampire Lovers
(1970)

Credits and Cast

Released September 1970; 91 minutes (U.K.), 89 minutes (U.S.); Technicolor; A Hammer Film Production; Released through American International Pictures

(U.S.) and MGM-EMI (U.K.); MPAA R; Filmed at Associated British Productions Studios, Boreham Wood, England. Director: Roy Ward Baker; Producers: Harry Fine, Michael Style; Screenplay: Tudor Gates; Based on the novel *Carmilla* by J. Sheridan le Fanu; Director of photography: Moray Grant; Editor: James Needs; Art director: Scott MacGregor; Production manager: Tom Sachs; Assistant director: Derek Whitehurst; Sound: Roy Hyde; Costumes: Brian Box; Music: Harry Robinson; Musical supervisor: Philip Martell; Recording supervisor: Tony Lumkin; Continuity: Betty Harley: Makeup supervisor: Tom Smith; Hairdressing supervisor: Pearl Tipaldi; Wardrobe: Laura Nightingale; Construction manager: Bill Greene; Dubbing mixer: Dennis Whitlock; Camera Operator: Neil Binney; Sound recordist: Claude Hitchcock.

Ingrid Pitt (Mircalla/Marcilla/Carmilla), Pippa Steel (Laura Von Spielsdorf), Madeleine Smith (Emma Morton), Peter Cushing (General Von Spielsdorf), Dawn Addams (The Countess), Kate O'Mara (Madame Perrodot), Douglas Wilmer (Baron Hartog), Jon Finch (Carl Ebbhardt), Kirsten Betts (First Vampire), John Forbes-Robertson (Man in Black), Harvey Hall (Renton), Ferdy Mayne (Doctor), George Cole (Roger Morton), Janey Key (Gretchen), Charles Farrell (Kurt the Landlord), Cat (Gustav).

Synopsis

> *The trouble with this part of the world is they have too many fairy tales.* —Madame Perrodot

Baron Hartog (Douglas Wilmer), whose sister has become a vampire, seeks his revenge on the Karnstein Family, who he believes were responsible. He destroys all but one—Mircalla Karnstein.

The story shifts to a party being given by General Von Spielsdorf (Peter Cushing). A countess (Dawn Addams) and her daughter Marcilla (Ingrid Pitt) are the special guests of the general. When the countess begs to be excused from the gathering due to news of a death in her family, the general offers to look after Marcilla while she is away. The countess agrees and Marcilla befriends the general's niece, Laura (Pippa Steele).

Marcilla gradually comes between Laura and her fiancé, Carl Ebbhardt (Jon Finch). Marcilla tells Laura that she loves her. Soon Laura begins to have nightmares and at the same time grows weaker until eventually she dies due to what the family doctor (Ferdy Mayne) describes as anemia.

Marcilla disappears after Laura's death but soon manages to become the house guest of the Mortons, who are neighbors of General Spielsdorf. Marcilla, who now goes by the name of Carmilla, befriends Morton's (George Cole) daughter, Emma (Madeleine Smith). Emma also starts to have nightmares and is beginning to lose her strength. When Emma's governess, Madame Perrodot (Kate O'Mara) becomes suspicious of Carmilla's unnatural affection for Emma, Carmilla seduces the governess and places the woman under her complete control.

Peter Cushing and Dawn Addams in an attractive greeting in Hammer's *The Vampire Lovers.*

Emma's condition worsens and Renton (Harvey Hall), the Mortons' manservant, suspects that Madame Perrodot is responsible. He sends for the doctor and orders that garlic be placed in Emma's rooms. Renton also sends word to Emma's father of her condition. Morton returns and meets Baron Hartog and General Spielsdorf, who tell him that Laura was a victim of a vampire and that Emma is in the same danger. They further explain that they suspect Carmilla is, in reality, Mircalla Karnstein, the last of a family of vampires who have terrorized the region for centuries. Morton agrees to join the vampire hunters.

Carl Ebbhardt, fearful for Emma's safety, rides on ahead to Morton's house and confronts Carmilla. He tries to fight her, but she simply vanishes before his disbelieving eyes and returns to the safety of her concealed grave at her ancestral castle.

The vampire hunters anticipate her flight and converge on the castle. They discover the hidden tomb and when it is opened find Carmilla at rest, her body free of the corruption of death. General Spielsdorf drives a stake through her heart and beheads the vampire, believing that with Mircalla's true death they have destroyed the last of the Karnsteins. However, a mysterious man in black is seen riding away from the crypt.

Commentary

> *Peter was the kindest colleague I have ever met in my 54 years in the business.* — Ferdy Mayne (December 1990)

Hammer Film's first entry in the subsequently called "Karnstein Trilogy," *The Vampire Lovers*, went into production on January 19, 1970, at Elstree Studios. Based on characters originally created by Joseph Sheridan le Fanu in his novella, *Carmilla* (originally published in 1871), producers Harry Fine and Michael Style had hoped to bring out the story's underlying sexuality. They succeeded quite effectively. *The Vampire Lovers* is opulent in Gothic atmosphere and sensuality — perhaps more so than in any of Hammer's previous attempts.

Ingrid Pitt, who played Carmilla, believed that the film's success was due to what she called director Roy Ward Baker's "restrained way of shooting it. You felt that the vampire did other things than lurk around drinking blood . . . [it was] not treated as (a) 'horror movie' with all the usual paraphernalia of creaking doors and rattling chains."[1]

Though a definitive version has yet to be made, Hammer's vision of Le Fanu's hauntingly beautiful tale is, at times, inspiring. The opening precredits sequence with vampire hunter Douglas Wilmer witnessing the spectacular corporealization of one of the undead is one example of Hammer at its classic best.

Roy Ward Baker's direction is laudable. His instinctual feel for the Gothic is evidenced in all his Hammer and Amicus works. *The Vampire Lovers* is further proof of his natural gift for breathing new life into those genre films which might otherwise have suffered in the hands of a lesser talent.

Baker recalled that he helped contribute to the film's unnatural atmosphere. "One of the supernatural touches I used in the film was when someone threw a dagger at Ingrid. I showed it going right through her, and we did that effect on the floor, not as an optical. There were some superbly photographed scenes of Ingrid moving through a cemetery as a ghost and one scene where I dissolved through a tapestry to show another room."[2] All of Baker's efforts, as well as those of the special effects and camera crew add immeasurably to the surrealism of the picture.

A first for Hammer was the main theme of the picture: a lesbian vampire. Screenplay author Tudor Gates told Randy Palmer:

> Once I'd decided what the interpretation of the *Carmilla* story would be, I simply decided to underscore it, particularly the lesbian undertone. Le Fanu, in his period, could not make that undertone any more clear than he did. I wanted to bring it out in the open. And to do that, I knew we would have to employ a certain amount of nudity in the film.... The doors of censorship were opening wide, and there was a complete new liberty in what could be allowed on film. Hammer had been making their productions deliberately more adventuresome and I wanted to make an up-to-date picture that would be able to employ this new permissiveness.[3]

Though many might call Tudor Gates' idea of nudity gratuitous, it was as tastefuly handled as could be expected. Whether or not it was necessary is pointless in retrospect. The fact remains that it was employed here for the first time, and, afterwards, Hammer never looked back. It was also the first time that a Hammer film was given an "R" rating upon its U.S. release.

All technical aspects of the film were extraordinary — in particular, set direction, music, and costumes. The film's lead performers were no less impressive. Ingrid Pitt carried her role with as much grace as she did vice. Although criticized by some as being too old for the part, these same critics may not have sensed the ever-present undercurrent of sensuality this very skilled actress was able to invest into her character and that she was able to do it with such obvious style. Pitt easily outclasses the production's novice thespians, Pippa Steele and Madeleine Smith, and even the more experienced Kate O'Mara.

In a surprising turn, all the key male members of the cast had relatively minor parts, notably, Peter Cushing, Douglas Wilmer, Jon Finch, and Ferdy Mayne.

Douglas Wilmer, noted for his appearances in such Hollywood favorites as *El Cid* (1961), *Jason and the Argonauts* (1963), and *The Golden Voyage of Sinbad* (1973) among many other fine performances, played Baron Hartog in the film. Hartog was a tragic character who had vowed to destroy every member of the Karnstein family after one of them corrupts his sister and turns her into a vampire.

TERROR and TORTURE EMBRACE IN UNHOLY BLOOD-LUST!

EVEN THE LIFELESS CAN LOVE. EVEN THE DEAD CAN DESIRE!

THE VAMPIRE LOVERS

AN AMERICAN INTERNATIONAL RELEASE Starring

R — RESTRICTED

AN AMERICAN INTERNATIONAL HAMMER FILM PRODUCTION

INGRID PITT · GEORGE COLE · KATE O'MARA and PETER CUSHING AS THE GENERAL

GUEST STAR DAWN ADDAMS SCREENPLAY BY TUDOR GATES · DIRECTED BY ROY WARD BAKER · PRODUCED BY HARRY FINE · CO PRODUCER MICHAEL STYLE COLOR BY MOVIELAB

© 1970 American International Pictures, Inc.

In addition to his film career, Wilmer is also known to British television audiences as the immortal Sherlock Holmes. Peter Cushing would later take over this role from Wilmer, appearing in the last sixteen episodes of the series, 1968–69. Wilmer was contacted about his association with Peter on the film and he remembered a particular day on the set when both he and Peter reminisced about the Holmes series.

> When I refused to continue in another series of "Sherlock Holmes" for the BBC (owing to a large amount of "unwisdom at the helm," so to speak), Peter took over for me. He agreed to the proposed reduced rehearsal schedule that had been "the last straw" for me.
>
> It was during *The Vampire Lovers* that I asked him how he had enjoyed doing the Holmes series. He replied tersely to the effect that he would rather sweep Paddington Station for a living than go through the experience again. He had my sympathies!

Yet another member of the distinguished cast of *The Vampire Lovers* was Ferdy Mayne, who deservedly earned his own form of immortality after his commanding performance as Count Von Krolack in Roman Polanski's horror-comedy farce, *The Fearless Vampire Killers* (1967) (U.K. title, *Dance of the Vampires*). Mayne has appeared in well over 110 feature films since he initially entered the business in 1943 and has known Peter Cushing since the early days of television.

Ferdy originally costarred with Peter in the 1953 six-part television serial entitled *Epitaph for a Spy* and recalled that during those early days of British television all the performances were done live. This particular broadcast was transmitted from the Alexandria Palace Studios, one of the BBC's first television facilities in London. Mayne recalled:

> In those days we did this on a Sunday and then repeated it the following Thursday. The "scenery" on the set was not as solid as it is today. At one point in the performance, I had to have an "angry exit" and I stormed towards the door leading out of the "drawing room" set and . . . I couldn't open the door! It was unyielding stuck! I pushed, made noises . . . cursed, and I couldn't make an exit! Peter, always a great improviser, said "Oh, allow me! There is another way out of this house. Let me lead you to it!" He then led me past the camera toward an apparent exit!
>
> Also, I remember that at another point in the play, I dried up! I couldn't remember my lines! I remember there was one way of dealing with it, and that was just to mouth the lines, which gave the impression to the audience, hopefully, that the sound had broken down. So I said anything that came to my mind, just mouthing them, and Peter again helped me out of another potentially disastrous situation.
>
> Peter was always there and was always helpful. He was such a conscientious artist. To look at his script was like looking at an opera libretto! All the detail work he had thought of. I think he was one of the most hard-working actors I have ever met in my long, long career. Peter was

a saint! I think he was the most saintly actor I ever knew. His friendliness and helpfulness, his charm. He was always in a good mood and he combined it by being a hard worker. But he never made it look as though it was hard work.

Ferdy Mayne also reminisced about his performance in *The Vampire Lovers* and a particular experience he had during the making of the film.

> I remember a dreadful story that happened to me during *The Vampire Lovers* that was produced by a friend of mine [Harry Fine]. I think I got the part because Harry pushed me into the part. The producers did say to me, "Do you ride?" In those days, one just lied! I said, "Of course I do!" figuring I would wing it when the time came. But this time it wasn't all that easy!
>
> *Vampire Lovers* had a young man in it whom Polanski used later on in his version of *Macbeth*, Jon Finch. Jon was an accomplished horseman. When it came to that great scene where we had to ride through the forest, I, as the doctor who had to accompany Jon, thought we were going to ride . . . slowly. But no! Not with Jon galloping away! I tried to follow.
>
> I did ask the producers to give me a *very old horse* and they did. I just couldn't get on with this horse. I cut a very self-conscious figure on it. Hoping that I could make this horse gallop or move faster, I held on to its neck and tried to encourage it, not only by using my heels, but my hands. Apparently, it was an old circus horse that was trained to go down on its knees when you touched a certain spot on its neck. And this was precisely what happened! It went down and as it did, I shouted, "CUT!" The director, who as an irate little red-headed Scotsman said, "How dare you! How dare you shout cut! You're an actor, you should get on with the job! I'll never employ you again!" And Roy never did employ me again! We stayed friends throughout the years, whenever I did manage to meet him, but I never got another job with him!

Ferdy Mayne is still very active in the business, although unfortunately for his American fans, his work nowadays is mostly overseas in Europe and, in particular, Germany. He has appeared in many television shows and, more recently, has worked on more than a few German series. Ferdy's daughter, Belinda, is also in the acting profession. Among her credits was the 1981 television movie, *Goliath Awaits* which was directed by Kevin Connor and also starred Christopher Lee and John Carradine.

Although *The Vampire Lovers* has to rank as one of Hammer's most impressive entries overall, its only serious drawback was the fact that such talented, veteran actors as Ferdy Mayne, Douglas Wilmer, and, of course, Peter were in what amounted to brief guest star appearances. Cushing's character, General Spielsdorf, does little aside from standing around looking serious and skeptical while Carmilla cavorts with his niece, Laura (Pippa Steele). However, while all three of these well-respected actors deserved so much better than what they eventually received, their contributions were nonetheless memorable.

Critiques for the film varied greatly. Kevin Thomas of the *Los Angeles Times* praised *The Vampire Lovers*, calling it "an excellent horror film — what makes for really good horror is not great quantities of blood and guts spilled across the screen (indeed all-out Grand Guignol fans will be disappointed), but the sense of pathos and loneliness surrounding the monster-heros ... a rare and pleasurable experience ... intelligence and taste...." How poignant director Roy Ward Baker makes it and what really fine performances he gets from most of his quite large cast." A. H. Weiler of the *New York Times* (February 1, 1971) agreed with Thomas, noting, "a departure from a hackneyed, bloody norm. It also is professionally directed, opulently staged and sexy to boot." However, Kathleen Carroll of the *New York Daily News* disagreed, saying, "Horror movies, like *The Vampire Lovers*, drain us of patience, not blood, for they are always so predictable." *New York* magazine's Judith Crist in her article, February 15, 1971, called it, "a luscious film for enthusiasts." Donald J. Mayerson of *Cue* (February 20, 1971) thought it was "Smoothly and stylishly directed by Roy Ward Baker ... this Hammer film has the classic constituents of teeth, fog, caresses, stakes through the heart, and garlic flowers. It also has a bevy of beautiful women and some decent acting." John L. Wasserman of the *San Francisco Chronicle* (October 29, 1970) was not easily impressed, however, reporting, "Peter Cushing, who struggles along in this sort of thing regularly, co-stars with a regular bevy of beauties, none of whom will ever be heard from again.... The director, whoever he may be, manages to present their principal assets with enthusiasm and regularity; the rest of the picture just sort of takes care of itself. There is a bit of humor, not much horror.... The plot, if you care, is not worth mentioning. But enough of this sex and violence." John Russell Taylor of *The Times* (September 4, 1970) apparently liked his vampires in the traditional mold, reporting that "apart from being terribly cobbled up in script and direction, [the film] makes the fatal mistake of trying to work Le Fanu's pre–Dracula vampires into the full, familiar vampire cosmology. It just won't go, since any child knows that proper garlic-fearing vampires shrivel in the sunlight, and require to be permanently staked through the heart rather than given a mere peremptory jab." "Rich" of *Variety*, in his September 16, 1970, review, thought the screenplay had "all the needed ingredients. Dark interior, eerie exteriors, shrieks in the night ... plenty of blood, etc. ... but this time the fairly flat dialogue doesn't provide much of the unconscious humor that usually gives a lift to this type of entertainment. Roy Ward Baker has directed it traditionally and the special effects boys, the music and ... technicolor lensing add to the atmosphere.... Cushing, Cole and Wilmer reveal worry, resource and incredulity at appropriate moments."

In a change of pace, Peter had a guest spot on the popular British television comedy-variety series, "The Morecambe and Wise Show." Peter's appearance was so well received that he was asked to return again and wound up being featured several times during the series' run.

Apparently there was a running gag in which Peter found himself caught up that involved the matter of his unpaid salary. Eric Morecambe and Ernie Wise always tried to avoid coming to terms with the problem by employing many diversified and devious means. Peter was eventually reimbursed for his services but not until the very last show was aired.

Notes

1. Ingrid Pitt, interview with Gary Dorst, *Midnight Marquee* 28.
2. Roy Ward Baker, interview with Philip Nutman, *Fangoria* 36.
3. Randy Palmer, "Lust for Horror," *Fangoria* 40.

The House that Dripped Blood
(1970)

Credits and Cast

Released April 1971 (U.S.); 101 minutes; Eastman color; An Amicus Production; Released through Cinerama Releasing; MPAA PG; Filmed at Shepperton Studios, England. Director: Peter Duffell; Producers: Max J. Rosenberg, Milton Subotsky; Executive producers: Paul Ellsworth, Gordon Wescourt; Screenplay: Robert Bloch, based on his short stories; Director of photography: Ray Parslow; Editor: Peter Tanner; Sound: Ken Ritchie; Art director: Tony Curtis; Assistant director: Peter Beale; Music composed and conducted by Michael Dress; Production manager: Teresa Bolland; Camera operator: Gerry Anstiss; Wardrobe: Laurel Staffell; Makeup: Harry Frampton, Peter Frampton; Continuity: Phyllis Townshend; Set dresser: Fred Carter; Dubbing Mixer: Michael Redborne; Dubbing editor: Nolan Roberts; Hairstyles: Joyce James; Titles by G.S.E. Ltd.

Link Story: John Bennett (Inspector Holloway), John Bryans (Stoker), John Malcolm (Police Sergeant). "Method for Murder": Denholm Elliott (Charles Hillyer), Joanna Dunham (Alice Hillyer), Tom Adams (Dominick), Robert Land (Psychiatrist). "Waxworks": Peter Cushing (Philip Grayson), Joss Ackland (Rogers), Wolfe Morris (Waxworks' Owner Jacqueline). "Sweets to the Sweet": Christopher Lee (John Reid), Nyree Dawn Porter (Ann Norton), Chloe Franks (Jane Reid). "The Cloak": Jon Pertwee (Paul Henderson), Ingrid Pitt (Carla), Geoffrey Bayldon (Von Hartmann).

Synopsis

> *That's what's wrong with your present-day Horror Films, no real-
> ism! Not like the old ones—the Great Ones! Frankenstein . . .
> Phantom of the Opera . . . Dracula! The one with Bela Lugosi,
> of course, not that new fella!* — Paul Henderson, Horror Film
> Star

Shortly after renting a country estate, horror film star Paul Henderson (John Pertwee) disappears and Inspector Holloway (John Bennett)
from Scotland Yard is called in to investigate. Inquiring at the local police
station, Inspector Holloway is told about the history of the house and
some of its former tenants — all of whom had tragic ends.

Method for Murder: A writer of horror stories, Charles Hillyer
(Denholm Elliott) leases the house and begins work on his latest novel.
The story concerns an escaped homicidal maniac named Dominick. Hillyer becomes so involved with his character that he suddenly begins to see
him — for real!

Hillyer's wife, Alice (Joanna Dunham) is greatly concerned for her
husband's state of mind and encourages him to see a psychiatrist. However, in the doctor's office, the psychiatrist is murdered by Dominick who
is, in reality, Alice's lover and an actor by profession.

Alice's plot to have her husband judged insane goes awry when Alice's
lover murders Charles along with the doctor and, taking his role a bit too
seriously, murders her as well!

Waxworks: The next tenant is a recently retired stockbroker, Philip
Grayson (Peter Cushing), who hopes to spend his remaining years enjoying his hobbies at the quaint country estate.

Shortly after moving in, Philip goes into town and visits the local wax
museum. He is shocked when one of the exhibits, the figure of Salome
carrying the head of John the Baptist, bears an uncanny resemblance to
a woman he had loved and lost many years ago.

This fact is not lost on Grayson's friend, Neville Rogers (Joss Ackland), who comes for a visit and also notices the striking resemblance.
Rogers, who it seems was also a rival for the woman's affections, becomes
obsessed with the waxwork figure.

Grayson learns that the proprietor of the museum modeled Salome
after his own wife who was executed for the murder of her husband's
(Wolfe Morris) best friend. When Rogers is murdered and Grayson discovers his friend's head on Salome's platter, he realizes that the waxworks'
owner, insanely jealous of any man admiring his wife even in death, was
the real murderer. Philip tries to escape but the owner, wielding an axe,
kills him. Grayson's head replaces that of his friend's in the exhibit.

Philip Grayson falls head over heels for Salome in Amicus' *The House That Dripped Blood.*

Sweets to the Sweet: John Reid (Christopher Lee) leases the house along with his eight-year-old daughter, Jane (Chloe Franks). Reid engages a governess, Ann Norton (Nyree Dawn Porter) who discovers that the child is very sheltered and lonely. The girl is not even permitted toys and when Norton buys her a doll, the girl's father severely berates her for it, throwing the doll into the fireplace. When the governess chastises Reid for his behavior, he explains that Jane's mother was a witch, an evil woman whom Reid believes passed on her wickedness to her offspring. His suspicions prove accurate when Jane fashions a likeness of her father in the form of a wax doll and disposes of it by throwing it in the fireplace, killing her father instantly.

The Cloak: Inspector Holloway then interrogates the real estate agent, A. Stoker (John Bryans), who rented out the house to its various tenants. The agent tells him about the house's latest tenant, a horror film star, Paul Henderson, who was obsessed with the supernatural and longed for a return to the classic age of horror film productions. Disgusted with the cheapness of his latest production, especially his own wardrobe, Henderson visits a mysterious antiques store in the hopes of finding an authentic-looking vampire's cloak. The owner of the shop sells him one for thirteen shillings.

During the next day's shoot Henderson, after donning the cloak, actually bites into the throat of his costar and off-screen mistress, Carla (Ingrid Pitt). Trying to make up for his blunder, Henderson takes Carla out for the evening. But when they return to his house for a nightcap, Henderson confesses that the cloak has mysterious powers. Carla seems unaffected until it is revealed that she is, in reality, a vampire and initiates Paul into the cult of the undead.

Inspector Holloway, skeptical of Stoker's story, visits the infamous house. After making his way into the cellar, Holloway is attacked by Henderson and Carla, who are now both vampires.

Commentary

> I think the genre has really been destroyed by ... producers who have substituted blood, gore and finally very obvious sex for the true feeling of terror and evil which can affect even the most sophisticated of us. Although in the case of my film perhaps these feelings were mostly undermined by the gimmick endings of the short stories themselves. If that strange figment of a troubled mind turns out to be just the wife's nasty boyfriend, how can we suspend disbelief in vampires and werewolves? — Director Peter Duffell, (June 9, 1971)[1]

Amicus' third horror anthology, *The House that Dripped Blood*, was originally supposed to go into production shortly after *Torture Garden* (1967) completed principal photography, but due to a shake-up at Columbia (the distributors for both films), *The House that Dripped Blood* was temporarily shelved. By 1970 producers Milton Subotsky and Max J. Rosenberg had renegotiated with Cinerama Releasing to distribute the film; however, the deal was contingent on the producers delivering Peter Cushing, Christopher Lee, and Ingrid Pitt to star in the film. They did, and *The House that Dripped Blood* finally went into production in the summer of 1970 at Shepperton Studios.

Along with costars Cushing, Lee, and Ingrid Pitt, *The House that Dripped Blood* also featured Denholm Elliott, Joanna Dunham, Nyree Dawn Porter, and John Pertwee—all equally distinguished performers—in key roles. Subotsky, well known in the industry for assigning his films to first-time feature filmmakers, signed Peter Duffell to direct. Duffell, who already had several award-winning documentaries and commercials among his numerous television credits (as well as some theatrical featurettes he had done in the 1960s) attracted Subotsky who was quite impressed with his previous work.

Duffell, who was interviewed by the authors, had nothing but praise for Subotsky.

> Milton is an extraordinary man.... He's got an absolutely photographic memory. You could mention almost any novel that he would have read ... as a possible film script, and he would immediately give you a breakdown of what the story was about.... It was quite extraordinary. I got on very well with Milton.... I remember that in the story with Chris Lee [*Sweets to the Sweet*] ... I had an idea for a scene where the little girl is being taken out by her nanny and they're talking about trees ... and the little girl suddenly points to a yew tree.... She talks about that tree as being an evil, magic tree.... The nanny [Nyree Dawn Porter] says: "Well, how do you know that?" And she says, she read it in a book and ... runs off.
>
> Now that was not in the original script. It was an idea of mine that I wanted to do. I mentioned it to Milton. He didn't think much of it, but I went out and shot it when I had a half an hour to spare one afternoon.... With the best of grace, Milton then said to me, "You were right. That's good. That works. We'll put it in." I thought that was extremely fair and nice of Milton because we had had a considerable argument about this scene. He couldn't see what I was getting at at all. Why I wanted to do it. He thought it was a horrible idea.... But then having seen it on film ... he was all for it. He was jolly good in that way ... a nice chap to work with.... Milton always liked this film as one of the better films turned out by the organization.

However, Peter Duffell was not as impressed with Subotsky's partner, Max Rosenberg.

> My feelings about Max Rosenberg are slightly different. I personally always loathed the title, *The House that Dripped Blood*, which in a way has been a little bit of an albatross around my neck ever since. I wanted to call the film "Death and the Maiden" which I think is a much more resonant and suggestive title ... it came from the fact that I used the Schubert String Quartet in the episode with Peter which I chose quite carefully as the music for that. I'm always very involved in the music in my movies, being a great music lover.... Rosenberg objected, disagreed with me. I begged him to change the title, but he refused. He said, as he put it, "In the marketplace it was a good commercial title." Well, maybe it was, but I still think it's a pretty cheap, trashy title and I think the film deserved better than that.
>
> Rosenberg always believed that Amicus worked as ... a two-tier operation. One tier, the lower one by implication, was the horror movie tier and the upper tier was the tier of serious movies ... which he dealt with, leaving Milton to deal with horror movies.

Duffell was very pleased with the actors chosen for the film, even though he admitted that he had little to do with the initial casting of the players.

It was nice to actually have both of them, Cushing and Lee, cast in straight roles and not as devils, devil worshippers, or vampire killers.... Just two straight human beings in this sort of macabre situation. My working relationship with all of them was splendid. They were always totally professional. I was very lucky in this film in a way because I didn't have any difficult actors at all. Everybody came in, did their bit in which-ever episode they were in, and did it with great professionalism, great charm and great cooperation. I've done a great number of films for televi-sion ... which is where I started. I certainly wasn't unused to working with actors but on a tight budget picture like that, it was a great relief having actors all of whom were totally professional ... and friendly.

Christopher Lee I worked with more recently. I did a big television mini-series called "The Far Pavilions."[2] We spent several weeks together in India working on that picture and I do see Chris quite a lot, actually. We don't live very far from each other and we occasionally visit socially. Chris has a habit of ringing me up and with his deep voice, saying on the phone, "Is this the world's most famous director?" To which I say, "Yes. Is this the world's most famous actor?" A sort of running gag.[3]

Peter, I always found, during what was, after all, a fairly short relation-ship on one movie, an extremely gentle, kind and sensitive person. There was, I think, a slight air of sadness about him at that time which subse-quently became very clear because that was the time when his wife [Helen], whom he loved very much indeed, and to whom he was totally devoted, was dying. I didn't know that until after the film was over. But in retrospect, I realize that possibly some of the slightly indrawn quality of Peter must have been due to the enormous personal stress he was suffering at that time.

As an actor, [Peter] was wonderful to work with, totally sympathetic, and listened to everything that one had to say as a director. It was, after all, my first feature and certainly my first and my last horror movie. Peter was, of course, a veteran of that kind of film. He presumably knew all the tricks of the trade ... but he was always most receptive to suggestions and we got on, I think, extremely well.

Cushing's segment, "Waxworks," was one of four short stories, writ-ten by Robert Bloch, which originally appeared in *Weird Tales* magazine. Bloch then adapted his story for Boris Karloff's "Thriller" television series during its 1961–62 season. However, his subsequent screenplay was quite different from the teleplay and had to be drastically altered in order to in-clude Peter's character, Philip Grayson.

In a letter to the *Wall Street Journal* movie critic, Joy Gould Boyum, Peter Duffell explained his participation in the formation of Grayson.

The "Waxworks" story was basically nothing more than a corny little contrivance to get Peter Cushing's head on a plate and this gave me the greatest problems. I decided to try and give the story a little resonance on the strictly human level by building up the loneliness of the character, taking refuge from the disappointments of life in his books, music and memories, and by introducing the theme of the unhappy love for the unattainable dead girl. I would like to have gone much further in this direction but I was not allowed to.

The nightmare sequence was a last-minute interpolation into the story, because I felt that so little happened and the obsessional thing needed building up more strongly and dramatically. There was really no time allowed in the schedule for it and I had to shoot it in less than a day.

Duffell also told the authors that he was greatly influenced by German Romantic painters like Frederick, whom he believed related tremendously to Gothic horror films. One of Frederick's paintings—which was reproduced in Lotte Eisner's book *The Haunted Screen*—gave him the inspiration for one scene in particular where Peter is seen standing alone by a riverside.

Sharp viewers may have noticed Peter leafing through some theater playbills at the beginning of the segment. Duffell explains. "I took them to the studio and suggested to Peter that this might be a nice sort of thing to do in the sequence. It wasn't in the script. It was something I put in. 'Have a look through these, Peter,' I said and he picked some out. He picked out the ones that we actually used . . . and did mildly mention to me that he was in those productions which I had seen. Of course, that's why I had the programs."[4]

Duffell contributed some of the other props used in the film as well. The castle set used in "The Cloak" belonged to his son, and some of the books and bric-a-brac seen in the house also came from his own personal collection. Furthermore, Duffell also admitted that he had some input concerning many of the "in jokes" that appeared throughout the picture which he says stemmed from his lifelong affection for horror films.

Peter Duffell's affection for the genre is more than obvious in *The House that Dripped Blood*. Although Bloch's trite endings are a bit annoying, the film can take credit for being one of those rare occasions where a true Gothic atmosphere was achieved within a modern-day setting— something that no other Amicus anthology was quite able to achieve. All production values were superior and the cast above reproach.

The majority of film critics who reviewed *The House that Dripped Blood* were enthusiastic. *The Sunday Times* (London, Dilys Powell, February 28, 1971) called it an "agreeable surprise . . . four stories by Robert Bloch . . . go to make up a lively and intelligent essay, far better than its title suggests, in horror and joke-horror. Peter Duffell, directing his first feature film, has dealt admirably with a cast including . . . Peter Cushing." Donald J. Mayerson wrote in *Cue*, "Don't be put off by this abattoiresque title. . . . This spook carnival from England is a witty, literate, campy and most of all, paralyzingly scary film—a work of art in the horror movie genre." "Robe" in *Variety* (March 3, 1971) called it "one of the most entertaining of its genre to come along in several years." Roger Ebert of the

Chicago Sun Times said, "*The House that Dripped Blood* understands horror." Kevin Thomas in his April 23, 1971 review for the *Los Angeles Times* wrote: "despite its lurid and misleading title, [the film] is many notches above today's usual horror fare. Richly atmospheric settings, muted color photography, an outstanding cast and competent direction ... do justice to Bloch's fine script, which deals with psychological terror rather than relying on the typical blood-and-guts formula." Judith Crist in her April 26, 1971, review for *New York* magazine called it "a fictional horror feast ... a collection of four little thrillers to revel in, beautifully conceived and excellently acted." The *New York Daily News* critic, Ann Guarino (April 22, 1971) wrote: "Horror fans will get their money's worth ... horror buffs should not overlook this one." And *Kine Weekly* reported that the film was "thoroughly enjoyable entertainment without a tedious moment."

Notes

1. Letter to movie critic Joy Gould Boyum of the *Wall Street Journal*.
2. Originally shown on the HBO cable television network.
3. Milton Subotsky originally wanted Lee to play the part of Paul Henderson in "The Cloak" segment but Lee evetually turned it down. The part went to Jon Pertwee, who was a popular name on British television for his role as Dr. Who.
4. *School for Scandal* (1948, 1949), *Richard III* (1948, 1949), *Hamlet*—Cushing appeared in the film version, directed by Laurence Olivier, in 1947.

I, Monster
(1970)

Credits and Cast

Released 1972 (U.S.); 80 minutes (74 minutes U.S.); Eastman color; An Amicus Production; Released through Cannon (U.S.) and British Lion (U.K.); MPAA PG; Filmed at Shepperton Studios, England. Director: Stephen Weeks; Producers: Max J. Rosenberg, Milton Subotsky; Screenplay: Milton Subotsky; Based on the novel *Dr. Jekyll and Mr. Hyde* by Robert Louis Stevenson; Production manager: Teresa Bolland; Assistant director: Al Burgess; Director of photography: Moray Grant; Camera operator: Robert Kindred; Sound: Buster Ambler; Editor: Peter Tanner; Makeup: Harry Frampton, Peter Frampton; Hairdresser: Joyce James; Continuity: Phyllis Townshend; Music composed and conducted by Carl Davis; Art director: Tony Curtis; Sound editor: Michael Redbourn.

Christopher Lee (Dr. Charles Marlowe/Mr. Edward Blake), Peter Cushing (Frederick Utterson), Mike Raven (Dr. Enfield), Richard Hurndall (Dr. Lanyon),

George Merritt (Poole), Kenneth J. Warren (Deane), Susan Jameson (Diane), Marjie Lawrence (Annie), Aimee Delamain (Landlady), Michael Des Barres (Boy in Alley).

Synopsis

As a psychiatrist and follower of the recently published works of Dr. Sigmund Freud, Dr. Charles Marlowe (Christopher Lee) has developed a serum which he hopes will, through this stepped-up process, prove Freud's theories concerning the triple elements that make up the human psyche—primitive drive or id, ego, and super ego. He tests the serum on some of his patients but notices that the character traits brought out are unpredictable and decides to experiment further only on himself until the serum is perfected.

With his first attempt, Marlowe is transformed into his alter ego, Edward Blake, a creature with no morals and no conscience. He becomes the perpetrator of a series of heinous crimes while under the influence of the drug. Marlowe's friends, Dr. Enfield (Mike Raven) and Mr. Utterson (Peter Cushing), Marlowe's lawyer, at first suspect that their friend is being blackmailed by Blake. Utterson is more than convinced of this when Marlowe arranges to have his will changed leaving Blake as sole beneficiary. But as the crimes mount and Utterson investigates further, he discovers that Blake and Marlowe are one in the same.

Though Marlowe had to physically administer the drug at first, he soon finds that Blake can emerge at will. As Blake, he also realises that Utterson knows of his association with Marlowe and can expose them. Blake attacks Utterson in the lawyer's home. During the struggle, Blake knocks over a kerosene lamp. The ensuing fire catches Blake's cloak and he rushes from the room to save himself, only to fall down a flight of stairs to his death.

As Utterson looks on, Blake changes back into his good friend, Dr. Charles Marlowe.

Commentary

Not the best film I've ever worked on. — Peter Cushing

I, Monster, based on the novel *Dr. Jekyll and Mr. Hyde* by Robert Louis Stevenson and produced by Milton Subotsky and Max J. Rosenberg (their twenty-fourth film), was shot at Shepperton Studios. Production began on October 19, 1970, with a six-week schedule.[1]

"Not the best film I've ever worked on," lamented Peter Cushing on his role as Dr. Utterson in *I, Monster*.

Taking into consideration the fact that Stevenson's book had been adapted for the screen before, Milton Subotsky, who wrote the screenplay, spoke about the project.

> I realized that *Dr. Jekyll and Mr. Hyde* had been done a lot of times, but I wanted to do the most definitive version of the book ever. I think we did exactly that, except that I changed the character's names (Marlowe/ Blake). It's the closest ever to the ... Stevenson story of any version made ... with only one [other] exception.... Stevenson had Dr. Jekyll hole up in his laboratory at the end, destroying it, where he is found dead.

I thought that was a rather tame ending, so I had him realize that Utterson [Cushing] was getting wise to him and he [Lee] dies in the attempt
to kill his once good friend ... the trouble with the picture is that in
sticking so close to the original we wound up with a film that was very
respectable and rather boring.[2]

Having the distinction of being Amicus' first period-setting film, *I,
Monster* has a magnificent Victorian-Edwardian look, with opulent, ornate sets. Costumes, color photography, and music are also in keeping
with the film's desired effect. Performances throughout are very good.
However, this does not save the film, whose major faults are the aforemen-
tioned screenplay and Stephen Weeks' poor direction.

After Peter Duffell (*The House that Dripped Blood*) turned down
Subotsky's offer to direct this feature (not being comfortable with Subotsky's idea to shoot the film in a variation of the 3-D process and not wanting to become typecast as a horror film director[3]), Subotsky turned to then
twenty-two-year-old Stephen Weeks. Weeks, whose previous work had
been in film shorts and documentaries and who had been suggested to the
producers by the film's star, Christopher Lee, had trouble making the
move up to a full-length feature film.

Subotsky told Chris Knight, "We had a director who didn't know how
to direct action scenes. Everything was fine until you [got] into an action
scene and ... nothing happens, because he didn't know what to do with
it. He didn't end up with the footage needed to cut what we had intended."[4]

Even though the film suffered on these levels, it must be stated that
Christopher Lee (especially as Blake) does give one of his best performances here. Because the book is basically a one-character study, naturally
Lee's dual-nature characters are the focal point of the film and, as such,
leaves little room for the other players to build on.

Cushing's character, Mr. Utterson, who is Marlowe's personal attorney and close friend, is pivotal to the story but is given little screen
time. His best scenes come at the end when Lee (as Blake) attacks Cushing
in the latter's home after Utterson discovers that Blake and Marlowe are
one in the same. Evocative of their confrontations in Hammer's *Dracula*
series, the film's climax is no less exciting due solely to Lee's and Cushing's
superior abilities as actors.

Among the assembled cast are some familiar faces — notably, Mike
Raven, who bears more than a slight resemblance to Christopher Lee, and
who was featured in Hammer's *Lust for a Vampire* (1971), George Merritt
(Poole), who also worked with Lee and Cushing in *Horror of Dracula*
(1957), and Kenneth J. Warren (Deane) who appeared in *The Creeping
Flesh* (1972).

It is also interesting to note that Michael Redbourn, who was the sound editor on the film, would later produce another Cushing-Lee film, *The Creeping Flesh.*

Cinefantastique reviewed the film:

> The only real weak point of the film [was] the basically dull script. The acting, photography, and the recreation of 1906 London are all very well done.... Christopher Lee did his usually splendid job as the Marlowe/ Blake character ... Peter Cushing had little to do as Utterson except question Marlowe on his theories and did both of these quite well.... One question really develops over *I, Monster:* Just why did Amicus choose to re-do the Stevenson work when so many renderings of it have been done already?[5]

Notes

1. Lion International Films publicity release.
2. Chris Knight, "The Amicus Empire," *Cinefantastique* 2, no. 4.
3. Source, Peter Duffell.
4. Knight, "The Amicus Empire," *Cinefantastique* 2, no. 4.
5. Mike Pitts, review, *Cinefantastique* 2, no. 4.

Twins of Evil
(1971)

Credits and Cast

Released June 1972 (U.S.); 87 minutes (85 minutes U.S.); Eastman color; A Hammer Film Production; Released through Rank (U.K.) and Universal (U.S.); MPAA R; Filmed at Pinewood Studios, England. Director: John Hough; Producers: Harry Fine, Michael Style; Screenplay: Tudor Gates; Based on the characters created by J. Sheridan le Fanu; Director of photogrpahy: Dick Bush, B.S.C.; Second unit photography: Jack Mills; Art director: Roy Stannard; Editor: Spencer Reeve; Production manager: Tom Sachs; Assistant director: Patrick Clayton; Sound: Ron Barron, Bill Trent, Ken Barker; Makeup: George Blackler, John Webber; Wardrobe: Rosemary Burrows; Hairdresser: Pearl Tipaldi; Music: Harry Robinson; Music supervisor: Philip Martell; Special effects: Bert Luxford.

Peter Cushing (Gustav Weil), Madeleine Collinson (Frieda Gellhorn), Mary Collinson (Maria Gellhorn), Kathleen Byron (Katy Weil), Damien Thomas (Count Karnstein), Isobel Black (Ingrid Hoffer), David Warbeck (Anton Hoffer), Dennis Price (Dietrich), Harvey Hall (Franz), Alex Scott (Hermann), Katya Wyeth (Countess Mircalla), Roy Stewart (Joachim), Maggie Wright (Alexa), Luan Peters (Gerta), Inigo Jackson (Abode Man), Judy Matheson (Abode Man's Daughter), Sheelah Wilcox (Lady in Coach), Kirsten Lindholm (Young Girl at Stake), Peter Thompson (Jailer).

Synopsis

The Devil has sent me twins of evil! — Gustav Weil

Gustav Wiel (Peter Cushing) and his Brotherhood, a fanatical group of witch hunters, ride deep into the forest to accuse a young woman who lives there of witchcraft. They burn her at the stake.

Soon after, recently orphaned twins, Frieda (Madeleine Collinson) and Maria Gellhorn (Mary Collinson) arrive by coach at the small middle European village of Karnstein. They are to live as the wards of their aunt Katy (Kathleen Byron) and their tyrannical uncle Gustav — a deeply religious and overzealous man who hates the power of the aristocracy and its sinful, evil decadence.

Frieda, the more daring of the twins, is almost at once bored with her new life and is anxious for thrills. She eventually finds her "spiritual twin" in the arrogant Count Karnstein (Damien Thomas) who, like Frieda, is also eager to find ever new amusements.

During a faked black mass ceremony, arranged for by the count's lackey, Dietrich (Dennis Price), the count dismisses all the players except for the "sacrifice," a young woman. Praying over the body, the count murders the girl in an offering to Satan. Karnstein's prayers are answered by the vampiric spirit of Mircalla Karnstein (Katya Wyeth), one of his ancestors, who initiates the count into the cult of the undead.

Maria and Frieda are enrolled at the village school, run by two teachers who are brother and sister, Ingrid (Isobel Black) and Anton Hoffer (David Warbeck). Anton, who is the school's choirmaster, is immediately drawn to the fiery Frieda and he falls in love with her. Though Maria is attracted to him, her feelings go unrequited. Frieda, however, is more interested in the count, and manages to steal away to his castle one night. They become lovers and Frieda is made a vampire.

Anton, who is familiar with the practices of witchcraft, devil worship, and vampirism but who doesn't believe they really exist, speaks with his intuitive sister about the Brotherhood and Gustav Weil's bloodthirsty hunt of young, innocent women. He threatens to expose them to the authorities, but Ingrid cautions him against the idea, knowing that he is attracted to Weil's niece. Anton's skepticism regarding local superstitions is painfully smashed when, soon after, Ingrid's body is brought to the school by Weil — the victim of a vampire's attack.

One night Frieda is caught attacking one of the members of the Brotherhood. She is imprisoned. The Brotherhood holds a trial and Frieda is condemned to death. Count Karnstein, however, arranges to have Maria put in Frieda's place, since no one in the village can tell the twins apart. Anton discovers the switch when Frieda, pretending to be her

Head of the Brotherhood, Gustav Weil, in Hammer's *Twins of Evil*.

sister, tries to attack him and he saves Maria minutes before her death at
the stake.

With the help of the villagers and the Brotherhood, Anton and Gustav — reconciled and allied in a common cause — go after Count Karnstein
and Frieda. Weil captures Frieda and beheads her but is in turn killed by
Karnstein. Anton impales the count with a lance and destroys him.

Commentary

> *I think what was most characteristic of Hammer was its great concern for quality.... Everything that they have produced was looked into to the extremes, and this must have been one of the main reasons for the success of their films. People who went to see them knew what to expect.* — John Hough, Director[1]
>
> *I am finding it very difficult to adjust myself — the whole purpose of my life is gone.* — Peter Cushing (June 1971)[2]

Twins of Evil went into production in the spring of 1971, and was Peter Cushing's first film appearance since the death of his wife, Helen Beck Cushing, on January 14. The physical and mental contrast between his appearances in *The Vampire Lovers*, the initial entry in the Karnstein Trilogy, and this film is not only strikingly apparent, but to fans a bit frightening as well. His character, Gustav Weil, seems, oddly enough, to reflect the actor's own personal inner torment. The spirit and passion which had consistently radiated from the screen whenever he was featured was conspicuously absent in this film. When the screen fills with Gustav Weil's face, showing his character's frustration and indecision, it is an all too real manifestation of Peter Cushing's own personal grief.

Weil wears the puritan black of his character's religious zeal but it is, in reality, Cushing's mourning colors. The blackness of his clothes greatly underscores his skin's sudden pallor and the sharp gauntness of his features speaks volumes about his state of mind. Peter's eyes are tiny mirrors of his heartbreak and anyone viewing the film who was also aware of his personal loss could not help but share in his sorrow.

Originally entitled "The Gemini Twins" and "Twins of Dracula," *Twins of Evil* was a significant departure from previous Hammer productions. Though still lavish in the Gothic style that made the company famous, its concept was more far-reaching than most audiences at the time might have realized. The film was more violent and sexually explicit than any previous Hammer production — despite cuts in the U.S. print — and hidden within the screenplay were some thought-provoking symbolisms that genre critics would have a field day exposing. Bruce Hallenbeck theorized that Cushing represented "authority, the hypocrisy of religion, the overly-protective parent.... [Damien] Thomas' character, on the other hand, represents the opposite extreme; a sort of ultra-decadent Hugh Hefner living in a perpetual state of ennui.... The twins themselves represent rebellious humanistic youth. Maria is like a flower child, but Frieda is an accident waiting to happen, the kind of girl who would nowadays be attracted to a motorcycle-riding hood."[3]

Kevin Thomas, reviewer for the *Los Angeles Times* (August 25, 1972) hailed *Twins of Evil* as "among the most sophisticated horror pictures ever

Newspaper publicity ad mat from *Twins of Evil* press book.

produced by England's Hammer films.... Though conceivably too mor-
bid and grisly ... for general taste ... [it] possesses the kind of bravura
style that should make [it] appealing to film buffs.... Not only [is the] film
distinguished by [an] exceptionally well-wrought script, but [it is] also
strong in richly detailed period atmosphere."

    Screenplay writer Tudor Gates talked about his views regarding the
film and director John Hough: "Hough ... had a nice flair for the Gothic.
There were some absolutely breath-taking shots in *Twins*. I wanted the

picture to have a new, modern look without losing the flavor for which Hammer had become famous and I think Johnny was able to accomplish this very well, especially in scenic composition."⁴ Gates also spoke about Peter Cushing: "Cushing turns in a memorable performance and the story of a repressed Quaker has a strong psychological base."⁵

John Hough, who would later direct Peter in the Yorkshire Television production of the series, "The Zoo Gang" (episode title: "The Counterfeit Trap") in 1973, had this to say about Hammer and his association with the production company, "I was very happy to be working with Hammer because they had always struck me as pioneers in the field. . . . To be at a studio as legendary as the Disney studio. . . . The people at Hammer did seem to feel that they'd had a good run and were coming to the end of an era. I never felt that way, I don't believe it today. Whether it's Gothic horror, or whatever, there will always be a market for a good picture."⁶

Damien Thomas, who played Count Karnstein, spoke about his personal approach to his character and what it was like working with Peter:

> I was hoping to draw some sympathy towards the vampire, that he was like any other person caught in a life situation, over which he has no control. He might have been just an ordinary chap if it had not been for a series of unfortunate events. Although later on he's clearly quite sick, and his sickness deteriorates. He turns into a beast, . . . a terrible, awful, helpless creature, a kind of embodiment of lust and disease and everything else.
>
> Peter Cushing was a delight to work with, and helpful. You see, I think the good actors are generous and helpful to their fellow actors.⁷

Another star of the film, Isobel Black, well known to fans from her appearance in Hammer's *Kiss of the Vampire* (1962) and who played Ingrid Hoffer in *Twins*, also talked about her memories regarding Peter: "I was greatly in awe of Peter Cushing, as was everybody, because, after all, he was 'The Man' of horror films." Black also remembered Peter's obvious state of mind during that time, "He was rather sad. He'd been very devoted to her [Helen]. He was very quiet . . . very melancholy. But . . . a charming man. Not the kind of person you'd expect to be in horror films."⁸

Most critical reviews of the film readily saw its uniqueness. "Jock" in *Variety* (London, October 20, 1971) reported, "above-average horror entry . . . settings, production values, camerawork and acting are all of a high standard. Casting is highly effective. . . . Acting as kingpin is veteran Peter Cushing as the sinister witch-hunter." Robert L. Jerome wrote: "Peter Cushing . . . gives the twisted witch-hunting uncle an almost sympathetic bent as he travels the lonely road of evil-doing in the Lord's name."⁹ Calvin T. Beck remarked that "The plotting is excellent in that the opposite worlds and forces of Good vs. Evil do not plummet into the cardboard-like simplistic depths of more routine horror-actioners. . . . [The] fusion of the austerity of Puritan morality, pesonified by Peter Cushing and his crusading followers, their spartan life-style and meeting hall, are in stark contrast with the dark Gothic mysteries of Karnstein's opulent but foreboding domain."[10] Andrew MacDougall reported "yet another Grimm-style exercise in fairy tale atmosphere, just what this genre needs more of."[11] And lastly the *New York Times* (A. H. Weiler, July 14, 1972) whose reviewer blunders, stating, "Credit the Hammer movie teams with providing a variation on standard horror themes. . . . In *Twins of Evil . . . comely twin sisters are turned into vampires* by that scion of a long line of old Mittle Europe's 'undead,' Count Karnstein, which probably is a first for the Cinema."

Notes

1. John Hough, interview with Alain Schlockoff, *L'Ecran Fantastique*. (Vol. unknown).
2. Letter to the Canadian Peter Cushing Club, general membership.
3. Bruce Hallenbeck, "The Karnstein Trilogy" *Little Shoppe of Horrors* 8.
4. Tudor Gates, interview with Randy Palmer, *Fangoria* 40.
5. Tudor Gates, interview, *Little Shoppe of Horrors* 4.
6. John Hough, interview, *Fangoria* 23. John Hough would direct three films for the Disney studio: *Escape to Witch Mountain* (1975), *Return from Witch Mountain* (1977) — the latter starring Christopher Lee — and *The Watcher in the Woods* (1980). Hough would also direct Peter Cushing in 1985's *Biggles — Adventures in Time* for Compact-Yellowbill Films.
7. Damien Thomas, interview, *Little Shoppe of Horrors* 4.
8. Isobel Black, interview with Bruce G. Hallenbeck, *Little Shoppe of Horrors* 10-11.
9. Robert L. Jerome, review, *Cinefantastique* 2, no. 3.
10. Calvin T. Beck, review, *Castle of Frankenstein* 19.
11. Andrew MacDougall, review, *Little Shoppe of Horrors* 8.

Tales from the Crypt
(1971)

Credits and Cast

Released March 1972 (U.S.); 92 minutes; Eastman color; An Amicus Production; Released through Metromedia (U.K.) and Cinerama (U.S.); MPAA PG; Location scenes filmed in London and Surrey, interiors at Shepperton Studios, England. Director: Freddie Francis; Producers: Max J. Rosenberg, Milton Subotsky; Executive producer: Charles W. Fries; Screenplay: Milton Subotsky; Based on stories from *Tales from the Crypt* and *Vault of Horror* magazines by William M. Gaines, editor; Director of photography: Norman Warwick, B.S.C.; Camera operator: John Harris; Lighting cameraman: Norman Warwick; Editor: Teddy Darvas; Art director: Tony Curtis; Sound: Pat Foster, Nolan Roberts, Norman Bolland; Assistant director: Peter Saunders; Music composed and conducted by Douglas Gamley; Bach's Toccata and Fugue in D Minor played by Nicholas Kynaston; Production manager: Teresa Bolland; Production supervisor: Arthur Stolnitz; Publicity: John Doran; Stills photographer: John Brown; Set decorations: Helen Thomas; Wardrobe: Bridget Sellers; Makeup: Roy Ashton; Hairstyles: Joan Carpenter; Production executive: Paul Thompson; Continuity: Penny Daniels.

Ralph Richardson (The Crypt Keeper), Geoffrey Bayldon (Guide). "All Through the House": Joan Collins (Joanne Clayton), Martin Boddey (Richard Clayton), Oliver MacGreevy (Maniac), Chloe Franks (Carol Clayton). "Reflection of Death": Ian Hendry (Carl Maitland), Susan Denny (Mrs. Maitland), Angie Grant (Susan), Paul Clere (Maitland's son), Sharon Clere (Maitland's daughter), Frank Forsyth (Tramp). "Poetic Justice": Robin Phillips (James Elliot), Peter Cushing (Arthur Edward Grimsdyke), David Markham (Edward Elliot), Edward Evans (Mr. Ramsay), Ann Sears (Mrs. Carter), Irene Gawne (Mrs. Phelps), Kay Adrian (Mrs. Davies), Clifford Earl (Police Sergeant), Manning Wilson (Vicar), Dan Caulfield (Postman), Robert Hutton (Mr. Baker), Melinda Clancy (Mrs. Carter's daughter), Stafford Medhurst (Mrs. Phelps' son), Carlos Baker (Mrs. Davies' son), Dog (Jamie). "Wish You Were Here": Richard Greene (Ralph Jason), Roy Dotrice (Charles Gregory), Barbara Murray (Enid Jason), Peter Thomas (Pallbearer), Hedger Wallace (Detective). "Blind Alley": Nigel Patrick (Major William Rogers), Patrick Magee (George Carter), Tony Wall (Attendant), Harry Locke (Cook), George Herbert (Old Blind Man), Carl Bernhard, Ernest C. Jennings, John Barrard, Chris Cannon, Hugo de Vernier, and Louis Mansi (Blind Men), Dog (Shane).

Synopsis

Five sightseers become separated from their tour group while visiting some ancient catacombs in England, though none of them can explain why they are there. Looking for a way out, they become trapped in a secret chamber located in one of the caves. It is here that they meet the crypt keeper (Sir Ralph Richardson). He probes each of their minds and they are forced to envision what the future holds for them as a result of their unrepentant greed, cruelty, and, in some cases, acts of murder.

The first story, "All Through the House," concerns an escaped homicidal maniac (Oliver MacGreevy), dressed in a Santa Claus suit, who terrorizes and eventually murders housewife (Joan Collins) who had just murdered her husband (Martin Boddey) on Christmas Eve.

The next play, "Reflection of Death," is about a man, Carl (Ian Hendry), who deserts his family for his mistress, Susan (Angie Grant). While attempting to drive out of town together, they are involved in an automobile accident. As a result, Susan is blinded, but Carl, though killed in the crash, cannot rest and he haunts all the places of his former life. Carl awakens to find that it was all a dream. Susan is at the wheel of his car driving them out of town when they are suddenly involved in a car crash.

The third tale, "Poetic Justice," concerns wealthy homeowners James and Edward Elliot (Robin Phillips and David Markham) who despise their kind, lonely neighbor—a junk man named Arthur Edward Grimsdyke (Peter Cushing). Grimsdyke is an old man who adores the neighborhood children. He entertains them after school with stories and repairs discarded toys for them to play with.

Deeming Grimsdyke's rundown house an eyesore in the community, the younger Elliot tries to harass Grimsdyke into selling his property—which has considerable land value—and moving away. After several unsuccessful attempts, he lights upon an idea which involves the upcoming St. Valentine's Day holiday. Elliot arranges for cards to be delivered to Grimsdyke, supposedly sent from everyone in town. Each card contains a cruel and vicious rhyme. As a result, Grimsdyke, heartbroken, takes his own life. But exactly one year later he returns from the grave to deliver his own heartfelt valentine.

The next morning the elder Elliot finds the body of his son and a message which reads:

> Happy Valentine's Day!
> You were mean and cruel
> Right from the start
> Now you really have no

Along with the poem is the still-beating heart of Elliot's son which Grimsdyke had ripped out of his chest in revenge.

The fourth tale, "Wish You Were Here," is a variation of "The Monkey's Paw." It concerns a wife, Enid Jason (Barbara Murray) who has bought a mysterious Chinese curio which has the power to grant three wishes. When her husband Ralph (Richard Greene), a ruthless businessman, is killed in an automobile accident, she uses the three wishes granted to her to bring him back from the dead. What she doesn't realize is that her husband died from a heart attack just before his car accident and that his body was embalmed. The embalming fluid keeps his body forever preserved, but he is in agony from the burning fluid. Enid tries to destroy him by chopping up his body, but now all the body parts have a life of their own as a result of her last wish.

The last story, "Blind Alley," is about a greedy, self-centered man, Major William Rogers (Nigel Patrick), who takes up a position as superintendent in a home for the blind. Unconcerned with the special needs of the blind, he uses the funds allotted to the inmates for his own purposes.

Grimsdyke and Jamie in Amicus' *Tales from the Crypt*.

When, as a result of neglect, one of the inmates dies, his fellow inmates devise their own form of revenge which puts Rogers in the position of learning what it is really like to be blind.

The film ends with the tourists attempting to leave the caves but instead finding that the only exit leads to a firey pit. Each of them realizes that they have descended into hell because of their sins.

Commentary

> *This little man, Grimsdyke, is totally lost without the physical presence of his wife. He tries to get in touch with her and that is the whole drive of the part. And the whole of the part was a combined spontaneity on the parts of the director and myself. . . . I think that relating to the part was partly responsible for the success of this character. I know how he felt.* —Peter Cushing[1]

In the spring of 1950, E. C. Comics editors Bill Gaines and Al Feldstein, looking for a new trend that would help them recover from a slumping comics market, introduced three new and decidedly different magazines. A legend was born that year, the horror comic.

Standing side by side with copies of *Superman* and *Classics Illustrated* on neighborhood candy store shelves were the premiere editions of *The Haunt of Fear*, *The Vault of Horror*, and *The Crypt of Terror*—all silently beckoning curious youngsters with their gruesome covers which depicted bloodcurdling, nightmarish creatures dregged up from ancient folklore as well as from some of the darker pits of the human imagination. The comics were an instant success with the younger set.

In November 1950, *The Crypt of Terror* was replaced by *Tales from the Crypt*. Like its sister comics, *Tales* also featured story narrators aptly named, "The Crypt Keeper," "The Vault Keeper," and "The Old Witch." Cameos of these horrifying apparitions appeared along the borders of each comic cover, laughing manically at youngsters who eagerly paid ten cents a copy to be terrified with tales in the blackest of comedy veins.

Alas, though fans of the magazines tried their best to keep parents blissfully ignorant of them—hiding the comics under beds and tucked carefully in the corners of crowded bedroom closets—eventually the older generation discovered them and, as usual, misunderstanding the true spirit of the stories, howled for their removal. With the help of "experts" like antiviolence psychiatrist and self-appointed watchdog, Fredric Wertham and Tennessee Senator Estes Kefauver, the witch-hunt began.[2]

In a paranoid era where communists were to be found lurking in every shadow and beneath nearly every rock, the adult public outcry eventually persuaded vendors and distributors into refusing to peddle the comics. Sadly, four years later, all three comics ended their run. The last issue of *Tales from the Crypt* (issue number 46) carried an editorial. In part it read:

> As the result of the hysterical injudicious, and unfounded charges leveled at crime and horror comics, many retailers and wholesalers throughout the country have been intimidated into refusing to handle this type of magazine. . . . Naturally, with comic magazine censorship now a

fact, we at E. C. Comics look forward to an immediate drop in the crime and juvenile delinquency rate of the United States. We trust there will be fewer robberies, fewer murders, and fewer rapes.

E. C. then went on to announce the formation of their newest "brainchilds," which included *Mad* magazine.[3]

Though parents and inquisitors alike heaved a collective sigh of relief, the national crime and delinquency rate continued to escalate. However, like any true legend, the horror comic refused to die. It merely went underground and in 1971, *Tales from the Crypt* would resurface in movie form under the loving auspices of Milton Subotsky and Max J. Rosenberg. Twisting the knife even deeper, upon its release in 1972, *Tales from the Crypt* would place second to, appropriately enough, *The Godfather* (1972) in the American box office top ten movie hits of the year in *Variety*. As the old crypt keeper might say, "Heh, Heh, Heh, kiddies. Always remember, revenge is sweet!"[4]

Producer Milton Subotsky described how the film originated.

> When I read *Tales from the Crypt* in the Ballantine paperback reprint I remembered reading it before, a long time ago. I went after Max [Rosenberg] to get the film rights to it. But it was very difficult . . . because money didn't interest Bill Gaines, who owned them. He was more interested in seeing a good film made from the material. The fun of it interested him. . . . I kept coming back to Max from time to time . . . and finally he met with Bill Gaines and they were able to work a deal.[5]

Part of the deal involved Amicus' promise not to violate the material. Subotsky felt that he and Roseberg had done a "faithful, almost reverential adaptaton" and indeed they had. The producers took their five tales from the pages of all three comics. "All Through the House," which starred Joan Collins, was adapted from *The Vault of Horror* (number 35, illustrated by Johnny Craig); "Reflection of Death," which featured Ian Hendry, was taken from *Tales from the Crypt* (number 23, illustrated by Al Feldstein); "Poetic Justice," starring Peter Cushing, had originally appeared in *The Haunt of Fear* (number 12, illustrated by Graham Ingels); "Wish You Were Here," starring Richard Greene, was also taken from *The Haunt of Fear* (number 12); and "Blind Alley," starring Nigel Patrick and Patrick Magee, had initially appeared in the last issue of *Tales from the Crypt* (number 46).[6]

In the same Chris Knight interview, Subotsky believed that the film's success was due to E. C. Comics' huge audience at the time and all those former kids who by the 1970s were now adults and had remembered them from their youth. Though he admitted that critically the film wasn't all that well received, it was Amicus' most financially successful film. It "had more audience appeal," Subotsky believed, and "things the audience liked to remember and talk about ... 'plums' like Nigel Patrick walking through the corridor of razor blades and Peter Cushing rising out of the grave."

Coincidentally, Peter Cushing was originally offered Richard Greene's segment, "Wish You Were Here." Cushing stated:

> When that script was sent to me ... I didn't like the part ... I couldn't see myself in that character. ... But I wanted to work. I wanted to be in this picture so I said to my agent, "What about this little old man," which in the original script was literally nothing. He didn't even have lines to say. The story as written was about the young man ... the villain [Robin Phillips as James Elliot]. So when the producer heard that that was the part I wanted to play he said, "Of course, let him have it!" ... So then I had to get together with Freddie Francis, the director, and virtually all of that part was ad-libbed.[7]

It is difficult to watch Peter Cushing as Arthur Grimsdyke without becoming emotionally involved with his performance. Even the most jaded of viewers could not help but notice that Cushing had bestowed upon his character his own heart and soul. How many of us can claim that they have never, at one time or another, been the victim of some sort of physical or emotional abuse? Grimsdyke strikes a cord in each of us and, though we may be loathe to admit it, his revenge from beyond the grave is something many might very well have wished to inflict on their own personal nemesis.

Film critic Dan Scapperotti said that "Poetic Justice" was "The best of the five tales starring Peter Cushing as the aged Grimsdyke. ... Freddie Francis ... [enlists] the finest performance from Cushing. The veteran actor ... presents a character both pathetic and noble. As the persecuted junk man, Cushing maintains his dignity as his world crumbles around him."[8]

About a year after the film opened worldwide, Peter was honored with two awards at the Second French Fantasy Convention (April 8–15, 1973). One eyewitness reported the proceedings thus:

> Peter Cushing won two medals, one as Best Actor; another especially for his work in *Tales from the Crypt*. He was very emotional and made a speech, in French. ... It was so kindly said that the audience [wildly] applauded him. I clearly saw tears in his eyes. Yes, Cushing is ... one of the most cooperative actors that I've met. He answered hundreds of questions, autographed ... stills, always smiling, always — even after one in the morning.[9]

Some of the film's critical reviews include *Cinema-TV Today* (November 7, 1972): "Freddie Francis makes the most of whatever opportunities the various stories give him to provide an eerie atmosphere and the cast do their best to make the characters live." *Variety* ("Vine," March 8, 1972) declared that it was "A generally excellent British suspense-horror package. . . . The tales are treated seriously and quite effectively handled for optimum suspense and horror. Subotsky's clever script, replete with some masterfully ironic twists, is engagingly helmed by Freddie Francis . . . with stylish mounting, evocative rich color camerawork, generally tight editing, appropriately Gothic music, absorbing characterizations etched by a line-up of solid British performers . . . the pic is an unusually entertaining shocker." The *New York Daily News* reviewer Ann Guarino hailed it, saying, "Horror fans should not miss this one — a thriller that will grasp your attention throughout as well as give you goosebumps along the way." The *Village Voice* (Richard McGuinness) said, "the transformation of comic book characters into portrayals of real actors works crisply." Joseph Gelmis of *Newsday* noted, "These five slickly packaged short stories . . . satisfy some of the current craving for ghoulish pleasures which is making TV's horror shows so popular today." Judith Crist, *New York* magazine (March 13, 1972), reported "For horror, during and after, I can't recall an anthology film quite so filled with it as *Tales from the Crypt*. . . . Joan Collins, Ian Hendry, Peter Cushing, Nigel Patrick, Patrick Magee and . . . Richard Greene . . . go through five juicy terror tales. . . . It's all done in very high style with polished performances and the excellent kind of physical production the genre too rarely gets. . . . Nothing is left to the imagination in this one." Barry Norman of *The Times* (September 29, 1972) obviously missed the point in his review, saying the film "is notable for wasting the talents of . . . performers. . . . The script might well have been lifted straight from the dialogue bubbles." Roger Ebert of the *Chicago Sun Times* (March 15, 1972) was more insightful in his evaluation: "the movie . . . featues good old horror-film superstars like Peter Cushing. . . . [The] visuals and decor have been planned in bright basic colors and gray, so they look something like comic panels." And Vincent Canby of the *New York Times* (March 9, 1972) gave it a left-handed compliment when he wrote, "*Tales from the Crypt* is not, strictly speaking, a horror film at all, although it has its share of silly supernatural effects. Its people are small and spiteful and their bad ends exhibit the kind of heavy morality I associate less with fine horror fiction than with cautionary literature designed to persuade children to brush their teeth."

I was most proud to be presented with two "Oscars" by . . . The 2nd French Convention of Fantasy Cinema: One for my part in *Tales from the Crypt* [Best Male Actor] and the other I was chosen as the most popular actor overall in France for this particular type of entertainment and service to the cinema in general. I feel deeply honoured, and went over to

Paris . . . for the presentation, to be met by a heart-warming reception. Terence Fisher was there too . . . he also received an award, as did Roy Ward Baker. [Peter Cushing, April 1973]

Notes

1. *The Monster Times* (vol. 1, no. 14), July 31, 1972. "A Tale from Behind the Crypt" by R. Allen Leider.
2. Author of *Seduction of the Innocent*, Fredric Wertham was a lifelong crusader against violence in all medias.
3. *The Monster Times* 1, no. 10.
4. Filmed in the fall of 1971, *Tales from the Crypt* had yet another resurgence when it became a weekly series on the HBO cable network and as of this writing, is still being produced.
5. Milton Subotsky, interview with Chris Knight, *Cinefantastique* 2, no. 4.
6. Calvin T. Beck, review of *Tales from the Crypt*, *Castle of Frankenstein* 18.
7. Peter Cushing, interview with R. Allen Leider, *The Monster Times* 1, no. 14.
8. Dan Scapperotti, review of *Tales from the Crypt*, *Cinefantastique* 2, no. 3.
9. Jean-Claude Michel, review, *Little Shoppe of Horrors* 3.

Dracula A.D. 1972
(1971)

Credits and Cast

Released November 1972; 95 minutes; color; A Hammer Film Production; Released through Columbia–Warner Brothers (U.K.) and Warner Brothes (U.S.); MPAA PG; Filmed at MGM-EMI Elstree Studios, England. Director: Alan Gibson; Producer: Josephine Douglas; Screenplay: Don Houghton; Director of photography: Dick Bush, B.S.C.; Art designer: Don Mingaye; Editor: James Needs; Continuity: Doreen Dearnaley; Sound editor: Roy Baker; Recording director: A. W. Lumkin; Dubbing mixer: Bill Rowe; Casting: James Liggat; Music composed by Michael Vickers; Musical supervisor: Philip Martell; Songs: "Alligator Man" by Sal Valentino, and "You Better Come Through" by Tim Barnes; Production supervisor: Roy Skeggs; Production manager: Ron Jackson; Special effects: Les Bowie; Makeup: Jill Carpenter; Hairdresser: Barbara Ritchie; Wardrobe supervisor: Rosemary Burrows; Assistant director: Robert Lynn.

Christopher Lee (Count Dracula), Peter Cushing (Professor Lorrimer Van Helsing and Lawrence Van Helsing), Stephanie Beacham (Jessica Van Helsing), Christopher Neame (Johnny Alucard), Michael Coles (Inspector), William Ellis (Joe Mitchum), Marsha Hunt (Gaynor), Janet Key (Anna), Philip Miller (Bob), Michael

Kitchen (Greg), David Andrews (Detective Sergeant), Caroline Munro (Laura), Lally Bowers (Matron), Rockgroup ("Stoneground").

Synopsis

> *Count Dracula! Look on me, Dracula. Look on me . . . and remember!* — Professor Van Helsing
>
> *Dig the music, kids!* — Johnny Alucard

One hundred years ago Lawrence Van Helsing (Peter Cushing) and his arch nemesis, Count Dracula (Christopher Lee), had a race with destiny — one that ended with a victory for Van Helsing — but it was not without payment in kind. Though the vampire hunter destroys Dracula, he is himself gravely wounded in the ordeal and succumbs. Van Helsing is laid to rest in a small London churchyard with only a simple marker to note this selfless hero's passing.

One hundred years later the descendant of one of Dracula's disciples, Johnny Alucard (Christopher Neame), manages to persuade a group of his friends to participate in a Black Mass. The ritual is held in the church where Van Helsing was buried a century ago. However, the church has fallen into decay and is slated to be torn down. The ceremony rises to a fever pitch and all but one of the group, Laura (Caroline Munro), flee. Alucard brings the count back to life and Laura becomes Dracula's first victim.

One of the frightened participants of the ceremony is Jessica (Stephanie Beacham) who lives with her grandfather, Professor Lorrimer Van Helsing (Peter Cushing). She learns of her friend's death when they are visited by Scotland Yard Inspector Murray (Michael Coles). Van Helsing is immediately suspicious when he hears the circumstances surrounding Laura's death. Later, his worst fears are confirmed when he determines that the name of Laura's "friend," Alucard, when spelled backward is Dracula! The professor offers to help the police.

Meanwhile, Dracula orders his disciple to bring Van Helsing's granddaughter to him. With her death, Dracula will have his ultimate revenge on the Van Helsings — ending their line by his own hand. Jessica is brought to Dracula but before he can complete the act of retribution he is interrupted by Van Helsing. Van Helsing manages to lure Dracula outside the church where he has dug a grave lined with wooden stakes. He flings a phial of holy water into Dracula's face and the vampire is momentarily blinded by the seering pain of the water on his skin. Dracula twists about in agony and falls into the grave where he is impaled. In a terrifying sequence, the vampire slowly begins to disintegrate.

Adversaries on-screen, best of friends off-screen, Christopher Lee and Peter Cushing in *Dracula A.D. 1972.*

Commentary

> *I think there is a certain amount of wry humor in this, from the point of view of the young people not really understanding the part I play of my generation. There's no conflict, there's great affection, but its just what I think they call today "the generation gap," which I think comes off extremely well in this picture, and there might be just a few smiles about that, no belly laughs.* — Peter Cushing[1]

With box office receipts starting to reflect general audience dissatisfaction with Hammer's more recent releases, Hammer head Michael Carreras was convinced that what the public wanted was fresh material and a new plot twist for his most famous (and profitable) character. Having previously entrenched Count Dracula firmly in the Victorian Era where Bram Stoker had originally given him birth, Hammer hired a new screenplay writer, Don Houghton, and instructed him to give Dracula yet another lease on life. Houghton decided to bring Dracula "Back to the Future."

Originally entitled "Dracula Chelsea 72" and "Dracula Today," production for *Dracula A.D. 1972* began in September 1971 at MGM-EMI's studio facilities at Elstree. Carreras stated there were "creative differences" between him and writer Houghton regarding the film's basic premise. "We had a new writer—Don Houghton— . . . and when we got down to modern sequences, we had battles galore. I would have liked the whole content of the modern Dracula to take place in a churchyard at midnight, since then you don't know where the devil you are. . . . But I was very strong in dragging in a deserted and empty churchyard as much as possible to give a midnight flavour, even though it was modern. . . . I will take the blame or accolade for that. . . ."[2]

Unfortunately, Carreras can assume the blame for much more than deciding which corner he was going to box Christopher Lee (Dracula) into this time. He should have realized that as soon as he brought just one twentieth-century character into Dracula's new domain the illusion of timelessness he wanted would have been shattered. By confining Dracula to the perimeters of the desanctified church he gave one the impression that Dracula was like some sort of spectral jack-in-the-box that popped up every time someone popped in! It also appeared as if Dracula suffered from agoraphobia, relegating his disciple (Johnny Alucard) to run shopping errands for him. Christopher Lee must have felt as ridiculous and helpless as his character. Though he gave it his best effort, it was no small wonder that after *The Satanic Rites of Dracula* (*Count Dracula and His Vampire Bride*), Lee wisely gave up on the Hammer series.

Peter Cushing fared a little better in his dual role. The flashback sequence, although chronologically inaccurate, was the high point of the film[3] but, unfortunately, not by much. Any other actor would have had a much harder time trying to convince audiences that his character, the current descendant of Van Helsing, was up to the vitality and bravado of his famous ancestor, especially after being out of practice for so many generations. The script made it seem as though the entire Van Helsing line had a sort of peculiar genetic link, uniquely inherent in their DNA makeup, that could be called to the fore to battle vampires with the spontaneity of a firefighter hearing an alarm go off! The modern Van Helsing, a professor of archeology (myths and legends of the occult were his specialty), would have been better played had he been the exact opposite—a disbeliever who scoffs at the very idea but who is forced to admit that the impossible has taken place.

What Hammer failed to realize in their transition to modern times was that nineteenth-century mores don't work in a twentieth-century setting. The suspension of modern prevailing attitudes should have been handled more delicately, not taken for granted. It was to Cushing's credit that he managed to pull it off as convincingly as he did. "This has been a particularly happy picture," Cushing stated. "I think we have a great director in Alan Gibson, who has wonderful ideas, and Dick Bush is doing a marvelous job . . . Don Mingaye's sets all round are beautiful, and such a lovely cast, all the young people are so marvelous."[4]

Technical credits, aside from an annoying soundtrack by Mike Vickers (formerly of Manfred Mann), were up to Hammer's usual high standards. Alan Gibson's direction on the whole was good, the exception being perhaps too much padding of some scenes. One example is the party-crashing scene, where Gibson goes out of his way to try to establish the antisocial attitudes of the kids and drags out the scene ad infinitum. Gibson does, however, manage to keep Stephanie Beacham from her tendancy to overact.

Another point concerns the supporting players. More consideration should have been taken in the selection of Alucard's cohorts. Although overall the acting was quite good, the actors themselves were too old for their parts and subsequently weren't very credible as the restless teens.

Stephanie Beacham had made quite an impression in *Nightcomers* (1971) and more recently appeared in a short-lived American television sitcom.[5] She had this to say about her association with Peter Cushing on the set: "I felt a touch of friendship with him that one is always grateful for. When you meet someone who is as kind, as well-meaning, as beautiful and generous as Peter Cushing, you feel very privileged."[6]

One of the most meaningful touches in *Dracula A.D. 1972* was the tender, very loving interplay between Jessica Van Helsing and her grandfather. This was beautifully projected throughout the film and full credit must be given to Peter for the subtlety of its execution.

A newcomer at the time, Caroline Munro, who played the hot-blooded worshipper Laura, remembers a more introverted Cushing during this time. She recalled that "Peter had then just lost his wife, so he was very quiet and withdrawn and terribly upset. Nobody had much contact with him, because he stayed in his dressing room when he wasn't filming."[7]

Genre fans were nearly unanimous in their disappointment with the film, prompting Carreras to comment in one press release for reporter Hugh Mulligan, "Fans are a large and traditional audience. They don't like you fooling 'bout with their legends or they get suspicious." Critics were generally more objective in their commentaries. Donald J. Meyerson of *Cue* (December 2, 1972) said, "Alan Gibson's direction has a proper mysterious tone, and Christopher Lee and Peter Cushing are consistently convincing in their now familiar roles." "Whit" in *Variety* (October 25, 1972) noted that the "film carries the type of chill ingredients any spectator associates with the living dead. . . . Cushing is persuasive as the professor . . . Gibson's direction is particularly effective in maintaining mood and spirit . . . production design . . . is . . . atmospheric. Special effects . . . add immeasurably." Kevin Thomas of the *Los Angeles Times* called it "a witty, successful attempt to bring the old Transylvanian vampire into present day London . . . it's a very tricky business to let Dracula go through his flamboyant paces in a modern setting." The *New York Times* reviewer Roger Greenspun (December 1, 1972) is quoted as saying that "it is gratifying to find even New Scotland Yard humbled before the steel-trap mind of Van Helsing." *Cinema-TV Today* commented that "Only Peter Cushing, moving serenely and sincerely through the thickest of trite dialogue and overanxious performances achieves moments of chilling conviction." The *New York Daily News* critic, Wanda Hale (November 30, 1972), said, "if you can't laugh at the stilted talk, you'll be bored stiff instead of scared stiff. . . . Peter Cushing makes the best show as the brilliant professor." And *The Advocate* insightfully reported that "Peter Cushing must be the most underrated actor in England, judging from the completely credible performance he gives armed with only the most cliché lines." Finally, Anita Earle of the *San Francisco Chronicle* (November 3, 1972) added that "By default, Peter Cushing carries the picture, what there is of it. Poor Cushing is required to look perfectly serious as he performs miracles of acuity such as the discovery that 'Alucard' backwards spells Dracula, therefore his granddaughter's friend Alucard is not to be trusted."

Notes

1. Peter Cushing, interview with Christopher Knight and Peter Nicholson on the set of "Dracula Today," *Cinefantastique*, (vol. 2 no. 2).
2. Michael Carreras, interview with Alan Frank, *Little Shoppe of Horrors* 4.
3. The flashback has Dracula being destroyed and buried in London in 1872, thirteen years *prior* to the onset of the first Hammer Dracula which took place in Middle Europe in 1885!
4. Cushing, interview with Knight and Nicholson, *Cinefantastique*, (vol. 2 no. 2).
5. After ABC television's "Dynasty" spin-off "The Colbys," was canceled, Beacham tried her luck with NBC television's series "Sister Kate." Unfortunately, it too was canceled by the network during its first season.
6. Stephanie Beacham, interview, *Bizarre* 3.
7. Caroline Munro, interview with Steve Swires, *Fangoria* 4.

Fear in the Night
(1971)

Credits and Cast

Released 1972 (U.K.), limited U.S. release 1972; 94 minutes; Color by Technicolor; A Hammer Film Production; Released through Anglo EMI Film (U.K.) and International Coproductions Release–Pisces Group (U.S.); Filmed at MGM-EMI Elstree

Studios, England. Director and producer: Jimmy Sangster; Executive producer: Michael Carreras; Screenplay: Jimmy Sangster, Michael Syson; Music composed by John McCabe; Editor: Peter Weatherley; Sound editor: Ron Hyde; Art director: Don Picton; Set dresser: Penny Struthers; Director of photography: Arthur Grant; Makeup: Bill Partleton; Hairdresser: Helen Lennox; Wardrobe: Rosemary Burrows; Assistant director: Ted Morley; Casting director: James Liggat; Music supervisor: Philip Martell; Production manager: Christopher Neame; Production secretary: C. Langley; Camera Operator: Neil Bibney; Assistant editor: P. Culverwell; Stills camera: G. Whitear.

Judy Geeson (Peggy Heller), Joan Collins (Molly Carmichael), Ralph Bates (Robert Heller), Peter Cushing (Michael Carmichael), Gillian Lind (Mrs. Beamish), James Cossins (Doctor), John Bown (First Policeman), Brian Grellis (Second Policeman).

Synopsis

Having recently recovered from a nervous breakdown, Peggy Heller (Judy Geeson) is preparing to meet her husband Robert (Ralph Bates) when she is attacked by a one-armed man the night before she's to leave the convalescent home. However, since there is no real evidence of the attack, no one believes her. Peggy leaves the next day to join her husband at his new post as an assistant teacher at a boys' academy. Peggy sets up housekeeping at the cottage she and Robert will share, which is conveniently located on the grounds of the school.

Robert introduces Peggy to the school headmaster, Michael Carmichael (Peter Cushing), whom she finds charming, but who also gives her an uneasy feeling. Peggy's also puzzled to learn that the school is unoccupied at this particular time of the year and she feels the school itself seems to be too pristine in appearance for an institution which had supposedly been in operation for many years.

When Robert leaves on a business trip, Peggy is once again attacked by the one-armed man. Soon after the attack, Peggy meets Carmichael's glamorous wife, Molly (Joan Collins), but they have little in common and Peggy doesn't encourage any relationship with her.

Robert, once again, has to leave on a business matter, but this time he gives Peggy a rifle for her protection. When Michael Carmichael visits Peggy at the cottage she notices for the first time that he has only one arm. Panicked, she shoots him, believing him to be her attacker. Robert returns to find the cottage empty and Peggy hidden in one of the boys' dorms. She refuses to tell him what happened. To persuade her to talk about her experience, Robert confesses that he is not a schoolmaster but is, in fact, Michael's nurse. He explains that Michael is mentally unbalanced due to a fire that had occurred at the school and which took the lives of some of the students. He also explains that during a rescue attempt, Michael lost his arm and later suffered a nervous breakdown which forced the

Professor Carmichael reminisces about happier times at the academy in Jimmy Sangster's *Fear in the Night.*

school to be shut down. Robert finally admits that the school has been transformed into an elaborate convalescent home for a man who will probably never recover.

Though Peggy still refuses to tell her husband about the incident, it is soon revealed that Robert and Molly are lovers. They had planned Peggy's relapse with this series of attacks so that when Michael finally did confront her, she would kill him. Once their plans were successful, Robert and Molly would be able to leave together with the money she would subsequently inherit while Peggy, charged with Michael's murder, would spend the rest of her life in an asylum. Peggy's continued silence jeopardizes their plans, however, and they resort to threats and physical violence to get her to tell them where she has hidden Michael's body since they are unable to locate it. Suddenly they hear the sound of the school's alarm bells. When Robert and Molly investigate, they realize that Michael is still alive and has been hiding somewhere in the school all along. Michael provokes Robert with only the sound of his voice coming from the school's PA system. In a rage, Robert shoots at a sudden movement in one of the rooms and, to his dismay, discovers that he has mistakenly killed Molly. Michael then kills Robert and hangs him from a tree in the schoolyard.

The police arrive but are unable to learn from Peggy what had transpired. Sadly, Peggy has finally succumbed to the mental illness she had once fought so hard to overcome.

Commentary

> *I think those days of type-casting are gone. I really don't think audiences will create another Peter Cushing and Christopher Lee. I think that era is past.... Cushing and ... Lee were not made Kings of Horror by Hammer but by the audiences.* — Ralph Bates[1]

Based on an earlier script by Jimmy Sangster entitled "The Claw," *Fear in the Night* went into production in November 1971 and was part of a double-feature release which Hammer planned to coin their "Women in Fear" series.[2]

With a meager budget of $282,000, Sangster, who also directed, had only five weeks to shoot the film. Sangster described the film as "a creep-around, bump-in-the-night kind of picture with no vast crowd scenes or special effects. We [had] to shoot an average of 3¼ minutes [of film] a day which isn't too difficult.... It's really only a four-handler, Judy Geeson, Joan Collins, Ralph Bates and Peter Cushing."[3]

Similar to other films such as *Gaslight* (1944), *Scream of Fear* (1961) (also written by Sangster), and *Diabolique* (1954), among others, *Fear in the Night* had nothing new to offer audiences. The see-through plot line left little to the imagination and characterizations were equally transparent. Both Geeson and Collins were too cast to type, and Ralph Bates, who was particularly disappointing as he wandered somnambulistic-like throughout, added new meaning to the term underplayed.

However, the only real crime committed in *Fear in the Night* was the casting of Peter Cushing in the throwaway role of Michael Carmichael. Amazingly, he was the only character to illicit any immediate audience sympathy — not bad considering the fact that he was supposed to be the main suspect in the piece! Audiences weren't fooled and Sangster should have realized that he was in trouble when he began stealing from himself! This lackluster script and Sangster's dull direction merely added to the ennui.

Ralph Bates reminisced about Cushing:

> Peter was my mentor for awhile then ... I had met him, publicity-wise, during *Horror of Frankenstein* (Hammer 1970). They shot some pictures of him on the set handing over the role to me.... Cushing is such a kind, good man. I try to get back to the theatre every so often and I went to do a play ... Peter was doing night filming and he bothered to come down

during the day to see a matinee, then rushed back and shot at night. That's the kind of generosity Peter has. He really is a gent and also a smashing actor. . . . The stuff he did before Hammer was amazing. There was a TV version of *1984* in which he played Winston Smith that still haunts me.[4]

Fear in the Night had a very limited release in the United States before being sold to television. Critical evaluations were rare, but *Cinema-TV Today* in its July 1972 edition called it "An acceptably exciting second feature for uncritical audiences. Except that the characters and the setting remain unchanged, I would have suspected that some mischance had resulted in a mix-up of two films of very different quality. Having painstakingly and effectively built up suspense and terror to the point of the headmaster's supposed death, the film suffers a sudden change of pace and loses all credibility in a breathless rush to reach its garbled conclusion."

Notes

1. Ralph Bates, interview, *Bizarre 3*.
2. The cofeature, filmed concurrently with *Fear in the Night* was *Straight on Till Morning* with Rita Tushingham and Shane Briant. The latter was clearly the better of the two films.
3. Jimmy Sangster, interview with Keith Dudley, *Little Shoppe of Horrors* 10–11.
4. Ralph Bates, interview with Bruce G. Hallenbeck, *Fangoria 55*.

Dr. Phibes Rises Again
(1971)

Credits and Cast

Released July 5, 1972 (U.S.); 89 minutes; Color by Deluxe, U.S. prints by Movielab; An American International Production; MPAA PG; Filmed at Elstree Studios, England, and on location in Spain. Director: Robert Fuest; Producer: Louis M. Heyward; Executive producers: Samuel Z. Arkoff, James H. Nicholson; Screenplay: Robert Blees, Robert Fuest; Based on the characters created by James Whiton and William Goldstein; Director of photography: Alex Thomson; Music: John Gale; Art direcor: Brian Eatwell; Sound: A. W. Lumkin, Les Hammond, Peter Lennard, Dennis Whitlock; First assistant director: Jake Wright; Editor: Tristan Cones; Production manager: Richard Dalton; Makeup: Trevor Crole-Rees; Wardrobe: Ivy Baker.

Vincent Price (Dr. Anton Phibes), Robert Quarry (Biederbeck), Valli Kemp (Vulnavia), Fiona Lewis (Diana), Peter Cushing (The Captain), Beryl Reid (Mrs.

Ambrose), Terry Thomas (Lombardo), Hugh Griffith (Ambrose), Peter Jeffrey (Inspector Trout), John Cater (Superintendent Waverly), Gerald Sim (Hackett), Lewis Flander (Baker), John Thaw (Shavers), Keith Buckley (Stuart), Milton Reid (Cheng), Caroline Munro (Victoria).

Synopsis

> *I suppose he never ... How can I put this? I suppose he never ...*
> *touched the bottle?* — Ship's captain to Biederbeck regarding the
> missing Mr. Ambrose

Dr. Anton Phibes (Vincent Price) has survived in a state of suspended animation for three years since his last exploits sent him into hiding (*The Abominable Dr. Phibes*, 1971). Now he has returned to continue his quest for a means to restore his wife (who died prematurely in an operation) to life. Phibes thinks he has found a way with the aid of an ancient Egyptian map which he believes will lead him to the tomb of a pharaoh, under which flows the sacred "river of life."

However, Phibes discovers that his precious map has been stolen. The culprit is Biederbeck (Robert Quarry), an enigmatic man who has managed to outwit death for many, many years by means of a secret elixir. Because he has run out of this very special antidote to death, Biederbeck is just as anxious to find the river of life as Phibes. Both set out for Egypt in a race to find the legendary canal.

Along the way, Phibes once again devises some ingenious methods to eliminate the members of Biederbeck's expedition using Scripture as a reference. However, it is Biederbeck's own mistress, Diana (Fiona Lewis) who proves to be Biederbeck's undoing. By using her as a hostage, Phibes manages to secure from Biederbeck the key that unlocks the gates to the sacred river.

Biederbeck, now beginning to age from lack of his life-prolonging elixir, looks on in defeat as Phibes — on a raft with his wife's coffin — sails down the river of eternal life.

Commentary

Originally scheduled under the working title, "The Curse of Dr. Phibes," production on this sequel to *The Abominable Dr. Phibes* began in November 1971. It was the first of a multipicture deal American International Pictures had signed with MGM-EMI at Elstree Studios, England. However, although interiors were shot at Elstree, some location work was done in Ibiza, Spain, utilizing its desert terrain to simulate the sands of

Peter Cushing as the ship's captain in *Dr. Phibes Rises Again*.

Egypt where both expeditionary teams (those headed by Phibes and Biederbeck) raced to locate the legendary river of life.

Returning as Anton Phibes was Vincent Price. Price, who has always
considered Phibes as one of his personal favorites, cunningly handled his
character with all the varying degrees of camp and menace that had become Phibes' hallmark.

Phibes himself is a fascinating creature—a modern-day Phantom of
the Opera who was as motivated by his all-consuming hatred and need for
revenge as was his pitiful counterpart.

Like the phantom, Phibes hides from the world in his underground domain. His surroundings are a curious combination of art deco–Bizarro World with a little Disneyland thrown in for good measure. It is here that Phibes' madness festers and eventually bears fruit. When the doctor finally emerges from his elaborate tomb, he sets in motion the methods and modes of his peculiar concept of retribution.

Robert Quarry, who shared top-billing honors with Price and who was already a favorite with genre audiences for his role in AIP's mega-hit, *Count Yorga, Vampire* (1970), handled the role of Biederbeck with equal effectiveness.[1]

Quarry, born in 1923, made his film debut in Hitchcock's *Shadow of a Doubt* (1943). Universal had placed him under contract to earn over $700 a week at the time. Later both MGM and Fox offered him contracts before he eventually signed with AIP and a five-year picture deal.

Quarry would work once again with Price and Cushing in *Madhouse* (1973). But aside from occasional appearances in films and guest shots on television series, Quarry's career suffered drastically after that. It seemed as if his fall from fame was fated to be as dramatic as was his rise.

Although he performed admirably, Peter Cushing's guest star role as the ship's captain, who interrogates Quarry over the sudden disappearance of Ambrose, was hardly more than a glorified walk-on with virtually no time to build any real characterization. Having immersed himself in work, Cushing appeared worn out from all the self-imposed pressures of this time. Literally filming *Fear in the Night* (1971) and *Phibes* back to back, and after having already completed work on three other films that year, Peter would continue his nonstop schedule with another starring role in *Horror Express* after work on *Phibes* was completed.

Among the supporting players for *Dr. Phibes Rises Again* — who all handled their roles deftly — were some actors who also appeared in other Cushing vehicles. Hugh Griffith (Ambrose), who had won an Academy Award for *Ben Hur* (1959), would later make an appearance in *Legend of the Werewolf* (1974). Was it mere coincidence that Griffith, who was alleged to have been an alcoholic, met his demise in the film by being drowned in a liquor bottle, or was it an in-joke among the production team? Keith Buckley (Stuart) would be one of the featured players in *Trial by Combat* (1975) and Caroline Munro, who had an unbilled appearance as Phibes' deceased wife, Victoria, also starred in *Dracula A.D. 1972* (1971) and *At the Earth's Core* (1976).

Producer Louis M. Heyward described the film's director, Robert Fuest, as having "a great sense of style and flair. He struck up a very good rapport with all the actors.... He conceptualized a lot, and he also had a very sly English sense of humor. He was a working director ... [and] was very conscious of budget."[2]

Heyward also commented that the script had a steadiness to it and that it was a very good one—the type of screenplay one could use in a scriptwriting class. Though he was sorry that the proposed third Phibes film ("Phibes Resurrectus") failed to materialize, Heyward admitted that black comedies of this type were very difficult to pull off: "You're treading a funny middle ground between humor and murder.... Precious few pictures have stayed on that tightrope."[3]

Although some of the critical evaluations for the film were negative, the vast majority of notices relished the picture's campiness. Kevin Thomas, in the *Los Angeles Times* (August 11, 1972), wrote, "*Dr. Phibes Rises Again*—but only to be shot down by a lousy script. Those who enjoyed the campy horror of *Abominable Dr. Phibes* are in a for a keen disappointment." The *New York Daily News* reviewer, Kathleen Carroll, felt "movies like this are always better the first time around.... We can only wish that Dr. Phibes had instead sailed away on the river of no return." The *San Francisco Chronicle* (Anita Earle) cited the film's brutality, obviously unaware of the fact that the screenwriters took their references from the Talmud. "The tortures Phibes puts his victims through this time around are less ingenious than revolting in their sadism." Vincent Canby of the *New York Times* (January 13, 1973), however, was less fault-finding in his review, stating that "Mysteriously, a lot of it works, probably because Robert Fuest, the director, knows just how long to hold an effect before it wilts.... I also liked the idea that a man, murdered by Phibes aboard ship, might wash ashore in a bottle.... The movie ... has such respect for fantasy that it never gets bogged down in explanation ... a lot of it shows a real awareness of style that is usually absent in the work of people who set out to exploit camp." Donald J. Mayerson of *Cue* (January 6, 1973) called it "Campy and enjoyable.... In this delightfully daffy sequel ... the various murders that Phibes must perpetrate are executed with such marvelous relish and macabre ingenuity that laughter and repulsion are joyfully linked." *British Monthly Film Bulletin* hailed the film saying, "It's refreshing to find a sequel that's better than its prototype." "Whit" in *Variety* (July 26, 1972) agreed, adding, "Sequel carries the same type of comedic gore that made [its] predecessor one of AIP's top grossers of 1971." *Film Review* (number 72) writer Paul Bradford mentioned that "*Phibes* ... has the same flair and flourish as its predecessor, thanks to the fact that it has the same fun-loving director."

Notes

1. Robert Quarry reprised his Yorga character in AIP's sequel, *Return of Count Yorga* (1971).

2. Tom Weaver, *Science Fiction Stars and Horror Heroes.*
3. Ibid.

Horror Express
(1971)

Credits and Cast

Released June 1972; 98 minutes (90 minutes U.S.); Eastman color (U.S.), Technicolor (Overseas); Cinemascope; A Granada Films–Benmar Productions coproduction; Released through Gala Productions (U.K.) and Scotia International (U.S.): MPAA PG; Filmed in Madrid, Spain, at Studios 70 Complex. Director: Eugenio Martin; Producer: Bernard Gordon; Story and screenplay: Eugenio Martin, Arnaud D'Usseau; Director of photography: Alejandro Ullea; Production supervisor: Jose Maria Ramos; Assistant director: Gil Carretero; Editor: Robert Dearberg; Art director: Ramiro Gomez Guadiana; Special effects: Pablo Perez; Music composed and conducted by John Cavacas; Sound: Antonio Ilan; Sound recordist: Jose Maria Ramos; Makeup: Julian Ruiz.

Christopher Lee (Professor Alexander Saxton), Peter Cushing (Dr. Wells), Telly Savalas (Captain Kazan), Silvia Tortosa (Irina Petrovski), Jorge Rigaud (Count Petrovski), Alberto de Mendoza (Pujardov), Julio Pena (Inspector Mirov), Alice Reinhart (Miss Jones), Angel Del Pozo (Yevtushenko), Helga Line (Natasha); also appearing: Jose Jaspa, Victor Israel, Vincent Roca, Juan Olaguibel, Jose Canalejas, Faith Clift, and Peter Beckman.

Synopsis

> *Miss Jones—I shall need your assistance!—* Dr. Wells to his assistant
>
> *Well, at your age, I'm not surprised!—* Jones to Dr. Wells, after noticing his lovely young dinner partner

China 1906. Professor Alexander Saxton (Christopher Lee) leads an expedition into the mountainous regions of Manchuria and, while exploring one of its many caves, comes upon the fossil remains of a creature— half man, half ape—which Saxton has estimated as being well over two million years old, and perhaps far older than that.

Taking the find back with them, the expedition returns to Peking, China, where it hopes to book passage on the Trans-Siberian Express to Moscow. While trying to secure a berth, Saxton meets an old colleague, Dr. Wells (Peter Cushing) and his assistant, Miss Jones (Alice Reinhart).

Doctors Wells and Saxon (Cushing and Lee) are about to make a fascinating discovery in this scene from *Horror Express*.

While Wells is attempting to discover the reason for Saxton's journey to China, a petty thief tries to break into the crate containing the fossil. He is later found dead—his eyes looking as though they had been boiled in his head. After a minor police investigation, the crate is loaded onto the train and the journey begins.

The trip proves to be an uneasy one from the start as strange noises and even stranger, inexplicable events take place in the baggage car that houses the crate. When Dr. Wells, curious about Saxton's find, bribes a baggage attendant to drill some holes in the crate so that he can have a look, the creature, now fully revived, escapes—killing the attendant.

When several of the passengers are murdered by the creature, Dr. Wells and Professor Saxton make some startling discoveries concerning the creature. They learn that the fossil houses an alien intelligence of pure energy that had traveled to earth from another galaxy and arrived on earth during its very beginnings. It managed to survive by using various earth species as hosts for its bodiless form. The creature has been gathering knowledge by absorbing the memories of its victims, boring through the eyes to the brain which then becomes smooth when all memories have been removed. They believe the alien has been marooned on earth for eons and has been waiting until man's technology evolved sufficiently so that it would be able to obtain the necessary materials to construct a spacecraft for the voyage home. Unfortunately, the alien also has the ability to enter the bodies of humans, assuming their identities. This allows the creature to move among the passengers virtually undetected.

When Wells and Saxton learn how to single out the creature from among the passengers, they are finally able to destroy it. Moving all the other passengers to the last railroad car, they unhitch the car moments before the train careens over a cliff.

Commentary

> I thought it was so clever of the producer who bought the two model trains used in the film, Nicholas and Alexandra . . . and then wrote a script around them. — Peter Cushing to John Bros-nan[1]

In December 1971 Peter Cushing went to Madrid, Spain, to begin work on *Horror Express* for producer-director Gene Martin. Appearing with Cushing was his friend and costar, Christopher Lee. *Horror Express* would mark their eighteenth appearance together in a feature film. Lensed at Madrid's new Studio 70 complex, *Horror Express* was only the fifth feature to be shot there and the first with a fantasy theme.[2]

Combining elements of horror, science fiction, intrigue, and with dashes of comedy thrown in for good measure, Gene Martin and Arnaud D'Usseau's screenplay works — but only up to a point. The claustrophobic atmosphere of a train racing along the desolate, snow-covered countryside on its way to Moscow, while carrying an extra passenger who turns out to be not of this earth, is interesting if not altogether original. If one substitutes the Trans-Siberian Express for a spaceship, *It: The Terror from Beyond Space* (1958) combined similiar elements in its plot line thirteen years earlier.

The film is also plagued with confusing questions of logic. For example, one has to wonder why an alien species, composed of pure energy, would have the need to construct a space vehicle to journey back to its home world.

As expected with most thin plots, the story quickly sinks into the quicksand of repetition. How many passengers can the alien take over in its ninety-eight minute running time? *Horror Express* turns into an elaborate version of the old shell game: a seemingly pointless endeavor, since scientists Saxton and Wells don't come up with a foolproof method of detecting the alien's host identity until minutes before the film ends, anyway.

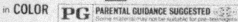

On the plus side the film has some imaginative makeup touches and special effects. Alejandro Ullea's muted photography is above average and fixes the proper mood. Period sets and costumes are also good. Gene Martin's direction is proficient. The movie also benefits from a fine music score by John Cavacas.

Cushing and Lee more than hold their own throughout the proceedings. As always, they are a welcome combination. It's amusing to watch them feed off each other and one has an impossible task trying to decide which of the two might have given the better performance.

Among the otherwise average supporting cast, Alice Reinhart, who plays Wells' assistant, Miss Jones, is noteworthy. However, Telly Savalas, in his portrayal as "Telly Savalas the Cossak" (Captain Kazan), could have been eliminated altogether. His all too obvious box office appeal seems to be the only reason for his character's appearance here.

Film critics were, for the most part, negative in their reviews. *Variety* ("Besa," October 25, 1972) stated, "Taut and well-paced throughout. Good thesping by international cast . . . though pic does attain some nice horrific moments and builds up tension quite nicely, the sci-fi angle is too labored, while the transfer of evil powers by a glowing eye is too childish for sophisticated audiences." *Cinema-TV Today* called *Horror Express*, "Enjoyable gory, inventive hokum for Horror fans." *Screen International* (June 1974) was favorable, saying, "Good value for money. . . . It is Gothic Horror on wheels, lightly sprinkled with in-jokes for the benefit of British audiences who can enjoy the understated wit. . . . Christopher Lee and Peter Cushing portray stiff upper-lipped Englishmen coping with a lot of hysterical foreigners." Dilys Powell in the June 23, 1974, edition of *The Sunday Times* noted that "The supernatural and medical horrors are enjoyably absurd . . . and it is always a pleasure to see Peter Cushing and Christopher Lee together." *The Observer* (Russell Davies, June 23, 1974) differed, however, saying, "You would need to be fanatically devoted to Cushing and Lee to get much more than a hollow laugh and a snooze out of *Horror Express*." *Time Out* (Chris Petit) reported that "Lee and Cushing at their most urbane ensure that it remains watchable." And Tim Lucas, who reviewed the film for *Cinefantastique* (volume 3, number 2) reported, "Despite the incredible nature of the film's story, it is enjoyable simply on the basis of its fast-paced action scenes."

After completing work on the film, Peter returned to England to make a guest appearance on a British radio program entitled, "Sounds Natural," where he discussed his passionate interest in the study of wildlife. Peter's curiosity began as a child when he initially began collecting bird's eggs, then moved on to bird's skeletons. Peter credits his brother David, as the impetus for what was to become a lifelong hobby for him.[3]

Peter remembered one occasion when he went on an outing with his brother and their mother. The brothers had spotted a kestrel's nest part-way down the face of a nearby cliff. Their mother arrived just in time to see David lowering his younger brother down the cliff side on the end of a rope. Peter recalled that it always seemed his fate to be involved in dangerous stunts and that his mother fainted on the spot.

Notes

1. Brosnan, *The Horror People.*
2. Scotia International Films publicity release.
3. Peter's older brother, David, who pursued a career in the agricultural field, passed away in 1988.

The Creeping Flesh
(1972)

Credits and Cast

Released March 1973; 89 minutes (U.S.); 92 minutes (U.K.); Eastman color; A Tigon British–World Film Services Production; Released through Columbia (U.S.); MPAA PG; Filmed at Shepperton Studios, England. Director: Freddie Francis; Producer: Michael Redbourn; Executive producers: Norman Priggen, Tony Tenser; Screenplay: Peter Spenceley, Jonathan Rumbold; Director of photography: Norman Warwick, B.S.C.; Music composed and conducted by Paul Ferris; Editor: Oswald Hafenrichter; Art director: George Provis; Sound: Norman Bolland, Ann Other, Colin Miller; Production supervisor: Geoffrey Haine; Assistant director: Peter Saunders.

Christopher Lee (Dr. James Hildern), Peter Cushing (Professor Emmanuel Hildern), Lorna Heilbron (Penelope Hildern), George Benson (Waterloo), Kenneth J. Warren (Lenny), Duncan Lamont (Inspector), Harry Locke (Barman), Hedger Wallace (Dr. Perry), Michael Ripper (Carter), Catherine Finn (Emily), Robert Swann (Young Aristocrat), David Bailie (Young Doctor), Maurice Bush (Karl), Tony Wright (Sailor), Marianne Stone (Female Assistant), Alexandra Dane (Whore), Jenny Runacre (Emmanuel's Wife), Larry Taylor, Martin Carrole (Warders).

Synopsis

Professor Emmanuel Hildern (Peter Cushing) confers with another doctor regarding his theory that evil is a disease, and he believes he has unwittingly unleashed that evil upon an unprotected world. As the young doctor listens attentively, Emmanuel tells his story.

While on an expedition to New Guinea, Hildern makes a discovery which leads him to believe that he has found the missing link in man's evolution—or an earlier race of homo sapiens, far superior to present-day man. He returns to England with his find—a gigantic skeleton.

With the help of his assistant, Waterloo (George Benson), Professor Hildern studies the skeleton to the exclusion of all else—even his daughter, Penelope (Lorna Heilbron). The professor feels that his findings will revolutionize all previously held theories of the origins of man and might even earn him the coveted Richter Prize—a prize his half brother, Dr. James Hildern (Christopher Lee), also hopes to win through his experiments on the origins of mental disorders which he has been conducting at the asylum he heads.

The brothers have long been rivals and when James informs his brother that he will no longer fund his expeditions, feeling they are non-productive, Emmanuel works even harder to prove he has made a significant find.

Returning to his laboratory, Professor Hildern prepares the skeleton for study. He begins by washing the hand of the remains with water, and to his amazement, tissue and skin begin to re-form on one of its fingers. Remembering some of the local native legends he had heard during his expedition, Emmanuel now believes that he has found the remains of "the Evil One," a god of ancient origin whom the natives say will return to earth when "the sky gods weep."

Cutting off the finger and examining a blood sample under the microscope, Hildern comes to the conclusion that if the creature's blood cells are the essence of evil, it might be possible to find a serum that would protect humankind from what he perceives to be the "disease of evil." By finding such an antidote, he believes it might also cure man of all of his evil manifestations, such as insanity.

Because Hildern's wife (Jenny Runacre) died in his brother's asylum, incurably insane, Emmanuel fears that his daughter might carry the tainted blood of her mother. He develops a serum and inoculates her with it. However, instead of protecting Penelope, it changes her from a kind, sweet young lady into a wanton and eventually a murderess.

Dr. James Hildern learns of his brother's find and comes to the conclusion that both of them are working along similar lines, which would jeopardize his chance for the Richter Prize. At first he threatens to expose Emmanuel for illegally experimenting on his own daughter, but when Professor Hildern remains unintimidated, James arranges for the skeleton to be stolen. However, on the way back to the asylum, James and his assistant are involved in an accident. The coach they are traveling in overturns. At the same time a sudden rainstorm develops and the Evil One is resurrected because the "sky gods have wept." Returning to Emmanuel's

Professor Emmanuel Hildern studies his incredible find in Columbia's *The Creeping Flesh.*

house, the creature searches for the missing finger Hildern had cut off and subsequently destroyed. The Evil One, however, finds a suitable replacement.

At the asylum Dr. James Hildern confers with the young doctor who has examined the professor and who concurs that Emmanuel is completely mad. Dr. Hildern tells his colleague that the professor has even gone so far as to believe that he, James, is his half brother and that another inmate, Penelope, is his daughter. When the doctor asks Hildern how long the professor has been at the asylum, Dr. Hildern replies that it has been three years — the same year he won the Richter Prize. The film ends with a close-up of Professor Hildern in his cell — begging the doctor to believe his story and with his left hand missing one of its fingers.

Commentary

> The Creeping Flesh ... *it's a pity the story did not hold too well.... So much can happen after shooting until the release, and daily rushes only given an overall impression of what to expect in the finished product.* — Peter Cushing (March 6, 1973)

Immediately following the completion of *Horror Express* in Spain, both Christopher Lee and Peter Cushing began work on *The Creeping Flesh* for then twenty-seven-year-old producer, Michael Redbourn, at Shepperton Studios.[1]

Redbourn, a former editor who turned to producing, had purchased the rights to the film in January 1971 but did not begin actual preparation until almost a year later. His decision to hold off production was made in order to be able to secure the right people for it. As Redbourn put it, "Until all the elements were just right." The "right elements" in this instance included signing Lee and Cushing, as well as director Freddie Francis to the project.

Although in some ways similar in plot line to *Horror Express*, *The Creeping Flesh* turned out to be by far the better of the two films. Peter Spenceley's and Jonathan Rumbold's screenplay gave the film two wonderful, complex characters, James and Emmanuel Hildern. Unlike Sexton and Wells in *Horror Express*, whose backgrounds are only briefly touched upon in the story, here Lee and Cushing play siblings (half brothers) whose relationship turns out to be anything but brotherly. Cushing's character, Emmanuel Hildern, not only finds a skeleton during his expedition, but he already has one back home — in his closet. His wife had been declared insane and wound up in his brother's asylum.

Professor Hildern has a daughter, Penelope (beautifully played by Lorna Heilbron), whom he virtually ignores in favor of his studies. He deliberately avoids telling his only child of her mother's fate and makes every effort to eradicate the woman's memory from his own life as well as his daughter's. Penelope is forbidden to enter her mother's rooms. She lives an extremely lonely and sheltered existence, a virtual prisoner in her father's house. At one point Penelope is discovered reading a penny romance. Emmanuel chastises her then takes the offending periodical away from her.

Emmanuel's deep-rooted fear that his daughter will genetically inherit her mother's madness leads him to irrational behavior. He injects her with a serum he has developed in the misguided hope of curing her. Yet he does this *before* Penelope even begins to show any signs of mental illness! Was Emmanuel himself insane all along?

Dr. James Hildern (Christopher Lee) has evidently been financing his half brother's expeditions but at one point advises Emmanuel that he will no longer contribute toward his brother's nonproductive pursuits. Why did Emmanuel withhold his obviously very imporant discovery? Was it because Emmanuel feared for what eventually did happen—that his own brother would attempt to steal the skeleton and claim it as his own? Did the skeleton ever actually exist? Or was the entire story the ravings of a madman who, in his own mind, believed that James was his brother and another inmate, Penelope, his daughter?

There were many unanswered questions in the film: many dark avenues not ventured along or at which there was only a brief glimpse. Though it does have flaws, it is also a film worthy of much debate and conjecture.

Although Cushing and Lee were obviously important to the film's appeal, director Freddie Francis must also be given credit here (along with a fine technical crew). Francis' trademark—his camera images—are quite evident throughout the production. A particularly impressive visual effect occurs during the flashback sequence when Emmanuel's wife begins to deteriorate mentally. Francis shows us a distorted image of the woman's face while everything else around her remains in sharp focus.

Freddie Francis reminisced about the film:

> That film had great style. I think one of the reasons for that was because it was produced by a very dear friend of mine, Norman Priggen. . . . Norman didn't know anything about horror films; he just knew about producing good films. Not to knock Hammer or Amicus, but I think this was one of the reasons why the film had good sets and all—because it wasn't the usual unit of people who were regularly attached to the horror film. It was pure chemistry. It was just one of those things that clicked when put together.[2]

Francis also had praise for his star, Peter Cushing.

> Peter was an extremely good actor. He adapts his talent to suit the genre. Quite honestly, most horror scripts are rubbish, but Peter can make you believe every word he says. I've had Peter do pages and pages of dialogue

which, if you got down and analyzed it, didn't mean anything. But Peter is able to get on the screen and recite this dialogue so that you believe he really knows what he's talking about. Consequently, you believe in the character. Chris Lee is a fantastic character, especially for the genre. The two of them together really work. I mean, if you want to make horror films . . . you can't do better than Peter Cushing and Christopher Lee. They have a wonderful chemistry on screen.[3]

Other cast members handled their secondary roles with efficiency. Of note were the cameo appearances of Michael Ripper as the crusty Carter; George Benson as Waterloo, who also appeared in *Horror of Dracula*; Scottish character actor Duncan Lamont as the inspector, who had made appearances in three other Cushing films — *The Evil of Frankenstein, Frankenstein Created Woman* and *Nothing but the Night*; and Harry Locke, the dockside bartender, who also worked in *Tales from the Crypt*.

Critically, *The Creeping Flesh*, like many of its predecessors, was received with mixed blessings. "Rino" in *Variety* (February 14, 1973) wrote, "*The Creeping Flesh* ticks too much like a grandfather clock to make the follicles quiver. But Freddie Francis' direction is sturdy, lean and perfectly paced, and the plotline, though convoluted as a seashell, acccelerates steadily to a neat, final jolt. . . . The entire cast is tops . . . without a hint of camp." *Films Illustrated* lauded it as "very much a return in class to the early Hammer Films . . . the film's real secret lies in its style." *Screen International* (1972) said, "The story is imaginative . . . the horrors are presented with considerable subtlety . . . and the moments of suspense are very well sustained. It is a film of quality; more convincing than most of its contemporaries." The *Village Voice* (William Paul) singled out Cushing in his review, saying, "Peter Cushing's performance as the mad doctor has a sufficiently Boris Karloff quality of wisely controlled near-overacting to make the whole thing locate itself on the far side of self-parody." *The Sunday Times* (March 4, 1973) critic Dilys Powell also singled out Cushing: "It employs the two pillars of our native horror cinema, Christopher Lee . . . and Peter Cushing, always good for a little laboratory work and here excelling himself as the anthropologist. . . . As a matter of fact, I thought Mr. Cushing gave one of his best performances; and the screenplay, . . . too, was on a higher level of invention than usual." *Cinema-TV Today* wrote, "For the more critical addicts, the plot may prove a little too intricate for those who expect horrors to be undemanding." Kevin Thomas of the *Los Angeles Times* (October 13, 1973) said, "under the blithe direction of veteran horror specialist Freddie Francis, Peter Cushing and Christopher Lee are mercifully as reliable as ever."

However, the "Blooper of the Year" must go to the *New York Times* reviewer Roger Greenspun who, in his commentary dated February 13, 1973, wrote, "*The Creeping Flesh* is fun and also pretty fancy. . . . There is a scary 3,000-year-old skeleton and some spooky lunacy, but the story mainly has to do with evil, which *Christopher Lee* has located under a microscope, like a disease germ, and for which he means to develop an antidote."

Notes

1. Location shooting was also done near Tower Bridge in London and at Thorpe near Egham, Surrey.
2. Freddie Francis, interview with Randy Palmer, *Fangoria* 30.
3. Freddie Francis, interview with Janrae Frank, *Monsterland*, December 1985.

Asylum
(1972)

Credits and Cast

Released October 1972 (U.S.); 88 minutes; Technicolor (U.K.) Eastman color (U.S.); An Amicus Production; Released through Harbor Productions (U.K.) and Cinema International (U.S.); MPAA PG; Filmed at Shepperton Studios, England. Director: Roy Ward Baker; Producers: Max J. Rosenberg, Milton Subotsky; Executive producer: Gustave Berne; Screenplay: Robert Bloch; Director of photography: Denys Coop; Editor: Peter Tanner; Sound: Norman Bolland; Art director: Tony Curtis; Music composed and conducted by Douglas Gamley; Assistant director: Anthony Waye; Camera operator: Neil Binney; Set decorations: Fred Carter; Special effects: Ernie Sullivan; Sound: Clive Smith, Norman Bolland, Robert Jones; Wardrobe: Bridget Sellers; Makeup: Roy Ashton; Hairstyles: Joan Carpenter; Production manager: Teresa Bolland; Continuity: Pamela Davis.

Patrick Magee (Dr. Rutherford), Robert Powell (Dr. Martin), Geoffrey Bayldon (Max Reynolds/Dr. Starr). "Frozen Fear": Barbara Parkins (Bonnie), Richard Todd (Walter), Sylvia Syms (Ruth). "The Weird Tailor": Peter Cushing (Smith), Barry Morse (Bruno), Ann Firbank (Anna), John Franklyn-Robbins (Stebbins). "Lucy Comes to Stay": Britt Ekland (Lucy), Charlotte Rampling (Barbara), James Villiers (George), Megs Jenkins (Miss Higgins). "Mannikins of Horror": Herbert Lom (Dr. Byron), with Tony Wall, Sylvia Marriott, Dan Jones, and Frank Forsyth.

Synopsis

> *Rest in pieces!* — Walter to his "late" wife, Ruth.

Dr. Martin (Robert Powell) arrives from London to apply for a staff position at the Dunsmoor Asylum. However, instead of being interviewed by the head of the institution, Dr. Starr, he is met by an associate, Dr. Rutherford (Patrick Magee). The doctor informs Dr. Martin that Starr has had a nervous breakdown and is now a patient. He further states that in order for Dr. Martin to get the preferred position, he must identify Dr. Starr from among the asylum's patients. If he is successful, he can have the job.

Dr. Martin, led by an orderly, Max Reynolds (Geoffrey Bayldon), is first introduced to a patient named Bonnie (Barbara Parkins). Searching for clues in order to make a proper identification, Dr. Martin questions Bonnie as to why she is a patient. She tells him that she and her lover, Walter (Richard Todd) had planned to be married but that his wife, Ruth (Sylvia Syms) refused to give him a divorce. In desperation, Walter murders his wife and, after dismembering the body, stores it in a basement meat freezer. Ruth, however, had been an avid follower of the dark arts and always carried a voodoo charm that granted her immortality. Returning from the dead, she murders her husband and, when Bonnie arrives, her reanimated parts attack her. Bonnie shows Dr. Martin her badly scarred face, telling him that she had tried to chop Ruth's dismembered arm off her face.

Dr. Martin consults Bruno (Barry Morse) next. Bruno is a tailor. he tells the doctor that in order to make his rent payment he consented to make a magical suit for a mysterious man named Smith (Peter Cushing). Following his strange instructions, Bruno delivers the suit as arranged, only to find that Smith was penniless and that he had spent his entire fortune on a very rare book of magic spells in order to bring his son back from the dead. He assures Bruno that once the suit restores his son, he will have the agreed-upon price. Frustrated, Bruno tells Smith that he will not give him the suit without the money. Smith pulls out a gun and they struggle. Smith is killed accidentally and Bruno returns home with the suit and the book. He tells his wife Anna (Ann Firbank) about the murder and that she must burn the suit immediately. Instead, she clothes the tailor's dummy, which she's named Otto, with it. Soon after, Anna and Bruno argue over whether or not he should go to the police and Bruno attacks her. Otto, hearing Anna's screams, comes to life. Bruno tells Dr. Martin that the dummy nearly killed him and that he must notify the authorities that Otto is still at large somewhere in the city.

Dr. Martin's third patient is Barbara (Charlotte Rampling), a recovering drug abuse patient. She is accused of murdering her brother, George (James Villiers), and her nurse, Miss Higgins (Megs Jenkins), but insists that her friend Lucy (Britt Ekland) is responsible for the deaths. Dr. Martin then meets Lucy, Barbara's alter ego.

Martin's last patient is Dr. Byron (Herbert Lom) who has devoted all his confinement into constructing mechanical dolls. He has made one in his own likeness and claims that he can transfer his soul into it, giving it life through the power of concentration.

Dr. Martin, outraged over the absence of any form of medical treatment for the patients, returns to Dr. Rutherford's office to refuse the post. While Rutherford discusses the only option open to the incurably insane — lobotomies — Dr. Byron successfully transfers his essence. The doll murders Rutherford and when Dr. Martin destroys it by stepping on it, the doll's chest cavity cracks open to reveal human entrails.

Dr. Martin rushes to get the orderly, but instead finds the real Max is dead and that Dr. Starr had assumed his identity. Martin tries to escape but is strangled by Starr. Soon after, another young doctor arrives at the asylum for an interview.

Commentary

> *I'm rather an impetuous gentleman with the wonderful name of Mr. Smith who goes to a tailor to get a suit made and that's all I can tell you.* — Peter Cushing to AP news feature writer Phil Thomas

Following up on the enormous successes of their last two anthologies, *The House that Dripped Blood* and *Tales from the Crypt*, Milton Subotsky and Max Rosenberg produced yet another multitale thriller, *Asylum*. The picture, which took fifteen weeks to shoot, went into production on April 15, 1972, and premiered in British theaters to sell-out crowds sixteen weeks after it had initially begun.

Amicus had once again assembled a sterling cast which included Robert Powell, Herbert Lom, Charlotte Rampling, Richard Todd, Patrick Magee, James Villiers, and Barry Morse. Peter Cushing worked with Morse in the second segment of Robert Bloch's screenplay, "The Weird Tailor."

This segment, which had originally aired on the NBC television series "Thriller" during its second season (1961–62) and was hosted by Boris Karloff, initially starred Henry Jones and George Macready in the roles of the tailor and Mr. Smith, respectively. The theatrical version was severely trimmed from the original teleplay (shown in a sixty-minute time slot). The teleplay had additional scenes and supporting players. Although they did not greatly detract from the filmed version, they gave much more insight into the motivations of the characters.

Two examples of this are Henry Jones' character, who is a mean-spirited man as well as a loser, and that of his wife, who is also far more developed in the teleplay. In the television version, Anna is portrayed as

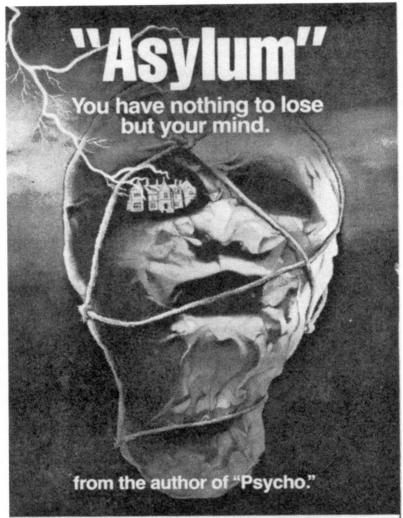

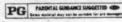

a lonely, mentally immature young woman who, because she is ignored by her husband most of the time, talks to her only friend, Hans, the tailor's mannequin. She is also a battered wife (in every true sense of the word). In the film version her character is so vaguely defined that Bruno's subsequent behavior toward her (he tries to strangle her, prompting the dummy to come to her defense) seems incongruous.

Roy Ward Baker, who was celebrating his twenty-fifth anniversary as a director, was assigned to direct *Asylum*. Baker, who had previously directed Cushing in *The Vampire Lovers* for Hammer and would follow up this feature with Amicus' *And Now the Screaming Starts*, was very pleased with his work on the film. Baker reminisced about his participation in the production.

> I think it's a very good film. It had an excellent script by Robert Bloch, very good stories in fact. The filming was very enjoyable and went smoothly. [However, he did note in the same interview that there was one minor difference of opinion citing Subotsky's partner as the instigator.] The only snag came during the editing when Max Rosenberg . . . saw it for the first time. . . . He didn't think the order of the stories was right and had the editor change them around because he believed that unless the distributors saw some action within the first ten or fifteen minutes they wouldn't be interested. Robert Bloch was not at all happy about the changes as he had carefully constructed the film to build up slowly, to have a cumulative effect. I think Milton Subotsky agreed with him and so did I, but the changes were made.[1]

Peter Cushing, who came to the United States on a rare two-week television and radio promotional tour to coincide with the film's October release, had this to say about his approach to his character, Mr. Smith:

> Acting for me must be an instinctive thing. . . . I believe that reactions must be instinctive rather than planned because I do not find planned reactions believable. Let's say that a part calls for the actor to react to the death of a loved one. The unschooled actor or director would have the character wailing, with tears streaming down his face moaning something like . . . "No . . . No . . . I can't go on . . . etc." Well that's not at all the way that everybody would react. When my own wife passed away I was very quiet . . . almost stunned. I was not hysterical as some director might have had me act in a similar part. Mr. Smith in *Asylum* loses his son and does not go to pieces. He quietly seeks a way to regain his son by means of this occult book and magic suit he had made. I don't approve of the occult business but the reaction of Smith is entirely my own based on my own experience and for that reason it is more believable than if I played it for histrionics.[2]

Peter portrays Smith with dignified grace—a sad, pitiful character who resorts to black magic to bring his beloved son back to life, willing even to kill the tailor Bruno to achieve his single-minded goal. Smith has lost the ability to reason rationally, succumbing to any temptation that might appeal to his own needs, and devoting his life and personal fortune to the misguided belief that once his son is returned to him, all will be made right in his life once again. Predictably, Smith suffers the ultimate fate as a result.[3]

Technical efforts were excellent all around. Notable were Ernie Sullivan's special effects which were quite impressive in the "Frozen Fear" and "Mannikins of Horror" stories. It was unfortunate in a way that they used a live actor to portray the tailor's dummy, Otto, in "The Weird Tailor" segment. It would have been interesting to see what magic Sullivan might have conjured up had the budget allowed for it.

A significant number of the film's reviews were quite favorable. The *Sunday Express* said it "offers addicts of mystery and imagination a splendid wallow. It's genuinely scary." Ann Guarino in the *New York Daily News* reported that Amicus' "latest multi-thriller again successfully strings together weird stories of murder . . . the film has a smashing twist ending that will delight horror fans . . . a professional job worth seeing if you can stand the chills." Kevin Thomas of the *Los Angeles Times* in his October 12, 1972, review said, "producers . . . Rosenberg and . . . Subotsky have again joined forces with writer Robert Bloch to create another high quality omnibus horror film . . . bolstered by solid performances all around. . . . [Asylum] is a noteworthy achievement for its genre and admirable for its lack of gratuitous gore. Once again Messrs. Rosenberg and Subotsky are to be commended for their consistent good taste." *Cinefantastique* (volume, number 4) reviewer Dan Scapperotti cited Baker and Cushing in his review, saying, "Director Roy Ward Baker . . . keeps the performances of the cast on a solid and serious base. . . . The cast includes such performers as . . . Peter Cushing. Cushing has appeared in all of Amicus Films of this type to date. No complaints here for whether hero, villain, or victim, his presence always adds to a scene . . . he brings to life the character and in some cases saves an otherwise dull story." John Russell Taylor of *The Times* (July 28, 1972) conceded that the film was "foolish but reasonable fun . . . Roy Ward Baker has done a nice glossy job." And *Variety* (August 2, 1972) spoke of *Asylum* as "a trim little chiller, with . . . polished performances and smooth direction. . . . All production values seem first rate." Though Tom Shales of the *Washington Post* was, for the most part, unimpressed: "just when the story is getting scary, its impact shatters with a weak ending." He did concede that this "new picture has some moments [which were] better than those of its predecessors." And critic Donald J. Mayerson of *Cue* concurred, saying, "The finale is a letdown. . . . This spook concoction eerily directed by . . . Baker . . . [makes for] dandy, spellbinding, storytelling."

Notes

1. Roy Ward Baker, interview with Philip Nutman, *Fangoria* 36.
2. Peter Cushing, interview with R. Allen Leider, *The Monster Times* 1, no. 17.
3. In the teleplay version Smith's son, played by Gary ("How to Make a Monster") Clarke, is killed during one of his father's black arts ceremonies. Ridden with guilt, Smith searches for a very rare book of magic that contains a spell to resurrect the dead. Ironically, he uses the same methods to achieve the opposite effect.

And Now the Screaming Starts
(1972)

Credits and Cast

Released May 1973; 91 minutes (87 minutes U.S.); Color; An Amicus Production; Released through Cinerama Releasing (U.S.) and Harbor Productions (U.K.); MPAA R; Filmed at Shepperton Studios, England, and on location at Bray, England. Director: Roy Ward Baker; Producers: Milton Subotsky, Max J. Rosenberg; Screenplay: Roger Marshall; Based on the novel *Fengriffen* by David Case; Director of photography: Denys Coop; Production manager: Teresa Bolland; Unit manager: Ivo Nightingale; Music: Douglas Gamley; First assistant director: Derek Whitehurst; Second assistant director: Lindsey Vickers; Camera operator: John Harris; Focus puller: David Wynn-Jones; Clapper/loader: Trevor Coop; Continuity: Betty Harley; Sound mixer: Norman Bolland; Boom operator: Michael Tucker; Sound camera operator: Peter Myers; Art director: Tony Curtis; Set dresser: Fred Carter; Construction manager: Jim Brown; Makeup: Paul Rabiger; Hairdresser: Mibs Parker; Wardrobe supervisor: Betty Adamson; Wardrobe: Dulcie Midwinter, Freddie McManus; Casting: Ronnie Curtis; Editor: Peter Tanner; First assistant editor: Tom Cornwall; Dubbing editor: Clive Smith; Stills cameraman: Barry Peake.

Peter Cushing (Dr. Pope), Herbert Lom (Henry Fengriffen), Patrick Magee (Doctor Whittle), Ian Ogilvy (Charles Fengriffen), Stephanie Beacham (Catherine Fengriffen), Guy Rolfe (Maitland), Geoffrey Whitehead (Silas), Rosalie Crutchley (Mrs. Luke), Janet Key (Bridget), Gillian Lind (Aunt Edith), Sally Harrison (Sarah), Lloyd Lamble (Sir John Westcliffe), Norman Mitchell (Constable), Frank Forsyth (Servant).

Synopsis

> *I live in horror that* this *is the child of a ghost!* — Catherine Fengriffen

England, 1785. Charles Fengriffen (Ian Ogilvy) arrives at his family estate with his young bride, Catherine (Stephanie Beacham). Catherine, unaware of a curse placed on the Fengriffens long ago, is raped on her wedding night by what she later claims was a horrifying, one-armed apparition. She is also unable to learn why she is suddenly the focus of so much subsequent supernatural hostility. The matter is equally complicated when Catherine learns that she is pregnant.

After the mysterious deaths of all those who attempt to explain the nature of the Fengriffen legend, Catherine decides to investigate herself. Taking a walk through the grounds of the Fengriffen estate, she comes upon a cottage where woodsman Silas (Geoffrey Whitehead) lives and questions him. Silas bears an uncanny resemblance to Catherine's phantom attacker, but Catherine is unsuccessful in learning anything from him.

Charles, who fears that his bride is losing her mind and who, on the surface, still stubbornly refuses to acknowledge the old folklore, invites a specialist in the field of mental disorders, Dr. Pope (Peter Cushing), to examine his wife. The doctor also tries to unravel the mystery.

After Catherine attempts suicide, Charles finally confides his long-suppressed dread to the physician. He tells Dr. Pope that during the tenure of his grandfather, Henry Fengriffen (Herbert Lom), Silas' father (Geoffrey Whitehead) (also named Silas) married and brought his virgin bride to their new home, the cottage Catherine had recently visited. Henry and some of his companions, drunk after an evening of carousing, paid a visit to the young couple on their wedding night. Fengriffen and the others began rudely taunting the young couple. As a joke, Henry claimed the ancient custom of *le droit du seigneur*. When Silas protested the claim and tried to attack Henry, the grandfather raped the woman and chopped off Silas' right hand for his insolence. Silas cursed Fengriffen and vowed that the next virgin bride of the family would suffer the same fate as did his defiled wife. Both Charles and Dr. Pope are unaware of the fact that Catherine has overheard their conversation concerning the legend.

Catherine gives birth to a son and when Charles sees that the child carries the same facial birthmark as Silas and that the child's right hand is missing, he, crazed with grief and outrage, seeks out Silas and kills him. He then exhumes the corpse of his hated ancestor and desecrates the body, smashing the skeleton to pieces.

Catherine at first rejects the child, but soon comes to accept it — with a kind of defiant, insane pride.

Commentary

The year 1972 proved to be a very busy time for Peter Cushing. During this prolific period he would reprise two of his most well-known and beloved characters — Professor Van Helsing in *The Satanic Rites of Dracula*

Dr. Pope tries to decipher the mystery of the Fengriffen curse in Amicus' *And Now the Screaming Starts.*

and Dr. Frankenstein in *Frankenstein and the Monster from Hell*, the latter for the last time. In all, Peter would make appearances in six productions, including a starring role with the newly formed company Charlemagne, begun by his close friend and costar, Christopher Lee. In fact, Cushing would costar with Lee in four of the six films made that year.

Ironically, four of these films dealt with madness in one form or another. *And Now the Screaming Starts* was one of those incursions that crossed that very thin line—but with a twist. It was also a ghost story.

The film, begun in July shortly after *Asylum* had completed production, also starred Stephanie Beacham (Peter's granddaughter in *Dracula A.D. 1972*), Ian Ogilvy, and Herbert Lom (who had also appeared in *Asylum*) in pivotal roles.

Described as a combination of *Rosemary's Baby* (1968) and *The Hound of the Baskervilles* (1958) (the latter film also dealt with a family curse being visited on future generations), Roy Ward Baker, who had previously directed Peter in *Asylum*, handled Amicus' period-setting film with style. Everything one could hope for in a typical Gothic mystery was not overlooked. However, unlike most Gothic romances which end up having all too human antagonists, this film plunged head first into the supernatural—a picture worthy to be listed among the giants of the genre, *The Haunting* (1963), *The Innocents* (1961), and *The Legend of Hell House* (1973).

The entire cast, with the possible exception of Stephanie Beacham, who overacts here on occasion, was first-rate. Herbert Lom, as the instigator of the curse, Henry Fengriffen, was the perfect choice for the role. He performed with just the right blend of amused indifference and, when called upon, chilling menace.

Peter Cushing as Dr. Pope has a relatively small role, when one considers that the original novel from which the film is based—*Fengriffen* by David Case—has the character not only participating throughout but narrating the book! However, Peter's soft-spoken and wonderfully underplayed persona, while graciously allowing the other actors to work around him, ended up becoming the focal point in every one of his scenes. While trying to appear unobtrusive, Peter does, in fact, transfix you with his presence on the screen and the audience finds itself anxious to learn just what he plans to do next. As always, it is a surprise. Though this is nothing new to those who have seen his films, considering his relatively small amount of on-screen time, Cushing's performance never fails to live on long after other players have faded in memory.

As for the technical aspects of the film, the first that comes to mind are the incredible interior sets. Both Tony Curtis as art director and Fred Carter as set dresser were outstanding. Curtis' interlocking sets permitted the camera to move easily from room to room with less edits to interrupt the flow. Denys Coop's photography was also commendable as was Douglas Gamley's appropriate score. Of equal merit was the house itself. The slow panning of the exterior of Oakley Court during the opening credits did much to invoke the tone of the play to follow.[1] The mansion, a brilliant example of the Gothic revival period built during the reign of Queen Victoria, made it seem a likely place for evil to dwell.

As for the screenplay, director Roy Ward Baker felt the film suffered somewhat because it was poorly written in certain respects.

> [It was] sad in a way because the film had a lot of potential. In essense it was a good story, a ghost story, the sort of material that has always appealed to me. It was very Gothic in that it dealt with the bride of a man called Fengriffen who is confronted with a series of unaccountable happenings. The film had a very interesting psychological base because the events could have been of her own imagining, but that wasn't brought out in the script. The motivation was not made clear from the start. It wasn't until half-way through the filming that I became aware of the fact that the husband . . . should have been established as impotent. That could have been a very important aspect . . . as it would have explained his bride's troubled state of mind after the weddng night . . . [but] as it turned out it . . . was nothing more than an anecdote.[2]

Milton Subotsky, one of the film's producers, felt differently about the sexual aspects of the film's underlying theme. "We've never had any sex in our films because I think it's boring to show it on the screen. It turns the audience into voyeurs and it's not what they are interested in unless they want to go to sex films. Normally, an audience wants to see a story, a plot, action, and they want to see what's happening. It's not prudish or anything like that."[3]

Reviews for the film, as usual, were mixed. *Cinefantastique* reviewer David Bartholomew (volume 3, number 2) wrote, "This film is a splendidly detailed filmic creation of a legend. . . . Roy Ward Baker's sturdy and energetic direction intrigue us with these strange goings on at the Fengriffen estate. . . . Baker manages to bring us . . . to a generally chilling climax. . . . The performances are quite good, notably Peter Cushing as Pope, a Freud cum Sherlock Holmes figure." The *New York Times* (A. Weiler, April 28, 1973) said, "Peter Cushing adds a singular bright note to the dark proceedings." "Robe" in *Variety* (May 9, 1973) also praised Peter's performance: "Peter Cushing, that ambidextrous terror film specialist who can play hero or villain with equal skill, here wears his white hat as the doctor . . . who ferrets out the cause of all the spooky goings-on in the Fengriffen household. . . . The film really moves when Cushing arrives on the scene." The *Los Angeles Times* (Kevin Thomas, May 5, 1973) had this to say about the film: "writer Roger Marshall has fashioned a simple, serviceable . . . screenplay . . . augmented by handsome authentic settings . . . gorgeous muted color cinematography . . . a fine, moody score and above all, the stylish, assertive direction of Roy Ward Baker. . . . The cast is uniformly satisfying . . . Peter Cushing lends dignity." And the *New York Daily News* reviewer Ernest Leogrande (April 28, 1973) said of the cast, "Peter Cushing, Herbert Lom and Patrick Magee, pros in such cinematic supernatural goings-on do their stuff with reasonable melodramatic restraint." *The Times*

Amicus' tribute to Hammer films?

(November 15, 1974), however, was not all that impressed: "[It] has a little more style mostly thanks to Denys Coops' elegant . . . camera work. Like beautiful girls from the Bronx, some good actors (Peter Cushing, Patrick Magee, Herbert Lom) are splendid until they have to open their mouths. As down-market horror films are now the principal staple of the British Cinema, one wishes that they could be taken out of the hands of dull, uninspired journeyman directors." While Donald J. Mayerson of *Cue* did not "recommend the movie to expectant parents," he did add that others "might enjoy the hair-raising and heir-producing effects [of] this juicy horror show."

Notes

1. Oakley Court, fondly familiar to Hammer Film aficionados, is now, sadly, a hotel and part of the Norfolk Capital chain in the United Kingdom. However, the exterior has remained virtually unchanged.
2. Roy Ward Baker, interview with Philip Nutman, *Fangoria* 36.
3. Milton Subotsky, interview with Chris Knight, *Cinefantastique* 2, no. 4.

Nothing but the Night
(1972)

Credits and Cast

Released October 1972 (U.K.), 1974 (U.S.); 90 minutes; Eastman color; A Charlemagne Production; Released through Fox-Rank (U.K.), Cinema Systems (U.S.); Filmed on location and at Pinewood Studios, London. Director: Peter Sasdy; Producer: Anthony Nelson-Keys; Screenplay: Brian Hayles; Based on the novel by John Blackburn; Music: Malcolm Williamson; Music director: Philip Martell; Director of photography: Ken Talbot; Camera: Ronnie Maaz; Editor: Keith Palmer; Production manager Tom Sachs; Art director: Colin Grimes; Sound: Danny Daniel, Cynl Taylor, Don Chalice; Makeup: Eddie Knight; Wardrobe: Rosemary Burrows; Continuity: Doreen Dearnaley; Hairdresser: Pat McDermott; Special effects: Les Bowie. Released in some U.S. markets as *The Resurrection Syndicate* and on video as *The Devil's Undead*.

Christopher Lee (Colonel Bingham), Peter Cushing (Sir Mark Ashley), Diana Dors (Anna Harb), Georgia Brown (Joan Foster), Keith Barron (Dr. Haynes), Gwyneth Strong (Mary Valley), Fulton Mackay (Cameron), John Robinson (Lord Fawnlee), Morris Perry (Dr. Yeats), Michael Gambon (Inspector Grant), Shelagh Fraser (Mrs. Alison), Duncan Lamont (Dr. Knight), Kathleen Bryon (Dr. Rose), Geoffrey Frederick (Computer Operator), Louise Nelson (Nurse), Robin Wentworth (Porter), Michael Selig, John Kelland (Reporters).

Synopsis

> *I dislike being put in my place — for you or anyone else.* — Sir Mark
> Ashley to Dr. Haynes

Colonel Bingham (Christopher Lee), a Special Branch officer, discovers a link between the deaths of three wealthy, elderly people — deaths that had been considered accidental. All three, as trustees of the Van Traylen Trust, had willed their fortunes to an orphanage sponsored by the trust off the Scottish Coast. One of the dead is the trust founder, Helen Van Traylen.

A bus carrying children from the orphanage crashes, and Mary (Gwyneth Strong) is hospitalized. Bingham confides to his friend Sir Mark Ashley (Peter Cushing), the hospital pathologist, that if the trustees on the bus had died, the trust would have been £5 million richer.

Anna Harb (Diana Dors) — a prostitute and paroled murderess — claims that Mary is her daughter and demands her release from both the hospital and the orphanage. Dr. Haynes (Keith Barron) is treating Mary and learns, through hypnosis, that she seems to have had a horrifying experience in a fire somewhere in America.

Joan Foster (Georgia Brown), a reporter, investigates Anna's claim. Dr. Haynes — against hospital regulations — allows Anna and Mary to meet, hoping that it will unlock the child's mind. However, Mary becomes violent at the sight of Anna who leaves, screaming threats. When Sir Mark enters Mary's room, he finds Dr. Haynes murdered with Anna's hat pin.

Mary is returned to the orphanage and is tracked by Anna who, in turn, is the object of a massive search headed by Bingham and Sir Mark. Panic sets in on the tiny island that houses the orphanage when explosives are stolen from a quarry. Terror erupts when a motorboat carrying five trustrees explodes.

The children prepare for the annual bonfire as Anna breaks into the grounds. Despite the discovery of a murdered child, the staff is unwilling to cooperate with the police.

Joan has joined the hunt, and she and Sir Mark listen to a tape made by Dr. Haynes of Mary's hypnotic nightmare. In the tape Mary confesses to starting a fire that killed a man named Vincent. Joan decides that Mary is somehow reliving events from trustee founder Helen Van Traylen's life — her husband Vincent died in a fire in America thirty years ago.

With the help of Dr. Knight (Duncan Lamont), Sir Mark examines the brain tissue of the trustees killed in the explosion. They were, he deduces, dead before the explosion.

After realizing that the trust employs two eminent brain specialists, Sir Mark comes to a staggering conclusion. The trustees, frightened of

Peter Cushing and Christopher Lee — nothing but the best in *Nothing but the Night*, a Charlemagne production.

death, are having their brain cells transplanted into the children. Mary no longer exists — she has become Helen Van Traylen.

Colonel Bingham fears that some explosives might turn up at the bonfire. He rushes to the scene and finds Anna dead inside a huge effigy that falls into the fire. He is mobbed by the "children" and overcome. "Mary" confesses to what Sir Mark has already discovered and announces her plan to kill Bingham to ensure their survival.

Sir Mark and Joan hover above in a helicopter and its blades fan the flames higher. "Mary" is set ablaze and leaps off the cliff into the sea. Silently, one by one, the others follow.

Commentary

Nothing but the Night was the first — and only — film produced by Charlemagne Productions. The company was formed by Christopher Lee and ex–Hammer producer-writer Anthony Nelson-Keys. Both men had presumably grown weary of Hammer's repetitive output in the early 1970s and wanted the opportunity to make the films *they* felt worth doing.

This commendable attitude, unfortunately, did not lead anywhere due to the failure of the initial film and the general fading of low-budget horror–science fiction films during the period.

Despite an excellent cast and intriguing story, *Nothing but the Night* did nothing at the box office. Poor distribution is an oft-used excuse for a film's failure, but in this case it is certainly justified. Christopher Lee commented in his fan club journal in 1973 that "I was thoroughly dissatisfied by the almost total lack of promotion and advertising of my film. . . . Even *The Godfather* would not have made money with a similar lack of marketing."

Upon its initial release it seemed to play primarily in Southern U.S. drive-in theaters and not, for whatever reason, in metropolitan areas. Its excellent title (taken from an A. E. Housman poem) with its unsettling vagueness was one of the film's strong points. Naturally, this was changed in some markets to the more explicit *The Resurrection Syndicate*. Even worse, it is now called *The Devil's Undead* on home video.

The film is definitely not for all tastes. Its plot is difficult to follow unless one is prepared to pay close attention to it (which may rule out the casual renter of a title like *The Devil's Undead*). However, those willing to stay with it after a rather talky first half will be rewarded.

In the film's publicity handouts, director Peter Sadsy emphasized that "this is not a horror film. Nor is it an excursion into a world of fantasy." Christopher Lee added, "The main purpose of a film is to entertain audiences. So why rob them of enjoyment by giving away the mystery, the surprise?"

Although one could argue with Peter Sadsy's somewhat pretentious disavowal of his film being in the horror category, Christopher Lee is on the mark. The solution to the mystery is indeed a surprise and unlike any one is likely to encounter.

Although Charlemagne did many things wrong, they certainly had the right idea when hiring the outstanding cast. Peter Cushing, second-billed (to the coproducer), has equal screen time to the star and makes the most of it. Although this attitude may seem somewhat repetitive, he is truly the best aspect of the film.

In the early scenes he goes against his usual image of steely control and is quite testy, losing his temper several times. He even barks at Christopher Lee! His precise and sincere reading of his lines adds credibility to the film's preposterous premise and makes it all believable.

Although Christopher Lee plays his stock authority figure character with little shading, the supporting cast comes through with high marks. Diana Dors and Gwyneth Strong are excellent as the weird mother and daughter. Location filming also adds to the production's feel of quality.

Due to the (oft-mentioned) poor distribution, *Nothing but the Night* was barely reviewed. Those reviewers who did manage to see it were unimpressed. Typical of the reviews was that of *The Guardian*. "The film progresses through some verbose but leaden dialogue from absurdity to absurdity."

Horror genre publications were also less than enthralled, feeling generally that the film was an interesting failure. Perhaps the film's weakest point is that everyone expected it to be so much better.

Frankenstein and the Monster from Hell
(1972)

Credits and Cast

Released 1973; 93 minutes; Color; A Hammer Film Production; Released by Paramount (U.S.); Filmed at MGM-EMI Elstree Studios, England. Director: Terence Fisher; Producer: Roy Skeggs; Screenplay: John Elder; Music: James Bernard; Music supervisor: Philip Martell; Director of photography: Brian Probyn; Art director: Scott MacGregor; Editor: James Needs; Sound recordist: Les Hammond; Production manager: Christopher Neame; Camera operator: Chick Antiss; Makeup: Eddie Knight; Continuity: Kay Rawlings; Wardrobe: Dulcie Midwinter; Hairdresser: Maud Onslow.

Peter Cushing (The Baron), Shane Briant (Simon), Madeline Smith (Sarah), David Prowse (The Monster), John Stratton (Asylum Director), Michael Ward (Transvest), Elsie Wagstaff (Wild One), Norman Mitchell (Sergeant), Clifford Mollison (Judge), Patrick Troughton (Body Snatcher), Philip Voss (Ernst), Christopher Cunningham (Hans), Charles Lloyd-Pack (Durendel), Lucy Griffiths (Hag), Bernard Lee (Tarmut), Sydney Bromley (Muller), Andrea Lawrence (Girl), Jerold Wells (Landlord), Sheila Dunion (Gerda), Mischa de la Motte (Twitch), Norman Atkyns (Smiler), Victor Woolf (Letch), Peter Madden (Coach Driver).

Synopsis

> *If I've succeeded this time, then every sacrifice will have been worthwhile.* — The Baron

Dr. Simon Helder (Shane Briant), a young admirer of Baron Frankenstein, is arrested shortly after taking delivery of a corpse from a body snatcher (Patrick Troughton). An unsympathetic judge (Clifford Mollison) sentences Simon to be committed to the Carlsbad Asylum, as the baron had been before him.

Arriving at the asylum in chains, Simon forces his way into the office of the director (John Stratton), who is unaware that Helder is an inmate. Simon learns that the baron had been a "guest," but is now dead.

Two brutal warders (Philip Voss, Christopher Cunningham) drag Simon off to be given a "bath" with a high-pressure fire hose. This torture is ended by the startling arrival of the prison physician, Dr. Victor (Peter Cushing), whom Simon immediately recognizes as the baron. Sarah (Madeline Smith), a beautiful mute, is instructed by the baron to tend to Simon's wounds.

Although the baron denies Simon's suspicions about him, he nevertheless recruits Helder after learning of the young man's medical knowledge. And, since the baron actually runs the asylum due to the director's incompetence, he gets what he wants.

Simon and Sarah (called the Angel by the patients) join the baron on his rounds. Tarmut (Bernard Lee), who creates beautiful wood carvings, and the professor (Charles Lloyd Pack), a violin playing mathematician, arouse Simon's sympathy. That night, unable to sleep, Simon witnesses the burial of Tarmut. He is minus his delicate hands.

Helder becomes obsessed with discovering what the baron is really doing and finds a secret laboratory behind a hidden door. He enters the laboratory and finds, housed in a cage, an incredible creature (David Prowse). More neolithic than human, the creature has no eyes but has the delicate hands of a sculptor.

The baron finds Simon in the laboratory and, with little choice, confesses the obvious. The creature was once an inmate named Schneider who was committed to the asylum for slashing people with broken glass. After Schneider's suicide attempt, the baron has kept him alive as a framework for a new creation . . . hence Tarmut's hands. Since his hands were badly burned, the baron uses Sarah to perform the surgery under his guidance. With Simon now in his confidence, this will no longer be necessary.

The professor, told by the baron that he will never be released, hangs himself in his cell. Simon, although digusted by the baron's role in the man's death, removes the professor's brain and places it into the creature's skull. The transplant seems to have gone well, until. . . . The creature's new brain, instead of controlling its body, is overtaken by Schneider's sheer physical force. It seizes a glass beaker, smashes it, and attacks Simon.

After subduing the creature, the baron informs Simon of his unthinkably grotesque plan—to mate the creature with Sarah! When Simon threatens to expose the plan to the director, the baron is amused. The director is Sarah's father—she lost the ability to speak after he assaulted her.

During the baron's absence, the creature escapes and kills the director. Surrounded by screaming inmates, it panics. Sarah, shocked back into

Peter's final performance as Baron Frankenstein in Terence Fisher's last film, *Frankenstein and the Monster from Hell.*

speech, rushes to protect it. The inmates, fearing for her life, attack the creature and destroy it.

When the baron returns, he quiets the inmates and returns with Simon to the laboratory. He confides to a disbelieving Helder that, although the experiment failed, he knows what went wrong and will begin again. Simon stares at the baron, horrified.

Commentary

When one compares the initial film of a popular series with one at or near the end, the result is usually the same—disappointment. Would, for example, *A View to a Kill* have spawned the James Bond series? Or how about *Tarzan and the Mermaids?* Perhaps *Andy Hardy Comes Home?*

Compared to the above, *Frankenstein and the Monster from Hell* isn't a bad film. While it's certainly no classic and not nearly the best of the series, the actor and director who started it all can go out unbowed. The film relies almost entirely on them and is not let down.

In his final performance as the baron, Peter Cushing takes the character about as far as he can go. Frankenstein is now truly mad and has lost whatever limited sense of proportion he ever possessed. His goals have become so twisted that they have become nonexistent. The cold brutality of his previous appearance has been replaced by an even colder sense of indifference. It is perhaps fortunate that the series ended here; it's difficult to imagine what direction it could have taken.

As usual, Peter Cushing threw himself—literally—into the role. When the script called for the baron to make a rather dangerous leap, Cushing refused the help of a stunt performer. His personal script was, as usual, a mass of alterations, dialogue changes, and small reminders on the playing of a certain scene.[1] Although this was his sixth performance in the part, it was not a part to be walked through.

The script was an interesting attempt to portray the twisted mind of the baron through his environment at the asylum. While not entirely successful, at least it was something a little different. Unfortunately, the sets lacked the realism of Hammer's late production designer Bernard Robinson. The miniature photography is not totally convincing, either.

David Prowse's make up as the monster—while pointing out the baron's madness, is not very well executed. Prowse (famous as Darth Vader) does succeed in gaining some audience sympathy despite his ludicrous appearance.

What really works here is the performance of Peter Cushing. "You cannot make a film like this without integrity. To make the audiences believe in you, you must believe utterly in what you are doing."[2] He certainly lives up to his words by rising above the material and delivering one of his best performances.

Joining Cushing in giving a fine performance was young Shane Briant, whose slightly off-center film personality is perfect for Simon Helder. Briant shared his thoughts with the authors:

> *Frankenstein and the Monster from Hell* was not by any means a great film. The majority of Peter's films were far better. I think the script was

pretty weak, but we struggled through the dialogue and gazed at the some-what ridiculous costume worn by David Prowse.

Peter was the most gentlemanly of gentlemen. He did all he could do to help me learn my craft (it was only my second film). Every now and then his dry sense of humor would surface and he'd make us all laugh. He was certainly a man whom everyone respected enormously and a man who was loved by the entire crew.

During the early 1970s, sex and violence were becoming more and more a part of the horror film. Peter Cushing commented, "Our film could not be compared with [A] *Clockwork Orange* and all its brutality, for instance. Audiences cannot identify with our characters. They are pure escapism. Our Frankenstein and Dracula films are simply fantasies. We are only out to entertain."[3]

This was to be Terence Fisher's last film, and it's a shame that it's not a better one. The victim of two car accidents (while a pedestrian!) Fisher only directed two films from 1969 until his death in 1980.

Having directed Peter Cushing thirteen times, he had as much to do with the actor's success as anyone. During their long association, both men had nothing but praise for each other. "The real task of the fantasy film director is to bring integrity of intention to his film making. I always ask for a similar response from my actors and I rarely fail to get it, especially from Peter Cushing."[4]

Summing up his role, Fisher remarked, "Of course, people go in thinking they'll have a good laugh. My job is to stop them. Dead."[5]

The Sunday Times (May 5, 1974) said, "We are back with something like the original horror myth; one is sorry for the monster. Peter Cushing, so elegant and his manner . . . so flawless that one can't help wishing him better luck." *Variety* (June 17, 1974) felt it to be "a good, tight little dual bill item with an economy of filmmaking that is missed in more ambitious efforts."

In most markets, the film was released with Hammer's *Captain Kronos — Vampire Hunter*.

Notes

1. Paramount press book.
2. *Hammer News*, October 1972.
3. Ibid.
4. "House of Horror — The Story of Hammer Films."
5. *Hammer News*, October 1972.

The Satanic Rites of Dracula
(1972)

Credits and Cast

Released January 1974 (U.K.), November 1978 (U.S.); 87 minutes; Color; A Hammer Film Production; Released through Columbia–Warner Brothers (U.K.) and Dynamite Entertainment (U.S.); MPAA R; Filmed at MGM-EMI Studios and on location in London. Director: Alan Gibson; Producer: Roy Skeggs; Associate producer: Don Houghton; Screenplay: Don Houghton; Director of photography: Brian Probyn; Camera operator: Chick Anstiss; Music: John Caeavas; First assistant director: Derek Whitehurst; Continuity: Elizabeth Wilcox; Sound mixer: Claude Hitchcock; Art director: Lionel Conch; Wardrobe supervisor: Rebecca Breed; Makeup artist: George Blackler; Hairdresser: Maud Onslow; Casting: James Liggat; Stills cameraman: Ronnie Pilgrim; Editor: Christopher Barnes; Production secretary: Sally Pardo; Dubbing mixer: Dennis Whitlock; Production manager: Ron Jackson; Music supervisor: Philip Martell; Special effects: Les Bowie. Title in U.S., *Count Dracula and His Vampire Bride*.

Christopher Lee (Count Dracula), Peter Cushing (Lorrimer Van Helsing), William Franklyn (Torrence), Michael Coles (Inspector Murray), Joanna Lumley (Jessica Van Helsing), Freddie Jones (Professor Keeley), Barbara Yu Ling (Chin Yang), Valerie Van Ost (Jane), Richard Vernon (Colonel Mathews), Maurice O'Connell (Hanson), Patrick Barr (Lord Carridine), Lockwood West (General Freeborne), Peter Adair (Doctor), Richard Mathews (Porter), Maggie Fitzgerald (Vampire Girl), Mia Martin (Vampire Girl), Finnuala O'Shannon (Vampire Girl), Pauline Peart (Vampire Girl), Marc Zuber (Mod C), Graham Reese (Guard), Ian Dewar (Guard), John Harvey, Paul Weston.

Synopsis

Five prominent men in the fields of business, government, and scientific research are under investigation by a top security branch of British Intelligence. When one of their field agents is picked up, near death, he tells his superiors a bizarre tale. It involves black masses and blood sacrifices at the country estate of Pelham House which had been under surveillance. The agent dies but photographs he had taken while on assignment are developed. One of the men in the photographs turns out to be the head of their department. Another photograph is mysteriously blank. The agency calls Scotland Yard in on the investigation. Inspector Murray (Michael Coles), upon hearing the circumstances involved in the case, contacts an expert in the field of the occult, Professor Lorrimer Van Helsing (Peter Cushing).

Murray discusses the case with the professor and soon they are joined by Van Helsing's granddaughter, Jessica (Joanna Lumley). She later

The reigning monarchs of terror—Christopher Lee and Peter Cushing on the set of Hammer's *Satanic Rites of Dracula.*

accompanies Murray to Pelham House. Unfortunately, both are caught trespassing by some of the strange inhabitants of the house.

Van Helsing, recognizing one of the men in Murray's photographs, a Professor Keeley (Freddie Jones), goes to visit his old friend at the biologist's laboratory in London. Van Helsing finds Keeley a very different man from the dedicated scientist he had known many years ago. Van Helsing ascertains that Keeley has been coerced into developing a new strain of bubonic plague—a virus that has no antidote and is capable of destroying all life on the planet. Van Helsing also learns that Keeley's work is being funded by the Denham Group of companies, which is owned by a man named D. D. Denham. Denham, it seems, is a man of strange habits who has never been photographed or seen in the daytime. After Van Helsing witnesses Keeley's assassination by an unknown assailant, he visits Denham's offices and discovers that the reclusive Denham is none other than his archenemy, Dracula (Christopher Lee)! The vampire king plans to release Keeley's virus on the world after making Jessica, who he is holding prisoner, his bride.

Dracula takes Van Helsing to Pelham House where the professor finds his granddaughter unconscious on an altar in one of the rooms. Van

Helsing is joined by the remaining officials who were under investigation —
all disciples of Dracula. One of the men, Porter (Richard Mathews), drops
the vial of plague he had been holding and as the others watch terror-
stricken, the man dies horribly from the deadly power of the virus.

Meanwhile, Inspector Murray escapes his captors and starts a fire in
the house which quickly spreads to the room where Dracula is holding
Van Helsing and Jessica. Van Helsing uses the fire to divert Dracula's attention away from Jessica and manages to escape when Murray arrives to
rescue Jessica.

While the fire continues to blaze inside, consuming Porter's body and
destroying the plague virus, Dracula pursues Van Helsing into a nearby
wood. He corners Van Helsing in an area surrounded by bushes. When
the vampire tries to reach Van Helsing, he unknowingly becomes entwined
in a hawthorne bush — which is purported to be fatal to the undead.

Van Helsing looks on as Dracula vainly struggles to free himself from
the unyielding branches of the hawthorne bush before he finally succumbs to its power and crumbles into dust.

Commentary

> Hammer Films are indeed making a further 'modern' version,
> which Christopher Lee and I started a few weeks ago. The title is
> "Dracula Is Dead . . . But Well and Living in London." Michael
> Coles is playing the part of the police inspector again — but my
> granddaughter is portrayed in this film by Joanna Lumley, as
> Stephanie Beacham had a prior engagement and her dates clashed
> with ours. — Peter Cushing (January 1, 1973)

> A woman wanted to know what Hammer Films used for blood.
> "Always the same thing, dear lady," Cushing replied, "Kensington
> Gore by Max Factor."[1]

Although Hammer eventually decided to release their latest, and
final "Christopher Lee as Dracula" opus as *The Satanic Rites of Dracula*,
it might have been far more fitting to have entitled it, "Dracula Meets Ian
Fleming," instead. This mish-mash of fantasy, vampire lore, and spy
thriller misadventure was the final blow not only to audiences but to one
of its stars, Christopher Lee, as well. "I'm doing the next one under protest," Lee told writer Don Glut of *Monsters of the Movies* magazine just
after the release of *Dracula A.D. 1972*. "I don't see the point." Lee added,
"I don't see what they hope to achieve. I think it's playing down to people."

Filmed at MGM-EMI Studios in London, with a six-week shooting schedule between November and December 1972, and with approximately
eight days of location shooting in and around London, Hammer was

perhaps blissfully unaware of the fact that while they were putting the finishing touches on their sequel to *Dracula A.D. 1972,* their previous release was floundering overseas at the box office. As a result, *The Satanic Rites of Dracula* would be shelved, sold, and resold for approximately six years before finally being released stateside by Max Rosenberg's Dynamite Entertainment with the absurd title of *Count Dracula and His Vampire Bride.* Had Hammer executives been listening, they might have heard a death knoll beginning to sound, loud and clear.[2]

Screenwriter Don Houghton, whose previous credits included screenplays for British television series such as "Emergency Ward 10" and "Dr. Who," showed, purely and simply, a total lack of inspiration in regard to his key characters. This, in turn, forced near-mechanical performances out of the film's leads. If Lee and Cushing seem to be walking through their roles, it is the script's lack of purpose and not any ineptitude on their parts.

Houghton's plan to have his suicidal Dracula extinguish all life on earth by means of a super plague might be exciting in a James Bond film but hardly has a place in the immortal vampire's scheme of things. The whole storyline is redundant in a way because Dracula himself is a plague, and although he may be the essence of evil, he's certainly not foolish enough to want to completely annihilate what he basically perceives as his food supply.

Although definitely hampered by Houghton's blueprint, director Alan Gibson did the best he could with the limited material he had at hand. However, like his cast, Gibson appeared to be bored with the whole thing. Any filmmaker knows that if a film's foundation is weak then the entire structure will collapse. This is precisely what happened with *The Satanic Rites of Dracula.* Peppering the film with a few new gimmicks wasn't sufficient to sustain what basically appeared to be a lack of interest. Viewing this film only made one long for the golden days of Hammer.

"Hege" in *Variety* (December 13, 1978) noted that *The Satanic Rites of Dracula* was "silly, dull and lack[ed] a sense of humor." *People Weekly* prophetically reported that "England's Hammer Films have, by now, about drained the life out of the genre." Kevin Thomas of the *Los Angeles Times* (November 24, 1978) noted that "Christopher Lee and Peter Cushing are back for yet anther round. . . . The film itself is routine Hammer horror fare but it's a pleasure to watch Lee and Cushing, both such polished actors, resume their familiar roles . . . a passible diversion for Horror fans." Ron Borst of *Photon* (number 27) cited that "although both Lee and Cushing are again reunited and manage to carry off their respective scenes with conviction and polish, their talents are sadly misused and they are unable to overcome an inane script with countless contrived and trite situations directed by Alan Gibson, a man who shows utterly no flair at all

Max Rosenberg's idea of dynamite entertainment!

for this genre. . . . Who but Peter Cushing could continually spout those often-heard lines about evil . . . and say them with such sincerity and finesse that they are of interest rather than so much tripe." Dilys Powell of *The Sunday Times* (January 20, 1974) noted that *The Satanic Rites of Dracula* "offer[ed] no great novelty, but then with the company of . . . Peter Cushing, the refined face always elegantly intent on the ridiculous action, I can do without novelty. . . . Even the Horror Film has grown more savage."

Notes

1. "'Case of Fantasy, Dear Boy,' says Sherlock Holmes," *Mid-Sussex Times,* February 8, 1973.
2. Locations for the film took place at High Cannons, a large country house in Hertfordshire—which was used to represent Pelham House in the film. Other locations: Shepherd's Bush in London, as well as London's West End, Piccadilly Circus, Pall Mall, St. James Palace, and Clarence House.

Madhouse
(1973)

Credits and Cast

Released 1974; 89 minutes; Color; An Amicus Production; Released through American International (U.S.), MGM (U.K.); Filmed at Twickenham and on location at Pyrford House, Surrey, and London Weekend TV Studios, Wembley. Director: Jim Clark; Producers: Max J. Rosenberg, Milton Subotsky; Executive producer: Samuel Z. Arkoff; Associate producer: John Dark; Screenplay: Greg Morrison; Based on the novel by Angus Hall, *Devilday*; Music: Douglas Gamley; Director of photography: Ray Parslow; Art director: Tony Curtis; Editor: Clive Smith; Sound recordist: Danny Daniel; Makeup: George Blackler; Hairdresser: Helen Lennox; Wardrobe: Dulcie Midwinter; Special effects: Kerss and Spencer.

Vincent Price (Paul Toombes), Peter Cushing (Herbert Flay), Robert Quarry (Quayle), Adrienne Corri (Faye), Natasha Pyne (Julia), Michael Parkinson (Interviewer), Linda Hayden (Elizabeth), Barry Dennen (Blount), Ellis Dale (Alfred), Catherine Wilmer (Louise), John Garrie (Harper), Ian Thompson (Bradshaw), Jenny Lee Wright (Carol), Julie Crosthwaite (Ellen), Peter Halliday (Psychiatrist).

Synopsis

> Sit down and watch one of your old movies — it might give you a laugh. — Herbert Flay

Has-been horror film star Paul Toombes (Vincent Price) is making a comeback after twenty years of scandal, disgrace, and mental problems. His career as a Hollywood star ended with the beheading of his fiancée (Julie Crosthwaite) at a party held in his honor. As a major suspect, Paul broke under the strain and was hospitalized. The killer was never found.

Now, through the efforts of old friend and writer Herbert Flay (Peter Cushing), Paul's famous character — Dr. Death — is being revived in a television series to be filmed in London. Paul is overjoyed to be reunited with Herbert who, with Toombes, created the character.

Unfortunately, Paul's problems are not over. On the voyage to England he is harassed by Elizabeth Peeters (Linda Hayden), a young actress, who wants Paul to "help her career." When he refuses, she makes it seem as if they were having an affair.

He is met at the pier by Julia (Natasha Pyne), a young publicity girl, who spirits him away. Unknown to Paul, the series producer is Oliver Quayle (Robert Quarry), a boorish, low-budget filmmaker who, years earlier, had used Toombes' fiancée in a porno film.

Paul stays at Herbert's country house and dozes off while watching one of his old films. He awakens to a recording of his singing "When Day Is Done" and investigates. He is horrified to discover a disfigured woman playing with spiders. Faye Carstairs (Adrienne Corri), a former costar, is now Mrs. Flay. An unhappy marriage led her to pick up young men — one of whom had an accident while driving her in his car and she lost both her beauty and her sanity.

What is more disturbing is the discovery of Elizabeth's body in a rowboat — murdered with a pitchfork. Paul is, again, a suspect.

Things go little better on the set. Carol (Jenny Lee Wright), his costar, is obnoxious, untalented, and Quayle's girlfriend. She and Paul quarrel, both during filming and later at a party. During a showing of one of Paul's old films, Carol is murdered by a figure dressed like Dr. Death.

Unsure as to whether he is actually guilty, Paul decides to quit the show, despite Herbert's pleas. After being questioned by the police, Paul is accosted by Elizabeth's foster parents who plan to blackmail him with a watch she stole from his stateroom.

Paul reconsiders and returns to the set. As the director (Barry Dennen) demonstrates a scene involving a falling bed canopy, he is crushed while Paul watches helplessly.

The blackmailers strike again and are lured into Herbert's house by a mysterious figure where they are murdered. Paul awakens to a phone call from Julia who has discovered new evidence.

When he goes to meet her at the studio he is accosted by a figure dressed as Dr. Death. Paul escapes, only to bungle his way onto an interview show which he had forgotten about. While the interviewer (Michael

Did they watch one of their old films? Peter Cushing and Vincent Price enjoy a good laugh on the set of *Madhouse*.

Parkinson) runs an old Toombes film ("Pit and the Pendulum"), Julia is murdered after reading a special replacement clause in the Dr. Death contract.

   Paul discovers her body and carries it to the set and sets it ablaze, filming the scene with the studio camera to appear as his death.

   The next day, Herbert—who gave up acting to create the Dr. Death character — fulfills the option clause and assumes the role. At home, while viewing the film of Paul's incineration, Herbert is horrified as Toombes walks through the screen. Flay screams that he always resented Paul's success and felt that he should have played Dr. Death all along. He is responsible for all the killings — past and present. Herbert attacks Paul with a sword, but is killed by Faye and falls into a pit of spiders.

As Faye reminds him that supper is ready, Paul painstakingly makes himself up as Herbert. Later, he and Faye enjoy a meal of sour cream and red herring.

Commentary

The long-awaited teaming of horror legends Peter Cushing and Vincent Price finally occurred with this violent but amusing film. Their teaming was a natural and it's hard to believe it didn't happen sooner (not counting *Scream and Scream Again* (1969) which hardly qualifies as a joint venture). Based on Angus Hall's novel *Devilday*, the film was originally titled "Revenge of Dr. Death" — a far better title than the vague *Madhouse*.

Joining the two stars was an up-and-coming horror actor of the period, Robert Quarry. Described as a "compact Christopher Lee," Quarry made his mark in *Count Yorga, Vampire* (1970). He is, not surprisingly, outclassed by the two veterans.

Vincent Price is perfectly cast as a somewhat hammy horror star. His horror stardom began more or less in director Roger Corman's Poe films of the 1960s, and Price commented on the set, "I think horror stories end up more successful if they're done the Corman way. By which I mean to say, letting the audience in on the secret that the actor is enjoying it."[1] He and Peter Cushing definitely transmitted their enjoyment and the audience realizes early on that they are not to take the film too seriously. Price continued, "Sometimes, however, a scene is so totally preposterous it is almost impossible to do. Yesterday dear Peter had to fall into a tank of spiders! It's very difficult to fall into a tank of spiders and be Brando!"[2]

Fortunately, it wasn't that much of a trial for Peter Cushing, for he confided to the authors, "I like spiders." He also liked working with Vincent Price and the Amicus company, which he described as "efficient and friendly."[3]

He found in Vincent Price a kindred spirit. He said of Price, "One of his great qualities as a gentleman is his manner and attitude to all who come within his orbit. No matter what their status, everyone received the same charming courtesy and attention."[4]

The film itself is a tribute to Vincent Price, showing clips from American International Poe films including *Tales of Terror* (1962), *The Raven*

(1963), and *The Masque of the Red Death* (1964). Although Price is clearly the film's star, Peter Cushing has considerable screen time and is not reduced to a minor role.

Despite a lively plot and spirited performances from the two old pros, *Madhouse* is a bit of a letdown. Filmed in very drab color, it looks cheap — much cheaper than it really was. One also might wish that a more serious film would have resulted from their pairing — perhaps a Poe story in period costumes.

That aside, the film is fun to watch despite less than rave reviews. *The Times* (November 15, 1974) found it to be "an atrocious Hollywood [*sic*] horror flick. . . . The makers had the wit to see that their material was ludicrous. . . . The result is not only inept, silly, nasty, but also rather camp." *Cinema-TV Today* (November 16) called it "a partially successful mixing of squeal-worthy shocks and in-jokes for film buffs." *Variety* (March 26) dubbed it an "inaptly titled but otherwise satisfactory horror entry . . . a tepid blend of shivers and snickers. . . . The nostalgia never becomes necrophilic."

Just before filming *Madhouse*, Peter Cushing appeared in an episode of British television's "The Zoo Gang" with John Mills.

In addition, he guest starred on "Magpie," "This Week in the West," and "Going for a Song."

Notes

1. *Famous Monsters of Filmland,* August 1974.
2. Ibid.
3. *The Monster Times,* June 1974.
4. *Bizarre 3.*

From Beyond the Grave
(1973)

Credits and Cast

Released March 1976 (U.S.), February 1974 (U.K.); 100 minutes (98 minutes U.K.); Color; An Amicus Production; Released through Columbia–Warner Brothers (U.K.) and Howard Mahler Films (U.S.); MPAA PG; Filmed at Shepperton Studios, England. Director: Kevin Connor; Producers: Milton Subotsky, Max J. Rosenberg;

Screenplay: Robin Clarke, Raymond Christodoulou; Based on four short stories from *The Unbidden* by R. Chetwynd-Hayes; Director of photography: Alan Hume; Music composed and conducted by Douglas Gamley; Editor: John Ireland; Art direction: Maurice Carter; Set decorations: Simon Wakefield; Special effects: Alan Bryce; Sound: Peter Keen, Peter Handford, Nolan Roberts; Wardrobe: John Hilling; Makeup: Neville Smallwood; Hairstyles: Miles Parker; Associate producer: John Dark; Production manager: Teresa Bolland; Assistant director: John Peverall; Re-release title: *The Creatures.*

Peter Cushing (The Proprietor). "The Gate Crasher": David Warner (Edward Charlton), Wendy Allnutt (Pamela), Rosalind Ayres (Prostitute), Marcel Steiner (The Face). "An Act of Kindness": Donald Pleasence (Underwood), Ian Bannen (Christopher Lowe), Diana Dors (Mabel Lowe), Angela Pleasence (Emily Underwood). "The Elemental": Margaret Leighton (Madame Orloff), Ian Carmichael (Reggie Warren), Nyree Dawn Porter (Susan Warren). "The Door": Ian Ogilvy (William Seaton), Leslie-Anne Down (Rosemary Seaton), Jack Watson (Sir Michael Sinclair); also appearing: Tommy Godfrey, Ben Howard, John O'Farrell, Dog (Mr. Hawkins).

Synopsis

> *Customers! Come in! Come in! I'm sure I have the very thing to tempt you. Also Bargains. All tastes catered for. Oh, and a big novelty surprise goes with every purchase. Do come in . . . . Any Time . . . . I'm always open!* — The Proprietor

Tucked away in a darkened alleyway somewhere in London, a quaint antique shop lures in five male customers. Each one sees something they want to own, but nearly all attempt to cheat the Proprietor (Peter Cushing) of its true worth. As a result, each will pay a terrible price for their deception.

The first customer is Edward Charlton (David Warner), who talks the proprietor into selling him an antique mirror for far less than its value. Later, Edward invites some friends over to a party and one of them remarks that the mirror really belongs in a medium's parlor. When one of them suggests that it might be fun to hold a seance, Edward agrees. However, during the ceremony, a demonic spirit (Marcel Steiner), who had been imprisoned in the glass, is inadvertently summoned and takes control of Edward's mind, forcing him to murder people for their blood. The spirit soon becomes strong enough to break free of its confinement and enters the world as a living being.

Offering Edward an alternative to execution or life imprisonment for his crimes, the spirit kills Edward and imprisons him in the mirror, to patiently await his summoning.

The next customer is a white-collar worker named Lowe (Ian Bannen), a simple-minded man who holds a mediocre job and who is further burdened with a demeaning wife (Diana Dors) and a precocious son. Lowe befriends a peddler named Underwood (Donald Pleasence), who is also a war veteran. Feeling a strange compulsion to impress the man, Lowe steals a British Distinguished Service Cross medal from the antique shop to show to the peddler. Underwood invites Lowe to tea and there he meets Underwood's daughter, Emily (Angela Pleasence). Lowe is immediately drawn to her and they begin an affair. However, Lowe is not aware of the fact that Emily is a witch and she uses her powers to kill Lowe's wife. After the murder, Lowe marries Emily but when she cuts into the figure of the bridegroom on their wedding cake, Lowe falls over, dead. Lowe's son is grateful that his prayers were finally answered, even if the methods were a bit unorthodox.

The third customer, Reginald Warren (Ian Carmichael) acquires an old but elegant snuff box after he deliberately switches the price tags with a cheaper box. On his way home he meets a clairvoyant named Madame Orloff (Margaret Leighton) who informs Warren that an elemental is sitting on his shoulder and that unless he rids himself of the invisible demon, it will eventually possess him completely. Warren is skeptical until that night when his wife (Nyree Dawn Porter) accuses him of trying to strangle her. The next day Reggie calls Madame Orloff and she performs an exorcism. The rite appears to be a success. However, later that night Warren and his wife hear strange noises from somewhere on the second floor. When Warren goes to investigate, he is thrown down the stairs. As he lies helpless his wife, now possessed by the elemental, kills him.

The fourth visitor to the shop is William Seaton (Ian Ogilvy), a writer, who offers the proprietor a fair price for a beautifully carved door which he installs in front of a closet in his study. However, when he opens the closet door, he is shocked to find that a strange, blue room has mysteriously replaced the cupboard space. Entering the room, Seaton finds the portrait of a nobleman in seventeenth-century attire and a diary. The diary contains the memoirs of Sir Michael Sinclair (Jack Watson), who claimed to be a sorcerer who attained immortality through human sacrifice. William is then confronted by Sinclair himself who threatens to take his soul and that of his wife, Rosemary (Leslie-Anne Down). William tries to flee the house with his wife but finds all the outside doors locked. Rosemary is lured into the room by Sinclair. William hacks away at the door with an axe and realizes that with each stroke, a portion of the room crumbles to dust. Eventually Sinclair himself is destroyed. Seaton and Rosemary barely escape with their lives as the room literally disintegrates all around them.

The last visitor to the shop is a petty thief who tries to rob the

The proprietor in Amicus' *From Beyond the Grave.*

proprietor of the day's receipts. However the robber trips over something
in the cluttered store and falls into a most unusual trunk whose lid is lined
with sharp spikes. As the lid slams down, trapping the thief, the proprietor
welcomes in his next customers, the audience.

Commentary

> Tony Blackburn once interviewed Peter Cushing on a BBC tele-
> vision show ("Ask Aspel" January 7, 1973) and asked Peter if he
> was ever frightened by horror films and if they ever gave him
> nightmares. "*No, I get nightmares if I eat cheese late at night!*" —
> Peter replied.

Peter Cushing's next venture into the supernatural originally had two different working titles: "Tales from the Beyond" and "Tales from Beyond the Grave." Production on the film began at Shepperton Studios on June 4th, 1973, for an eight-week shoot. As was typical of most Amicus films during this time, the budget was set at $500,000. MGM had originally considered releasing the picture, then backed out. Warner Brothers decided to take up the film's U.S. distribution but there were problems. Milton Subotsky offered an explanation: "We made a film called *From Beyond the Grave*.... Well Warner Bros. bought it for U.S. release and they [weren't] going to distribute it to cinemas — they [were] going to sell it directly to television! AIP wanted to take it over and some other distributors tried to take it over, but the terms Warners asked were too big."[1] Eventually, Warners sold their U.S. rights to Howard Mahler Films who released the film in 1976.[2]

According to Subotsky, horror films on limited budgets were suffering a decline in box office profits. An average $500,000 production might only take in $800,000 in receipts. Yet a distributor would have to spend over $650,000 for advertising, publicity material, and cost of prints. So, in essence, the film might end up suffering a loss in excess of $350,000. Of course, no one could accurately predict how well any given film might do on the market, but if this was the prevailing measuring device, it would certainly account for one of the reasons why the film had problems finding a release and why none of the major studios wanted to chance taking on the picture at the time — unless they needed a tax write-off.

What is indeed tragic is that *From Beyond the Grave* was one of the best Amicus had ever produced. Every facet of its production was first-rate and it was brilliantly directed by Kevin Connor in this his first feature film project.

Based on four short stories by R. Chetwynd-Hayes from his anthology, *The Unbidden*, writers Robin Clarke and Raymond Christodoulou effectively brought the stories to life. The film also had the benefit of an exceptional cast which included: Margaret Leighton, Donald and Angela Pleasence (father and daughter), David Warner, Ian Bannen, Ian Ogilvy, Nyree Dawn Porter and Peter Cushing.

Although similar to *Dr. Terror's House of Horrors* (1964), in that his character guided the film's framework story line, Peter seemed to be thoroughly enjoying himself in his role as the eerie proprietor of a rather unusual antique shop called, appropriately enough, "Temptations Ltd." Sporting bushy eyebrows and a Yorkshire accent, Peter appeared harmless enough on the outside. However, as it turned out, he was hardly your average shopkeeper!

An interesting postscript to this production would occur years later with the premiere of the syndicated television show, "Friday the 13th." This well-made Canadian based import used a very similar subplot for its weekly, hour long series. Like *Tales from the Crypt, From Beyond the Grave* would prove to have a lasting impact in the industry.

Critical evaluations of the film included *The Times* (David Robinson, February 22, 1974) reporting that *From Beyond the Grave* was "an omnibus horror film, its stories linked by an over-elaborated notion of Peter Cushing as a fate figure, presiding over a curio shop whose stock . . . lands its unwary purchasers in very strange pickles. Kevin Connor directs it with a certain verve but the best moments are Margaret Leighton's extravagances as a post-arcate medium." The *New York Post* reviewer, Winston, in his March 4, 1976, review "Found the very fine cast convincing." The *Independent Film Journal* (E.P., March 17, 1976) added, "A devilishly entertaining group of tales . . . well acted, possesses some infectious humor along with a fair amount of chills . . . the violence is more suggestive than graphic." *The Observer* critic Russell Davies (February 24, 1976) remarked that "Though I am already fed up to the back fangs with Satanic rites and such FBTG struck me as a better-class creepie. . . ."

Donald J. Meyerson of *Cue* was particularly hostile, reporting that "this is not the horror film anyone has been waiting for . . . forgettable . . . hokey routine stuff. . . . Kevin Connor's listless and dismal direction . . . [made even the] outstanding British cast look like has beens." Linda Gross of the *Los Angeles Times* said, "good actors whose talents are wasted . . . in [an] incredible, incoherent and incomprehensible screenplay . . . tacky . . . silly . . . the stuff that nightmares not movies are made of." The *New York Daily News* critic Kathleen Carroll wrote "[the] British-made horror movie has about as much thrills to offer as a tea party. . . . However . . . it does feature a surprising array of talent."

The *Chicago Sun Times* (Roger Ebert, November 3, 1975), however, seemed to have a feel for the true nature of the film, unlike fellow critics. "Horror with more fun than gore . . . the British do these things with a certain style and would rather amuse and scare us than disgust us. . . . It's an anthology of four different horror stories, tied together by a common thread. This time, it's a little antique shop presided over by the one and only Peter Cushing, wraithlike, rubbing his hands together and looking suitably sinister. . . . What's nice about Rosenberg and Subotsky productions . . . they're not so heavy on the blood and gore as most of Hollywood's el-cheapo, sleazo garbage . . . as tales from graves and crypts go, these go quite far enough."

The *New York Times* (Richard Eder, March 4, 1976) reported, "The episodes in *Grave* are crude and obvious. Each punch is telegraphed, each twist is a stranglehold. They over-compensate with blood for their lack of deftness."

However, *Cinefantastique* editor Frederick S. Clarke (volume 4, number 4) in his review called it "the very best film Amicus has ever produced . . . with a strong script as its base . . . allows the main virtues of the British Cinema—top-notch performers and craftmanship in sets, costuming and related arts—to operate at their fullest potential. An impeccably chosen cast is headed by Peter Cushing."

For those of you who are curious and have wondered where "Temptations Ltd." is actually located, here's the address: 4 Pornthorp Mews, London WC 2. Or, you can call at 555-9901 for store hours. However, if you happen upon something you'd like to buy, don't haggle over the price!

Notes

1. Milton Subotsky, interview, *Bizarre* 4.
2. Warner Brothers retained joint overseas distribution rights with Columbia. Warners also released the film on video in 1986.

The Beast Must Die
(1973)

Credits and Cast

Released April 1974; 93 minutes; Technicolor; An Amicus Production; Released through Cinerama Releasing (U.S.), British Lion (U.K.); MPAA PG; Filmed at Shepperton Studios, England. Director: Paul Annett; Producers: Max J. Rosenberg, Milton Subotsky; Associate producer: John Dark; Screenplay: Michael Winder; Based on the novel by James Blish, *There Shall Be No Darkness*; Music: Douglas Gamley; Production manager: John Davis; Director of photography: Jack Hildyard, B.S.C.; Art director: John Stoll; Assistant director: Richard Jenkins; Camera operator: Derek Browne; Sound mixer: Ken Richie; Continuity: Phyllis Townshend; Wardrobe supervisor: John Hilling; Makeup: Paul Rabiger; Hairdresser: Bobbie Smith; Editor: Peter Tanner; Special effects: Ted Samuels; Set dresser:

Herbert Westbrook; Casting director: Thelma Graves; Executive producer: Robert Greenberg.

Calvin Lockhart (Tom Newcliffe), Peter Cushing (Dr. Christopher Lundgren), Charles Gray (Bennington), Anton Diffring (Pavel), Marlene Clark (Caroline Newcliffe), Ciaran Madden (Davina Gilmore), Tom Chadbon (Paul Foote), Michael Gambon (Jan Jarmokowski), Sam Mansaray (Butler), Andrew Lodge (Pilot), Carl Bohun (First Hunter), Eric Carte (Second Hunter), Sultan (Werewolf).

Synopsis

Millionaire and big game hunter, Tom Newcliffe (Calvin Lockhart), has assembled an odd group of guests to his isolated country estate. Newcliffe believes that one of his guests is a werewolf and he informs them that with the benefit of the highly sophisticated monitoring equipment he has acquired, he will hunt down the creature and destroy it. Newcliffe further states that the werewolf hidden among them will have to make itself known since over the next three evenings the moon will be full.

However, Newcliffe's task may not be easy since any one of his guests could ultimately turn out to be his prey. The hunter's suspects include Professor Christopher Lundgren (Peter Cushing), who is an expert on werewolf legends and knows their habits and customs as well as how to identify and destroy them; Pavel (Anton Diffring) who originated from Central Europe where the legends first began and who is employed by Newcliffe as his assistant in tracking the werewolf and its prey; Bennington (Charles Gray), a disgraced British diplomat, whose former aides all mysteriously disappeared; Paul Foote (Tom Chadbon), an artist and reputed sadist who had been accused of painting macabre paintings of people just before they met violent deaths; Jan Jarmokowski (Michael Gambon), a concert pianist who had allegedly been caught eating human flesh; Jan's mistress, Davina (Ciaran Madden); and Caroline (Marlene Clark), Newcliffe's wife.

During the first night of the full moon Pavel is killed. Newcliffe announces that all his guests are to remain confined to the estate over the next two nights or until the werewolf is destroyed. The next night, after an argument with his wife Caroline, Newcliffe stalks the werewolf from a helicopter until the beast is cornered in a barn. Caroline arrives with the couple's pet dog, who is mortally wounded in a fight with the beast. Newcliffe's helicopter pilot (Andrew Lodge) is killed by the werewolf as it makes its escape. Newcliffe returns to the house to check on the remaining guests and finds Bennington, whom he had strongly suspected, dead — another victim of the lyncanthrope.

Dr. Lundgren wonders which of his dinner companions is a werewolf in Amicus' *The Beast Must Die.*

On the last night Newcliffe is determined that "the beast must die!" He gathers all the remaining suspects in his living room and forces each guest to put a silver bullet in his mouth (werewolves are allergic to silver and will transform if they come into contact with the metal). Each of his guests proves to be immune. Caroline, however, does not. She transforms and Newcliffe is forced to kill his own beloved wife.

Newcliffe is shocked by the revelation until he suddenly remembers that his wife was present in the barn when the werewolf attacked their dog. It could only mean one thing—there were two werewolves! A scream is heard and Newcliffe finds Davina bending over the mutilated body of Paul Foote. Newcliffe discovers that Jan Jarmokowski is missing and while Dr. Lundgren agrees to look after Davina, Newcliffe goes after Jan. He traps the werewolf on the grounds near the house and kills the beast after a struggle. However, when Newcliffe returns to the house, where Davina and Lundgren are waiting, he discovers that he has been bitten by Jarmokowski. Now he too will become a werewolf.

Newcliffe commits suicide, using his last silver bullet. The sound of the gun blast reverberates throughout the house.

Commentary

> *People sometimes look at me as if I were a monster.... I can't*
> *understand why. Never harmed a fly. And I love animals.* — Peter
> Cushing[1]

The Beast Must Die was not the first time that Amicus had attempted to deal with the werewolf legend. In 1964, *Dr. Terror's House of Horrors* set aside one if its five minitales for a lyncanthrope. However, it was the first and only occasion that the production company devoted a full-length film to the subject.

Based on James Blish's novel *There Shall Be No Darkness*, Milton Subotsky and Max J. Rosenberg hired screenplay writer Michael Winder to adapt Blish's book and assigned first-timer Paul Annett to direct. They also hired two previous Oscar winners, cinematographer Jack Hildyard and art director John Stoll, to head up the technical crew.[2]

Production began on July 16, 1973, at Shepperton Studios with a cast that included such well-known veterans as Anton Diffring and Charles Gray. However, the producers signed Calvin Lockhart, a black actor whose prior credits (all nonhorror) included *Cotton Comes to Harlem* (1970), to the lead. No doubt this strategy was due to the tremendous success American International Pictures had recently had in America with *Blacula* (1972), an exploitation film that featured an all black cast, headed by the distinguished Shakespearean actor William Marshall, and which would eventually lead to a string of similarly formatted B-pictures in the 1970s. But, unlike Marshall, who handled his role as the Afro-vampire king with dignity, Lockhart, as the multimillionaire big game hunter who is searching for a werewolf, seemed far too pulpish to suit most viewers. In fact, none of the characters managed to endear themselves to the audience, and only two effected any modicum of audience empathy — Marlene Clark, who played Newcliffe's wife, Caroline, and Michael Gambon, the "haunted" pianist, Jan Jarmokowski. Ironically, both turn out to be the werewolves in the piece.

The film suffers on many levels. It takes much too long to build and is painfully repetitive. With all the high-tech tracking equipment Newcliffe has at his disposal, he has his guests pass around silver candlesticks and bullets to try to ferret out the beast. Evidently, silver reacts like a geiger counter when it comes into contact with a werewolf! To make matters worse, this trick is repeated no less than three times during the film's ninety-three-minute running time!

Another sore spot concerns the werewolf itself. This film takes the cheap way out and features a German Shepherd in a not-so-clever disguise as the monster. Covered in goat's hair and wearing what seems suspiciously like a feather boa around its neck to give it bulk, the beast looked about as intimidating as a toy poodle! In one scene where it supposedly attacks Newcliffe's helicopter pilot, the actor appeared as though it was too much to do to stop the dog from playfully knocking him over and licking him to death! The only true atmospheric shot of the werewolf comes when it appears on the skylight roof of the house before it crashes through the glass and attacks Pavel (Diffring). Unfortunately, this is hardly sufficient to sustain audience interest.

Gambley's Euro-jazz music score grates on the nerves and only succeeds in further minimizing the film's overall effect. Subotsky might have fared better had he shot the film without a soundtrack and hired live organ music instead.

However, the worst offense of all comes from the unforgivable misuse of the acting talent assembled for the film. Charles Gray and Anton Diffring are cast in roles which any recent dramatic arts school graduate could have handled with ease.

Peter Cushing, who plays Dr. Lundgren, the expert on werewolves, is reduced to giving textbook lectures on werewolf folklore. That is when he's not required to lurk about and hopefully throw audience suspicion his way as the prime suspect for the totally inane werewolf break gimmick employed at the end of the film. Cushing, who took the time to study recordings in order to master a Norwegian accent and who instructed makeup artist Paul Rabier to give his face the appropriate wolfish cast, invested more in the film than it warranted. The one-minute break, which occurs just prior to revealing the werewolf's true human identity, was both stale and annoying. Whatever continuity the film could be credited for was lost with this ridiculous attempt at audience participation. Viewers would have been far more satisfied with a tighter script and more imagination in plotting. Instead, what they got was a poor-cousin version of *The Most Dangerous Game* with some Agatha Christie minced in.[3]

Appraisals of the film seemed to concur that Winder's screenplay was the picture's major fault. Linda Gross in her April 27, 1974, review for the *Los Angeles Times* said, "Michael Winder's screenplay rambles confusedly and is bogged down with schlock gimmicks and red herrings." Vincent Canby, of the *New York Times* (March 23, 1974) in his article entitled "Who Says They Don't Make 'B' Movies," called it "An English horror film with a difference: Black Calvin Lockhart plays the monomaniacal tycoon who invites an ill-sorted group of guests ... in order to find out which one of them is a werewolf. Like so many English horror films, the movie looks much better than it is." *Variety* reviewer "Whit" (April 24, 1974), called it "a contrived but suspenseful British import.... Michael Winder never completely makes his characters believable in his screenplay.... Peter Cushing is an expert on the subject whose discoursing sets the stage.... Camera work ... is above standard.... Art Direction is a superlative plus."

Cinefantastique critic David Bartholomew (volume 4, number 4) predicted that "This new werewolf movie from Amicus continues that particular British Studio's further decline . . . screenplay juggles too many familiar elements with too little dexterity. . . . Novice film director Paul Annett . . . allows an excellent cast including Peter Cushing and Anton Diffring foolishly to override the proceedings." And in *Black Oracle* (number 9), John E. Parnum said,

> The idea of the story is interesting . . . the classic Werewolf yarn modernized with touches of . . . *And Then There Were None* and that RKO thriller, *The Most Dangerous Game*. If you look closely enough, you may even see touches of "Mission Impossible." . . . With the exception of Lockhart who overacts embarrassingly, the cast is quite good, especially Peter Cushing . . . and Marlene Clark as Lockhart's wife who is appalled at her husband's intimidations towards their guests, a kind of insulting Sadism that certainly does not endear us to the hero of the story. . . . It's all very difficult to decide with whom to identify in this . . . story . . . finding the "good guy" is more of a puzzle than finding a Werewolf.

In the same year Peter made a guest appearance on "The Amazing World of Kreskin," a British (and later American) television broadcast, hosted by mentalist Christopher Kreskin. During the broadcast, Kreskin briefly interviewed Cushing regarding his film career and then asked him to participate in some card tricks. Cushing was then asked to write something on a sheet of paper in secret. Kreskin burned the paper and then rubbed the ashes on his arm. The name Helen appeared. Peter was quite astounded over the trick and confirmed that it was indeed his late wife's name which he had written down. "My appearance in 'The Amazing World of Kreskin' has already been taped. I went up to Newcastle-upon-Tyne to do the programme a few weekends ago. . . . Christopher Kreskin is indeed amazing, but I fear people will think his 'act' is faked. I assure you it is not." (July 25, 1973, letter to the authors).

Notes

1. Cinerama Releasing Corporation production notes.
2. Cinematographer Jack Hildyard was an Oscar winner for *Bridge on the River Kwai*, art director John Stoll earned an academy award for *Lawrence of Arabia*.
3. Incredibly, *Howling V — The Rebirth* (1989) would employ a very similar plot line for its fifth rehash. This rendering features a Hungarian count who invites several people to his isolated mountaintop castle because one of them just happens to be a werewolf whom he ultimately plans to destroy. Ho hum!

Legend of the Seven Golden Vampires
(1973)

Credits and Cast

Released September, 1974 (U.K.), 1979 (U.S.); 89 minutes (83 minutes in U.S.), origi-
nally 110 minutes; Color; Panavision; A Hammer–Shaw Brothers Production; Re-
leased through Columbia– Warner Brothers (U.K.) and Dynamite Entertainment
(U.S.); MPAA R; Filmed in Hong Kong. Director: Roy Ward Baker; Producers: Don
Houghton, Vee King Shaw; Screenplay: Don Houghton; Directors of photog-
raphy: John Wilcox, B.S.C., Roy Ford; Editor: Chris Barnes; Assistant editor: Larry
Richardson; Special effects: Les Bowie; Martial arts sequences staged by Tang Chia,
Lui Chia-Liang; Camera operator: Roy Ford; Sound recordist: Les Hammond;
Continuity: Renee Glynne; Production secretary: Jean Walter; Boom operator:
Tommy Staples; Assistant to producer: Christopher Carreras; Production mana-
ger: Chua Lam; Art director: Johnson Tsau; Assistant director: Erh Feng; Makeup:
Wu Hsu Ching; Hairdresser: Peng Yeh Lien; Props master: Li Wu; Costumes: Lui
Chi-Yu; Unit manager: Shen Chung; Floor manager; Peng Cheng; Sound editor:
Frank Golding; Composer: James Bernard; Music supervisor: Philip Martell. Title
in U.S., *The Seven Brothers Meet Dracula*; Working title: "Dracula and the Seven
Vampires.".

Peter Cushing (Professor Van Helsing), David Chiang (Hsi Ching), Julie Ege
(Vanessa Buren), Robin Stewart (Leyland Van Helsing), Shih Szu (Mai Kwei), John
Forbes-Robertson (Dracula), Robert Hanna (British Council), Chan Shen (Kah),
James Ma (Hsi Ta), Lui Chia Yung (Hsi Kwei), Feng Ko An (Hsi Sung), Chen Tein
Loong (Hsi San), Wong Han Chan (Leung Hon).

Synopsis

Transylvania 1804. A lone pilgrim makes his way through the countryside and enters a seemingly deserted castle. There he meets Dracula —
king of all vampires. Dracula (John Forbes-Robertson) offers the priest
eternal life but when the man agrees, Dracula kills him and takes possession of his body to hide his true identity.

The story shifts to Chungking circa 1900. Professor Van Helsing (Peter
Cushing) is lecturing students about the old Chinese legend of the village
of Ping Kuei and the seven golden vampires. One of the students, Hsi
Ching (David Chiang) seems particularly interested in what the professor
has to say concerning vampire lore. Later, Hsi Ching meets with Van Helsing and offers proof that the legend is not fantasy but fact. He also tells
Van Helsing that the golden vampires still plague the village of Ping Kuei,
his home. He, along with his five brothers and sister offer to escort Van
Helsing and his son, Leyland (Robin Stewart) to the village where it is
hoped Van Helsing can free its people from the curse.

The expedition leaves the next day but with an additional member,

Professor Van Helsing lectures students on Oriental vampire lore in Hammer's
Legend of the Seven Golden Vampires.

Vanessa Buren (Julie Ege), a widow touring China, whom Leyland had
rescued the night before from the unwanted advances of a local warlord,
General Yang Shih-Fan. Shortly after they begin their journey, the group
is attacked by some of General Shih-Fan's men but they are quickly dispatched by Hsi Ching and his siblings, who are all masters of the martial
arts.

    The night before reaching the village of Ping Kuei, the party camps
in a large cave where they are suddenly attacked by the vampires and their
zombie armies. Before the battle ends, three of the vampires are destroyed.

    The next day Van Helsing and the others reach their destination and
start to make preparations for the next vampire attack. It comes that night
and many are killed, including Vanessa Buren, who is attacked by one of
the vampires and who becomes one of the undead. Hsi Ching, who had
fallen in love with her, destroys Vanessa and then, in remorse over the loss
of his love, kills himself. His sister, Mai Kwei (Shih Szu) is abducted by the
last remaining vampire and is taken to the vampire's lair in a deserted
temple.

    Van Helsing and Leyland pursue her there and Leyland destroys the
last golden vampire. However Dracula, who had been commanding the

vampires, confronts his nemesis, Professor Van Helsing, and they battle. Van Helsing, once again, is triumphant.

Commentary

> I'm being asked to write quite a number of "Forewords" for various publications recently, and have completed two. One of a book entitled A History of Hunting to be published by the League Against Cruel Sports, and the other The Sherlock Holmes Scrapbook, compiled by Peter Haining. I imagine both will be in the book-shops by Christmas time. — Peter Cushing (May 8, 1973)

> As soon as I finish The Beast Must Die, I fly to Hong Kong to make a picture for the Hammer-Shaw combined company. It is called Legend of the Seven Golden Vampires in which I play "Professor Laurence Van Helsing." The schedule is for 6–7 weeks and the director is Gordon Hessler. No other casting has been announced yet. — Peter Cushing (June 20, 1973)

> I am making several model film sets for the proposed Hammer private museum. — Peter Cushing (October, 1973)

With so much negative audience reaction to Hammer's updated Dracula films, *Dracula A.D. 1972* and *The Satanic Rites of Dracula*, Hammer returned their vampires to a period setting for their next film production, *Legend of the Seven Golden Vampires*. Coproduced with the Shaw Brothers Company, the picture began shooting on October 22 in Hong Kong.

Replacing Gordon Hessler as director was Roy Ward Baker, and almost immediately upon his arrival in Hong Kong the problems began.

> That was a real disaster ... I nearly went mad trying to make that film. The filming conditions were not properly explored and there was a great deal of misunderstanding between [all] parties concerned ... what they [Shaw Brothers] did ... was shoot by the Italian principle. They shoot in a silent studio, not a sound stage, and [then] dub the sound in after the film has been shot. They usually release their own pictures in 6 or 7 different languages. The studios were just iron sheds. If a dog barked outside that's what we got — people fighting with a dog in the background. Absolutely insane. I expected to film in a sound stage and they didn't understand. ... We thought they were mad and they thought we were....
>
> The other main problem was the script. It wasn't even finished by the time we arrived in Hong Kong, which is always the kiss of death as far as I'm concerned. That film was not a happy experience by any means.[1]

Eventually, what had initially been planned as a ten-week production and postproduction schedule, ended up taking over twenty-one weeks to complete.[2] During this time the Shaw Brothers had also insisted on incorporating Dracula into the story, citing Dracula's popularity in many Asian countries as the reason for their demand. Hammer had no choice but to comply. They supplemented the screenplay with a precredits sequence as well as a new ending—to allow for the additional character—and added John Forbes-Robertson to the cast. Unfortunately, these needless additions would prove to be the weakest points in what was otherwise an entertaining and innovative film.

Hammer's idea to create a film based on Far Eastern vampire lore was indeed a novel concept. It could have also afforded the filmmakers with a whole new medium to explore—a series of films based upon the various legends of the undead which prevailed around the world.[3] Unfortunately, due to continuing problems with overseas distributors and waning audiences for martial arts films during this time (among other reasons), Hammer would never have the opportunity to realize this contingency.

Legend of the Seven Golden Vampires combined Eastern and Western technicians as well as actors, all of whom performed their tasks with varying degrees of success. Aside from John Forbes-Robertson (who overacts appallingly in the film) as Dracula, and Robin Stewart (who achieves the complete opposite) as Van Helsing's son, all other key players handled their respective parts competently. Peter Cushing, in his final performance as Van Helsing, was equally comfortable with his character in the Far East as he was in the mountains of Transylvania and gave audiences another fine portrayal.

Key technical credits were all up to Hammer's established excellence—notably Les Bowie's special effects, and the martial arts sequences staged by Tang Chia and Lui Chia-Liang. James Bernard's score, while more than vaguely familiar in spots, was once again a memorable one. John Wilcox's and Roy Ford's photography also deserves special mention.

Don Houghton's otherwise standard screenplay is highlighted with imaginative touches, especially the flashback sequence dealing with the legend and the Alamo-style battle sequences between Van Helsing's expedition group and the vampire warlords.

Roy Ward Baker's direction manages to overcome the difficulties he experienced at the onset. The result is another aptly handled directorial effort that had just the right amounts of action and imagery to satisfy most viewers.

Legend of the Seven Golden Vampires premiered in London during the first week of September in 1974. The list of the top ten movies of that week in *Cinema-TV Today* showed *Legend* in third place within days of its opening. In November 1975 the film was shown in New York City during the Second Famous Monsters Convention to a capacity crowd. The audience gave the film a standing ovation. It was unfortunate that

The interior of the vampire temple. Peter's model set from *Legend of the Seven Golden Vampires*.

representatives from the three U.S. distributors who had previously bought the rights to the film and then subsequently abandoned it were not present to see this particular audience's reaction.[4]

Critical evaluations for *Legend of the Seven Golden Vampires* included *The Sunday Times* (Dilys Powell, August 25, 1974) who reported that the film "has vampires with nobs on, oriental vampires with gilt heads versus exponents of the Martial Arts. It would be tedious were it not for the distinguished presence of Peter Cushing as a Dracula-hunter and for some advanced exercises in the practice of vampire-disintegration which has long been a feature of the genre." "Cano" in *Variety* (June 4, 1975) wrote, "[the movie] transplants the vampire story to China with attendant variations." *Cinefantastique* (Bill Kelly, volume 9, number 1) reported "[a solid performance by Peter Cushing]. Though older now, the vampire-hunter is as keen and alert as ever . . . [although he] doesn't completely overcome the restrictions of the exploitation format. But in those moments when the film truly springs to life, it shows what screen fantasy is capable of." *Films Illustrated* noted, "it doesn't take itself seriously — fatally, I think . . . [there are] few redeeming features." *Little Shoppe of Horrors* (Dennis

Fischer, number 8) observed, "The attempt to do something different gives the production an added freshness."

Shortly before leaving for China, Peter Cushing filmed an episode of "Orson Welles Great Mysteries" for Anglia Television. The episode was entitled "La Grande Bretèche" and costarred Susannah York as his wife, the Countess de Merret. The episode eventually aired in America on November 23, 1973.

Peter had also been approached by Hammer's Michael Carreras to create several model sets for their proposed Hammer Museum. Among the film sets Peter was asked to make were "Dracula's Castle," *One Million Years B.C.*, and a set from another of their films, *When Dinosaurs Ruled the Earth*. Peter did complete work on one from *Legend of the Seven Golden Vampires* and described how he went about its creation. "'The Vampires' Temple' took five weeks to complete—with much burning of midnight oil, because I had to finish it by a certain date. I make everything myself except the figures, which are especially constructed from sketches I submit to a firm who specializes in such things. Cardboard, paper and Balsa wood are the main materials I use, but if you look closely at the seven candle-stands, for example, you might detect a 2½" nail, various nuts, washers and page-binders. The scale is ½" representing one foot." Unfortunately, the remaining sets were never completed when plans for the museum fell through.

Notes

1. Roy Ward Baker, interview with Philip Nutman, *Fangoria* 36.
2. Chris Barnes, "*Legend of the Seven Golden Vampires*," *Little Shoppe of Horrors* 4.
3. Hammer had planned to film another Van Helsing adventure set in India if *Legend of the Seven Golden Vampires* proved popular with audiences.
4. Warner Brothers, Cannon, and AIP all dropped their options to release the film in the United States. It was eventually bought by Max Rosenberg's Dynamite Entertainment—who trimmed the running time, reedited and retitled the film before releasing it in 1979.

Shatter
(1973)

Credits and Cast

Released 1974 (U.K.), January 1976 (U.S.); 90 minutes; Color; A Hammer Film Production in association with Shaw Brothers Productions; Released through Avco

Embassy; Filmed in Hong Kong. Director: Michael Carreras; Producers: Michael
Carreras, Vee King Shaw; Screenplay: Don Houghton; Directors of photography:
Brian Probyn, John Wilcox, Roy Ford; Sound: Les Hammond; Continuity: Renee
Glynne; Production manager: Chua Lam; Production secretary: Jean Walter; Art
director: Johnson; Dubbing editor: Dennis Whitlock; Assistant to producer: Chris-
topher Carreras. Released in U.S. as *Call Him Mr. Shatter.*

Stuart Whitman (Shatter), Ti Lung (Tai Phah), Lily Li (Mai Mee), Peter Cushing
(Rattwood), Anton Diffring (Leber), Yemi Ajibade (M'Goya), Liu Ka Yong, Wang
Pei Chi (Bodyguards), Ya Ling (Leber's Girl), Lo Wei (Howe).

Synopsis

> *The breakthru movie that mixes martial arts with mob-style vio-
> lence!* — Avco Embassy publicity

General M'Goya (Yemi Ajibade), president of the East African state
of Badawai, is murdered by Shatter (Stuart Whitman), an international hit
man. After also killing an aide and stealing his document case, Shatter flies
to Hong Kong to be paid.
  After an attempt on his life on a Hong Kong street, Shatter learns
from Rattwood (Peter Cushing), a British security agent, that the U.S.
government did not order the hit as Shatter presumed. Rattwood orders
him to leave Hong Kong, and when he hesitates, has him brutally beaten.
Shatter is nursed back to health by Tai Phah (Ti Lung), a martial arts instructor, and Mai Mee (Lily Li), a hostess who becomes his lover.
  After a second attempt on his life — arranged by Leber (Anton Diffring), a bank manager — Shatter hires Tai Phah as his bodyguard. He then
allows himself to be kidnapped by Rattwood's team and is taken to a secluded spot where, with Tai Phah's help, he easily overcomes them. By
roughing up Rattwood, Shatter learns that the Badawai was actually gov-
erned by a crime syndicate with Leber supplying arms paid for with drug
money. M'Goya was killed and replaced by Dabula (also Yemi Ajibade),
his more cooperative twin. Shatter was duped into thinking he was working for the United States.
  The stolen document case contains a list of drug-processing labs, and
Rattwood offers $25,000 for it — and Leber's death. Shatter refuses the
deal and attempts to sell it back to Leber for $1 million. The exchange is
botched and Mai Mee is killed by Leber's men.
  Shatter and Tai Phah go to a Macao casino where, on the top floor,
Leber has an office. Shatter confronts Leber but is overpowered. He is to
return to Badawai — minus his vocal chords — with Dabula to stand trial for
M'Goya's murder. Tai Phah breaks into the room and, during the struggle,

Secret Agent Rattwood plays into the hands of Shatter (Stuart Whitman) in Hammer's *Shatter*.

Shatter shoots Dabula. As he falls, he collides with Leber and the pair crash through a window to their deaths.

With no optons left, Shatter makes the exchange with a smirking Rattwood, who leaves the hit man with his money and his troubled conscience.

Commentary

In a January 1974 letter to the authors, Peter Cushing remarked, "I returned from Hong Kong on Boxing Day, December 26, after nearly ten weeks in China. I completed two films out there — Van Helsing in *Dracula and the Seven Golden Vampires* and Rattwood in *Shatter*."

"*Shatter* was, unfortunately, a bad picture, no question about it . . . badly conceived from the start."[1] This perceptive review is from a man who should know — producer-director Michael Carreras. As half of a two-picture deal between England's Hammer Films and the Shaw Brothers of Hong Kong, *Shatter* was a radical departure from what Hammer did best.

In addition to the problems one would expect in an East-West coproduction, original director Monte Hellman was replaced in midstream by Carreras. Quentin Falk reported that "Hammer is remaining tight-lipped about the reasons for Hellman's exit so far into the schedule and would only comment that it was by 'mutual agreement' with Carreras and the Shaws."[2]

Despite many flaws, *Shatter* does have plenty of action and, for what it's worth, is no worse than any other kung fu film of the period. Ti Lung is an acceptable Bruce Lee type for martial arts fans, and Stuart Whitman is satisfactory as the world-weary hit man. It's not his fault that the part, by then, had become a cliché. Anton Diffring, in a small role, is properly chilly as the lead villain.

Peter Cushing delivers a brief but interesting performance as Rattwood. Although on the right side of the law, his character is so obnoxious that when Shatter slaps him around, he gets — and deserves — little audience sympathy. Since this was Peter Cushing's last feature film for Hammer, it is unfortunate that their long — twenty-three films — and successful association should end with such an indifferent film.

Shatter was not widely released or reviewed. *Variety* (January 14, 1976) did not think much of it except for Peter Cushing's "expertly cynical performance."

Peter Cushing was quite active on radio, with guest appearances on "Woman's House," and "PM" in addition to playing in "The Man Who Hated Scenes" — a segment of "The Price of Fear" hosted by Vincent (who else?) Price.

Notes

1. Michael Carreras, interview, *The House of Hammer* 7.
2. Quentin Falk, *Cinema-TV Today*, November 16, 1974.

Tendre Dracula
(1974)

Credits and Cast

Released 1974 (France); 90 minutes; Color; A Vincent Malle–Renn Production; Filmed in France. Director: Pierre Grunstein; Executive Producer: Jerome Kanapa; Director of photography: Jean-Jacques Tarbes; Camera: Bernard Noisette; Music: Karl-Heinz Schager; Screenplay: Justin Lenoir, Harold Bray, Pierre Grunstein; Sound: Antoine Bonfanti; Editor: Anne Marie Deshayes; Art director: Jean-Pierre Kohutsuelko; Set design: Jean Gourmelin. Also called *La Grand Trouille* (*The Big Scare*).

Count MacGregor? Cushing in Pierre Grunstein's *Tendre Dracula*.

Peter Cushing (MacGregor), Alida Valli (Heloise), Miou-Miou (Marie), Nathalie Courval (Madeline), Bernard Menez (Alfred), Stephen Shandor (Boris), Julien Guiomar (Producer), Percival Russel (Abelard).

Synopsis

> *Without romance, my dear young friends, we are lost . . . we are all lost.* — MacGregor

Alfred (Bernard Menez) and Boris (Stephen Shandor), two script-writers, are summoned to the Paris office of a television producer (Julien Guiomar). His problem; horror star MacGregor (Peter Cushing) no longer wants to play horror.

The "boys" are writers for a romantic series that would better suit MacGregor's current state of mind—he wants to become a romantic star. Alfred and Boris are to change the concept of the program to merge horror and romance: then comes the hard part—they must convince MacGregor.

The duo drive to MacGregor's isolated castle with two (supposed) actresses, Marie (Miou-Miou) and Madeline (Nathalie Courval) to assist them. MacGregor and his wife Heloise (Alida Valli) entertain them with a lush meal and music provided by Abelard (Percival Russel).

The situation begins to deteriorate. Boris becomes fascinated with MacGregor's makeup kit, which reminds him of the career which he abandoned. He dies while playing Russian Roulette . . . or does he? No, it's just an extremely realistic makeup job. Abelard injures himself chopping wood and Madeline looks after him — until he buries an axe in her back. Heloise whines about practically everything while MacGregor talks — endlessly — about romance.

A flashback shows MacGregor as a child with his aged grandfather (Peter Cushing). The horrors the child witnesses — including the old man's death — reveal why MacGregor is, well MacGregor.

The producer and a film crew have secreted themselves on the grounds to capture these events on film. After apparently dying, MacGregor awakens to — endlessly — proclaim his love for Heloise. Leaving the crew to amuse themselves at an orgy, MacGregor and Heloise walk, hand in hand, to a section of the castle that is actually a rocket and blast off into space.

Commentary

In a career as long as Peter Cushing's, it would be impossible not to have appeared in a few poor films. Certainly *Magic Fire, Sword of the Valiant,* and *Night of the Big Heat* are far from classics. *Tendre Dracula,* however, makes these films seem like *Citizen Kane* (1941). It is a truly wretched, embarrassing experience and is the nadir of the excellent actor's career.

Horror comedies seldom work well; after *Young Frankenstein* (1973), the list is a short one. The fact that *Tendre Dracula* was filmed in France makes it even more difficult to appreciate. French humor often mystifies an English or Amerian audience; remember, this is the country that regards Jerry Lewis as a genius. So, to be fair, perhaps the film works better with a French audience.

Also, to be fair, the video the authors viewed was dubbed into English. So much for excuses — it's difficult to imagine the film being watchable in any form.

Joining Peter Cushing in this ill-conceived venture is another excellent performer who has done — and deserves — much better. Alida Valli (*The Third Man,* 1949) valiantly tries, as does Cushing, to overcome the ludicrous script, inept costars, and nonexistent direction. One feels degraded watching two stars of their standing associated with an embarrassment like this. The full frontal nudity of the two starlets seems out of place in a Peter Cushing film, as does the scene in which he spanks one of them!

Peter Cushing entered the production with high hopes. In a January 1974 letter to the authors he wrote, "It is a fantasy comedy and if the French can imbue it with their usual elegance, it could be very amusing with perhaps a touch of pathos here and there. We shall see what we shall see."

In an October letter, however, he seems to have had some justified misgivings. "I've not seen it myself yet—and I only hope it has turned out well. It's an 'odd' film, I think—and may not be to everyone's taste."

An actor must work, naturally, and the experience did give Peter Cushing a few weeks in France. The only other thing to be grateful for is that the film was not widely shown. Making matters worse—if possible—is that Cushing looks absolutely magnificent in his Dracula costume and one is forced to speculate as to what he could have done in a "straight" performance as the count.

Variety (August 28, 1974) generously allowed that the film "seems undecided about its outlook and genre," and that the leading role was "played with dispatch by Peter Cushing."

Peter Cushing was a popular television guest in 1974, appearing on "Film 74," "Horizon," "This Is Your Life," and "Christ—What Was He Like?"

The Ghoul
(1974)

Credits and Cast

Released June 1975 (U.K.); 93.5 minutes; Eastman color; A Tyburn Film Production; Released through Fox-Rank (U.K.); Filmed at Pinewood Studios, England. Director: Freddie Francis; Producer: Kevin Francis; Screenplay: John Elder (Anthony Hinds); Production manager: Ron Jackson; Director of photography: John Wilcox, B.S.C.; Art director: Jack Shampan; Music composed by Harry Robinson; Musical supervisor: Philip Martell; Costume designer: Anthony Mendleson; Film editor: Henry Richardson; Continuity: Pamela Davies; Assistant art director: Peter Williams; Assistant director: Peter Saunders; Camera operator: James Bawden; Sound mixer: John Brommage; Wardrobe supervisor: Bridget Sellers; Makeup: Roy Ashton, Jimmy Evans; Hairdresser: Joan Carpenter; Assistant to the producer: Lorraine Fennell.

Peter Cushing (Dr. Lawrence), John Hurt (Tom), Alexandra Bastedo (Angela), Gwen Watford (The Ayah), Veronica Carlson (Daphne), Don Henderson (The Ghoul), Stewart Bevan (Billy), Ian McCulloch (Geoffrey), John D. Collins (Young Man), Dan Meaden (Police Sergeant).

Synopsis

During a party in the 1920s in England, host Billy (Stewart Bevan) challenges his friend, Geoffrey (Ian McCulloch), to a car race. His friend accepts the wager. Along with their girlfriends Daphne (Veronica Carlson) and Angela (Alexandra Bastedo), the two men set off for Land's End.

Billy and Daphne eventually gain a substantial lead but have to abandon the race when their car runs out of gas. Billy goes off in search of fuel and, when he fails to return, Daphne leaves the car to look for help. She encounters a very strange young man named Tom (John Hurt) who abducts her. Later, she manages to escape from him and meets an elderly gentleman, Dr. Lawrence (Peter Cushing), who offers her the shelter of his manor house — an oasis in the midst of the surrounding dangerous marshland. Grateful for his protection, Daphne accepts the doctor's offer but that night she is brutally murdered.

The next day Geoffrey and Angela, concerned for their friends, begin their search but learn from the local police that Billy died when his car went over a cliff and that Daphne's body was never found. Geoffrey continues the search and questions Dr. Lawrence, who tells him that Daphne had stayed with him but left for London by bus. Geoffrey prepares to leave, intent on following Daphne but has trouble starting his car; and now Angela has also disappeared. Tom shows up and offers to help but during their conversation Tom admits that he works for Lawrence and that he did not see either of the girls leave. However, before Geoffrey can get any more information, Tom runs off. Geoffrey chases him into the swamp where Tom slips and falls into a pit of quicksand. Using the urgency of Tom's plight, Geoffrey promises to free Tom if he reveals the truth. In desperation, Tom tells Geoffrey that Dr. Lawrence keeps a "thing" in his house — a disgusting creature thought only to exist in legend. A monster that eats human flesh — a ghoul! Geoffrey frees Tom and they rush back to the Lawrence house.

Geoffrey confronts Lawrence who, under pressure, tells him that the flesh-eating ghoul is his son. Lawrence had been living in India with his wife and son. While they were there, his son became friends with a local Indian prince — a perverted degenerate that corrupted and transformed his beloved son into a vile, hideous creature. Lawrence brought him home and has been protecting him ever since. Geoffrey rushes upstairs to search for Daphne and Angela but is fatally stabbed by the creature.

Angela, who had been abducted earlier by Tom and had been kept prisoner in one of the upstairs bedrooms, is once again confronted by him. Tom tells her that Geoffrey is dead and tries to attack her. Angela struggles with him and is able to knock him unconscious just as the ghoul (Don Henderson) enters the room. The creature moves over to Tom's motionless

Dr. Lawrence contemplates "the thing in the attic" in Tyburn's *The Ghoul*.

body and, using an ornamental dagger, begins to hack away at Tom's body. Lawrence follows his son into the room and shoots the ghoul. He then turns the gun on himself. Angela flees from the house, hysterical over the horors she has just witnessed.

Commentary

> *Peter was offered the part by phone when he was in Hong Kong recently, "I'd just got back from the studios one evening when my phone rang and a young man, who sounded as though he was downstairs in the hotel lobby, introduced himself as Kevin Francis, Freddie's son, whom I'd last seen as a boy. He was ringing from London to ask if I would star in* The Ghoul *under his father's direction. Of course, I was delighted to accept."* — Peter Cushing: Tyburn Film Production Publicity Manual

Once work had been completed on *Shatter*, Peter returned to England. Several weeks after his return, production began on *The Ghoul*, for Kevin Francis' newly formed film company Tyburn, in March 1974, at Pinewood Studios.[1]

Not to be confused with the Boris Karloff film of the same name, produced in 1933 by Gaumont-British Productions, *The Ghoul* was based on a new screenplay by John (Anthony Hinds) Elder and bore no relation to the original Roland Pertwee, John Hastings Turner, and Rupert Donning adaptation.

Along with Peter Cushing, who was cast as the ill-fated Dr. Lawrence, Kevin Francis chose John Hurt for the role of Lawrence's mentally defective gardener, Tom Rawlings. Hurt, who was well on his way to becoming an internationally known actor, chose the role because he felt the script had "a good, well-written part" and because he had "always wanted to do a proper horror film."[2] Many of the film's reviews would single out Hurt's performance, even though most were not as generously inclined toward the film itself.

Also cast in lead roles were Gwen Watford, primarily a stage actress who occasionally made the foray into television and film work; Alexandra Bastedo, who was previously seen in William Castle's *13 Frightened Girls*[3] and *Casino Royale*; and Veronica Carlson who, through her appearances for Hammer Films, remains a cult favorite today. *The Ghoul* would mark her final feature film appearance in England before relocating to America where she now lives with her husband and three children.

In an interview for this publication, Veronica Carlson related her impressions of Peter both as an actor and as a man:

> The first thing that hits you forcibly about Peter is his kindness and his gentleness. He's got an overwhelming sensitivity which makes you open up to this man. Nobody that meets Peter can dislike him. It doesn't matter what your feelings are for what he does, you can't dislike the man ... Peter's got such grace. He stands so tall, not necessarily physically in his person. He's got such a wonderful aura about him. He commands this wonderful feeling of respect, so he lends credibility to anything he does.

Veronica Carlson enjoyed playing her character, Daphne, whom she described as "an airhead. A flapper. The typical twenties character ... a sort of 'quality' Englishwoman having a wonderful time."

When asked about the car race, Veronica remembers spending a morning in one of the back projection rooms, "I was sitting at the wheel pretending to drive. The car was the genuine old thing, difficult to drive. I drove away, that sort of thing, out of camera view but the actual race was done by a stuntman.... You could tell!"

Carlson also remembers the day that Peter broke down on the set. She referred to the scene where she and Peter were in Dr. Lawrence's drawing room and the doctor was recounting to Daphne the tragic story of his wife's suicide in India. During this scene, Peter held a photograph of his character's wife which also happened to be a portrait of his real wife, the late Helen Beck Cushing. It was during the filming of this particular scene that Peter became so emotionally involved with his character and the circumstances of his own personal tragedy that he was unable to separate the two. "[E]verybody on the set was weeping by the time Peter had finished that. He had to go to his dressing room and we were all so shaken because his grief was so real. It was so exposed for everybody to see and nobody likes to have their weeping open to human view. It's such a humiliation, no matter how justifiable the cause. It makes me go goosebumps just thinking about it."

According to Carlson, the director, Freddie Francis, saw that Peter was becoming too involved in the scene yet did not stop the cameras, "I know Freddie had to . . .! He saw what he was getting from Peter was good stuff, good footage. He wanted to get as much as he could, I suppose."

What remains a mystery is the fact that this particular footage was eventually cut from the final print. Carlson could offer no explanation for this decision. It can only be assumed that the decision was made out of respect for Cushing.

According to Tyburn's publicity department, Peter had suggested the use of Helen's photograph to represent his on-screen wife. It was taken in 1941 when Helen was in her mid-thirties. "A photograph was needed to represent 'Mrs. Lawrence.' I asked if one of my beloved Helen might be used and Freddie Francis thought it a splendid idea. . . . It was a warm comfort to know she was actually 'appearing' in a picture with me. Another of 'Mr. Lawrence' when young was required . . . which the stills department enlarged from a negative I had in the family album."[4] Evidently, at the end of the production, producer Kevin Francis made Peter a gift of his wife's photograph housed in a beautiful silver frame.

Kevin Francis spoke about Peter and expressed his admiration for him: "he's been my idea of a star for years and I've seen almost every horror/terror film he's ever made. . . . No matter who or what else is in the scene with him, it is Peter who catches the eye and holds it. Add to this Peter's unfailing courtesy and professionalism and the fact that he's just about the finest technician I've ever come across and you have a star of the first magnitude."[5]

Although *The Ghoul* was never released theatrically in the United States and was only recently made available in video format, it was in general release in England in June 1975. One British review of the film came from David Robinson of *The Times* (May 30, 1975), who wrote "directed by Freddie Francis from a screenplay by John Elder . . . [*The Ghoul*] is a tidy reworking of the old horror conventions without excessive concentration on the physical aspects of murder and cannibalism. It can even claim a couple of well developed characters, played by John Hurt and Peter Cushing and some good period staging . . . the film manages to give the exteriors with empty rural roads and eerie old mansions, an authentic twenties look." However, Dilys Powell, in her *Sunday Times* review (June 1, 1975) felt differently than her weekday counterpart: "I have long thought that no film can be all bad if it includes Mr. Cushing. But one has to make exceptions, and this may be the moment ... no wonder poor Mr. Cushing, trying to keep the ghoulish presence dark, does a good deal of praying." In the *Daily Mirror* Arthur Thirkell (June 5, 1975) wrote, "Cushing is superb and he gets excellent support from John Hurt as an odd odd-job man." Marjorie Bilbow (June 8, 1975) of *Cinema-TV Today* reported that "With a stalwart cast working overtime to put flesh on the dry bones of the pedestrian script, the plot keeps moving under its own momentum. All the action—from the car race to the murders—has pace and suspense." The *Sunday Telegraph* reviewer, Tim Hutchinson, wrote, "Francis has the experience to take his leisure time in building up the circumstantial detail leading to the ultimate ugliness and his writer, John Elder, convincingly suspends our disbelief by putting the whole tale in the never-never void of Wooster's 1920s.... The denouncement is not quite so aghast-making as the buildup, but there's a really oppressive sense of claustrophobia and the conflict between different faiths is believably delineated within the fantasy's circumstance." "Pit" in *Variety* (June 6, 1975), in his evaluation gave the film perhaps its most accurate appraisal: "As a visual mood piece, *The Ghoul* plays nicely enough, being loyal in that respect to the Gothic horror traditions. It even has genre veteran Peter Cushing doing a dependable turn. But an old-fashioned armrest gripper it isn't, being far too tame for its own good.... What misfires is the John Elder script, which moves from A to Z without generating much excitement and surprise in between. On the positive side is assured acting and Jack Shampan's impressive set decoration.... Cushing is dependable in an ambiguous but essentially goody role while Hurt creates a convincing case for institutions with iron bars.... The seasoned hand of director Francis is evident throughout; all he lacked was more suspenseful plotting. All technical credits, including the Eastman color photography by John Wilcox are likewise polished."

A month after Peter completed work on *The Ghoul*, he made a guest star appearance, along with Joanna Dunham, in the Group Three television production of "Space 1999." Filmed at Pinewood Studios, the episode was entitled, "The Missing Link." Peter described his character "Raan" as being "508 years old—but I hasten to add that I don't have to look that age because the planet Zenno where he lives is 5 million light years away from Earth, and the Zennites span of life is 10 times longer than Earthmen's."

In October 1976, Peter Cushing was awarded Best Actor honors at the International Festival of Science Fiction and Terror at Sitges, Spain, for his portrayal of Dr. Lawrence in *The Ghoul*.

Notes

1. *The Ghoul* was Tyburn's second film production. *Persecution* (U.S. titles *Sheba* and *The Terror of Sheba*), made in 1973, was Tyburn's initial feature release.
2. Tyburn publicity manual.
3. Bastedo appeared under the name, Alexandra Lendon Bastedo in this 1963 exploitation disaster released by Columbia.
4. Peter's age in his photograph was 24.
5. Kevin Francis, interview, *Children of the Night* 1, no. 2.

Legend of the Werewolf
(1974)

Credits and Cast

Released October 1975 (U.K.); 90 minutes; Eastman color; A Tyburn Production; Released through Rank; Filmed at Pinewood Studios, England. Director: Freddie Francis; Producer: Kevin Francis; Screenplay: John Elder (Anthony Hinds); Production manager: Ron Jackson; Director of photography: John Wilcox, B.S.C.; Art director: Jack Shampan; Music composed by Harry Robinson; Musical supervisor: Philip Martell, Film editor: Henry Richardson; Continuity: Pamela Davies; Production assistant: Lorraine Fennell; Assistant art director: Brian Ackland-Snow; Assistant director: Peter Saunders; Camera operator: Gerry Anstiss; Sound mixer: John Brommage; Wardrobe supervisor: Mary Gibson; Makeup: Jimmy Evans, Graham Freeborn; Hairdresser: Stella Rivers; Assistant to the producer: Janet Neal.

Peter Cushing (Professor Paul Cataflanque), Ron Moody (Zookeeper), Hugh Griffith (Maestro Pamponi), Roy Castle (Photographer), David Rintoul (Etoile), Stefan Gryff (Inspector Max Gerard), Lynn Dalby (Christine), Renee Houston (Chou-Chou), Marjorie Yates (Madame Tellier), ·Norman Mitchell (Tiny), Mark Weavers (Young Etoile), David Bailie (Boulon), Hilary Labow (Zoe), Elaine Baillie (Annabelle), Michael Ripper (Sewerman), Patrick Holt (Dignitary), John Harvey (Prefect of Police), Pamela Green (Anne-Marie), Sue Bishop (Tania), James Mc-Manus (Emigré Husband), Jane Cussons (Emigre Wife).

Synopsis

Sometime during the mid–nineteenth century, a group of poor refugees is slowly making its way across Central Europe when it is set upon by wolves. All are killed except an infant boy, who is carried off by the pack and reared by them.

Years later, a traveling circus headed by Maestro Pamponi (Hugh

Griffith) and his wife, Chou-Chou (Renee Houston), find the boy in the forest. The boy is a strange physical combination of man and beast and the maestro sees a golden opportunity to exploit the child. Pamponi names the boy and incorporates him into the show as their star attraction — "Etoile, the Wolf Boy" (Mark Weavers).

Etoile remains with the show for several years, but as he grows into manhood, he loses his wolfish look and therefore his former appeal. He is later forced to leave the circus when one night, during a full moon, Etoile (David Rintoul) undergoes a terrifying transformation and savagely murders Pamponi's assistant, Tiny (Norman Mitchell). Etoile flees to Paris where he finds work at a small zoo when the zookeeper (Ron Moody) notices the young man's unusual affinity for the animals, especially the wolves.

One day Etoile meets Christine (Lynn Dalby) who, along with some friends, is a regular visitor to the zoo during her lunch hour. Etoile and Christine are drawn to one another and soon form a close, personal relationship.

However, the relationship is threatened when Etoile learns that Christine is not a servant as he was led to believe, but a prostitute working in a local brothel. Outraged, Etoile attacks one of her patrons and murders him. The victim, a local dignitary (Patrick Holt), is brought to the morgue where police pathologist Paul Cataflanque (Peter Cushing) and Inspector Gerard (Stefan Gryff) examine the body and are bewildered over the ferocity of the attack.

When more equally savage murders are reported, Cataflanque comes to the conclusion that a wolf is responsible and begins his own investigation into the crimes.

A break in the case occurs when one of Etoile's victims survives long enough to describe the incredible appearance of his attacker. At first Paul is skeptical, but when he realizes that the murder took place during the full moon he concludes that a werewolf is loose in Paris. He also deduces that the werewolf must be using the sewers of Paris as his escape route since he is never seen by any of the local citizens.

Loading his pistol with silver bullets, Paul searches the sewers for the killer and is confronted by the beast who, surprisingly, begs for his help. In a show of trust, Paul drops his gun but other police arrive on the scene and wound Etoile. The werewolf manages to escape and returns to his lodgings where Christine is waiting. Though she is terrified at the sight of Etoile in his transformed state, she tries to offer him comfort. Inspector Gerard and Paul, who have been tracking Etoile's escape route, confront him. Gerard, who had retrieved Paul's gun, shoots the werewolf. As he lies dying, the werewolf transforms back into the handsome, tragic Etoile.

Pathologist Paul Cataflanque and his assistant Boulon (David Bailie) gaze at the werewolf's latest victim in Tyburn's *Legend of the Werewolf.*

Commentary

> My next picture will be for Tyburn Productions — and once again directed by Freddie Francis — entitled Legend of the Werewolf. — Peter Cushing (July 13, 1974)

> A few weeks ago I made a record for Hammer's Legend of the Seven Golden Vampires which includes music and sound effects from the film. — Peter Cushing (September 25, 1974)

Tyburn Films, riding the crest of a short-lived wave, began production on *Legend of the Werewolf* on August 19, 1974, at Pinewood Studios.

Along with Peter Cushing, who was cast as police pathologist Paul Cataflangue, were Ron Moody, Hugh Griffith, Roy Castle, and Michael Ripper (the latter two in brief cameos), as well as newcomers David Rintoul and Lynn Dalby.

John Elder, who had also scripted *The Ghoul* for Tyburn, returned with his new adaptation on werewolf folklore and Freddie Francis was back as the film's director.

The day after filming began at Pinewood, a timber wolf, used in the film's opening scenes, escaped from its cage and headed for nearby Black

Park.[1] Producer Kevin Francis, attempting to dissuade any fears, told reporters that the wolf had been raised in captivity and had never had to kill for its food. So while the local police went in search of the runaway wolf, Francis called in its understudy and went on with the production. The event drew national attention and even made the front page of *The Times*.[2] As they say, any publicity is good publicity.

John Elder's screenplay for *Legend of the Werewolf* offered some interesting plot twists in its attempt to provide a fresher approach to an otherwise tapped-out werewolf filmography. Elder borrowed from various sources for his character, Etoile. History has recorded stories (varying in degrees of factual data to support them) of children raised in the wild by animals. This theme, which had previously been very successful for authors such as Edgar Rice Burroughs in his *Tarzan* series, can be traced as far back as ancient times and the legend of Romulus and Remus.

However, Elder never fully explains how Etoile came to become a werewolf other than the fact that he was raised by wolves and assumes wolf-like ways when under extreme stress. Although *Legend of the Werewolf* stretches the credibility factor beyond the obvious, the film does manage to keep the proceedings stimulating throughout.

Production properties are slim but the film has some good performances. Equally well done was the werewolf makeup, similar to that used to excellent effect in Hammer's *Curse of the Werewolf* (1960), and which carries equal leverage here.

Peter's character, Paul Cataflanque, is quite a fascinating combination of biting cynicism and (to make things interesting) kindheartedness. He has little patience for any and all authority figures, yet places his own life in jeopardy when he finally confronts the werewolf in the sewers under Paris and offers to help the pitiful creature. This in itself is quite a reversal of roles for Cushing who in previous films was often cast as the antagonist of the supernatural.

Both *The Ghoul* and *Legend of the Werewolf* were never released theatrically in the United States. Like the former, *Legend* was eventually released here in video format. However, *Legend of the Werewolf* did have a world premiere showing on October 27, 1975, at the New Victoria Cinema in London. Among the attendees were Kevin and Freddie Francis, Peter Cushing, Renee Houston, and Lynn Dalby, in addition to various Fox–Rank Organization executives.

Critical evaluations of the film include *Screen International* (November 8, 1975) who reported that *Legend of the Werewolf* was recommended

> For the fans for whom any werewolf is better than no werewolf. A cumbersomely plotted hotch-potch of incidents, accents, and illogicalities.

The half-hearted attempt to rationalize the werewolf myth is not developed and does nothing for the story beyond giving Hugh Griffith and Renee Houston something to do.... The special effects of Etoile's transformation into the werewolf and his killings are convincingly horrific; otherwise the only consistently pleasing element is the performance of Peter Cushing who gives the imperturbable pathologist a tongue-in-cheek insouciance that is a joy to watch.

The *Sunday Telegraph* cast its vote saying, "it's a horror movie that can be awarded only one snarl." *The Sunday Times* (Dilys Powell, October 26, 1975) noted that "with his fur on the werewolf looks agreeably like Jean Marais in *La Belle et La Bete*. And it is always a pleasure to see Peter Cushing, elegant, bland, playing, as the police surgeon, with his customary and admirable earnestness." *Little Shoppe of Horrors* (number 4) reviewer Chris Wood said,

The film is evocative of the early Hammer pictures.... Tyburn seems to have given an additional "gloss" to the film whilst retaining all that was good about the Hammer pictures.... John Elder's script and the direction of Freddie Francis bring out some excellent performances from the cast ... the greatest pleasure ... is the performance of Peter Cushing. The man is a professional through and through.... We are treated to Peter's quick comic wit and zest for life ... with a tenderness and love of his work.

Tyburn Pictures had planned to produce several films after *Legend of the Werewolf*. Some of these included "The Golem," "By the Devil ... Possessed," "Dracula's Feast of Blood," "The Phantom Coachman," and "The Satanist"—the latter based on the Dennis Wheatley novel and which was to star Peter Cushing.

Director Freddie Francis was optimistic about Tyburn's future when he spoke to interviewer Susan Munshower for *Monsters of the Movies* (number 1) saying, "If one can go by the present indication, it certainly looks as if Tyburn Films will steam past Hammer and Amicus.... I hope Tyburn gets up there and doesn't make their mistakes."

Unfortunately, all Tyburn's proposed projects were dropped when they failed to find overseas distributors for their last two productions. It seemed the only thing Tyburn would have in common with Hammer and Amicus was the fact that within a year after the release of *Legend of the Werewolf* both Amicus and Hammer would be producing their final fantasy films. As for Tyburn, they never really had a chance to compete nor were they given the opportunity to show audiences what they might have been capable of accomplishing under more favorable conditions—a sad commentary of the times.

Notes

1. The *Sun* (August 21, 1974): "Where's our Werewolf?"
2. *The Times* (August 22, 1974): "Runaway Wolf Shot: A police marksman yesterday killed a wolf which escaped on Tuesday (August 20, 1974) from Pinewood Film Studios near Iver, Buckinghamshire."

Shock Waves
(1975)

Credits and Cast

Released 1975; 84 minutes; Color; A Joseph Brenner–Zopix Production; Filmed in Florida. Director: Ken Wiederhorn; Producer: Reuben Trane; Screenplay: Joan Harrison, Ken Wiederhorn; Music: Richard Einhorn; Director of photography: Reuben Trane; Underwater photography: Irving Pare; Editor: Norman Gay; Production design: Jessica Sack; Makeup: Alan Ormsby; Production manager: Doug Kauffman; Sound: Steve Manners.

Peter Cushing (Commandant), Brooke Adams (Rose), Fred Buch (Chuck), Jack Davidson (Norman), Luke Halpin (Keith), D. J. Sidney (Beverly), Don Stout (Dobbs), Clarence Thomas (Fisherman), John Carradine (Captain); Sammy Graham, Preston White, Reid Finger, Mike Kennedy, Donahue Gullory, Jay Maeder, Talmedge Scott, Gary Levinson, Robert Miller (Zombies).

Synopsis

> We created the perfect soldier from cheap hoodlums and thugs and a good number of pathological murderers and sadists as well ... [as] creatures more horrible than you can imagine ... not dead, not alive, but somewhere in between. — The Commandant

During World War II, Nazi scientists developed a race of zombie-like soldiers that needed no food, rest, or weapons. They were indestructible killing machines and not one of them was ever captured.

Off the coast of present-day Florida a small rowboat is spotted by a fisherman (Clarence Thomas). In the boat, near death, is Rose (Brooke Adams), who remembers the events which led up to her being set adrift.

Along with Chuck (Fred Buch), Norman (Jack Davidson), and Beverly (D. J. Sidney), Rose had chartered a ship — the *Bonaventure* — for a cruise. The third-rate yacht has a third-rate crew consisting of the captain (John Carradine), Keith (Luke Halpin), and Dobbs (Don Stout).

After experiencing unnatural sky conditions, the *Bonaventure* is rammed by the shell of a freighter and both ships run aground near an island. Released from the freighter's hold are the "Death Corps"—living corpses that have survived since World War II.

The next morning the captain is found drowned near the island's shore. Abandoning the *Bonaventure*, the survivors search the island and find a decrepit hotel with one occupant—a former ss commandant (Peter Cushing). He curtly refuses to help them, but becomes frightened when the freighter is mentioned.

While gathering supplies from the *Bonaventure*, Dobbs is drowned by a blonde, goggled ss man. His corpse is found clutching a Nazi emblem.

Back at the hotel, the commandant explains that he was in charge of the zombies and was ordered to dispose of them as the war was ending. He sunk the freighter and found refuge on the island, but they have returned.

After ordering his "guests"—at gun point—to leave the island, the commandant searches for his "men." They are now beyond his control, and one drowns the commandant as he drinks from a pool.

One by one, the rest are hunted and drowned until only Rose and Keith are left. When they are almost free in the *Bonaventure*'s rowboat, Keith is pulled out and drowned. Rose, alone in the boat, drifts aimlessly until rescued by a fisherman.

She awakens in a hospital—insanely scrawling nonsense in a notebook and mumbling incoherently.

Commentary

Originally titled "Death Corps" this was a very low-budget—but effective—production filmed in Florida. It was the first of two teamings of Peter Cushing and John Carradine, although the two veterans shared no scenes and, in fact, never met during the production. As a cost-saving measure, the film was photographed in 16mm and all of Peter Cushing's scenes were shot in four days (out of a six-week schedule).

On the set as a stills photographer was Fred Olen Ray, today a successful and prolific maker of action-horror films (*The Tomb*). He shared his memories with the authors.

> Peter was not well known by the rest of the cast and crew, and he initially kept pretty much to himself. Things got off to a bad start when he broke a tooth on the plane and he was afraid he would hold up the shoot. While most stars spend a lot of time asking others to do things for them, he spent much of his time fixing coffee for the crew and helping the ladies through the swamp. During breaks I would ask him questions which

he would graciously answer, but he preferred talking about his late wife. The filming was done under very difficult conditions, like crabs crawling up the camera legs.

Famed producer Richard Gordon (*Corridors of Blood,* 1958) had worked with Peter Cushing in *Island of Terror* (1966) and was instrumental in securing Cushing for the film. He told the authors that "Ken Weiderhorn [the director] contacted me for advice on doing a low-budget horror film—what actors to go for, and whatever. I suggested Peter Cushing and put Ken in touch with Peter's agent."

Most of the production company had little or no experience in making a feature film. "I knew it was a new and young company," recalled Peter Cushing, "and I felt if my name could help them at all it would be a good thing to do. I might have made a mistake doing "Death Corps," but I don't think it shall do me any harm and it certainly won't do that company any harm."[1]

Cushing was correct. His name on the marquee and his solid performance are, as so often, the best things that the film has to offer.

While by no means a classic, *Shock Waves* has much to recommend it. The acting of the young cast is quite good—especially Brooke Adams in the lead. Peter Cushing's screen time is relatively short and the cast does its best in his frequent absences. The film aspires to do no more than frighten and is often successful.

Decked out in ratty clothing and Alan Ormsby's unpleasantly realistic scarface makeup, Peter Cushing has never looked less dashing on screen. Despite the hurried schedule and bare-bones budget, he as always, delivers a professional performance. Unlike others who have found themselves in similar circumstances, Cushing never comes across as feeling superior to his material or audience.

First-time director Ken Weiderhorn does a commendable job and makes what could have been a standard exploitation far better. John Carradine keeps things moving with his performance as the crusty captain but, unfortunately, does not survive until Peter Cushing enters the film. The underwater photography of the walking dead is quite eerie and produces a few unnerving images.

As one might expect, press coverage and reviews were quite limited. The *Miami Herald* did report, however, that "Peter Cushing refused to go anywhere without first stopping at the International House of Pancakes for a stack of buckwheats."

Peter Cushing made a rare American television appearance on Tom Snyder's "Tomorrow" program in New York. He was the special guest of the *Famous Monsters of Filmland* magazine convention and appeared on the program to promote the event.

Cushing also made guest appearances on the following radio programs: "Capitol Annual," "Night of Horror," "About London," "Star Sound," and "Weekend."

Note

1. Peter Cushing, interview with Steve Swires, *Famous Monsters of Filmland*, August 1978.

Trial by Combat
(1975)

Credits and Cast

Released 1975; 88 minutes; Color. Director: Kevin Connor; Producers; Fred Weintraub, Paul Heller; Screenplay: Julian Bond, Steve Rossen, Mitchell Smith; Story: Fred Weintraub, Paul Heller; Music: Fred Cordell; Director of photography: Alan Hume; Production design: Edward Marshall; Editor: Willy Kemplen; Production manager: Eva Monley; Stunts: Peter Brace; Wardrobe: Rosemary Burrows; Construction manager: Vic Simpson; Makeup: Eddie Knight; Hairdresser: Ramon Gow; Camera: Jimmy Devis. Also called *A Dirty Knight's Work*; video title, *A Choice of Weapons*.

John Mills (Bertie Cook), Donald Pleasence (Sir Giles Marley), Barbara Hershey (Marion), David Birney (Sir John Gifford), Margaret Leighton (Ma Gore), Peter Cushing (Sir Edward Gifford), Brian Glover (Sidney Gore), John Savident (Oliver), John Hallam (Sir Roger), Keith Buckley (Herald), Neil McCarthy (Ben Willoughby), Thomas Heathcote (Tramp), Bernard Hill (Blind Freddie), Alexander John (Lawyer), Diane Langton (Ruby), Roy Holder (William Redfield), Una Brandon-Jones (Martha Willoughby).

Synopsis

> *But to kill him—that's outrageous—that's mob law! It endangers all that our order stands for!*—Sir Edward Gifford

An armored knight on horseback gallops across a plain and into a castle where a joust is to take place—a trial by combat to determine the fate of William Redfield (Roy Holder). If he survives the joust against Sir Giles Marley (Donald Pleasence), he will be freed. However, Sir Giles is his superior and Redfield is savagely killed.

"A dirty knight's work." Peter Cushing and Donald Pleasence in *Trial by Combat*.

As the corpse is covered with a banner, Sir Edward Gifford (Peter Cushing) emerges from the forest — in modern dress! Sir Edward is, like the assembled knights, a member of the Order of Avalon — a club dedicated to preserving the code of chivalry. Sir Giles, however, has gone a step further — using the joust as a method of disposing of those he feels have gone unpunished for their crimes.

When Sir Edward voices his horror at what has occurred, he is met by the icy stares of the "knights." One of them draws his sword and advances, killing Sir Edward.

Sir Edward's son John (David Birney), investigating his father's death, is joined by Bertie Cook (John Mills), a retired commissioner of police. While raised in the traditions of knighthood and chivalry, John is living in the present and is skeptical of the motives of the Knights of Avalon.

John learns that Sir Giles has now replaced Sir Edward as leader of the order. He is aided in his inquiries by Sir Giles' attractive secretary, Marion Evans (Barbara Hershey). She leads John and Bertie to discover the order's vigilante activities and to learn of their next victim.

Sidney Gore (Brian Glover), a London gangster, is next on the list. When contacted by John and Bertie, he naturally lends his support.

Unfortunately, he and Bertie are captured by the order. In an effort to free them, Marion — showing more courage than sense — tries to free them by attacking the mounted knights with her car.

John, when he learns of the trio's capture, goes to the castle. Following the traditions of chivalry, he announces himself as their champion and demands the right to a trial by combat. Using the ancient weapons, he defeats several knights of the order, but his final opponent is Sir Giles.

After a lengthy sword fight, Sir Giles gets the better of John and escapes on horseback, only to be impaled on the spikes of the lowering castle gate.

Commentary

Peter Cushing's guest star billing is a bit misleading — he is killed off before a tardy popcorn buyer has an opportunity to find a seat. Typically, he invests even a performance of such short duration with an intensity that makes itself felt.

Trial by Combat has much of the feel of an episode of television's "The Avengers" and is enjoyable on the same level. It is also just about as easily forgotten.

A fine cast was assembled in support of David Birney who, while more than adequate, lacks the charisma and self-mockery to really pull off the role in the style of Patrick MacNee.

Joining Peter Cushing was old friend and frequent costar John Mills. They first appeared together in *The End of the Affair* (1954), and Sir John played Watson to Cushing's Holmes in the television film "Masks of Death" (1984).

Peter Cushing credits Sir John with giving him the necessary push to write his autobiography. In the preface, Cushing writes "my dear friend John Mills, who by his encouragement and example, finally persuaded me to take the plunge and record these memoirs, which I had started originally as a form of therapy, with no intention of making them public. He threatened never to work with me again if I didn't."

Sir John, in a letter to the authors, gave the following appreciation of Peter Cushing: "Peter Cushing was a pleasure to work with; he is a most dedicated actor and one always had a feeling of great security because Peter always turned up on the first day of shooting absolutely word and letter perfect. I have never known any actor more popular on the set and I am delighted that you are writing a book about him — it is high time!"

Peter Cushing describes his experience in *Trial by Combat* as "the cozy idea of my being used as a sandbag by a group of narrow minded knights—in armour—who took it into their heads to charge at me full tilt and en masse, plunging their lances in my midriff."[1]

Tom Milner, in *The Observer* (May 23, 1976) was not enthralled. "The idea behind this silly thriller might conceivably have served as an episode for television's "The Avengers." Interminably padded out, wretchedly executed, it expires long before continuing to intimate in the last few minutes that it was really intended to be tongue-in-cheek all along."

Peter Cushing was again quite active on television and radio, appearing in both England and America. His British television work included guesting on "Haunted," "The Amazing World of Cinema," "Beyond Tomorrow," and "Looks Familiar."

Note

1. Cushing, *Past Forgetting.*

Land of the Minotaur
(1975)

Credits and Cast

Released October 1977 (U.S.); 94 minutes (88 minutes U.S.); Color; A Getty Pictures-Poseidon Films Production; Released through Crown International (U.S.) and Poseidon (U.K.); MPAA PG; Filmed on location in Greece. Director: Costa Carayiannis; Producer: Frixos Constantine; Executive producer: Nick Morrison; Screenplay: Arthur Rowe; Director of photography: Aris Stavrou; Music: Brian Eno; Song: "The Devil's Men" by Karl Jenkins, sung by Paul Williams; Music supervisor: Gordon T. Chambers; Editor: Barry Reynolds; Art director: Petros Copourallis; Sound: Jon Blunt, Trevor Pike; Associate producer: Herbert Luft; Production manager: Pantellis Filiphides. Title in U.K., *The Devil's Men.*

Donald Pleasence (Father Roche), Peter Cushing (Baron Corofax), Luan Peters (Laurie Gordon), Nikos Vewrlekis (Ian), Costas Skouras (Milo Kay), Vanna Revilli (Beth), Bob Behling (Tom Gifford), Fernando Bislani (Police Sergeant Vendris), Anna Mentgosrani (Widow), Christina (Grocer's Daughter), Orestes Vlahos (Shopkeeper), George Veulis (Chauffeur), Jane Lyle (Milo's Girlfriend), Meira (Maid), Jessica (Mrs. Zagros), Ea Cosma, Lambrinos (Victims).

Synopsis

Hidden underground in a mountainous village somewhere in Greece is a secret temple. The villagers worship a demon god from ancient times

Director Costa Carayiannis has apparently just seen the daily rushes and pleads his case with the cast of Poseidon's *Land of the Minotaur.*

called "The Minotaur"—a demigod, half man, half bull, who, according to Greek mythology, was the son of Pasiphae and who was slain by Theseus, the hero of Attica.

These ceremonies are presided over by the village's most influential citizen, Baron Corofax (Peter Cushing), an exile from the Carpathian Mountains of Romania, who acts as high priest to these modern Minoans.

For many years villagers have worshiped their god, undisturbed, offering human sacrifices to the minotaur in return for its protection. However, reports of disappearances have brought curious outsiders who threaten their ceremonies and their very existence.

Father Roche (Donald Pleasence) is the pastor of a neighboring village and is also a professor of archaeology. After several of his students disappear in the vicinity of Baron Corofax's village, he is convinced that the town is possessed by an evil older than time. With the help of a former student, Milo Kay (Costas Skouras), now living in New York as a private detective, and Laurie Gordon (Luan Peters), who has come to Father Roche to find her missing boyfriend, Tom Gifford (Bob Behling), they discover the location of the secret temple.

Using the power of the Christian ritual of exorcism, they are able to

HALF MAN – HALF BEAST
TRAPPED IN A WORLD FORGOTTEN BY TIME

destroy the demon and his evil followers. The only participants who are spared are the village children, whose souls, Father Roche explains, are incorruptible.

Commentary

> *I fly to Greece shortly to make a film entitled* The Devil's People *with Donald Pleasence.* — Peter Cushing (November 11, 1975)

After an extremely successful guest of honor appearance in New York at the Second Annual Famous Monsters Convention sponsored by Warren Publications (November 1975), Peter flew to Greece to begin work on *Land of the Minotaur* for Getty Pictures, and Poseidon.

Originally announced under such working titles as "The Devil's People" and "The Demon," *Land of the Minotaur* went into production with an approximate budget of $650,000 and signed Donald Pleasence, Luan Peters, and Costas Skouras, in addition to Peter Cushing, as its featured stars.

Producer Frixos Constantine, who had hopes that one day his country might be known as the "Hollywood East" of the world, shot the film entirely on location in Greece. However, if the content and quality of *Land of the Minotaur* was any indication of what a Hollywood-Greek style film had to offer, Hollywood West had little to worry about concerning Constantine's proposed pipe dream.

The film itself is a preposterous labyrinth of false starts and dead ends. It's tediously predictable and gleefully flaunts scripter Arthur Rowe's total lack of imagination. None of his characters, unfortunately, were ever able to escape the first dimension and one becomes painfully aware that a five-minute plot cannot be stretched into a ninety-four-minute running time.

Technically, *Land of the Minotaur* fares even worse. The sound quality is literally a disaster and dubbing is so poorly done that even though Cushing and Pleasence are speaking English on film, their lip movements are off synch on the soundtrack! Editing is even worse, with scene changes cutting into dialogue (a prerogative normally deferred to local television hacks!).

Both Donald Pleasence and Peter Cushing are hideously squandered in this "Greek tragedy." Cushing's character, Baron Corofax, simply described as a Carpathian in exile, keeps the local yokels in line with regularly scheduled human sacrifices. The baron commands a band of hooded lackeys who parade about the village nightly reminding one of a KKK convention in downtown Athens! As if this isn't bad enough, the promised minotaur monster turns out to be nothing more than a diminutive fire-breathing statue which annoyingly repeats the same phrases over and over again like some demented "Teddy Ruxpin."

Pleasence, cast as a priest from a neighboring village named Father Roche, appears to be the only character present with a molecule of sense, and he spends most of his time babbling about demonology! New York detective Milo Kay, played by Costas Skouras, serves absolutely no purpose in the play. What should have been a very strong character merely blunders about uselessly, leaving the dirty work up to Roche. One wonders why the good priest sent for Milo in the first place since only a Christian exorcism could finally rid the village of its demonic possession and Roche seemed fully aware of this from the beginning!

John Stanley of the *San Francisco Chronicle* (December 10, 1977) summed it up, calling *Land of the Minotaur* "a film without logic or characterization and its location photography is without distinction. The movie is far beneath the talents of both actors [Pleasence and Cushing], and one hopefully assumes they accepted the assignments solely to enjoy an extended holiday in Greece." *Screen International* (September 18, 1976) reported that the film was "a garbled tale with a modicum of suspense . . . so stupid that any self-respecting demon would reject them as not worth the bother of coming all the way from Hell. . . . As usual, Peter Cushing adds a touch of elegant evil." Linda Gross of the *Los Angeles Times* (September 16, 1977) acknowledged that "The movie is . . . distinguished by the presence of two seasoned actors, Donald Pleasence and Peter Cushing, starring as obvious opposite symbols of good and evil. . . . Rowe's screenplay is even more obvious . . . the dialogue is regurgitated mumbo jumbo about the ever-present struggle between the forces of good and the devil. The direction of Costa Carayiannis is staid, failing to provide an atmosphere of terror in spite of scary and sadistic moments . . . location shots of ancient Greek ruins are picturesque but the village itself lacks a specific sense of locale." *Cinefantastique* (volume 7, number 2) referred to *Minotaur* as "a weird, . . . hybrid of fifties and sixties fantasy film clichés and seventies gore. Cushing fends for himself (and rather well) in his first totally unsympathetic role in years."

Cushing, who always adored children yet was never blessed with any of his own, appeared in a popular BBC program called "Jim'll Fix It," hosted by Jimmy Saville. Described as a make-a-wish show, this particular segment featured three youngsters who had asked if they might meet their favorite horror film star.

One child's wish was to *scare* Peter, so the show's makeup department was called upon to offer assistance in turning the boy into a monster. Peter promptly jumped out of his seat, on cue, when the boy crept up along side of the actor and shouted the obligatory "Boo!"

At the Earth's Core
(1976)

Credits and Cast

Released June 1976 (U.S.); 90 minutes; Movielab color; An Amicus Production; Released through American International (U.S.) and British Lion (U.K.); MPAA PG; Filmed at Pinewood Studios, England. Director: Kevin Connor; Producers: John Dark, Max J. Rosenberg, Milton Subotsky; Executive producer: Harry N. Blum; Screenplay: Milton Subotsky; Based on the story by Edgar Rice Burroughs; Camera operator: Derek Browne; Production designer: Maurice Carter; Art director: Bert Davey; Set dresser: Michael White; Special effects supervisor: Ian Wingrove; Editors: John Ireland, Barry Peters; Music compsoed by Mike Vickers; Production manager: Graham Easton; First assistant director: Jack Causey; Second assistant directors: Guy Travers, Andy Armstrong; Continuity: Doreen Soan; Lighting cameraman: Alan Hume; Construction manager: Vic Simpson; Stunts arranger: Joe Powell; Sound mixer: George Stephenson; Makeup: Neville Smallwood, Robin Grantham; Hairdresser: Joan Carpenter; Wardrobe: Rosemary Burrows; Dubbing editor: Jim Atkinson; Property master: Bert Hearn; Stills photographer: Albert Clarke; Executive in charge of production for Edgar Rice Burroughs: Robert M. Hodes; Unit publicists: Mike Russell, Peter Letsis; Production services: Midcore Ltd.

Doug McClure (David Innes), Peter Cushing (Dr. Abner Perry), Caroline Munro (Dia), Cy Grant (Ra), Godfrey James (Ghak), Sean Lynch (Hooja), Keith Barron (Dowsett), Helen Gill (Maisie), Anthony Verner (Gadsby), Robert Gillespie (Photographer), Michael Crane (Jubal), Bobby Parr (Sagoth Chief), Andree Cromarty (Slave Girl).

Synopsis

> *They're so excitable — like all foreigners!* — Dr. Abner Perry (describing the Sagoths)

During a test run of a gigantic earth-burrowing machine called "the Iron Mole," its inventor Dr. Abner Perry (Peter Cushing), along with his former student and investor, David Innes (Doug McClure), hope they will be able to use this invention to tap into the earth's natural resources at depths previously unattainable. However, as the machine makes its way through the solid rock of a mountainside in Wales, something goes awry and the Mole takes a downward turn — plunging the two men into the bowels of the planet — the earth's core.

Disembarking from the Mole, Perry and Innes find themselves in a lost world, the fabled land of Pellucidar. They are soon made the prisoners of the Sagoths, a primitive tribe of half-human creatures who are the minions of the giant lizard-like birds called Mahars. The Mahars rule Pellucidar by enslaving the people of its various tribes and terrorizing them. They communicate with the Sagoths through telepathy. The Sagoths provide the Mahars with a constant supply of new slaves who are also the lizard birds' main food source. On their journey to the Mahars' city, Perry and David meet Princess Dia (Caroline Munro). David and Dia fall in love.

Soon after their arrival in the city, David escapes and joins forces with Ra (Cy Grant), after saving his life from a maneating plant. Together they convince the various tribes to stop their in-fighting and to join forces against the Mahars.

David and the tribespeople return to the city. Using the Mahars' power source as a catalyst, they are able to destroy the Mahars. The people of Pellucidar are freed from the yoke of their oppressors, and as a result they also find a way to live together in peace and harmony.

David and Dr. Perry, with the help of the grateful Pellucidans, make repairs on the Mole and prepare to leave. But when David asks Dia to come back with him, she refuses — knowing that she would never be able to adjust in David's world. Innes and Perry board the Iron Mole and return home — this time arriving on the surface via the front lawn of the White House in Washington, D.C.

Commentary

> *I am now working with Doug McClure on* At the Earth's Core *from the Edgar Rice Burroughs story, which is by way of a sequel to the higly successful* The Land that Time Forgot *and is produced by the same company who made that film — Amicus — also the same director — Kevin Connor. I play Dr. Abner Perry. . . . It will take about twelve weeks in the studios at Pinewood and involves a lot of special effects.* — Peter Cushing (January 27, 1976)

> At the Earth's Core *was completed on schedule which involved a lot of extra work in the evenings and on weekends, as a delivery date has been promised in the States for early Summer. 95% of the picture will need dubbing, and this I've yet to do. . . . I do hope [everyone will] understand that the character of "Abner Perry" is very different on celluloid than in print.* — Peter Cushing (April 1976)

Utilizing seven of Pinewood's studio stages and special effects rigs, Amicus attempted to recreate the alien landscape of fantasy writer Edgar Rice Burroughs' first book about the subterranean continent he had dubbed Pellucidar.[1] Production notes made during the filming describe one of the sound stages as having "huge forests with creeper-clad trees which towered towards the gantries high above; rock, mountainous vistas

The zany Dr. Abner Perry in Amicus' *At the Earth's Core.*

and barren dust-filled deserts seemed to fade away to a distant magenta horizon; plasterers' shops and modellers' departments were proliferated with hideous half-completed creatures, cloying vegetation and hideous fungi . . . 'the Iron Mole' itself, an intricate model complete with opening doors, a gyrating nose-cone, rotating cutters and its own miniature steam-engine on rails, is a breathtaking work of art itself."

Pellucidar must have seemed a long way off for production designer Maurice Carter, who started as an interior designer at Harrod's, the world-famous department store in London. After finding his way into the film industry in 1934, Carter would eventually be involved in over 100 feature films—one of which was *The Battle of Britain* which required him to assemble the fleet of 150 Spitfires and Messerschmitts used in the production. Working closely with special effects supervisor Ian Wingrove and his team, Carter was able to re-create the monsters and landscapes of Burroughs' imagination after many months of frustrating work and much experimentation. The results were a strange mixture of the vaguely familiar and the utterly bizarre!

At the Earth's Core was a highly imaginative and beautifully photographed film. It obviously made the most of its limited budget and naturally, with a little more backing, could have given way to stop-motion animation instead of those men-in-the-rubber-suits that were actually used. But for all its lean funding, the film proved to be more entertaining than expected.

Direction and pacing were good enough to keep its main target audience — children and the young at heart — from becoming bored with the simplistic plot line. It was pure escapism and if one went along with the deliberately campy premise, it was quite a romp! Those who expected *Journey to the Center of the Earth* were in for a sore disappointment. *At the Earth's Core* tried to provide a fresher approach and one not meant to be taken seriously on any level. To that end it succeeded brilliantly.

Peter Cushing's corny one-liners were a delight and a definite focal point. Abner Perry was such a drastic departure from his previous characters (even Dr. Who) that many genre fans were unprepared for this zany and wildly eccentric professor. Cushing admirers, however, found Perry charming and a joy to watch — accentuating yet another facet of Peter's unlimited range as an actor.

Cushing himself was happy with the opportunity, finally, to show audiences that he could handle slapstick just as easily as he could any other medium. In a letter dated November 20, 1976, Cushing imparted the following as a result of all the favorable feedback he had been receiving: "It was most encouraging and gratifying to learn the general reaction to *At the Earth's Core* and 'Professor Abner Perry'; I'm so glad it gave such pleasure. The script was 90% action, so most of the dialogue had to be invented as we went along."

However, as much as Peter enjoyed his performance and the film as a whole, producer and screenplay writer Milton Subotsky was outraged. He lashed out at the director for what he felt was his total dissatisfaction with the film's final outcome:

> Kevin Connor is too ambitious. His taste is not that good and it was all his taste in *At the Earth's Core*. You can make a total studio film. We did that with our Dalek films. He didn't at all.... My own feelings are that you can't make a monster film with men in rubber suits. They changed my script entirely on that film. The last refuge of a tired imagination is an explosion at the climax and they've used it twice so far.

Critical evaluations, on the whole, were in Kevin Connor's favor and generally went along with the film's send-up premise. David Sterritt of the *Christian Science Monitor* (September 8, 1976) reported, "*The Earth's Core* movie is not respectable . . . it is very silly. It seems to know that it is silly though. At times it even pokes fun at itself, as when the old scientist never forgets his umbrella no matter how tough the situation gets.... Snazzy editing enlivens some sequences, but most of Kevin Connor's directing seems the visual equivalent of Burroughs' awful prose." *Variety* reporter "Mack" (June 23, 1976) offered, "an okay fantasy adventure film for the kiddie and drive-in markets . . . a fast-paced, slightly tongue-in-cheek tale. . . . Special Effects, while on the economical side, are good enough to hold interest through stretches of thin plotting in Subotsky's script . . . [which] harks back to a simple and unabashed kind of adventure formula which unfortunately isn't much used any more. . . . . Kevin Connor keeps the right balance of humor and straightforward adventure in the story, never making the fatal mistake of condescending to his plot or his audience. . . . [The] film has a nicely stylized visual look overall." Dilys Powell, *The Sunday Times,* said in her review (July 18, 1976), "the best comedy is played straightfaced as Peter Cushing plays it in *At the Earth's Core.* . . . Mr. Cushing is the elder explorer, armed only with an umbrella and insatiable scientific curiosity. The excellent special effects . . . deserve to be curiously studied, and the whole thing would make a good outing for the intrepid young." The *New York Times,* however, was openly hostile. Reviewer Richard Eder in his (August 28) account said, "the movie is a kind of no-talent competition in which the acting, the script, the direction and the camera work vie for last place." A similar sentiment was shown by Bill Kelley of *Cinefantastique,* who singled out Cushing's performance in particular: "This one is just about rock bottom, making the most juvenile excesses of Toho and Daier seem positively scintillating by comparison. . . . Abner Perry (an appallingly embarrassing performance by Peter Cushing) far from realizing Burroughs' careful blend of eccentric inventor and determined scientist, is transformed into a buffoon-like grandfather figure and foil for even the most inconsequential cast member. . . . While no Cushing performance is without interest, he hasn't received so much as a clue from Connor, who must have allowed him to experiment on his own." In contrast, *Black Oracle* (number 10) reviewer John Parnum said, "Subotsky's screenplay contains some humorous lines for Cushing which are even funnier because of his delivery . . . the problem is that fantasy fans have become a bit pompous in their expectations. . . . Watching *At the Earth's Core* is like watching a Thanksgiving Day parade. We all know the floats are not real. Why not let the child in us enjoy them?" And finally *Screen International* (July 17, 1976) said, "The film begins splendidly with an exciting trip to the Earth's core that is reminiscent of the best of Jules Verne. Henceforth, it is disappointing. . . . Doug McClure looks positively cheesed off with the whole business."

Critics notwithstanding, *Screen International* (December 18, 1976) listed *At the Earth's Core* as eighteenth in its list of the top British box office hits of the year.

Doug McClure, who was interviewed by Mike Munn (*The Greatest Show Beneath the Earth*) on the set, expressed his thoughts about what it was like to work with Peter: "I've never worked with anyone like him in my life. By the time you've finished a film with Peter you find you have a lot of feeling for him. You just can't walk away from him very easily. He's a brilliant actor. His range of comedy is unbelievable."

In *Fangoria* (number 4), Steve Swires spoke with Caroline Munro who told him about her impressions of Cushing: "he really enjoyed the movie because it was a departure from his normal roles. Peter is a very sweet and sensitive man.... He's very quiet and unspoiled—so unlike a star. I defy anybody who's met him to say a bad word about him."

Note

1. *At the Earth's Core* was the first book of a trilogy written by Burroughs. The other 2 books in the series were *Pellucidar* and *Tanar of Pellucidar*.

Star Wars
(1976)

Credits and Cast

Released May 25, 1977; 119 minutes; Technicolor; A Lucasfilm Production; Released through 20th Century Fox; MPAA PG; Filmed in Tunisia, Guatemala, California (Death Valley), and at Elstree Studios, England. Directed and written by George Lucas; Producer: Gary Kurtz; Director of photography: Gilbert Taylor; Second unit photography: Carroll Ballard, Rick Clemente, Robert Dalva, Tak Fujimoto; Music composed by John Williams; Orchestrations by Herbert W. Spencer; Performed by the London Symphony Orchestra; Editors: Paul Hirsch, Marcia Lucas, Richard Chew; Production designer: John Barry; Art direction: Norman Reynolds, Leslie Dilley; Second unit art direction: Leon Erickson, Al Locatelli; Set decoration: Roger Christian; Special photographic effects supervisor: John Dykstra; Special production and mechanical effects supervisor: John Stears; Production illustration: Ralph McQuarrie; Sound: Stephen Katz, Derek Ball, Don MacDougall, Bob Minkler, Ray West, Robert Litt, Michael Minkler, Les Fresholtz, Richard Portman, Sam Shaw, Robert R. Rutledge, Gordon Davidson, Gene Corso; Stunt coordinator: Peter Diamond; Casting: Irene Lamb, Diane Crittenden, Vic Ramos; Titles: Dan Perri; Costumes: John Mollo; Makeup: Stuart Freeborn, Rick Baker, Douglas Beswick; Production controller: Brian Gibbs; Production supervisor: Bruce Sharman; Assistant directors: Tony Waye, Gerry Gavigan, Terry Madden; Miniature and optical effects unit—photography: Richard Edlund, Dennis Muren, Bruce Logan; Composite optical photography: Robert Blalack; Matte artist: P. S. Ellenshaw; Production supervisor: George E. Mather; Effects illustration and design: Joseph Johnston; Chief model maker: Grant McCune; Animation and rotoscope design: Adam Beckett; Electronics design: Alvah J. Miller; Additional optical effects: Modern Film Effects, Ray Mercer Company, Van Der Veer Photo Effects, Master Film Effects, De Patie-Freleng Enterprises.

Mark Hamill (Luke Skywalker), Harrison Ford (Han Solo), Princess Leia Organa (Carrie Fisher), Peter Cushing (Grand Moff Tarkin), Alec Guinness (Ben Obi-Wan Kenobi), Anthony Daniels (C3PO), Kenny Baker (R2D2), Peter Mayhew (Chewbacca), David Prowse/James Earl Jones (Lord Darth Vader), Phil Brown (Uncle Owen Lars), Shelagh Fraser (Aunt Beru Lars), Jack Purvis (Chief Jawa), Alex McCrindle (General Dodonna), Eddie Byrne (General Willard), Drewe Henley (Red Leader), Dennis Lawson (Red Two-Wedge), Garrick Hagon (Red Three-Biggs), Jack Kalff (Red Four-John "D"), William Hootkins (Red Six-Porkins); Angus McInnis (Gold Leader), Jeremy Sinden (Gold Two), Graham Ashley (Gold Five), Don Henderson (General Taggi), Richard le Parmentier (General Motti), Leslie Schofield (Commander No. 1).

Synopsis

Charming—to the last!—Grand Moff Tarkin

Somewhere in a galaxy far away from our own, the inhabitants of every star system have been systematically subjugated by the Galactic Imperial Army. One of the army's governors, Grand Moff Tarkin (Peter Cushing) and his lieutenant, the evil Lord Darth Vader (David Prowse and James Earl Jones) are vigorously trying to stamp out a small group of resistance fighters. These rebels are led by Princess Leia Organa (Carrie Fisher).

Having stolen the plans for a massive weapon of destruction known as "The Death Star" (a type of planet killer), Princess Leia is captured— but not before she entrusts her faithful robot servant, R2D2 with the blueprints. R2 and his "friend" C3PO, another robot, are sent to find the one man whom Leia feels can help in the struggle—Ben Obi-Wan Kenobi (Alec Guinness)—the last of the famed Jedi Knights.

Along the way the robots befriend a young man named Luke Skywalker (Mark Hamill) and a space pirate known as Han Solo (Harrison Ford). Luke and the robots find Obi-Wan, who trains Luke to become a Jedi.

With the imperial forces on their trail, they manage to free the princess and are successful in getting the Death Star blueprints to the other leaders of the resistance movement.

In a daring raid Luke, using the powers of "the force" Obi-Wan taught him, saves the galaxy by destroying the Death Star.

Commentary

In April, I am to take part in The Star Wars *with Sir Alec Guinness, directed by George Lucas for Lucasfilm Ltd.... playing 'Governor Moff Tarkin.'*"—Peter Cushing (March 19, 1976)

Grand Moff Tarkin: the role that introduced Peter Cushing to a new generation of fans, in George Lucas' *Star Wars*.

No one can deny that *Star Wars* was both a visual and technical masterpiece. Although perhaps not on an intellectual par with films such as *2001—A Space Odyssey* (1968), *Star Wars* was an unprecedented success with the masses. Audiences, which included all age groups, did not leave theaters looking confused while they hopelessly pondered the heady symbolism of black granite monoliths and fetal star babies floating in the womb of space. *Star Wars* crowds left their local movie houses happily rejuvenated and anxious to return again for subsequent viewings. If worldwide audience satisfaction is the bottom line of any feature film's existence, then *Star Wars* indeed had no rivals. As any industry spokesperson will readily admit, entertainment is what the business is all about and *Star Wars* most certainly was pure diversion.

Star Wars was shot on a budget that by today's standards would be considered quite modest. Figures range from between $7 and $9.5 million. However, within a mere two weeks of its release on May 25, 1977, *Star Wars* had already grossed $8.5 million and broke house records in every theater in which the film was shown during its premiere engagement. It would eventually become one of the top-grossing films of all time.

Star Wars went into production in March 1976. After approximately eighteen days of location shooting in Chott Djerid, Nefta and Matmata, Tunisia, the cast and crew returned to EMI–Elstree Studios in London for the final fifteen weeks of interior work. The picture was completed after several months of postproduction special effects work while a second unit was dispatched to Death Valley, California, and Guatemala for more location filming.

Peter Cushing joined the cast during its fourth week at Elstree Studios on May 8, 1976. He had chosen to work on the film because, in his own words, "my criterion for accepting a role isn't based on what I would like to do. I try to consider what the audience would like to see me do [and] I thought kids would adore *Star Wars*."[1] His instincts were absolutely right.

Peter had originally been approached by writer-director George Lucas to portray Obi-Wan Kenobi but when the two men finally met Lucas changed his mind, feeling that Peter would be much more effective in the role of Governor Tarkin. Peter accepted, not having much of a choice. Lucas felt that he was drawn to such notable actors as Cushing and Guinness because, as he put it, "They're good actors and they're more or less by nature like the characters in the story. The important thing about a movie like *Star Wars* is that it be believable to an audience and that they identify with the characters and these actors, because of who they are, bring believability to the situations."[2]

Though Peter confessed he wasn't much of a science fiction fan, he did the best he could with the lines he was given. He also admitted outright that he didn't understand all the technical jargon. "I wasn't alone," Peter said, "Many of the stagehands came up to me and asked: 'What is all this about? I can't understand a word of it.' I told them: 'Neither can I. I'm just saying the lines and trying to sound intelligent!'"[3]

Cushing remembers feeling a sense of defeatism with regard to his

The first film in the subsequent Star Wars trilogy.

work in the film, blaming the special effects that surrounded all the actors for drawing away audience attention from their characterizations. However, these fears were very quickly doused when letters began pouring in from all over the world praising his performance.

George Lucas himself praised Peter's talents: "Peter Cushing . . . is a very good actor. . . . He's got an image that is in a way quite beneath him, but he is adored and idolized by young people and people who go to see a certain kind of movie. I feel he will be remembered fondly for the next 350 years at least."[4]

Though audiences could feel a noticeable drop in room temperature whenever Governor Tarkin appeared on-screen, actor Dave Prowse, who portrayed one of Tarkin's evil henchmen, Darth Vader, had quite a different story to tell behind the scenes, especially during the filming of Tarkin's interrogation of Princess Leia (Carrie Fisher) on board his Death Star spaceship.

> The interesting thing about Peter was he had a lot to do with Carrie Fisher. It was . . . Fisher's really first major film . . . and he went out of his way to show her the ropes. When there would be some dialogue between [them], he'd turn around and say, "Look Carrie, if I stand here, I'm going to get my shadow on you and you're not going to be seen in a very good light, etc. . . . So what I'll do, I'll move around so I'm in the shadow and you're in the light.[5]

This was a typical example of Peter's artistic intuitiveness. By keeping Leia's face bathed in brightness she retained her character's essential goodness of purpose. Tarkin, evil personified, remained a shadowy figure and one not clearly defined until just the right moment in order to build suspense and, hopefully, take the viewer by surprise.

However, as ruthless and blindly ambitious as Governor Tarkin may have been portrayed, one of his cohorts, General Tazzi, better known off camera as actor Don Henderson, gave the authors a different perspective of his friend Peter Cushing.

> My recollection of working with Peter is that he is a man of immense charm, old-fashioned manners, politeness and a 100% professional! I have *never* heard him swear, be rude to anyone, offend anyone nor say a bad word about any person, whatsoever.
> Peter always stands up when a lady enters, shakes hands with everyone in greeting. When he turns up for work, and despite ill health in latter years, he was always cheerful. He was always word-perfect with his lines, and his professionalism was like a diamond. He is an old-fashioned Gentleman.

Henderson also remarked that during the making of *Star Wars* Peter was given a pair of black knee-high jackboots to wear as part of his costume that, unfortunately, didn't fit. "Peter," Henderson recalled, "had to have all his scenes shot from the waist up so that one couldn't see that he was actually stomping about, being incredibly evil, while actually wearing a pair of red and pink bedroom slippers! Everyone involved in the scene had great difficulty keeping a straight face!"

Star Wars was reviewed by nearly every major publication in the world. Some of its national reviews included "Murf" in *Variety* (May 25, 1977) who hailed it as "a magnificent film.... Like a breath of fresh air ... sweeps away the cynicism that has in recent years obscured the concepts of valor, dedication and honor.... Both Guinness and Peter Cushing bring the right measure of majesty to their opposite characters.... This is the kind of film in which an audience, first entertained, can later walk out feeling good all over." Stanley Kauffmann of *New Republic* (June 20, 1977) said, "This is Lucas' tribute to Flash Gordon.... *Star Wars* is an unabashed, jaw-clenched tribute to the chastity still sacred beneath the middle-aged spread." Joseph Glemis in *Newsday* (May 27, 1977) reported that it was "An escapist masterpiece—one of the greatest adventure movies ever made." *Time* (Gerald Clarke and William Rademaskers, May 30, 1977) called it "A grand and glorious film ... a subliminal history of the movies wrapped in a riveting tale of suspense and adventure ornamented with some of the most ingenious special effects ever contrived for film ... one of the swiftest two hours on celluloid." Ron Pennington of the *Hollywood Reporter* predicted that "*Star Wars* will be thrilling audiences of all ages for a long time to come.... Cushing and Guinness are outstanding in their respective roles." Charles Champlin of the *Los Angeles Times* called it "The year's most razzle-dazzling family movie—an exuberant and technically astonishing space adventure." Kathleen Carroll of the *New York Daily News* was equally impressed, saying it was "an absolutely breathtaking achievement ... radiates a surprising amount of warmth." The *New York Times* reviewer Vincent Canby noted, "the true stars of *Star Wars* are the people who were responsible for the incredible special effects." Conversely, Molly Haskell of the *Village Voice* commented that "at the risk of sounding like ... a prissy 14-year-old, dammit, the picture is childish, even for a cartoon." Overseas, *The Times* (George Perry, October 2, 1977) praised Peter in its review, saying, "Peter Cushing, splendid as ever as the wicked Grand Moff Tarkin."

Star Wars earned ten Academy Award nominations that year, including the coveted Best Picture category. Unfortunately, it lost to Woody Allen's *Annie Hall*. However, *Star Wars* did collect seven Oscars— Original Score, Visual Effects, Sound, Costume Design, Editing, Art Direction, and a special achievement for Special Sound Effects Editing (an award Lucas shared with Steven Spielberg's entry, *Close Encounters of the Third Kind*).

With the release of *Star Wars* the industry had a new role model and an extremely tough act to follow. The film's monumental repercussions are still being felt today. No longer were many of the past's innovators in the field being mentioned. The one name on everyone's lips now was George Lucas.

Personally, Peter Cushing was delighted to be involved in another smash hit. "To have two such achievements in an actor's life is quite extraordinary.... I was so lucky to work for Hammer when they started ... and then, I was fortunate again to be in *Star Wars*, however small my role was.... My only disappointment was that poor old Tarkin was blown up at the end, which meant I couldn't appear in the sequels!"[6]

Notes

1. Steve Swires, "Peter Cushing—The Baddie with a Heart of Gold," *Starlog* 96.
2. 20th Century Fox, publicity release.
3. Swires, "Peter Cushing—The Baddie with the Heart of Gold," *Starlog* 96.
4. George Lucas, interview, *Rolling Stone* 246 (August 25, 1977).
5. Dick Klemensen, "Darth Vader Lives" (interview with David Prowse), *Little Shoppe of Horrors* 4.
6. Swires, "Peter Cushing—The Baddie with the Heart of Gold, *Starlog* 96.

The Uncanny
(1976)

Credits and Cast

Released April 1978 (U.K.); 88 minutes; Color; A Cinevideo-Tor Production; Released through Rank (U.K.) and Astral Bellevue Pathe (Canada); Filmed on location in Senneville, Canada, Panavision Studios, Montreal, and Pinewood Studios, London, England. Director: Denis Heroux; Producers: Claude Heroux, Rene Dupont; Story and screenplay: Michael Parry, Milton Subotsky; Director of photography: Harry Waxman; Music: Wilfred Josephs; Conducted by Philip Martell; Production design: Wolf Kroeger, Harry Pottle; Titles: Robert Ellis; Production supervisor: Claude Leger; Editors: Peter Weatherley, Keith Palmer, Michael Guay; Costumes: Nicoletta Massone, Joyce Stoneman; Assistant directors: Justine B. Heroux, Jack Casey; Executive producers: Harold Greenberg, Richard R. St. Johns, Robert A. Kantor; Special effects: Michael Albrechtoen; Makeup: Brigette McCaughey, Tom Smith; Assistant art directors: Stephen Reichel, Peter Childs; Camera operators: James Bauden, Jean Marie Birquet; Sound recordists: Ron Seltzer, Ron Barron; Sound editor: Jack Knight; Sound mixer: Gordon K. McCallum; Cat handler: John Holmes; Production manager: Jim Brennan; Production assistant:

Liz Taylor; Continuity: Georgina Hamilton; Hairdresser: Pat McDermott; Production assistant; Sam Williams; Still photographers: Albert Clarke, Attila Dory; Canadian publicity assistant: Prudence Emery.

Link Story: Peter Cushing (Wilbur Gray), Ray Milland (Frank). Malkin Story: Susan Penhaligon (Janet), Joan Greenwood (Miss Malkin), Simon Williams (Michael), Roland Culver (Wallace). Black Magic Story: Alexandra Stewart (Mrs. Blake), Chloe Franks (Angela), Katrina Holden (Lucy), Donald Pilon (Mr. Blake), Renee Giraud (Mrs. Maitland). Film Studio Story: Donald Pleasence (De'Ath), Samantha Eggar (Edina), John Vernon (Pomeroy), Sean McCann (Inspector), Jean LeClere (Barrington), Catherine Begin (Madeline).

Synopsis

> We let them prowl about just as they please. Hardly noticing them. And all the time they're watching us. Spying on us. Making sure that we behave. — Wilbur Gray, Author

Wilbur Gray (Peter Cushing), a writer of books concerning unusual phenomena, visits book publisher Frank Richards (Ray Milland) with his latest manuscript. The book fully documents cases of previously unsolved murders. Gray is convinced these deaths were perpetrated by cats, whom he is certain are to this day still a danger to mankind. His hope is that if the book is published it will warn humans about these manipulative and scheming felines.

The first case takes place in 1912. A wealthy and bedridden elderly woman, Miss Malkin (Joan Greenwood), contacts her lawyer to have her nephew, Michael (Simon Williams), whom she describes as a worthless spendthrift, cut out of her will. Instead, she wishes to leave her considerable fortune to her cats. Miss Malkin's maid, Janet (Susan Penhaligon), however, is Michael's lover and together they plot to murder Malkin and destroy the only remaining copy of the new will. Janet is caught by Miss Malkin when she attempts to take the document and Janet murders her. Miss Malkin's cats witness the murder and, in turn, kill both Janet and Michael to secure their inheritance.

The second story takes place in Quebec 1975. A young girl is sent to live with her aunt and uncle when both her parents are killed in a plane crash. Lucy (Katrina Holden) arrives with her pet cat, Wellington. Lucy's cousin, Angela Blake (Chloe Franks), an over-indulged child, is jealous of Lucy. When she sees Lucy's devotion to her pet and the fact that the animal disturbs her mother (Alexandra Stewart), who is a meticulous housewife, Angela blames the animal for damage she has caused. The cat is taken away to be destroyed. But since the animal is really a witch's familiar (Lucy's mother was a practitioner of the black arts), it returns and with the

Wilbur Gray faces his worst fears in *The Uncanny.*

help of a book of magic spells, Lucy uses sorcery to shrink Angela to the size of a mouse and then kills the child by stepping on her. Mrs. Blake arrives a short time later and, seeing the mess on the floor, scolds Lucy. She then proceeds to clean up what she thinks is some red paint.

The third story involves a horror movie actor in the 1930s, Valentine De'Ath (Donald Pleasence), whose actress wife is killed "accidentally" on the set of his latest film "Dungeons of Horror." She is quickly replaced by Valentine's protégé Edina Hamilton (Samantha Eggar), who is also his mistress. Valentine returns home with his paramour only to discover that his late wife's cat, whom he despises, has given birth to a litter of kittens. Valentine drowns the litter and vows to get rid of the mother as well.

After a disastrous day on the set, Valentine offers to stay late and coach Edina for the next day's shoot. On the torture chamber set Valentine is rehearsing with Edina while she is inside an iron maiden. The cat suddenly appears, leaps onto the iron maiden which slams shut, impaling Edina on its iron spikes.

The next morning one of the film's executives, Pomeroy (John Vernon), finds Valentine seated at his dressing room table — dead. His tongue has been torn out and the cat is seen playing with it!

Hoping that he has convinced Richards, Wilbur leaves the manuscript with the publisher and starts for home when he is killed by some stray cats who have been waiting for him. Richards' cat, Sugar, hypnotizes his master into throwing the manuscript into the fireplace, where the book is quickly consumed by the flames.

Commentary

> *My recent visit to Los Angeles ... was as sudden and brief as when I went to Florida last year. I must admit the jet lag did hit me this time and I fear my performance suffered from it. However, Paul Michael Glasser and Sally Struthers will more than make up for any lapse on my part. I think they'll be splendid as Mr. and Mrs. Houdini, and the screenplay is fascinating.* — Peter Cushing (July 31, 1976)

> *I play "Wilbur Gray" in the [Cinevideo-Tor] production, The Uncanny, which is a series of "cat" stories, my character linking them together. Ray Milland and Donald Pleasence also star, and it was directed by Denis Heroux in Montreal.* — Peter Cushing (November 20, 1976)

A few months prior to filming *The Uncanny*, Cushing was summoned to Los Angeles to film the ABC Television presentation of "The Great Houdinis." Peter would come full circle with his appearance in the film as Sir Arthur Conan Doyle, having already immortalized Doyle's most famous literary character (Sherlock Holmes) in both motion pictures and in the BBC television series based on the logical super sleuth.

Costarring with Peter in the film were many well-known television and motion picture personalities including: Ruth Gordon, Bill Bixby, Vivian Vance, Maureen O'Sullivan, Nina Foch, Jack Carter, Wilfrid Hyde-White, and Clive Revill. Though frequently embellished with fictionalized events, it was nonetheless a very entertaining and at times dramatic biography of one of the world's most famous magicians.

Produced to coincide with the fiftieth anniversary of Houdini's death, ABC originally aired the film on Friday, October 8, 1976. It would also be Peter's first American made-for-television movie.[1]

One of Peter's costars, Clive Revill, who also has had a long and varied career, had nothing but praise for Peter when the authors approached him for his observations: "[Peter Cushing has] my intense admiration as an actor who has provided an enormous amount of pleasure to audiences all over the world and has endured as one of the truly great character actors of our time."

Maureen O'Sullivan, who played Mrs. Conan Doyle, told the authors that her scenes with Peter were rushed because he was evidently due to fly home to England later in the day, but she remembers him as being "a charming man."

In the mid–1970s the Canadian motion picture industry was practically at a standstill. The Canadian government attempted to stimulate more foreign investments in Canadian-European coproductions by passing the Quebec Cinema Act in 1975. It was hoped that more foreign film companies would take advantage of Canadian locales—as well as Canadian technicians—to help their depressed market. Five countries in all signed agreements at the time: Israel, France, Italy, West Germany, and the United Kingdom. As a result, the fourth film to go into production under the act was *The Uncanny*, a Cinevideo of Canada and Tor Production of the United Kingdom coproduction.[2]

Budgeted at $1.1 million, *The Uncanny* started shooting on November 16, 1976, in Montreal for approximately four weeks. In December the production moved to Pinewood Studios in England where filming and postproduction mixing were completed.[3]

Tor Productions, headed by Claude Heroux and Milton Subotsky (Subotsky's last film with Amicus, coproduced with Max Rosenberg, was *At the Earth's Core*), based their stories on an anthology Subotsky had written entitled *Beware of the Cat*. Subotsky spoke about his involvement on the project:

> I was asked to do an anthology based on my stories. . . . [However,] we changed the idea to three and not five stories and the title became ["B-R-R!"]. The third story was to be a comedy. . . . Rene Dupont made a deal, I got coproducing credit and editing rights so I went to Montreal to work on the cast. Vincent Price turned me down. So did Peter Cushing and Christopher Lee . . . Cushing relinquished when he found out it was one of my pictures—he hadn't realized.[4]

Evidently the picture ran into some serious postproduction problems as Subotsky explained in the same interview: "The director, Denis Heroux, was the brother of the coproducer and he was terrible. He covered the film in master shot. . . . Nothing matched—we could only make one cut! They hadn't edge-numbered. I fired the editor and hired Michael Guay. . . . The whole thing was an appalling mess. I worked on the third story and the framework and found later that Heroux had reedited it and was proud of what he'd done! It was a miracle we got a final print."

During the time Peter Cushing was in Canada he was interviewed for a local Montreal newspaper (*The Gazette*, Friday, November 19). He told reporter Dane Lanken that he found it amusing that he was being interviewed in his hotel room at the first-class Ritz Carlton, "Whereas the last time I was in Montreal, I was staying around the corner at the YMCA." Peter was, of course, alluding back to 1941 when he had left Hollywood for Canada to find transportation home to then war-torn England. According to the article, Peter made his way to Halifax where he was finally able to secure passage on the SS *Tilapa*. "Someone had just deserted," Cushing told Lanken, "and I asked if I might take his place. The captain asked what I did and I replied that I was an actor, and he said, 'Oh my God, you can look after the ship's cat.' Which I did, and a mere eighteen months after leaving Hollywood I was back home." The irony of Cushing's story was that thirty-five years later Peter would return to Montreal to star in a film *about* cats.

Peter plays an author named Gray who has written a book in which he has carefully documented several previously unsolved murder cases. His theory is that ordinary house cats were responsible for the crimes. Gray tries to convince his publisher, Frank Richards (played by Ray Milland), that these so called harmless house pets are, in reality, not only well organized but they are also able to communicate with one another telepathically. Wilbur Gray firmly believes that through their cunning they are thus able to control their environment. Wilbur cites three such cases and these form the basis for the anthology. The film ends with Gray being killed by an organized group of felines who then force Frank Richards to destroy the author's manuscript before it can be published and alert other humans.

As expected, the film turned out to be as ridiculous as its story line. *The Uncanny* had little to offer audiences beyond some fair performances and mediocre production. What is obvious is that Peter Cushing would not have participated in the film at all had it not been for his loyalty to the film's producer, Milton Subotsky. Although he gives yet another gripping performance as the neurotic writer, the film was hardly worthy of him.

Critically, *The Uncanny* was not well received. *Screen International* (April 22, 1978) called it "A run-of-the-mill mixture of straight and camped up horrors.... There are no surprises ... unlikely to endear the film to cat lovers." *Variety* panned it saying, "There's nothing to recommend this one beyond its cheapness."

Notes

1. Harry Houdini died October 31, 1926. Peter was in Hollywood May 12–15, 1976.
2. Canadian Film Development Corporation.
3. Locations for *The Uncanny* were done in Senneville, Canada, and at Panavision Studios, Montreal.

4. Milton Subotsky, interview with Alan Jones and Mike Childs, *Cinefantastique* 6, no. 3.

Battleflag
(1976)

Credits and Cast

No official release date; 120 minutes; Color; An Ottokar Runz Production in association with Thalia Film (Hamburg) and Orfeo Productions (Madrid); Filmed October–December 1976 in Spain and Vienna, Austria. Director: Ottokar Runze; Executive producers: Karlheinz Mannchen, Mario Morales; Screenplay: Herbert Asmodi; Director of photography: Michael Epp; Music: Hans Martin Majewski; Set and costume design: Peter Scharff; Editor: Tamara Karabelten; Sound: Christian Dalchow; Casting: Otto Boris Dworak; Assistant director: Helmut Christian Gorlitz. European title *Die Standard.*

Simon Ward (Menis), Siegfried Rauch (Bottenlauben), Viktor Staal (Anton), Veronica Forque (Resa), Gerd Bockmann (Anschutz), Robert Hoffman (Klein), Wolfgang Preiss (Oberst), Peter Cushing (Hackenberg), Jon Finch (Charbinsky), David Robb (English Officer), Lil Dagover (Erzherzogin), Maria Perschy (Mordax), Friedrich Ledebur (General), Rudolf Prack (Lakai), Hans Thimig (Hofbeamter).

Synopsis

Menis (Simon Ward), a cadet, arrives in Belgrade at the end of World War I when a retreat by the empire has been ordered.

He meets Resa (Veronica Forque), a princess, at a concert and they fall in love. She decides to stay in Belgrade to be near him as he and his regiment must stay to protect the city.

His regiment is made up of non–Austrians who were drafted and have little loyalty to the royal family of Habsburg. The officers, including Major Hackenberg (Peter Cushing), are oblivious to the situation and, when the city is attacked, the regiment breaks rank. Many of those who remain are slaughtered and the regiment's battleflag is stolen by the attacking force.

The remaining members of the regiment sacrifice their lives to retake the banner — and their honor — so it can be presented to the Habsburgs.

Menis and Resa take the recovered battleflag to the palace in Vienna as it is being evacuated. Unable to obtain an audience with the royal family, Menis gives the torn banner to a servant to present when it is more

Peter Cushing rides at his peril in *Battleflag.*

convenient. As he and the princess leave, the servant tosses the flag into a fireplace.

Commentary

Battleflag was the first of four post–*Star Wars* films that seem to have completely vanished (the others being *Hitler's Son* [1977], *Touch of the Sun* [1978], and *Black Jack* [1981]).

All four were made outside the friendly confines of the United Kingdom or the United States, which goes some way in explaining their lack of availability. *Battleflag* and *Black Jack* were filmed in Spain, *Hitler's Son* in Germany, and *Touch of the Sun* in Zambia. However, countless films are made in non–English speaking countries and find their way to America or England.

In an October 1976 letter to the authors, Peter Cushing's secretary — Mrs. Joyce Broughton — wrote, "Mr. Cushing is in Spain filming *Battleflag* with Simon Ward and Jon Finch. He plays Major Von Hackenberg and I don't expect him back for some considerable time. It is possible that he may also be going directly to Canada or South Africa when the above is finished, depending on the possibility of two films which may materialize."

The possible Canadian film turned out to be *The Uncanny* (1976) — another poorly released venture — and the African film was *Touch of the Sun.*

Costar Simon Ward had this to say: "Apart from guest appearances by Peter Cushing and Jon Finch, I was the only English speaking actor in the cast. It was a very odd experience, because it was shot in three languages, and I had never worked on a production like it before. In the film, there was all this German and all this Spanish going on and as I cannot speak a word of either language, it was rather difficult to know what to do."[1]

The February 4, 1978, issue of *Screen International* listed *Battleflag* as one of Ward's films of the previous year, but no mention of a general release could be found.

Variety (May 25, 1977) reviewed the film at the Cannes Festival on May 19. The less than positive review shows, perhaps, why the film was not picked up by a distributor for a general release.

> A great deal of money was invested in Ottokar Runzes' *Battleflag* with the aim of capturing a commercial market at home and abroad. But this tale of the Austria-Hungary monarchy and a young cadet officer believing in the limited tradition of the Austrian Empire loses credibility as it goes along, particularly in so far as the love story and action sequences are concerned. Chances are poor for box office return unless picture is recut to save embarrassment for awkward script and thesp rules. [The film is] properly lensed and has some lovely location scenes. The condemnation of duty for its own sake also has relevance. . . . A few strong cameo roles by famous actresses and actors help.

The film's poor reception at Cannes undoubtedly resulted in a poor, if any, distribution deal. The film now seems lost.

Other than the three English actors, there is only one other recognizable name in the film. Incredibly, Lil Dagover, who starred in *The Cabinet of Dr. Caligari* (1919), is featured in a cameo.

Peter Cushing's memories of the film are quite limited. His role was, apparently, a small one—he is listed eighth in the cast—and comments only that he rode a horse "at my peril."[2]

Peter Cushing appeared as a guest on the television show "Clapperboard" and guest starred as Von Claus on one episode of "The New Avengers" ("The Eagle's Nest").

Notes

1. Simon Ward, interview, *Screen International*, June 4, 1977.
2. Cushing, *Past Forgetting*.

Hitler's Son
(1977)

Credits and Cast

Previewed January 1979 (U.K.), no known release for U.K. or U.S.; Color; A Naxos Film Production; Filmed at Arri Studios, Munich, and on location in Bavaria, Germany. Director: Rod Amateau; Producer: Dr. Gerd Goring; Screenplay: Lukas Heller, Burkhard Driest; Director of photography: Michael Marszalek; Editor: Murray Jordan; Camera: Georg Mondi; Production supervisor: Dieter Nobbe; Production manger: Klaus Keil; Location manager: Oliver Hengst; Set dresser: Klaus Haase; Sound: Peter Beil; Makeup: Uschi Borsche; Costume design: Siegbert Kammerer; Art director: Herbert Strabel. Known as "Return to Munich" during production.

Bud Cort (Willi), Peter Cushing (Haussner), Heinz Bennett (Ostermayer), Leo Gordon (Tuennes), Felicity Dean (Valeska), Dieter Schidor (Sommer), Anton Diffring (Gernheim), Til Kiwe (Dr. Puttkammer), Peter Kern (Jodl), Wolf Golden (Giesbert), Toni Cacciotti (Gunther), Burkhard Driest (Muller), Lynn Cartwright (Aunt Annie), Herbert Fox (Albrecht), Rolf Zacher (Ratman), Eduard Linkers (Postmaster).

Synopsis

Adolf Hitler and Eva Braun, it seems, had a child. Christened Willi (Bud Cort), the boy was raised in a desolate mountain area near Munich by an ss officer.

Peter Cushing and Bud Cort in the ill-fated *Hitler's Son.*

Willi grows up blissfully unaware of his parentage — or much else, for that matter. At age thirty-three he is an illiterate woodcarver, still living in the mountains until. . . .

A new right-wing party is attempting to gain power in Germany. Its leader, Heinrich Haussner (Peter Cushing) has learned of Willi's existence and feels that he, if properly manipulated and exploited, could greatly aid the party. With the help of his chauffeur Tuennes (Leo Gordon), Haussner begins the search.

But Willi comes to him. Finally leaving the mountains, Willi arrives, an innocent, in Munich. Even when he learns that his father was Adolf Hitler he is unmoved — the name means nothing to him. His innocence is sorely tested in a series of misadventures involving a dissipated old woman (Lynn Cartwright) and a beautiful young girl (Felicity Dean).

Unfortunately, Willi loses his birth certificate which, even more unfortunately, is found by Haussner. When Willi continues to insist that he is Hitler's son, he is committed to a mental institution.

Willi is eventually kidnapped by Haussner, who feels that the young man should lead the party. He is taught his father's mannerisms and speech patterns and given a similar haircut. A mustache completes the illusion.

At the party's preelection convention, Willi is the keynote speaker. The fate of the party, of Germany, of the world, hangs in the balance. But Haussner has forgotten one key element. Although Willi looks, acts, and speaks like Hitler, he still thinks like Willi—a happy, innocent child.

Commentary

Hitler's Son is the second of Peter Cushing's 1970s films that could be considered "lost"—the authors could find no trace of a general release or review. As of the writing of this book, the film has not surfaced on video, but one never knows!

This is not surprising. A comedy involving Hitler and Nazi Germany seems like a fairly risky enterprise. Author Colin Vaines stated, "How it will fare commercially . . . remains to be seen. But there is at least one market which [screenwriter Burkhard] Driest is not holding out great hopes for—Germany."

Driest commented, "Everybody in Germany turned the film down. Not one of these money guys was prepared to finance a picture . . . which made fun of Hitler. They were repelled by the idea. So because of the difficulties we faced, we eventually traveled abroad and got it privately financed."[1]

Unfortunately, the money guys were apparently correct—the film did not attract an audience outside of Germany, either. "Our film is directed against . . . Prussian spirit. So although I think the English speaking countries will enjoy a comedy about Hitler's son," Driest concluded, "it's very doubtful that the Germans will."[2] Perhaps this might be true in the 1990s, but Driest badly over- (or under-) estimated his audience.

The release of *Hitler's Son* had been originally announced for May 1, 1978, but this did not occur. Principal photography was to have ended by Christmas 1977 with a final cut to be prepared in Munich. Postsynching was to have been completed at England's EMI Elstree Studios. Its budget was $5 million.[3]

A second preview was announced for January 1979 in London to "gauge an audience reaction before negotiations are opened for U.K. distributions."[4] One can guess what form the reaction took.

"It's a comedy," Peter Cushing said. "I do play comedy, you know."[5] This makes the film's vanishing act even more frustrating. In a career as lengthy as his, Cushing has had few enough opportunitites to show this side of his talent.

Making matters worse, he was forced to withdraw from the cast of a film that was actually released. In an October 1977 letter to the authors, Peter Cushing stated, "I am making a guest appearance in a film entitled

Seven Cities to Atlantis. My part is Atraxon, Imperator of the supreme council." A January 1978 letter followed. "The schedule of *Hitler's Son* clashed badly with *Seven Cities to Atlantis* which prevented me appearing in the latter film."

Based on the production notes, *Hitler's Son* looks like a quality film. Coauthor Lukas Heller was involved in the scripting of *The Dirty Dozen* (1967) and *Whatever Happened to Baby Jane* (1962). Art director Herbert Strabel was an Oscar winner for his work on *Cabaret* (1972). Director Rod Amateau had a string of American television successes including "The Burns and Allen Show." The cast, in addition to Bud Cort and Peter Cushing included Anton Diffring. So what went wrong?

Judging good taste from bad is often an impossible task for filmmakers. One may doubt that a Hitler comedy is within the bounds of audience acceptance, but then there is Mel Brooks' *The Producers* (1968). So who can tell?

Notes

1. Burkhard Driest, interview, *Screen International,* April 8, 1978.
2. Ibid.
3. *Screen International,* November 19, 1977.
4. *Screen International,* January 1, 1979.
5. Robert Musel, "Noted Actor Feels Sorrow," *Pennsylvania Reporter.*

Touch of the Sun
(1978)

Credits and Cast

Released September 13, 1979 (Africa only); No known release in Europe or the United States; Color; Released through 20th Century-Fox; Filmed in Zambia. Director: Peter Curran; Producer: Elizabeth Curran; Screenplay: Peter Curran, George Fowler.

Peter Cushing (Potts), Oliver Reed (Nelson), Keenan Wynn (The General), Bruce Boa (Coburn), Sylvaine Charlet (Natasha), Edwin Manda (Emperor Sumooba); with: Melvyn Hayes.

Synopsis

An American space capsule lands—unexpectedly—in central Africa. Emperor Sumooba (Edwin Manda) captures the spacecraft and demands a huge ransom for its return. Lieutenant Nelson (Oliver Reed), the general (Keenan Wynn), and CIA agent Coburn (Bruce Boa) are sent to retrieve it. They learn that the capsule was downed by a sun-powered weapon in a plot engineered by Sumoomba and his aide Natasha (Sylvaine Charlet). Complicating the situation are a diminuitive Tarzan-type (Melvyn Hayes) and Commissioner Potts (Peter Cushing).

Potts is a somewhat confused excolonial official who was left behind at his post when World War II ended. He is, incredibly, unaware that the African states have achieved independence and carries on as before!

Commentary

Touch of the Sun is another of Peter Cushing's "lost films" from the latter part of his career. As far as the authors can determine, the film was never shown in the United States.

Filmed in Zambia, Africa, the production began on June 19, 1978, and was scheduled for an eight-week shoot.[1] Peter Cushing joined the production on July 27. A screening of the film in a rough-cut version was held at the Cannes Film Festival in May 1979 and its premier was announced for Lusaka, Zambia, for October 24. This was to celebrate the nation's fourteenth anniversary of independence.[2]

The actual premier took place on September 13. It was released through 20th Century–Fox in Africa with "other territories open and repped through the William Morris Agency."[3] Apparently, there were no takers, for the film seems not to have surfaced in either America or the United Kingdom.

This comedy-adventure was the first international film to be shot in Zambia and, as such, received a good deal of coverage in the local press. Here is a sampling:

The *Zambia Daily Mail* (July 28, 1978) home news section was headlined, "Top Film Star Jets In" and informed its readers that "Peter Cushing of *Star Wars* and Dracula fame arrived in Lusaka yesterday to join international film stars—Oliver Reed, Keenan Wynn, and Sylvaine Charlet—in the *Touch of the Sun* film which is currently being shot in the country. The 65-year-old actor who has 42 years of acting experience, arrived looking as cheerful as ever and visibly unaffected by the Zambian weather."

The August 5 edition noted that Oliver Reed and Keenan Wynn took part in a charity walk to a raise money for needy Zambian children. Peter Cushing was described as "an international star of *Star Wars*, Frankenstein, and Sherlock Holmes fame."

A publicity handout (August 2) entitled "Cushing in Central Africa" revealed the following:

Peter Cushing is trapped in Zambia in *Touch of the Sun*.

A full grown 450 lb. lion flung itself against its cage bars, bared its inch-long teeth, and snarled deep rumbling warnings as Peter Cushing strode down the steep rocky path close beside it, followed by co-star Oliver Reed.

"I am not afraid of it, with those steel bars between us, but I do hate to see an animal caged," said Cushing, when the cameras stopped turning and he was able to take a chair under a brilliant scarlet poinsettia bush.

Peter Cushing is a retiring personality whose monstrous deeds on the movie screen in Frankenstein films are hard to reconcile with the fragile looking gentleman of 65 who is inclined to describe himself as an old age pensioner from the tiny English seaside village of Whitstable in Kent.

Between takes, Cushing sits quietly alone in his own sea of tranquility and people constantly drift up to talk to this popular though retiring person. Someone says he is looking slightly tanned after a week in Zambia. "I'm afraid not, it's only a little make-up," he smiles.

The quiet Zambian temperament appeals to Cushing, a courteous and unassuming man who finds the local peole gentle, sympathetic, and more inclined to be content without the luxuries of life than their European counterparts.

Peter Cushing just waits for his next call to act as the slightly bush-crazy Potts. He talks of his English garden and his hobbies, but is really interested only in getting back to work and on to the next scene. And on to the next film, about the Arabian Nights, when this one is over.

Edwin Manda, starring as the emperor, was a local actor and singer. In all, over fifty Zambians acted in the film. Location shooting included the Victoria Falls, the Kafue River, and the countryside surrounding Lusaka.

Why the film was never properly released remains a mystery. Adequately budgeted at £1.5 million[4] it boasted an interesting cast and a novel premise. Perhaps it will, like many other little seen films, resurface on video.

Notes

1. *Screen International*, June 1978.
2. *Screen International*, July 1978.
3. *Variety*, September 2, 1979.
4. *Screen International*, July 1978.

Arabian Adventure
(1978)

Credits and Cast

Released November 1979 (U.S.); 98 minutes; Color; Dolby stereo; An EMI–Badger Films Production; Released through Associated Film Distribution (U.S.) and Orion-Columbia (overseas); MPAA G; Filmed at Pinewood Studios, England. Director: Kevin Connor; Producer: John Dark; Screenplay: Brian Hayles; Production supervisor: Graham Easton; Production assistant: Lorraine Fennell; Producer's assistant: Joanna Gunnell; Continuity: Doreen Soan; Director of photography: Alan Hume, B.S.C.; Music: Ken Thorne; Camera operator: Derek Browne; Sound mixer: Dennis Nisbett; Boom operator: John Samworth; Production designer: Elliot Scott; Art director: Jack Maxsted; Set decorator: Terry Ackland-Snow; Scenic artist: Ernest Smith; Special effects supervisor: George Gibbs; Special effects: Richard Conway, David Harris; Matte effects: Cliff Culley; Process projection: Charles Staffell, B.S.C.; Costumes: Rosemary Burrows; Chief makeup: Robin Grantham, Yvonne Coppard; Chief hairdresser: Stella Rivers; Editor: Barry Peters; Dubbing editor: Jim Atkinson; Unit publicist: Catherine O'Brien; Casting: Allan Foenander; Stills: Albert Clarke.

Christopher Lee (Alquazar), Milo O'Shea (Khasim), Oliver Tobias (Prince Hasan), Special Guest Appearances — Peter Cushing (Wazir al Wuzara), Capucine (Vahishta), Mickey Rooney (Daad el Shur). Emma Samms (Princess Zuleira), Puneet Sira (Majeed), John Wyman (Bahloul), John Ratzenberger (Achmed), Shane Rimmer (Abu), Hal Galili (Asaf), Elizabeth Welch (Beggarwoman), Suzanne Danielle (Eastern Dancer), Athar Malik (Mahmoud), Jacob Witkin (Omar the Goldsmith), Milton Reid (Genie), Cengiz Saner (Abdulla), Marcel Steiner

(Ayyub), William Sleigh (Aziz), Andrew Bradford (Ajib), Albin Pahernik (Asham), Stuart Fell (Alvi), Gurdial Sira (Akbar), Dan Long (Cell Guard), Tim Pearce (Zaeed), Benjamin Feitelson (Selim the Waterseller), Omelia Warland (Handmaiden), Michael Watkins (Fruitseller), David Freedman (Ali), Colin Howells (Felah), Bobby Parr (Pulan), Alf Mangan (Sulan), Eddie Tagoe, Sonny Caldinez, Robert Labassiere, Clive Curtis, Danna Amici, Roy Stewart (The Nubians).

Synopsis

> *For her, I'd achieve the impossible!* — Prince Hasan of Bagdad

Hidden in a mountainous region of Arabia lies the troubled city of Jadur which is ruled by the evil wizard, Alquazar (Christopher Lee). Alquazar seeks to become all-powerful but he can only achieve his goal when he possesses the Rose of Elil — whose ultimate powers of magic can make him invincible. However, the only one who can journey to the mythical isle of Elil and pluck the rose is one who is pure of heart.

Alquazar believes he has found such a man when Prince Hasan (Oliver Tobias), the son of the Sultan of Bagdad, arrives in Jadur to seek the hand of the Princess Zuleira (Emma Samms). Alquazar offers her in marriage if the prince can find and bring him back the rose.

Along with an orphaned boy Majeed (Puneet Sira), who journeyed to Jadur in search of a better life, and Alquazar's spy Khasim (Milo O'Shea), sent to double-cross the prince when the rose is located, the three journey to the Isle of Elil on a magic carpet. After many adventures, which include evil genies, mechanical fire-breathing monsters, and horrible swamp creatures who guard the rose in its hidden garden, Majeed obtains the magical flower. The boy also thwarts Khasim's plot to kill the prince and steal the rose for the caliph.

Using the rose's magic, Majeed and Hasan return to Jadur and join forces with those seeking freedom from the tyranny of Alquazar. The evil caliph is ultimately destroyed and Prince Hasan and Princess Juleira, as the new rulers of the city, promise the people of Jadur that they will govern its citizens with wisdom and fairness to all.

Commentary

> *My appearance in* Arabian Adventure *is only that of a "guest star," and although my dear friend Christopher Lee is playing one of the leading parts, we do not meet in the film. I had dinner with him and his family during its making, and it was nice to see them again, and to catch up with his news since last we met.* — Peter Cushing, September 1978

Peter Cushing as the Wazir al Wuzara in the John Dark production, *Arabian Adventure.*

With the box-office success of *At the Earth's Core,* which made the *Variety* list of that year's fifty top-grossing films, producer John Dark and director Kevin Connor began production on yet another collaboration (their fifth), *Arabian Adventure.* In a complete departure from their previous film ventures, Dark and Connor looked to the fairy tales that had emanated from the Middle East centuries ago, using "A Thousand and One Nights" as the basis for their latest vehicle.

Scripted by Brian Hayles, who also wrote the screenplay for *Warlords of Atlantis* and borrowing heavily from earlier screen adaptations, *Arabian Adventure* proved to be enjoyable but only on the most rudimentary of levels. Certainly it was not so much the fault of Dark's and Connor's knowledge of filmmaking, but owing more to their choice of subject matter. The bottom had already been scraped clean with *Arabian Nights* film fare and nearly every major studio had had its day with similar adaptations. There just wasn't any more to add that had not already been done in one form or another. Even the special effects, which promised to be its main draw after the impressive cast, couldn't save this minor, mediocre effort. There is little to commend here.

Primarily geared for the juvenile set, its main stars were eleven-year-old Puneet Sira and a monkey.[1] Emma Samms, then eighteen, was typical window dressing and added very little to the proceedings. Christopher Lee appeared properly bored with the whole thing and looked as though he decided, quite rightly, to take the money and run. Cushing's role as the deposed leader of Jadur, Wazir al Wuzara, was so minute that one wonders why he didn't opt to stay at home and sit this one out completely! It certainly did absolutely nothing for his career and only outraged fans who expected to see more of him than was eventually delivered. After the enormous success of *Star Wars*, it seems a mystery as to why Cushing consented to do this particular film other than out of loyalty to Dark, Connor, and Lee. His character is devoid of any substance and leaves one with the impression that it was thrown in at the last minute and could have just as easily been eliminated had Cushing been unable to appear due to a prior commitment.

There are two minor points of trivia concerning *Arabian Adventure*. The first deals with supporting cast member John Ratzenberger, who went on to become a regular cast member on the NBC television sit-com "Cheers." The other was the return of Milton Reid, a Hammer alumni, who appeared as the evil genie.

Critics were fairly uniform in their observations. The *New York Times* reviewer Vincent Canby (November 21, 1979) called it "a sweet-spirited, bargain-basement variation on the sort of film that reached its peak of splendor in 1940 with Alexander Korda's *The Thief of Bagdad*." In *Variety* "Pit" (May 30, 1979) astutely called it "*Star Wars* with flying carpets in lieu of space ships. . . . The action is strickly stagebound and looks it, but the kids will lap up the gaudy settings." In *Cinefantastique* Dan Scapperotti (volume 9, number 2) noted that "Flying carpets, fire-breathing monsters, a murderous genie, an evil wizard, an enchanted island, and a magic mirror fail to save *Arabian Adventure* from being just another routine kiddie matinee feature.... Peter Cushing, in a cameo appearance as the imprisoned deposed leader of Jadur, [is] in fine form." And the British *Daily Telegraph* reviewer, Patrick Gibbs, reported in the July 20, 1979 edition, "Kevin Connor's *Arabian Adventure* appears to take a number of elements from the Arabian Nights tales such as flying carpets and a jewel which works wonders for its owner and hope they will integrate into something exciting and comprehensible ... a muddled tale of the middle ages in, presumably, the Middle East."

In addition to *Arabian Adventure*, Peter also provided the voice-over narration for director Rodney Holland's thirty-three-minute film short entitled *The Detour*. Shot entirely on the Mediterranean island of Malta, Holland's 35mm featurette was privately financed by several local residents and cost approximately $60,000 to produce.

Holland described his film as "an occult thriller" which concerns the adventures of a twelve-year-old boy named Dominic (John Galdes) and his pet pharaoh hound, Rameses, whom the boy learns bears an uncanny resemblance to effigies of the ancient Egyptian dog-headed god, Anubis — Guardian of the Dead.

Other cast members for the Barkarow production included Narcy Calamatta, a local Maltese television personality, and British actor and stage director, Adrian Rendle.

The technical team assembled for the film included editor Tony Lawson, art director and cowriter John Branston, director of photogrpahy Ivan Strasburg, second unit cameraman Richard Day, executive producer Jeremy Holland (Rodney's brother), and featured a musical score written specifically for the film by Adrian Wagner, the great-great-grandson of composer Richard Wagner.

Note

1. Ernest Leogrande, *New York Daily News* (November 21, 1979), aptly observed that "Puneet Sira, as the focal character ... makes Sabu look like a torrent of emotion. The monkey is a champ scene stealer."

Mystery on Monster Island
(1980)

Credits and Cast

Released April 1981; 100 minutes; Eastman color; Dinavision; A Fort Films-Almena Films (U.S., Spain) Production; Released through 20th Century–Fox (U.S.);

Filmed in Puerto Rico, Canary Islands, and Spain. Director and producer: Juan Piquer Simon; Associate producers: Tonio Moi, Jose Barby; Production executive: Francisco Ariza; Production Consultant: Dick Randall; Screenplay: J. Grau, J. Piquer, R. Gantman; Based on the novel by Jules Verne, *Robinson's School*; Music: Alfonso Agullo; Director of photography: Andre Berenguer; Visual effects, production design: Emilio Ruiz; Art director: Gumet Andres; Costume design: Toni Pueo; Sound: George Stevenson; Camera: Ricardo Navarrete; Mechanical effects: Basilio Cortijo; Models: Gonzalo Gonzalo; Makeup: Pedro Camacho; Horsemaster: Miguel Pedregosa.

Terence Stamp (Taskinar), Peter Cushing (Kolderup), Ian Serra (Jeff), David Hatton (Mr. Artelett), Gasphar Ipva (Carefinotu), Blanca Estrada (Dominique), Ana Obregon (Meg), Frank Brana (Birling), Gerald Tichy (Captain Turkot), Daniel Martin (Croft), Luis Barboo (Stanton), Manuel Pereiro (Kraus), George Bosso (Brown), Ioshio Murakami (Sehng-Wu), Paul Naschy (Flint).

Synopsis

> *I can assure you it will be a trip you will never forget.* — William Kolderup

A group of cutthroats, including Flint (Paul Naschy), find a cache of gold on a tropical island. A battle ensues and one of the men ignites a box of explosives. The force of the explosion causes a lava eruption which covers the gold and kills all but one of the men.

He is rescued by the crew of a three-master and is brought to his employer — Taskinar (Terence Stamp). The wounded man tells of the incidents on the island before dying. Disgusted at the loss of the gold, Taskinar sets sail for San Francisco, but vows to return.

In San Francisco, America's richest man — William Kolderup (Peter Cushing), outbids Taskinar at an auction. The prize — the mysterious island. The price — $5 million.

At his estate, Kolderup makes plans to announce the engagement of his young nephew Jeff (Ian Serra) and Meg (Ana Obregon). Jeff, however, is unsure of the marriage. He wants to experience adventure and make his own way — not as Kolderup's nephew — before marriage. Meg and Kolderup agree.

Kolderup arranges for Jeff and his teacher, Mr. Artelett (David Hatton) to cruise the world on *The Dream*, part of Kolderup's fleet. Observing the departure, with a sneer, is Taskinar.

On the ship Jeff begins to show evidence of his impending adulthood when he stands up to the captain (Gerald Tichy) who wants to throw Sehng-Wu (Ioshio Murakami), a stowaway, overboard. He is tested again when a dense fog envelopes the ship and the crew is found murdered. As

Jeff and Artelett peer over the railing, they are suddenly attacked by a group of manlike fish monsters. To make matters worse (if possible) *The Dream* is on fire. Jeff and Artelett jump overboard and are washed up on the shore of the mystery island.

The castaways soon find a third person—the beautiful Dominique (Blanca Estrada). They are then joined by a fourth. Carefinotu (Gasphar Ipva) has escaped from cannibals and is a valuable addition to the group. Their survival skills are tested when they are attacked by a huge prehistoric monster. Complicating an already complicated situaton are a group of hooded men and Jeff's discovery of the gold.

The hooded band captures the castaways and threatens to kill them unless Jeff tells them the whereabouts of the gold. A nearby volcano erupts, creating a diversion, and the castaways escape.

Jeff is in for an even greater shock when Carefinotù makes a startling confession. He was hired by Kolderup to play the part of a castaway, and the monsters and explosions are mechanical devices, contrived to test Jeff's manhood. But the hooded men were not part of the plan.

As prearranged, Kolderup and Meg arrive in the supposedly destroyed *Dream* and are reunited with an angry Jeff. His anger dissolves when Kolderup explains that the dangers—although false—were real to Jeff and he faced them bravely. As Jeff realizes the truth of Kolderup's remark, they are attacked by the hooded thugs. Their leader is Taskinar.

After capturing the castaways and crew of *The Dream*, Taskinar reveals that he plans to kill them all for the gold—all of them but Dominique, who is in league with Taskinar. They are saved, however, by a convenient explosion staged by Sehng-Wu, and Jeff is ready to return to San Francisco to marry Meg.

Commentary

Despite many criticisms one could level, *Mystery on Monster Island* is rather enjoyable, even if one feels a bit guilty afterward.

The driving force behind the film was producer-director-author Juan Piquer Simon. He adapted Jules Verne's novel, *Robinson's School*, for the screenplay—a rather unlikely title! He had previously adapted the same author's famous *Journey to the Center of the Earth* for a 1976 film, *Where Time Began*.

Location filming in Puerto Rico, Spain, and the Canary Islands adds immeasurably to the rather slight story. The Victorian costumes and San Francisco sets are convincing, giving the film a quality look that is rather surprising. The press book claims an eighteen-week shooting schedule which, judging from the results, seems accurate.

The film's main drawbacks are the awkward — very awkward — "comedy" scenes with David Hatton and the less than inspired acting of young Ian Serra. The monsters are initially disappointing and fake looking, which is exactly the point. One is left feeling a bit embarrassed in criticizing the effects after the truth is learned at the film's conclusion.

Old pros Terence Stamp and Peter Cushing are excellent, but offscreen for the rather long middle section of the film. Their confrontations at the beginning and end are probably the best moments. Cushing, as usual, looks and acts like a Victorian gentleman — in this case the richest man in America. His delivery of Kolderup's speech to his nephew about accepting adult responsibilities is quite moving and seems too realistic for a basically silly film like *Mystery on Monster Island.*

Terence Stamp plays the evil Taskinar with just the right touch of glee and villainy and makes the viewer wish he was given more screen time.

Veteran European horror star Paul Naschy could hardly have had less screen time — he is killed off in the opening sequence — making one wonder why he was cast at all.

Variety (April 4, 1980) liked the film, calling it an "Entertaining action filled treatment of the Jules Verne yarn . . . it's good fun, and pic should appeal to a wide range of audiences."

Peter Cushing's real triumph of the year — and decade — in the Hallmark Hall of Fame production for television of "A Tale of Two Cities" went typically unnoticed. This superb production starring Chris Sarandon (as both Charles Darnay and Syndey Carton) is, to the authors' tastes, the best version of the Dicken's classic. As Dr. Manette, unjustly imprisoned in the Bastille, Peter Cushing delivers an outstanding performance, leaving one stunned at the lack of critical response in the United States.

Fortunately, the British were more responsive. When asked why his work in theatrical films was dwindling, Cushing replied, "I just didn't like the films I was being offered. Most of it was pure pornography. And also, there hasn't been a great deal happening here. Of course, one has to go where the work is, which is abroad, mostly. But I prefer England. I've always loved this country and always will."[1]

Commenting on the story, Peter Cushing said, "This sort of thing is very difficult to do because Dickens was a very verbose writer and he devoted a whole chapter to the gallows scene. On screen, it lasts one minute."

When informed that the production would soon be leaving for a two-week location shoot in Paris, Cushing was not enthralled. "I'm not looking forward to that. . . . I'm always miserable away from home. I would much rather spend the summer by the seaside at my cottage."

Discussing his role as Dr. Manette, Peter Cushing gave some insight into his career.

> I'm the goodie in "A Tale of Two Cities." But, you know, I've rarely played anything else.... We've had no rehearsal time.... You seldom have the luxury of read throughs with the whole cast. Film is such a spontaneous medium, whereas in the theatre you rely on rehearsals. I love the theatre, but I don't think I would have the energy to do it now. It's ironic, but the repetition would be too much for me. People are often surprised that since I played the Grand Moff Tarkin in a cult film like *Star Wars* that the fan letters don't come from younger audiences. I still get the same ones from people who remember me from the old Hammer films.

Peter Cushing finished the year, strangely enough, with one last role for Hammer. The studio, now little more than a name, was no longer headed by the Carreras family. The new regime (Brian Lawrence and Roy Skeggs) moved into television production with "The Hammer House of Horror." Cushing appeared as a less than beneign pet store owner in "The Silent Scream."

Note

1. Peter Cushing, interview with Mike Mann, *Photoplay*, October 1980.

Black Jack
(1981)

Credits and Cast

No official release; A Diffusion sa Production/Cinespaña; Director: Max Boulois; Screenplay: Max Boulois; Director of photography: Domingo Solano.

Peter Cushing, Claudine Auger, Hugo Stiglitz, Max Boulois, Brian Murphy, Fernando Sancho, Eduardo Fajardo, Jose Bodalo, Andres Resino.

Commentary

Black Jack has proven the most difficult of Peter Cushing's films to research. It was almost certainly never theatrically released in America or the United Kingdom (or, probably, anywhere else). A search of *Screen*

International magazine proved fruitless, as did a letter of inquiry to the production company. It simply seems to have vanished without a proper release.

Variety (May 13, 1981) reported that *Black Jack* would be screened at the Cannes Festival on May 18–21 to attract potential distributors. One can guess its reception.

Peter Cushing received top billing in a cast that included only Claudine Auger as a recognizable (to American or British audiences) name. This, naturally, did not help the film's chances.

Max Boulois apparently failed in an Orson Welles–like gambit as actor, director, and writer. His film may have had a European release, since it was filmed in Spain with a mostly Spanish cast. It could even resurface on a Spanish language television station or on video. However, since it is now over ten years since the film was made, this is unlikely.

Peter Cushing has no idea what happened to *Black Jack*. He recalls very little since his stint on the film only took a few days and he probably never saw it in its edited form. He does not mention it (other than listing it in his filmography) in either of his two volumes of autobiography.

The artwork in the *Variety* advertisement leads one to believe that the plot involved a casino robbery. If so, there have certainly been more than enough plots on that line and one wonders why they bothered.

Peter Cushing is pictured in a tuxedo — looking very dapper — at a black jack table. Sadly, that is all we can give you. We tried, but . . . .

House of the Long Shadows
(1982)

Credits and Cast

Released 1982; A Golan-Globus Production; Released by the Cannon Group. Director: Peter Walker; Producers: Menahem Golan, Yoram Globus; Screenplay: Michael Armstrong; Based on Earl D. Bigger's novel *Seven Keys to Baldpate* and George M. Cohan's stage production; Director of photography: Norman Langley; Music: Richard Harvey; Editor: Robert Dearberg; Art director: Mike Pickwood; Makeup: George Partleton; Camera: John Simmonds; Production manager: Jeanne Ferber; Sound: Peter O'Connor; Wardrobe: Polly Hamilton, Alan Flying.

Vincent Price (Lionel Grisbane), Christopher Lee (Corrigan), Peter Cushing (Sebastian Grisbane), John Carradine (Lord Grisbane), Desi Arnaz, Jr. (Kenneth Magee), Sheila Keith (Victoria Grisbane), Julie Peasgood (Mary Norton), Richard Todd (Sam Allyson), Louise English (Diana), Richard Hunter (Andrew), Norman Rossington (Stationmaster).

Synopsis

I've never been a particularly courageous man and the events of
this evening have been most distressing. —Sebastian Grisbane

American author Kenneth Magee (Desi Arnaz, Jr.), a rather shallow, self-satisfied young man, accepts a wager from his English publisher Sam Allyson (Richard Todd). Kenneth claims that he can write a Gothic novel in twenty-four hours—a better one than *Wuthering Heights*. At stake is $20,000.

Sam suggests that Kenneth write the novel in the seclusion of Baldpate Manor, located in an isolated section of Wales. The manor has been empty for forty years.

Somewhere in Wales, Kenneth stops for directions at a railway station. Inside are a young couple—Diane (Louise English) and Andrew (Richard Hunter)—on vacation. As they chat, a strange old woman enters—and leaves—mysteriously.

After getting accurate directions from the stationmaster (Norman Rossington), Kenneth arrives at the manor and begins his novel. Investigating the large house, he is startled by the sudden appearance of Victoria (Sheila Keith), and her father, Elijah (John Carradine)—the caretakers. As Kenneth explains his presence, he spots the old woman from the station skulking through the house. She is unmasked—literally—as Catherine (Julie Peasgood), a beautiful young girl.

Catherine warns Kenneth that he is in danger from a terrorist organization, but he refuses to believe it. His feelings are justified when he discovers that Catherine is really Mary Norton—Sam's secretary. He also learns that there are no caretakers.

As Mary is leaving to find a hotel, she encounters Sebastian (Peter Cushing), who explains that he has stopped for shelter. Kenneth is becoming suspicious.

The next apparition is Lionel Grisbane (Vincent Price), who voices his displeasure when Kenneth interrupts his soliloquy. Lionel is a former owner of the manor, recently returned from America.

While inspecting some paintings, Kenneth and Mary learn the truth—the quartet are a family, reunited after a long separation. But there is one portrait missing.

Enter Mr. Corrigan (Christopher Lee), who is the new owner of the manor. Corrigan reveals that he is going to tear down the house and build an industrial development. He also wants the Grisbanes to hold their reunion elsewhere.

As the evening wears on, Kenneth learns the secret of the Grisbanes. In 1939 young Roderick destroyed the family when he viciously attacked

Peter Cushing in *House of the Long Shadows.*

a pregnant girl. The family passed judgment on Roderick—he has been sealed in his room for forty years. The family separated after the murder, but has now rejoined to free Roderick.

When they enter the room, Roderick is gone! Elijah suffers a heart attack and dies from the shock.

Corrigan finds Diane and Andrew outside and brings them into the house as the problems begin to multiply. Victoria is found dead—her throat slit by a piano wire. Diane, after a nasty argument with Andrew, goes upstairs and washes her face—with acid. Andrew chokes to death on poisoned wine and, during a search for Roderick, the hysterial Sebastian is found hanged. Needless to say, Kenneth has written little.

Events take another turn for the worse when Corrigan announces that he is, in fact, Roderick and that Lionel actually killed the pregnant girl. This night is to be Roderick's revenge. This said, Roderick hacks Lionel to death with an axe.

Kenneth attacks Roderick and kicks him down a flight of stairs. Narrowly missing being beheaded, Roderick dies, impaled on his axe.

Suddenly, the previously killed "houseguests" return to life to everyone's amusement—including Mary. Especially amused is Sam, who appears, chuckling, on the balcony.

Later, at Sam's victory party, "Roderick" and "Lionel" insult each other, as "Victoria" congratulates "Sebastian's" hysterical behavior. All concerned are, in reality, actors hired by Sam to prevent Kenneth from writing the novel. Kenneth accepts his humiliation with style.

He admits that he has learned a valuable lesson and plans to abandon the trash he has been writing and produce a truly good novel.

Back at Baldpate, dawn has broken as Kenneth finishes his Gothic mystery. As he collects his check from Sam in a posh restaurant, he confesses that even with his story's twist ending, it seemed real and he enjoyed the experience.

As he leaves the restaurant, he tears up the check and meets Mary Jameson, Sam's "real" secretary. They leave together, passing a waiter with a more than passing resemblance to Lionel Grisbane.

Commentary

Following in the tradition of *House of Frankenstein* (1944), *House of the Long Shadows* proves the law of diminishing returns: the more horror stars in one movie, the less one enjoys each performance. There are usually few enough good parts in the average horror film to warrant the "all-star" approach, and this is no exception. When you've got four stars, someone—if not everyone—gets short-changed. Of course, it's nice to see your favorites together, but...

The plot is actually a revamping of an old comedy thriller, *Seven Keys to Baldpate* by Earl Derr Biggers (creator of fictional detective Charlie Chan) and dramatized by the legendary George M. Cohan. Of the many film versions, the best known are a 1917 silent with Cohan, a sound version (1929) with Richard Dix, and its 1947 remake with Phillip Terry. There have, of course, been many variations that do not credit the source novel.

"We've all worked together before," said Vincent Price of his three costars, "but never as a foursome. It was sort of a joyful class reunion. This isn't a horror movie. Today's horror films are just too far out and gruesome for people like us. This is an old-fashioned thriller."[1]

Christopher Lee agreed. "There's nothing subtle about an axe falling onto somebody's face. There is nothing left to the imagination of the audience."[2]

The thrills are indeed there, but one is somehow left expecting more. Perhaps the producers felt that audiences of the 1980s would not accept a straight Gothic thriller and camped up the plot a bit more than necessary.

Vincent Price immediately established the film's tone in his first appearance when he asks not to be interrupted while soliloquizing. His performance parodies his image established in the Roger Corman–Poe series of the 1960s which, to some critics, were parodies themselves.

Christopher Lee, as one might expect, plays things a bit straighter and delivers the film's best performance. Norman Langley's photography often catches him looking, strangely enough, like Dracula.

John Carradine has the least to do of the four stars and makes only a slight impression on the viewer. He, like his younger costars, bemoaned the current state of the horror film when compared to the old days. "When we did them, we had good actors, good scripts and good sets."[3]

Peter Cushing's role as Sebastian was amusingly written and performed. Sebastian is a self-admitted coward, and it's quite a treat to see Cushing cringing for a change. At the film's conclusion, Sheila Keith (as Victoria) congratulates Sebastian on his phony emotional breakdown. "I can see why you were always known as Waterworks," she says. Cushing replies, "Some called me the Big Drip."

Playing the pivotal role of author Kenneth Magee was Desi Arnaz, Jr. He is quite good and more than holds his own with the old pros. Arnaz shared his experiences with the authors.

> I grew up watching Peter Cushing as the hero in Dracula movies where he represented the forces of good winning over evil. When I finally met him during the filming, he exemplified goodness in that he was very polite, had a good sense of humor, and was very supportive of me.
>
> I enjoyed listening to Mr. Cushing and Mr. Lee tell stories about the making of the Dracula movies in which they played arch-enemies but in real life were the closest of friends.
>
> Another aspect of his character that I will always admire is this—he never wasted words but when he did speak it was always something worth listening to. I liked him very much and am thankful I had the opportunity to work with and learn from him.

Variety (June 24, 1983) felt that the film "could have been scarier, wittier and more mocking." Leslie Halliwell opined that it was "too restricted in script and production to be really effective" while *The Guardian* called it "a horror flick which basks in the Hammer tradition without in any way understanding it."

Notes

1. Cannon publicity release.
2. Ibid.
3. Ibid.

Sword of the Valiant
(1982)

Credits and Cast

Released 1984; 110 minutes; Fujicolor; A Cannon–Golan Globus Production; Released through Cannon; Filmed in Ireland. Director: Stephen Weeks; Producers: Menahem Golan, Yoran Globus; Executive producers: Michael Kagan, Philip Breen; Screenplay: Stephen Weeks, based on ancient legends; Director of photography: Freddie Young; Editor: Richard Marder; Music: Ron Geesin; Sound: George Stephenson; Production design: Maurice Fowler; Set design: Val Wolstenholme; Costume design: Shuna Harwood; Action sequences: Anthony Squire; Special effects: Nobby Clarke.

Miles O'Keefe (Gawain), Cynelle Claire (Linet), Leigh Lawson (Humphrey), Sean Connery (The Green Knight), Trevor Howard (Arthur), Peter Cushing (Seneschal), Ronald Lacey (Oswald), Lila Kedrova (Lady of Lyonese), John Rhys Davies (Fortinbras), Douglas Wilmer (The Black Knight), Brian Coburn (Vosper), Emma Sutton (Morgan la Fay), Bruce Liddington (Sir Bertilak), Wilfred Bramwell (Porter).

Synopsis

She should be worth a pretty . . . a very pretty ransom. — Seneschal

At a Christmas celebration King Arthur (Trevor Howard) bemoans the general lack of courage and daring among his knights. His fears are proven to be justified with the sudden arrival of the Green Knight (Sean Connery) who wishes to play a deadly game.

Any knight who dares may have one swing of the axe at the head of the Green Knight. Should he fail to behead his victim, the roles will be reversed. When there are no takers, the aged king accepts the challenge to preserve the honor of Camelot. Suddenly, Gawain (Miles O'Keefe), a squire, accepts the challenge. In gratitude Arthur knights the young man.

Gawain delivers a powerful blow to the Green Knight, cutting his head from his body. But, magically, the Green Knight replaces it upon his shoulders.

The Green Knight is not without sympathy and, noting the young man's courage, decides to spare him — for a year. At that time he will return to end the game. He also gives Gawain an out — if he can decipher the meaning of a mysterious riddle, the debt will be canceled.

Accompanied by Humphrey (Leigh Lawson), Gawain goes in search of the meaning of the riddle, and of life itself. His travels lead him into many adventures as he encounters the Black Knight (Douglas Wilmer), the evil sorceress Morgan (Emma Sutton), and, in the magical city of Lyonese, the beautiful Linet (Cynelle Claire).

His most dangerous encounter, however, is with the depraved Oswald (Ronald Lacey) and the more sophisticated but equally dangerous Seneschal (Peter Cushing). The two decide to abduct Linet, with whom Gawain has fallen in love.

Oswald is the son of the powerful Fortinbras (John Rhys Davies) and Seneschal plans to place Linet's fate in the absent ruler's hands.

When Fortinbras returns to his castle, an argument is raging with Sir Bertilak (Bruce Liddington) over some disputed land. The crafty Seneschal offers Linet in exchange for the land.

Unknown to Linet, Gawain has infiltrated the castle and, with the help of Friar Vosper (Brian Coburn), attempts to rescue her.

Unfortunately, the drunken Oswald gets to her first. As he enters her tower prison, he accidentally sets a fire which, apparently, kills them both.

Gawain discovers that Linet has been saved by Bertilak and, with her help, prepares for his fast approaching encounter with the Green Knight, with only half of the riddle solved. After killing Oswald — who survived the fire with horrible burns — Gawain goes with the Green Knight to meet his fate.

When the Green Knight delivers the death blow, he is distracted by a sash that Linet presented to Gawain and misses the target. In the ensuing battle, Gawain is victorious, reducing the Green Knight to dust. With the knowledge gained from his experiences, Gawain now knows the riddle's meaning.

Gawain and Linet are reunited, but she tells him that they must part — her place is at Lyonese. Before Gawain's startled eyes, she transforms into a bird and flies off.

Commentary

If you think that Sean Connery is incapable of pulling off a role in which his skin is painted green and his beard adorned with branches and sequins, think again. Unfortunately, the main (if not the only) reason to see this lackluster film is to take in Connery's commanding presence.

The physical aspects of *Sword of Valiant* are fine, and the supporting cast, in addition to Sean Connery, is populated with some fine actors. What prevents the film from being enjoyable is the incredibly episodic script and the lead actor, Miles O'Keefe.

O'Keefe is certainly up to the physical action required of him, but he lacks the panache needed for such a role. To be fair, Errol Flynn in his prime probably could not have saved the film, and Miles O'Keefe is miles from Errol Flynn.

The long wait to see Peter Cushing could be much better spent by doing practically anything else and, when he finally appears, the rewards are limited. Cushing's role is poorly defined and sketchily written, and even he is unable to do anything with it. His purpose is simply to advance the plot (such as it is) by kidnapping the heroine, and he plays it as well as it could be played.

He manages to create some tension in a well-acted scene in which Ronald Lacey (as Oswald) is firmly put in his place, but that is about the extent of his performance that is worth noting.

It is unfortunate that Peter Cushing was unable to find better roles in better films during this period. The simple truth is there are simply not an abundance of parts written for men of Cushing's age. Even in the wake of *Star Wars*, Peter Cushing accepted roles in only eleven theatrical films. One can only wonder about those he turned down.

Stephen Weeks, who directed Peter Cushing in the ill-fated *I, Monster*, was not pleased with the film's distribution. An April 5, 1989, article in *Variety* revealed that "Stephen Weeks and his production company have sued the Cannon Group for falsely reporting revenues from distribution of the film *Sword of the Valiant* and failing to adequately promote and distribute it. Weeks and Stephen Weeks Company Ltd. claimed their damages are in excess of $750,000."

Sword of the Valiant is not a worthless film, and it does have several things to recommend it. It's filled with action sequences that play rather well, and more or less convincingly recreates the period of King Arthur's court. And, can any film with Sean Connery, Trevor Howard, and Peter Cushing be all bad?

Variety (December 5, 1989) called it "a fanciful but uneven retelling of the Arthurian legend of Sir Gawain and the Green Knight, previously made by the same director (in an unrelated 1972 film). Cannon production and release boasts an impressive cast but is unlikely to turn on contemporary audiences. Special effects are cutesy and not up to current standards."

Top Secret
(1983)

Credits and Cast

Released 1984; 90 minutes; Metrocolor; An Abrahams-Zucker-Zucker Production; Released through Paramount. Directors: Jim Abrahams, David Zucker, Jerry Zucker; Producers: Jon Davison, Hunt Lowry; Screenplay: Jim Abrahams, David Zucker, Jerry Zucker; Director of photography: Christopher Challis; Editor: Richard Gribble; Music: Maurice Jarre; Sound: Derek Bali; Art director: John Fenner; Costumes: Emma Porteous; Choreography: Gillian Gregory; Special effects: Nick Atlder; Special music: Stuart Freeborn; Stunts: Joe Powell.

Omar Sharif (Cedric), Jeremy Kemp (General Streck), Lucy Gutteridge (Hilary), Val Kilmer (Nick Rivers), Peter Cushing (Proprietor), Michael Gough (Dr. Flammond), Warren Clarke (Colonel Van Herst), Tristam Jellinek (Major Crumpler), Billy J. Mitchell (Martin), Jim Carter (Deja Vu), Major Wiley (Porter), Gertan Klauber (Mayor), Richard Mayes (Biletnikov), Vyvyan Lorrayne (Madame Berger-one), Nancy Abrahams (Pregnant Woman), Ian MacNeice (Blind Man), John Sharp (Maitre d'), Harry Ditson (Du Quois), Eddie Tagoe (Chocolate Mousse), Christopher Villiers (Nigel).

Synopsis

?uoy pleh I yaM — Bookstore Proprieter

A famous American rock star, Nick Rivers (Val Kilmer), goes to East Germany as a guest at a cultural festival. The festival, however, is a blind to divert the world's attention from a political takeover of West Germany by General Streck (Jeremy Kemp).

Dr. Flammond (Michael Gough), a famous scientist, has been imprisoned by the general and is being blackmailed to create a secret weapon to aid in the takeover. If he refuses, his daughter Hilary (Lucy Gutteridge), will be killed.

As Hilary tries to find and free her father, Cedric (Omar Sharif), a British agent, fails at the same task in a rather bizarre manner—he is crushed inside his car into a cube three feet high!

Nick and Hilary meet by chance in a restaurant and are attracted to each other. He decides to join forces with her to save her father. They are helped by a bookstore proprieter (Peter Cushing) to find the local resistance members. This rather surly group is made up of Du Quois (Harry Ditson), Deja Vu (Jim Carter), and Chocolate Mousse (Eddie Tagoe). Their leader is Nigel (Christopher Villiers), a former lover of Hilary.

After many ludicrous adventures (including an attack by surfers and an underwater western-style bar fight), the resistance group parachutes

into the prison and rescues Dr. Flammond. With Nick and Hilary, he
boards a plane to freedom.

Commentary

In 1980 the team of Zucker, Abrahams, and Zucker broke up audiences and broke new ground in screen comedy with *Airplane!* Using a
style of anything for a laugh — reminiscent of the early Woody Allen — the
film spoofed practically everything and was a worldwide success.

Four years later the same style was used to destroy several other film
clichés — the spy drama and the rock and roll musical.

As anyone who has seen it can attest, it is pointless to discuss the plot,
which is either nonexistent or incomprehensible. There is no specific
time frame — World War II and Elvis-style rock and roll occur simultan-
eously. The jokes — both verbal and visual — are delivered in hit-and-miss
style with machine-gun rapidity. If off-the-wall humor is your thing, it's excellent. If not, well . . .

Two newcomers, Val Kilmer and Lucy Gutteridge, are perfect as the
leads. Kilmer, only twenty-four, has the aplomb of a veteran and pulls off
his ridiculous role in style. Gutteridge plays it straighter with equal results.
But it was not their performances that most audiences were interested
in — the main attraction was to see Omar Sharif, Michael Gough, and Peter
Cushing make fools of themselves.

Peter Cushing appears in the obligatory scene in spy films in which
a "contact" is made to gain information (and clue the audience in as to
what is going on). Suffice it to say that the audience, watching this scene,
is not enlightened to any degree.

When first seen, Cushing is looking through a magnifying glass which
distorts his eye — reminding one of a similar scene in *The Curse of Frankenstein.* When the glass is lowered, his eye remains gigantic! This brilliant
bit is followed by a scene in which Peter Cushing and the young stars
acted . . . backward.

"Forewards, backwards, sideways, it's all the same to me," said Peter
Cushing. "I've done so many pictures by now that I just try to do what's
asked of me to the best of my abilities and trust that all is well. My scene
in *Top Secret!* was a very interesting exercise in technique and I enjoyed
it very much."[1]

Although the scene itself is very funny, the events that followed are
not. Peter Cushing developed severe pain in his eye that he assumed was
a reaction to the makeup.

"I thought it was just an oversized stye," Cushing recalled, "very painful. So I lay down — I put some Optrex in it and lay down on the couch

hoping it would go away, but it didn't. And the next thing I knew I was being carted off to Kent and Canterbury Hospital. They diagnosed that I had cancer of the prostate gland which is also affecting this eye. My dear secretary's [Joyce Broughton] husband rang up the doctor and said, 'How long do you give him?' 'A year, eighteen months at the outside.' That was 1982 and I wasn't told this until six months later—and I had never felt better in my life."[2]

Peter Cushing, through the courage and iron will he had so often portrayed on screen, beat the odds. Since his victory over cancer he has been "a bit tired now and unfortunately I can't work as much as I would like to."[3]

Due to his physical condition, he was forced to withdraw from Tyburn's *The Abbot's Cry*—a Sherlock Holmes film. With typical modesty, he gives as the reason, "I think I would let everyone down, including myself."[4]

Peter Cushing's lone television appearance during 1983 was an excellently—and humorously—played cameo as Professor Copeland, Helen Keller's writing instructor in "Helen Keller—The Miracle Continues." This 20th Century–Fox production for American television was known in England as "Helen and Teacher."

Notes

1. *Top Secret!* press kit.
2. "Peter Cushing—A One-Way Ticket to Hollywood," a Tyburn Production for BBC Television, 1989.
3. Ibid.
4. Ibid.

Biggles—Adventures in Time
(1985)

Credits and Cast

Released 1986 (U.K.), January 29, 1988 (U.S.); 108 minutes; Color; A Compact-Yellowbill Film in association with Tambarle; Released (U.S.) by New Century–Vista; Filmed on location in and around London and at Pinewood Studios. Director: John Hough; Producers: Kent Walwin, Pom Oliver; Executive producer: Adrian Scrope; Director of photography: Ernest Vincze, B.S.C.; Production designer; Terry Pritchard; Music by Stanislas; Editor: Richard Trevor; Coexecutive producer: Paul Barnes-Taylor; Screenplay: Kent Walwin, John Groves;

Based on characters created by Captain W. E. Jones; Song "So You Wanna Be a Hero" sung by Jon Anderson; Associate producer: John O'Connor; Makeup: Eddie Knight; Production manager: Sally Shewring; Production Coordinator: Christine Fenton; Location finder: Martin Bruce-Clayton; Script supervisor: Lorely Farley; Lighting cameraman: Ernest Vincze; Camera operator: Neil Binney; Focus: Martin Testar; Second unit director-cameraman: Terry Cole; Clapper loader: Terry Nightingall; Grip: Nick Pearson; Production buyer: Leslie Fulford; Assistant art director: Peta Bietton; Art dept. Assistant: Christopher Townsend; Storyboard artist: Denis Rich; Sound mixer: Peter Pardo; Sound recordist: Stan Haines; Sound recordist (second unit): Dan Grimmel; Assistant editor: Hazel Harste; Costume designer: Jim Acheson; Wardrobe: Barry Bristow; Hairdresser: Tricia Cameron; Property master: Arthur Wicks; Supervisor special effects: David Harris; Stills photographer: John Brown; First assistant director: Peter Cotton.

Neil Dickson (Biggles), Alex Hyde-White (James Ferguson), Fiona Hutchison (Debbie Stevens), Peter Cushing (Captain William Raymond), Marcus Gilbert (Eric Von Stalhein), William Hootkins (Chuck), Alan Polonsky (Bill), Francesca Gonshaw (Maria), Michael Siberry (Algy), James Saxon (Bertie), Daniel Flynn (Ginger).

Synopsis

> *Time Travel is not unknown in history. There's evidence that it happens more often than anyone suspects!* — Air Commander William Raymond

Jim Ferguson (Alex Hyde-White), president of Celebrity Dinners, is visited in his home by a well-dressed elderly gentleman who asks him some strange questions about his current well-being and if anything out of the ordinary had recently occurred. Jim is immediately suspicious of the mysterious man and excuses himself. Returning to the living room, Ferguson is in the process of preparing a speech for the company's latest line of frozen dinners when suddenly he finds himself transported to a World War I battlefield. There, amid the heat of battle, he meets Biggles (Neil Dickson) — a World War I flying ace and spy for the British government.

As mysteriously as he found himself in another time and place, Ferguson finds himself transported back to his own time. Jim goes to London and once again meets with the elderly man whom he had encountered earlier, retired Air Commander William Raymond (Peter Cushing). Ferguson learns that he and Biggles are what Raymond terms "Time Twins" and that he is fated to meet Biggles from time to time — especially in periods of great personal stress. Raymond cannot fully explain or understand why the phenomenon occurs. Raymond asks Jim to try to come to grips with his extraordinary experiences and to assist Biggles any way he can. He tells Jim that the future depends on his cooperation. Shortly after his visit,

Former Royal Flying Corps' Commander William Raymond in John Hough's
Biggles – Adventures in Time.

Ferguson is once again back in time when he gets caught up in the flying
ace's adventures—both in the early twentieth century and in his own
time.

Biggles' mission is to obtain information concerning the Germans'
latest secret weapon. He discovers that the device has the power to use
high sound frequency levels to disrupt the molecular structure of matter,
turning its intended target into dust.

With the help of a police helicopter (which Biggles refers to as a "flying windmill") hijacked by the two daredevils in the present time, Biggles
returns to the past. Using the copter's built-in PA system, he bounces the
sound waves created by the weapon back onto the device and successfully
destroys it and the facility housing the machine. Biggles returns to his out-
fit a hero, and Ferguson returns to the future, but his adventures with Biggles are not quite over.

Commentary

"Biggles" was a member of the Old Royal Flying Corps during World War I, before it became the Royal Air Force. . . . I play his commanding officer as he looks today. My character is described as "young 80." I thought: "Well, thank you for the young!" —Peter Cushing[1]

W. E. John's fictional hero, James Biggleworth—the subject of nearly 100 books—had originally been a Disney project as far back as 1980 with Dudley Moore being considered for the title role. However, Disney's plans never materialized and Biggles went into a sort of limbo until 1985 when Compact-Yellowbill and the Tambarle film group announced that a Kent Walwin and John Groves screenplay adaptation of John's World War I flying ace would finally commence filming on January 21 under the direction of John Hough. Hough, whose previous credits included *The Legend of Hell House* (1973) and who had earlier made quite an impression with audiences and critics alike for his stylish handling of Hammer's *Twins of Evil* in 1971, completed *Biggles* in just under ten months. This included a seven-week film shoot with locations in London, Bedfordshire, and Northants, England.

One of the stars of the film, Alex Hyde-White (son of the distinguished actor, Wilfrid Hyde-White), who portrayed the reluctant time-traveler James Ferguson, told the authors that Peter Cushing was the first actor he had worked with on the film and that *Biggles* was his first feature film experience. He recalled that "London was snowy and cold. Peter was playing the part of Colonel Raymond, Biggles' commanding officer during the First World War. Only problem was this was in modern day. I was a New York business man thinking he was potty, telling me that I would have to go back to WWI to meet and aid my time-twin, Captain Bigglesworth. . . . On a particularly chilly evening near the docks, while filming out my open apartment front door, there was an ominous crack of lightning and thunder. Peter took it as his cue and entered the shot. He knew how to take advantage of the moment."

Appearing along with Cushing and Hyde-White was Neil Dickson as Captain Bigglesworth. Dickson, who later went on to appear in the syndicated television series "She-Wolf of London" as one of its stars, was the perfect choice for the dare-devil flyer cum special agent. His rugged good looks and restrained cavalier approach lent itself well to the part.

Cushing as Commander William Raymond retains an air of mystery throughout the film—softly underplaying his character, yet giving one an undeniable impression of inner strength and quiet resolve as he coordinates events of the past and present from his unorthodox headquarters at Tower Bridge in London.

Biggles is, without question, only light entertainment aimed at younger audiences. However, all age groups might get some enjoyment out of the film. What motion pictures had been lacking for many years were true cinema-style heroes that youngsters could rally around. Both Captain Bigglesworth and Jim Ferguson tried to help fill that void.

The acting is collectively very good and direction is up to Hough's usually high standards. The story and screenplay are somewhat simplified but this is expected due to the film's target audience. What *Biggles* suffers from the most is its obviously limited budget. The lack of high-tech imagery, which films like *Star Wars* and *Alien* exploited and which changed the look of sci-fi films for all time, made *Biggles* seem pale and unappealing to most overseas distributors. As a result, *Biggles* had a very limited theatrical release in the United States. Audiences here had been spoiled by all the glittering and dazzling special effects that *Star Wars* and others offered. *Biggles* could never hope to stand up against such pressure and soon faded back into the limbo from which it had previously sprung.

Although the majority of U.S. cinema audiences were virtually unaware that *Biggles* was in existence until its video and cable television releases, it was reviewed by *The Times* and the *Los Angeles Times*. *The Times* (David Robinson, May 23, 1986) reported,

> Just when British films seem to be doing so well, *Biggles* comes along to show the other side of things. It might for a start appear an odd decision to put Biggles on the screen at this juncture. How many of today's filmgoers remember Captain W. E. John's hero? Once committed, though, the flying ace might have been made over into a sort of period James Bond. Instead there is a misguided and inept attempt to give the film an appeal for imagined mid–Atlantic teenage audiences. The central character is a boyish N.Y. businessman of 1986 who keeps falling through a time warp and getting caught up in random adventures of Biggles and his pals on the Western Front, 1917. The script is witless, the direction is showy and the performances of the twin heros . . . are weakly amiable. The principal consolation is . . . Peter Cushing.

The *Los Angeles Times* (Sheila Benson, January 29, 1988) wrote,

> I cannot swear that the books . . . whip their hero back and forth from past to present, but [the film] certainly does, at an exhausting clip and with no special panache. . . . British born director John Hough has done a dozen or more films . . . but it is his memorable television success, "The Avengers" that should be closest in wit and irony to *Biggles*. The fact that it's not is only one of the disappointments of the film, which is depth charged with disappointment. Certainly Hough has assembled good actors including the elegant Peter Cushing. . . . But with a cheesy plot, . . . and time travel giving everyone whiplash, there's no time to savor the present or the past or the incongruities of one seen by the other.

Biggles was honored with a royal charity premiere in London attended by the Prince and Princess of Wales. Alex Hyde-White was present at the performance and remembered it fondly.

> On the 22nd of May in 1986 we had a Royal premiere at the Leicester Square Empire Theatre. This was, of course, my first time being presented as it was for Neil and the others. One somehow had the feeling that this was not Peter's first time. The Princess and Prince of Wales made their way down the queue toward the actors, where I stood next to Peter Cushing. Peter, upon receiving Princess Diana's hand graciously bowed and kissed it. A most gallant gesture indeed. I never would have thought of it had he not done it. And having done it there was no way I could not follow suit and be deprived of so wonderful a memory. So I received the Princess' hand with a bow and a kiss; which is a bit of a breach of protocol, really, for a young man to do. A picture of that moment sits atop our piano with Peter twinkling next to me, looking most reassuringly my way.

Hyde-White was generous in his praise of his friend and mentor.

> Peter's professional courtesy and respect for the craft of acting has no parallel as far as I can tell. He speaks with modesty of his many accomplishments and his rich and varied life. He treats everyone he meets to the joy of discovery that he keeps firmly in his grasp at all times.
>
> Anyone with such obvious sense of occasion, with such grace of carriage and a measure of talent can be a great performer. Peter's strength, his unique quality that all actors strive to attain and retain, is his complete and utter natural honesty. Not modesty, nor humility — although he strikes many as both that — but honesty in the sense that he gives everything its due. From the seasoned director to the writer trying to protect his own work, which with Peter isn't difficult because he always tries to say what is written, where some actors try anything but. However, from one young actor playing his first movie lead there will always be a thank you to Peter Cushing for being who he is. Peter, whether he tries to or not, always helps people through their day or through the job. He will even be the first to rise to get one a cup of tea.
>
> Peter has a love of life and respect for humanity that we were all fortunate to be around. We all were better for having worked with Peter. His spirit is fascinating. A piece of it is alive in my memory and one can only assume that he has affected countless more in some similar manner or surely the world would be a more difficult place in which to live.

Note

1. Steve Swires, "Peter Cushing — Stitcher of Limbs, Staker of Hearts," Part 2, *Starlog* 100.

New Beginnings

Peter Cushing, An Autobiography

My biography is indeed in the process of being written, but it will be a long, long time before it is published. I started it many months ago, but I really haven't any talent as an author. Many writers had expressed an interest to embark upon such a work, and I have enlisted the help of one of them. The compilation is — perforce — very sporadic, as both of us have other things to do which take up most of our available time. Such is the unpredictable nature of my profession — it is not possible to plan too far ahead, as I seldom know from one week to the next where I may be or what I will be doing. [Peter Cushing, March 28, 1973].

Even as far back as 1973, Peter Cushing had been contemplating having his life story published. However, due to his pressing film schedule at the time, Peter had to forego any serious pursuit of the project until almost eleven years later when, in 1984, his friend Sir John Mills urged him to finish the work and find a publisher.[1]

Peter had initially begun work on his autobiography in 1971, shortly after the death of his wife Helen. However, at that time he had no expressed purpose in mind other than as a form of therapy.

Ironically, on the day Peter finished work on the last chapter, he received a phone call from author Michael Hardwick whose publishers Weidenfeld and Nicolson seemed very enthusiastic over his proposal to chronicle Cushing's story. Hardwick must have been as disappointed as Peter was surprised to learn that he already had a publisher waiting in the wings!

Peter Cushing, An Autobiography went on the market in March 1986. It proved to be an immediate best seller and was subsequently reprinted in a paperback edition. Peter found himself in great demand throughout England which involved book-signing tours as well as several radio and television interviews to promote it.[2]

Coincidentally, the National Film Theatre in London had been running a retrospect of Peter's films entitled, "A Talent To Terrify." The month-long series had begun on March 1 and featured such films as: *The Curse of Frankenstein, The Abominable Snowman of the Himalayas, Horror of Dracula, The Hound of the Baskervilles, The Brides of Dracula, Night Creatures, She, Corruption,* and *The Creeping Flesh.*

On the last day of the series, Tuesday, March 25, Cushing himself made a personal appearance at the South Bank Theatre where he was interviewed by Wayne Drew to a capacity audience.

Past Forgetting—Memoirs of the Hammer Years

In the vast majority of cases whenever an actor publishes his or her autobiography fans are generally more than delighted with the prospect. Not so Peter Cushing fans, who were disappointed that their favorite thespian had devoted so little background to his prestigious film career or an emphasis on his Hammer films. As vocal and passionate as his admirers are known to be, these devoted masses let their disappointment be known to the author.

Cushing, ever sensitive to his fans' reactions, penned an unprecedented companion volume for Weidenfeld and Nicolson entitled *Past Forgetting—Memoirs of the Hammer Years,* which was published in 1988.

Once again, Peter found himself involved in a book-signing junket. The response to this subsequent publication was so spectacular that on more than one occasion bookstores literally ran out of copies and found themselves scrambling to track down additional books. According to one local newspaper article, the demand at Whitstable's Pirie and Cavender Bookshop was so great that a second autograph session had to be arranged a week later to accommodate all those who had to be turned away. The owner of the shop told reporters that "Everyone hopelessly underestimated Peter's popularity. . . . We have cleaned out the publisher's warehouse of every last copy!"

Peter Cushing and Her Majesty, the Queen of England

On December 30, 1988, only hours before being officially notified that he was to receive the prestigious OBE (Most Excellent Order of the British Empire), Peter Cushing was involved in an accident and was rushed to Canterbury's Chaucer Hospital where doctors determined that he had suffered a fractured thigh.

Cushing, seventy-five years old at the time, had been cycling in his hometown of Whitstable when an unleashed dog ran out in front of his bicycle. Swerving to avoid the animal, Peter was thrown from the bike.

After an emergency operation in which his broken femur had to be pinned, Cushing spent three weeks in the hospital and another few weeks convalescing at the home of his secretary, Joyce Broughton, and her family.

On Wednesday, March 22, 1989, Peter, with the aid of a cane for minor support, was presented to Queen Elizabeth II at Buckingham Palace to receive his honor.[3] Peter was said to have been in fine form for the event, smiling and joking with the many reporters who had gathered to chronicle the affair.

Overwhelmed by all the cards and letters he had received from all over the world in response to his accident and the award, Peter wrote a letter to the *Whitstable Times*:

> I have been deeply touched by the reactions of people ... and wish I could write to each and every one to thank them individually. But I am afraid that would not be possible, so I do hope they will accept my profound thanks through this letter, which was written with a sincere and very full heart.
>
> I suppose I am an incurable romantic, because I would liked to have "slain a dragon" ... and saved the Queen's life, or done some other brave deed which would make me feel I really deserve this honor.
>
> But I love this country of ours and its people so very much and am deeply proud of this recognition, because it must mean that I have done something during my life for it and for them.

Several months after his accident, Peter decided to give up his daily bicycle rides and donated the conveyance — which he described as "being like its present owner, a bit battered" — to a local conservation group who, in turn, planned to raffle it during one of their fundraising drives.

The Great Hip Race and "A One-Way Ticket to Hollywood"

On June 4, 1989, the British Orthopedic Association's Wishbone Appeal, hoping to raise $10 million for research, organized a walkathon which they promoted as "The Great Hip Walk."

Forty-two walks were scheduled throughout the United Kingdom and Peter Cushing, who had himself recovered from hip surgery, was asked to lead the Canterbury chapter's event.

Over 280 people began their walkathon at the St. Lawrence Cricket Ground, off Old Dover Road at 11:00 A.M. and raised more than $10,000 during their three-lap walk.

That evening, British television's channel 4 aired a tribute to Peter entitled "Peter Cushing — A One-Way Ticket to Hollywood" which showcased

Peter Cushing leads the pack in the British Orthopedic Association's Wishbone Appeal walkathon held in Canterbury, June 4, 1989. (Photograph taken by Anita Clarke.)

Cushing's fifty years in the acting business. The Tyburn production featured numerous film clips during the hour-long program which highlighted his film and television career and also included a delightful one-on-one interview with the show's host, Dick Vosburgh.

Peter Cushing, Rock Star?

In the spring of 1990 a British Rock group called War Fare composed a collection of original songs entitled "Hammer Horror."

Released by FM-Revolver Records, the record company commissioned Christopher Lee and Peter Cushing to pen the album's liner notes. In tribute to Hammer's most famous luminaries, War Fare titled two of their compositions "Baron Frankenstein" and "Prince of Darkness."

Tudor Tearoom Profiles

Ever since Peter Cushing became a permanent resident of the tiny seaside hamlet of Whitstable, he quickly endeared himself to the town's residents. Local Whitstablians greeted the day and Peter Cushing when-ever he went out on his routine bicycle rides or walks.

One of Cushing's favorite haunts was Harbour Street's Tudor Tea-room, where he could be found on many an afternoon chatting with the customers and sketching cameos of some of the tearoom's more colorful patrons.

After a time Peter had collected so many of these caricatures that in 1990 a book was published by Seaway Press entitled *Peter Cushing's Tudor Tea Room Profiles* which contained some of these hilarious pen and ink drawings. As expected, all profits from the sale of this very special collec-tion were donated to charity.[4] According to the publisher, this book was such an enormous success that two additional volumes were subsequently issued.

"This Is Your Life, Peter Cushing" (ITV 1990)

In February 1990 Thames Television's long-running series, "This Is Your Life" honored Peter Cushing with a tribute to his film and television career. Many of Peter's former coworkers made an appearance to pay trib-ute to him and in some cases to offer anecdotes. Among those gathered were Anthony Hinds, Sir James Carreras (the former head of Hammer Films), Kevin Francis (head of Tyburn Films), Christopher Lee (who was in New York City at the time and sent a videotaped message), Sir John Mills, Caroline Munro, Ursula Andress, Joanna Lumley, Peter Ustinov, Dave Prowse, David Rintoil, Fiona Armstrong, Peter Gray, Freddie Jones, and Ernie Wise.

Film clips were shown throughout the program. Among the movies featured were *The Curse of Frankenstein, Horror of Dracula, The Hound of the Baskervilles, The Satanic Rites of Dracula, At the Earth's Core, Star Wars,* and B.B.C.'s teleplay, *1984.*

For the Love of Helen (TVS 1990)

Not long after his tribute on "This Is Your Life," Peter appeared on the British television series, "The Human Factor." In a one-on-one inter-view with the show's producer and host, Peter Williams, Peter Cushing treated his audience to a mini-autobiographical sketch of his life off-screen. The discussion included a showing of some of Peter's magnificent artwork, family photographs, and a deeply personal look into his religious beliefs as well as his relationships with his parents, brother, and his late wife, Helen.

Human Conflict

On December 29, 1990, to commemorate the fiftieth anniversary of the Battle of Britain, BBC Radio Kent aired an original drama, written by Michael Bath and starring Peter Cushing, entitled *Human Conflict*.

Bath, who also produced and directed the play, based his semibiographical melodrama on Air Chief Marshal Hugh Dowding, the man who invented radar and subsequently orchestrated the now venerated World War II air battles. Bath concentrates on the successful plot by some of Dowding's jealous peers to have him discredited and eventually dismissed from his high-level military position during the conflict. As a result, Dowding's important contributions were nearly forgotten by his fellow countrymen.

Peter Cushing plays one of Dowding's former RAF pilots, a fictional character who, over the years, had been leading a one-man crusade to reveal the truth behind this plot and vindicate his commanding officer.

Prior to its broadcast, the nine cast members gathered at Cushing's seaside Whitstable home to record the play. Other featured performers included: Julie First (The Reporter), Ronald Fraser (Trafford Leigh-Mallory), David Angus (Sir Douglas Bader), Douglas Blackwell (Sir Winston Churchill), and Alan Dobie (Hugh Dowding).

British reporter Melody Foreman hailed the broadcast in her January 3, 1991, review. Among her comments she wrote, "The story was brilliantly told by Mr. [Peter] Cushing, and his co-stars.... It really was a bonus to hear ... Mr. Cushing on the air again. He really is one of the truly great theatre artists of Britain."

MC Cushing

In a world where normally anyone over the age of thirty is immediately classified by its younger generations as "the nearly, dearly departed," the mere thought of a seventy-eight-year-old rap singer would send most teens into a tailspin! But if anyone can help bridge that generation gap, Peter Cushing can, and has! In November 1991 he released his first dance-rap single entitled "No White Peaks."

Based on an original poem by Peter Kayne, "No White Peaks" reflects the feelings of a homesick Gulf War soldier who sees the horrors of war and longs for his home in the snowclad mountains.

Peter revealed the record's genesis: "The poem was sent to me by this young chap ... Peter Kayne. He and a friend ran a small recording company in Bolton, and Kayne had entertained the troops during the Gulf War. He was so upset by what he saw and felt ... he wrote the poem and asked me if I'd record it, and then they'd add something like "Auld Lang Syne" behind it and release it for Christmas."[5]

Peter agreed to do the recording. Meanwhile, another record company (Assegai Records) heard the recording and approached Peter and Kayne to do a dance version of it.

"When they told me it was rap music I thought it was something that was wrapped up like a parcel," Peter joked. "Then they told me to watch 'Top of the Pops' to find out what I had let myself into."[6]

Peter and Kayne agreed to allow the dance mix and on November 11, 1991, the recording went into general release in England.[7]

"I must admit that it's not really my scene," Peter told *Terror Magazine*, "but I can see what young people like in it. . . . I was worried that the marriage of an anti-war poem with the frivolity of a dance record would lose the overall message but I think it's worked out quite well."

Cushing's View

On Thursday, January 30, 1992, the *Whitstable Times* made the following announcement: "A small part of Whitstable is to take the name of one of the town's best loved and most famous residents, Peter Cushing. The veteran actor and his late wife Helen will be remembered forever when a new sea-viewing platform is named 'Cushing's View.'"

Peter was understandably thrilled and deeply honored when he heard the news and said it was the best thing that had happened to him since his OBE. A special plaque is to mark the spot and will read, "Presented by Helen and Peter Cushing who love Whitstable and its people so very much."

The idea for the platform originated with another local resident, Joseph Vaughn, an ardent supporter for senior citizens' rights and who had suggested that a raised area with slopes for easy access by the elderly and disabled be installed at Keams Yard, which overlooks the bay. Vaughn took his proposal to the town council two years ago and also suggested that it be named after Peter in order to, in his words, "hold in memory forever the unique and famous resident of Whitstable who has given so much pleasure to all." The council agreed to the proposal and planned to hold an official opening and dedication ceremony once the project was completed.

Peter has also donated one of his garden benches to be permanently installed on the site. "The only thing is," he quipped, "I'm an incurable romantic and there is only room for two on my bench!"

Peter Cushing unveils a nameplate for the Citizen Advice Bureau in Whitstable in 1990.

You Can't Keep a Good Actor Down!

As far as the majority of Peter Cushing admirers were concerned, *Biggles — Adventures in Time* (1985) marked the end of his unique and distinguished film career. All of us were resigned to the fact that Peter Cushing had apparently stepped aside to allow younger talent their own moments in the sun. However, very few actors really retire, and when one is speaking about a living legend, one hopes that the respite might be short-lived.

Although Peter is well past the age and health status required by motion picture and insurance companies overseas, Tyburn Films and producer Kevin Francis were willing to forgo the risk and plans are in the works to film a television movie entitled *A Heritage of Horror*.

Cushing revealed a portion of the plot line: "It's a wonderful fantasy about an old actor who wants to play *King Lear* and no one will touch him because they don't think it's a very commercial idea. He sets about showing them that it is and eventually succeeds. It's very funny and a little bit scary in places."[8]

In a letter to the authors Peter added, "It's such an excellent script and one of the best parts to come my way. . . . A great personal tribute."

Let us hope that this is indeed a new beginning and that the last chapters of the films of Peter Cushing have yet to be written.

Notes

1. Sir John Mills had costarred with Peter in the Tyburn made-for-television movie, "Masks of Death" (1984). The two actors had previously worked together in *The End of the Affair* (1954) and *Trial by Combat* (1975).

2. Peter made television appearances in "Pebble Mill at One" (March 24, 1986) and "Coast to Coast" (March 26, 1986). He also had a guest spot on BBC's "Radio Two—The John Dunn Show" (March 20, 1986) to promote the release of his autobiography.

3. "Founded in 1917, chiefly to recognize service by civilians in the first world war, it is now the most widely conferred on civilians or service personnel for public services or other distinctions. The Grand Master is the Duke of Edinburgh [Prince Philip]. There are two divisions, military and civil. Ranks in the Order, which is open to both sexes, and the customary abbreviations are ... O.B.E.—officer. Chapel of the order is located in St. Paul's Cathedral, London." This quote is taken from *Honours and Titles in Britain,* London: Foreign and Commonwealth Office by Reference Services, Central Office of Information, London, September 1982.

4. Peter Cushing, *Peter Cushing's Tudor Tea Room Profiles,* Canterbury, Kent: Seaway, 1990.

5. Peter Cushing, interview with Jerry Ewing, *Terror Magazine* 2. As of this writing, there were plans to release an American version using "The Battle Hymn of the Republic" as background music. Release of the British version has been held up until Easter 1992.

6. *Daily Record,* December 7, 1991.

7. Assegai Music 1991; marketed and distributed by the Total Record Company; words by Peter Kayne; music by Andrew T. Mackay, arranged and produced by Andrew T. Mackay for the Gor-Mac Music Organization; recorded at Mac's Love Parc and Battery Studios; mixed at Battery Studios; executive producer Tosca for Ascot Productions; cover design by Justin Greenleaf at Nice Art; and background vocals by Janet Cofie (formerly with Odyssey and Sister Sledge).

8. Peter Cushing, interview with Jerry Ewing, *Terror* 2.

Epilogue

Life after Death is an absolute certainty. It is the only factor which makes any sense of *this* life. In a sense, it will be a form of reincarnation; we go on to better things in a better sphere, reunited with those we love who have gone before. Therefore, I would have nothing changed, only hoping that I've learned the difference between right and wrong during this phase of existence and been forgiven my sins, so as to deserve acceptance amongst that cloud of witnesses. "For whosoever believeth in me, shall have everlasting Life."

Peter Cushing

Selected Bibliography

Books

Brosnan, John. *The Horror People*. New York: St. Martin's, 1976.

Buscombe, Edward. *Making "Legend of the Werewolf."* London: British Film Institute, 1976.

Clarens, Carlos. *An Illustrated History of the Horror Film*. New York: Putnam, 1967.

Cushing, Peter. *Peter Cushing, An Autobiography*. London: Weidenfeld and Nicolson, 1986.

_____. *Past Forgetting — Memoirs of the Hammer Years*. London: Weidenfeld and Nicolson, 1988.

_____. *Tales of a Monster Hunter*. London: Futura, 1978.

Davies, David Stuart. *Holmes of the Movies*. Foreword by Peter Cushing. New York: Bramhall House, 1976.

Druxman, Michael B. *One Good Film Deserves Another: A Pictorial Survey of the Film Sequels*. South Brunswick, N.J.: A. S. Barnes, 1977.

Falk, Quentin. *Travels in Greeneland*. London: Quartet, 1984.

Frank, Alan. *The Movie Treasury. Horror Movies: Tales of Terror in the Cinema*. London: Octopus Books, 1974.

_____. *The Movie Treasury. Monsters and Vampires: Spine-Chilling Creatures of the Cinema*. London: Octopus Books, 1976.

Gifford, Denis. *A Pictorial History of Horror Movies*. London: Hamlyn Books, 1973.

Halliwell, Leslie. *Halliwell's Film Guide*. New York: Charles Scribner's Sons, 1987.

Haining, Peter. *The Dracula Scrapbook*. New York: Bramhall House, 1971.

_____. *The Sherlock Holmes Scrapbook*. Foreword by Peter Cushing. New York: Bramhall House, 1974.

_____. *The TV Sherlock Holmes*. London: W. H. Allen, 1986.

Hutchinson, Tom. *Horror and Fantasy in the Movies*. New York: Crescent Books, 1974.

Katz, Ephraim. *The Film Encyclopedia*. New York: Crowell, 1979.

Lee, Christopher. *Tall, Dark, and Gruesome*. London: W. H. Allen, 1977.

McGee, Mark Thomas. *Fast and Furious: The Story of American International Pictures*. Jefferson, N.C.: McFarland, 1984.

Mank, Gregory William. *Karloff and Lugosi*. Jefferson, N.C.: McFarland, 1990.

Olivier, Laurence. *On Acting*. New York: Simon and Schuster, 1986.

Palmer, Scott. *British Film Actors' Credits, 1895–1987*. Jefferson, N.C.: McFarland, 1988.

Parfitt, Gary, ed. *The Films of Peter Cushing*. England: HFCGB, 1975.

Pattison, Barrie. *The Seal of Dracula*. New York: Bounty Books, 1975.

445

Phillips, Gene D. *Graham Greene: The Films of His Fiction*. New York: Teacher's College Press, Columbia University, 1974.

Pirie, David. *A Heritage of Horror: The English Gothic Cinema, 1946–1972*. New York: Avon Books, 1973.

_____. *The Vampire Cinema*. New York: Crescent Books, 1977.

Pohle, Robert W., Jr., and Douglas C. Hart. *The Films of Christopher Lee*. Metuchen, N.J.: Scarecrow, 1983.

_____. *Sherlock Holmes on the Screen*. South Brunswick, N.J.: A. S. Barnes, 1977.

Richards, Jeffrey. *Swordsmen of the Screen*. London: Routledge and Kegan Paul, 1977.

Silver, Alain, and James Ursini. *The Vampire Film*. South Brunswick, N.J.: A. S. Barnes, 1975.

Waller, Gregory A. *The Living and the Undead*. Champaign: University of Illinois Press, 1986.

Weaver, Tom. *Interviews with B Science Fiction and Horror Movie Makers*. Jefferson, N.C.: McFarland, 1988.

_____. *Science Fiction Stars and Horror Heroes*. Jefferson, N.C.: McFarland, 1991.

Weldon, Michael. *The Psychotronic Encyclopedia of Film*. New York: Ballantine, 1983.

Periodicals

Bizarre. Pit Company, Asheville, N.C. Editor and publisher, Sam L. Irvin.

Black Oracle. Baltimore, Md. Editor, George Stover.

Castle of Frankenstein. North Bergen, N.J. Editor and publisher, Charles F. Kane.

Children of the Night. Kansas. Editor, Derek Jensen.

Cinefantastique. Oak Park, Ill. Editor and publisher, Fred S. Clarke.

Famous Monsters of Filmland. New York. Publisher, James Warren; editor, Forrest J Ackerman.

Fangoria. Starlog Communications International, New York. Publisher, Norman Jacobs; Editor, Anthony Timpone.

Fantastic Films. Evanston, Ill. Editor, Michael Stein.

Films Illustrated. London, England. Editor, David Castell.

Gore Creatures/Midnight Marquee. Baltimore, Md. Publisher, Gary J. Svehla.

The Halls of Horror. London, England. Top Sellers.

The House of Hammer. London, England. Editor, Dez Skinn.

L'incroyable Cinema. Editors, Harry Nadler and Marie Nadler.

Little Shoppe of Horrors. Des Moines, Ia. Editor and publisher, Dick Klemensen.

Monsterland. Studio City, Ca. Editor, Forrest J Ackerman.

Monsters of the Movies. New York. Editor-in-chief, Marv Wolfman.

The Monster Times. New York. Publishers, Larry Brill and Les Waldstein; editor, Allan Asherman.

Photon: Brooklyn, N.Y. Editor and publisher, Mark Frank.

Starburst. London, England. Editor, Alan McKenzie.

Starlog. New York. Publishers, Norman Jacobs and Kerry O'Quinn.

Index

Italic page numbers indicate photographs.
Peter Cushing's film titles and their alternate forms are set in boldface.

447

Milton Keynes UK
Ingram Content Group UK Ltd.
UKHW031627270824
447500UK00024B/392